BURT FRANKLIN: BIBLIOGRAPHY & REFERENCE SERIES 88

THE ARTHURIAN MATERIAL
IN THE CHRONICLES

THE ARTHURIAN MATERIAL
IN THE CHRONICLES

Especially Those of
Great Britain and France

By

ROBERT HUNTINGTON FLETCHER

Second edition, expanded by a
bibliography and critical essay
for the period 1905-1965

by

ROGER SHERMAN LOOMIS

BURT FRANKLIN
NEW YORK

Published by LENOX HILL Pub. & Dist. Co. (Burt Franklin)
235 East 44th St., New York, N.Y. 10017
Reprinted: 1973
Printed in the U.S.A.

Burt Franklin: Bibliography and Reference Series 88

The Library of Congress cataloged the original printing of this title
as follows.

Fletcher, Robert Huntington.
   The Arthurian material in the chronicles, especially those of
Great Britain and France. 2d ed., expanded by a bibliography and
critical essay for the period 1905-1965, by Roger Sherman Loomis.
New York, B. Franklin 1966.

   ix, 335 p. 24 cm. (Burt Franklin bibliography and reference series, no. 88)
   "Originally published in 1906."
   Bibliography: p. 333-335.
      1. Arthur, King (Romances, etc.) 2. Literature, Medieval—Hist. & crit.
I. Loomis, Roger Sherman, 1887-   ed. II. Title.
PN685.F45 1966   809.933   66-20679
ISBN 0-8337-1153-9

PREFACE

The general object of this book, as the title indicates, is to show what Arthurian material is contained in the European chronicles, especially in those of Great Britain and France. Somewhat more than two hundred chronicles (including those mentioned on page 177) are here treated, and they range in date from the middle of the sixth to the end of the sixteenth century. No one would claim for the chronicles an importance in Arthurian literature proportionate to their number and the length of the period to which they belong ; nevertheless, their contribution seems to me well worth considering, even apart from the fact that the *Historia* of Geoffrey of Monmouth is to be reckoned among them. Some of my friends tell me also that the study may be of interest to historians for the side-light which it throws on the methods of the chroniclers.

I have interpreted the term " Arthurian material " as including everything that appears in the pseudo-history of Britain from the accession of Constans, whom Geoffrey introduces as the son of the second Constantine and elder brother of Aurelius and Uther, to the death (or disappearance) of Arthur. At first thought this may seem to be beginning too early, but the discussion will make it clear, I think, that the stories of Arthur's immediate predecessors are too intimately connected with his own to be separated from it.

I have meant to make my investigations complete, as nearly as circumstances allowed, for the chronicles of Great Britain and France.[1] I do not claim to have treated those of other countries adequately, though I doubt if anything further of real importance to the subject is to be found in them.

---

[1] I have mentioned in the notes the unpublished manuscripts known to me which, to judge by the descriptions of them, may contain Arthurian material, but which, for one reason or another, I have not been able to consult ; and for the benefit of possible future investigators I have listed them all together under one entry in the index.

iii

In the case of each chronicle I have aimed, first, to give a correct general idea of what it says of the subject, and second, to mention all particular features which are in any way important. As regards this second aim, however, entire evenness and consistency of treatment were scarcely to be hoped for. It must sometimes have happened that I have failed to take note, in connection with one chronicle, of some point (generally, I hope, a minor one) to which I have called attention in speaking of another. Perhaps it is only fair to ask readers to remember, apropos of this and some other aspects of the book, that in work involving considerable minute detail it is even harder than in other cases to avoid, in manuscript, imperfections which become apparent enough in print.

From the nature of the case, in some parts of the study, especially in the whole of the earlier portion, my work has consisted chiefly in summing up and combining the conclusions of previous writers. In the later sections, however, this has not been true, and the subject as a whole has never before received systematic treatment. I have meant to give credit in the notes for suggestions which I have adopted from others, but, as all students know, this is not always possible. For help received from two standard works, namely Potthast's *Bibliotheca Historica Medii Aevi* and the *Dictionary of National Biography*, a single general acknowledgment here must suffice, for the most part.

The book was originally prepared as a doctoral dissertation, and was submitted to the Faculty of Harvard University in May, 1901. In the following academic year it was corrected and enlarged by research in London, Oxford, and Paris, and was entirely rewritten. It was substantially complete in its present form and was put into the hands of the publishers early in 1903. The subsequent delay in bringing it out has been unavoidable. Certain relevant articles which have appeared in the meantime are noticed in an appendix. Mr. W. W. Newell's important paper *Doubts concerning Nennius* (*Publications of the Modern Language Association*, 1905, XX, 622 ff.), however, reached me too late to be considered.

The abbreviations which I have employed are, I believe, generally conventional and easily understood. In references large Roman numerals designate volumes, small Roman numerals books (*libri*).

"Ward" means the *Catalogue of Romances in the British Museum* by H. L. D. Ward; "Hardy," Sir Thomas Duffus Hardy's *Descriptive Catalogue of Materials relative to the History of Great Britain and Ireland* (Rolls Series); "Geoffrey," without further description, is always Geoffrey of Monmouth. In making citations from his *Historia* I have ordinarily used three sets of numerals, which refer respectively to book, chapter, and line of San-Marte's edition.

In regard to the names of characters in the Arthurian story, my general principle has been to reproduce in all cases the spellings used by the writer under discussion; but the printed proof shows me that I have often failed to do so. In the index all variant spellings, except those sure to be recognized at first glance, are entered and referred to a normal form, generally the one most widely current in the literature of the subject. For the names of the chroniclers I have used sometimes Latin, sometimes vernacular forms, because I am sure that in this case familiar usage is a better guide than theoretical consistency.

I am under the greatest obligations to three of my teachers and friends at Harvard. Professor Kittredge and Professor Schofield have given me most generous assistance at all stages of my work, and Professor Sheldon during the process of publication. I owe to them all very many suggestions and emendations which cannot be separately specified. Indeed, I could hardly explain the nature and extent of my indebtedness to Professor Kittredge, in particular, unless possibly to some of those who have had the same privilege of writing and publishing a book under his supervision. Professor Schofield, besides, first suggested the subject to me, and parts of the book were written in connection with his Arthurian seminary. It is hardly necessary to add, however, that for all errors and faults I alone am responsible. I am glad also to acknowledge great kindnesses received from Alfred Nutt, Esq., and special help from Professor Robinson of Harvard. Other obligations are mentioned in the notes. Of course I am indebted in the usual but very real way to the authorities of the libraries where I have worked, chiefly the Harvard University Library, the British Museum, and the Bibliothèque Nationale.

My first preface would be incomplete without mention of the name of Professor Richardson of Dartmouth College. Professor Richardson has had no direct connection with this book, but it is to him that I owe the beginning of my permanent interest in English studies, and he has been to me for years a constant friend and helper in matters professional as well as nonprofessional. I am very glad to have the opportunity of making him even this slight acknowledgment.

R. H. F.

HANOVER, N.H.
November 28, 1905

CONTENTS

vii

ARTHURIAN MATERIAL IN CHRONICLES

CHAPTER I

THE BEGINNINGS OF THE STORY

I. THE UNDOUBTED HISTORICAL FACTS

THE Arthurian stories, like the other great romance cycles of the Middle Ages, rest, however slightly, upon the unquestioned facts of a genuine historical period. With these facts, accordingly, the present discussion must commence. They are exceedingly few, because very little that could well be forgotten, especially as regards the British interests, with which alone we are directly concerned, has escaped the confusion and darkness of the time.[1]

Scarcely more than this, then, is certain. Even long before the departure of the Roman legions from Britain in the beginning of the fifth century, the Scots and Picts from the north, and the Germanic pirates from the east, had begun to make persistent incursions upon the people of the island. When the military forces of the empire were finally withdrawn, the power of resistance seemed to go with them; and, though the Britons recovered themselves and fought with determination, they were unable to keep off the invaders. Not many decades passed before the Germans permanently established themselves, first in the southeast, and then all along the eastern and southern coasts; and from that time on they

---

[1] A notable article on the period is that of Thurneysen in *Englische Studien*, 1895, XXII, 163–179, " Wann sind die Germanen nach England gekommen?" References will there be found to contemporary authorities.

fought their way steadily forward, occasionally meeting with a serious check, but seldom losing anything that they had won.   In comparison with this settled policy of conquest, the ravages of the Scots and Picts soon ceased to have importance.   It is to the century of the struggle which began with the first actual Germanic settlement that the Arthurian stories historically belong.

Some further details about the period may be accepted without much hesitation, but they are only to be inferred from the chronicles here to be considered, which may now be allowed to speak for themselves.[1]

---

[1] It will be convenient to give here a brief bibliography of the special books and articles which deal with the history of the period and with its historians.   Many of these are thoroughly scientific, but others present most ridiculous theories. G. and N. stand respectively for *Gildas* and *Nennius*.   When these initials are not followed by page numbers, the index of the book in question will indicate where the relevant discussion is to be found.   No additional bibliography will hereafter be necessary for Gildas, but for the special controversy about Nennius references will be given later (pp. 8–9).

Anscombe, *St. Gildas of Ruys*, 1893, pp. 29–67. — Anscombe, Stevenson, and Nicholson, letters in London *Academy*, 1895, Sept. 14–Dec. 14.   G. — d'Arbois de Jubainville, *Merlin est-il un personnage réel?* (*Rev. des Questions Hist.*, 1868, V, 559–568).   G. — W. H. Babcock, *Two Lost Centuries of Britain*, Philadelphia, 1890. — Beddoe, *Races of Britain*, Bristol and London, 1885.   G. 35–36. — W. Edwards, *The Settlement of Brittany* (*Y Cymmrodor*, 1890, XI, 74–82).   G. — Elton, *Origins of English History*, 1882. — Freeman, *Norman Conquest*, I, 11, note, etc. — Green, *Making of England*, New York, 1882.   G. 19–25, etc., and in general, chaps. 1–3. — Guest, *Origines Celticae*, 1883, II, 154–157, 165–166, etc. — Haigh, *The Conquest of Britain by the Saxons; a Harmony of the Historia Britonum*, etc., 1861. — Algernon Herbert, *Britannia after the Romans*, 1836.   G. xiv–xx, 40 ff., etc.; N. xx–xxii, 21, etc.; id., *Cyclops Christianus*, 1849, 212–216. — A. Holtzmann, in *Germania*, 1867, XII, 268–274. — Kemble, *Saxons in England*, 1849, I, 10, 11, 14 (another ed., 1876). — A. de La Borderie, *L'Historien et le Prophète des Bretons, Gildas*, etc., Paris and Nantes, 1884; id., *La Date de la Naissance de Gildas* (*Rev. Celt.*, 1883, VI, 1–13); id., *Hist. de Bretagne*, Rennes, 1896, I, 230 ff., 384–390, 409–414.   G. — Lappenberg, *Anglo-Saxon Kings*, English translation, ed. 1845, pp. 100–104 (ed. 1881, I, 57–58); id., *Geschichte Englands*, ed. 1834, I, xxxviii.   G. — Lipsius, in Ersch und Gruber's *Encyclopädie*, Sec. I, Bd. 67, pp. 231 ff., Leipzig, 1858.   G. — J. Loth, *L'Emigration bretonne en Armorique*, Rennes, 1883.   G. 27, note, 44. — Abbé Luco, *Histoire de St. Gildas de Rhuys*, Galles, 1869. — P. Paris, *Mémoire sur l'ancienne chronique dite de Nennius*, Paris, 1865. — Petrie and Sharp, *Monumenta Historiae Britanniae*, 1848, Introd. to G. and

II. Gildas

The first elements of the Arthurian story, scarcely recognizable as such, appear in the earliest of the chronicles of Great Britain, the *De Excidio et Conquestu Britanniae* of Arthur's contemporary, the almost legendary Gildas.[1]

Our absolute knowledge of Gildas is limited to what we can gather from his own book. He was born in the year of the battle of Mount Badon, probably very soon after the beginning of the sixth century;[2] was an ecclesiastic, probably a monk; crossed the sea to Armorica, like other Welsh saints of the time; and in Armorica, at the earnest request of his friends, composed his treatise. It seems quite safe to add that he was not only a thoroughly Romanized Roman citizen, but a vehement partisan in the struggle for supremacy which the conditions of the time, and a few hints of his own, justify us in supposing to have taken place, among the Britons of the period, between a Roman and a native faction. Some additional details may also be accepted with various degrees of confidence. The reverence which not only led to Gildas's canonization and has

---

N., pp. 59–68, 106–114. — Beale Poste, *Britannia Antiqua*, 1857. G. 5, 19 ff., 48–80; N. 6, 17–48. — Rhŷs, *Celtic Britain*, London, 1882. — Rhŷs and Jones, *The Welsh People*, 1900, p. 105. — P. Roberts, *The Chronicle of the Kings of Britain* (translation of *Brut Tysilio*) *with Dissertations on the History attributed to Gildas*, 1811. — San-Marte (A. Schulz), *Die Arthur Sagen*, 1842. G. 4–5; N. 5–6. — K. W. Schoell, *De Ecclesiasticae Britonum Scotorumque Historiae Fontibus*, Berlin and London, 1851. G. 1–20; N. 29–37. — Skene, *Four Ancient Books of Wales*, 1868. G. 44 ff., 77 ff.; N. 37–40; id., *Celtic Scotland*, 1876. G. 1, 117, 144, 150–151, etc.; N. 146–148. — Stephens, *Literature of the Kymry*, 2d ed. G. 9. — Stubbs, *Constitutional History*, I, 67, note. G. — Sharon Turner, *History of the Anglo-Saxons*, 1797; ed. of 1840, Paris, I, 99, 107, 117–119. G. — Thos. Wright, *Biographia Britannica Literaria*, *Anglo-Saxon Period*, 1842. G. 115–135; N. 135–142; id., *Essays on Archæological Subjects*, 1861, pp. 202 ff.; id., *Celt, Roman, and Saxon*, 1852. G. 389. — Zimmer, *Nennius Vindicatus*, Berlin, 1393, pp. 287 ff.

[1] The standard edition is that of Mommsen, in *Mon. Germ. Hist., Auct. Antiquissimi*, XIII, *Chron. Min.*, III, Berlin, 1898, pp. 1–110. The existing fragments of Gildas's other writings are also given there. For manuscripts, see also Hardy, *Descriptive Catalogue*, I, 132–137, 318. The most accessible English translation is that of Giles in his *Six Old English Chronicles* (Bohn Library).

[2] The date of this battle is a much-disputed point.

associated his name with scores of localities in Brittany, but designated him during the greater part of the Middle Ages as "Sapiens"
and ascribed to him the authorship of various books which, whether
real or imaginary, were certainly not written by him, is part of a
very ancient tradition.   This tradition appears at its fullest in two
characteristic mediæval "Lives," belonging respectively to the
eleventh and twelfth centuries; and their agreement in certain
points allows us, in spite of their generally extravagant tone, to
draw upon them to some extent for information.   There are also a
few plausible entries in Welsh and Irish annals.[1]   On these authorities we may hold it as quite possible that Gildas was the son of
some petty British king, perhaps of the lord of Alclud (Dumbarton);
that he was, for his time, a great scholar; that he preached elo-
quently in Ireland as well as in Britain and Armorica; that he
wrote his *De Excidio* not long before 547, went to Ireland about
565, and died about 570.

Gildas's main theme is the denunciation of the British people (and
especially the reigning princes) for their sins, — which, he declares,
have brought upon them all their past and present misfortunes, —
and the exhortation to repentance, which alone may restore to them
the favor of God.   But he begins, by way of introduction, with a
brief sketch of the history of the island from the earliest period to
the "last victory," which has occurred in his own time.   His fragmentary summary of events before the Saxon invasion is notable
chiefly for his excessive laudation of the Romans as the protectors
and benefactors of the Britons, and his equally unvarying deprecia-
tion of the Britons as destitute of any praiseworthy qualities.   He
arrives at the Arthurian period after writing at length of the
intolerable devastations of the Scots and Picts.

At last, he says,[2] in the midst of a brief interval of prosperity, came the
sudden report that these northern enemies were to make a new and more

---

[1] These "Lives" are edited by Mommsen together with the *De Excidio;* see
also F. Lot, *Rom.*, XXVII, 564–573; and for the manuscript of the life ascribed
to Caradoc, Hardy, I, 153, Nos. 437 ff.; *Annales Cambriae* (see pp. 31 ff., below),
ann. 565 and 570; *Annals of Ulster*, ed. Hennessy, Dublin, 1887, I, 62, ann. 569
(which is really equivalent to 570).   [2] Chaps. 22 ff.

formidable invasion. At the same time a terrible pestilence devastated the country. Then all the counsellors were blinded, together with the haughty tyrant [whom he does not name], and they called in the abominable Saxons [whom he has not previously mentioned]. [Here, and throughout the whole of this part of the narrative, Gildas exhausts the superlatives of vituperation in characterizing the invaders, both old and new, who are to him only ferocious beasts.] The Saxons came in three ships, answering the call, and first established themselves, at the command of the ill-starred tyrant, in the eastern part of the island. Their successful settlement brought others after them. On the pretense that they were to engage in dangerous battles for the Britons, they demanded rations. The granting of these stopped their mouths for some time; but at last they complained that enough was not given them, and threatened, unless they should be treated with more liberality, to devastate the whole land. This, in fine, increased by fresh accessions, they proceeded to do, laying waste the country almost everywhere, from sea to sea. Some of the inhabitants were killed; some surrendered themselves to slavery; some fled to lands across the sea; some hid in the recesses of the mountains.

After an interval, when the spoilers had returned home, the remnants of those who had not been brought under the yoke rallied, were joined by many of the others,[1] and, seeking the help of God, successfully attacked the victors. This was under the leadership of Ambrosius Aurelianus, a discreet (*modestus*) man, who alone of the Roman race had escaped the disasters of that epoch. His parents, who had been rulers,[2] had been slain. His descendants, says Gildas, have greatly degenerated at the present time.

After this the struggle went on with varying success until the year of the siege of Mount Badon. Here occurred the last slaughter of the barbarians, and one of the greatest of all. In spite of the cessation of the conflict with the foreigners, civil wars still continue.

Hereupon he turns to the main part of his subject.

In determining what facts may be accepted on Gildas's authority, it is first necessary to form an opinion as to his trustworthiness. Now certainly the general impression which he makes is not such as to inspire confidence. No reasonable person can question his sincerity, or fail to sympathize with him in his grief at the folly and

---

[1] Such seems to be the meaning of Gildas's *reliquiae, quibus confugiunt undique de diversis locis miserrimi cives* (chap. 25).

[2] *Purpura nimirum indutis.*

iniquity of his people, who, as he believes, are madly and wantonly wrecking their national existence and their eternal salvation. Even his violent, chaotic style may be viewed with leniency as the fittest expression of his despair. Yet it is impossible not to see that his attitude is absolutely uncritical. His historical sketch is merely used to point the moral of his argument, and his injustice to the Britons is carried to the last extreme. It is even possible that he was taking part in a controversy between the regular and the irregular clergy.

In those details, too, where personal feeling plays no appreciable part, Gildas is grossly inaccurate. This appears in several of his statements about the Roman period. It also appears in his account of subsequent events, especially in three points: — (1) speaking of the first part of the struggle with the Saxons, he implies that the latter had not appeared in Britain until they were summoned by the native leaders; (2) he asserts that very soon after their arrival they overran the whole island; and (3) he says that somewhat later they returned home. Indeed, his observation that the battle of Mount Badon, the last special event which he records, occurred in the year of his birth, is equivalent to the admission that he was not strictly contemporary with any part of the period included in his historical sketch. He takes pains to note at the outset that his authority is not written records, since all such have been destroyed, but oral tradition as it exists across the sea, the insufficiency of which he himself allows. Clearly he refers here to the reports, necessarily very unjudicial, of the Britons who had fled to Armorica.

Yet, notwithstanding all this, no competent scholar has ever held that Gildas's narrative is to be thrown aside as devoid of historical value. For it is evident that the definite facts which he mentions are only those of prime importance, which, however much they may have been distorted, could scarcely have been wholly falsified; and even his obvious misstatements can be explained on the ground that he is speaking in very general terms, with an exaggeration inevitable to a despondent man of ardent temperament. Even when he says that the Saxons returned home, he may very possibly mean only that they retired to the eastern part of the island, after pillaging more territory than they could then hold. It seems safe, on the whole, to accept as true from Gildas's account as much as this: that sometime toward the middle of the fifth century a king of the Britons enlisted the German pirates as auxiliaries against the Scots and Picts; that, after the alliance was broken (as it was sure to be before long) and the Germans had begun to appear in greater numbers, the first notably successful stand against them brought into prominence, perhaps as chief leader of the Britons, an able general of Roman birth (or at least belonging to the Roman party), Ambrosius Aurelianus;[1] that after this the war went on with varying fortunes for a considerable period, until a decisive British victory at the siege of Mount Badon checked the progress of the invaders for more than forty years; and that, in the interval of relief, the Britons, according to their former habits, carried on civil wars and made no serious effort toward reform.

Gildas's characterization of Ambrosius is too laudatory to be taken at its face value, especially in view of the fact that he is the only leader of the Britons whom Gildas anywhere mentions without dispraise. It seems almost certain that Gildas is repeating an exaggerated tradition of the Roman party, which would naturally ascribe to its leader more credit than was his due.

It is now time to consider a point of great importance, — namely the fact that, although Gildas covers the whole period of the Arthurian story, he does not even mention the one figure which later became of overshadowing importance. That he does not ascribe to Arthur anything of the fame and characteristics which are afterward associated with him, need occasion no surprise; but the entire omission of his name raises a more vital question: Had Arthur actually no historical existence?

That such a conclusion is not necessary appears from various considerations. Gildas is not attempting to write a complete history and he systematically omits almost all names. In any event, Arthur, if he was an actual person, is to be connected, as appears from Nennius, with the period ending with the battle of Badon, and

---

[1] As Professor Rhŷs thinks, he may very likely have held one of the chief military offices in Britain as established by the Romans, which offices may very well have continued in existence down to this time (see p. 29, below, with note 1).

that battle (to judge from Gildas's own words) was so well known in his time that the specification of its hero would have been super-fluous. Moreover, it was contrary to Gildas's declared purpose to praise any distinctively British leader, since every sentence of that sort would detract from the force of his relentless arraignment of the entire nation.

As to whether or not there was an historical Arthur, then, Gildas affords absolutely no evidence, and his whole record of the period of the Arthurian story may be summed up as follows. He tells of the calling in of the Germans by a tyrant whom he does not name, very briefly indicates the general course of events during the entire period, and supplies the figure of Ambrosius Aurelianus (his most important contribution) and the fact of the victory at Mount Badon. Even in this meagre list we almost ought to disregard the first incident; since in most later versions of the story it was Nennius's account of that episode which was adopted, and Nennius says that the Germans came by chance, not by invitation. Indeed, Gildas's whole relation to the Arthurian story is purely accidental, due to the fact that as the only contemporary historian of the epoch he necessarily mentions incidents which were sure to be incorporated in later accounts.

III. The *Historia Britonum* of Nennius

Far more contributive than the work of Gildas to the Arthurian tradition, and for the chronicles the real foundation of the whole, is the second of the extant sources, — that strange compilation, the *Historia Britonum* which goes under the name of Nennius.[1]

---

[1] The standard edition is the critical one of Mommsen in the same volume with his Gildas, pp. 113–219, which is noticed in *Rev. Celt.*, XVI, 106–108, and in other periodicals mentioned below. Other important editions are: that of W. Gunn from the Vatican MS., London, 1819; that of Jos. Stevenson from the Harl. MS., London, 1838; that of San-Marte in his *Nennius und Gildas*, Berlin, 1844; J. H. Todd's *Leabhar*, etc., *The Irish Version with English Translation*, Dublin, 1848; Hogan's Irish version from the *L. na Huidre*, Todd Lect. Ser., Dublin, 1895. There is an English translation by Giles in *Six Old English Chronicles*. For manuscripts, see Mommsen, and Hardy, I, 318 ff. The following

The problems of authorship and composition raised by the numerous and inconsistent manuscripts of this disordered collection of annals, chronicle, and tradition can never be fully solved; but a great deal of light has been shed upon them by the prolonged discussion begun some years ago by Professor Zimmer. What may now be considered as probably proved, so far as the present subject is concerned, may be briefly stated.

Sometime in the seventh or eighth century, a Briton (of what region cannot be certainly known), the son of a certain Urbgen, or Urbgehen, put together extracts from a Life of St. Germanus (which had apparently been composed in the south of Britain) and matter relating to the genealogy and history of the Britons. He wrote very briefly up to the period of the Saxon Conquest, when he entered into details. In the year 679 there was compiled in the North (whether or not by the same author, and whether or not as a part of this same work) a genealogy of the English kings of the island, especially those of the North, and a history of affairs there,[1] which, as it began, apparently, at about the year 540, may have been intended as a supplement to the historical sketch of Gildas. If not originally, at any rate as early as the seventh or eighth century, these two documents were joined together, making a version of which, if it ever existed by itself, no copy now remains. By 796, or not long thereafter, a manuscript of this version [2] was taken, together with supplementary sources, by some one (apparently Nennius) who was a native of South Wales, on the borders of Hereford and Brecknock-Radnor, as the basis of a new edition.[3]

---

are the most significant discussions: K. W. Schoell, *De Ecciesiasticae Britonum Scotorumque Historiae Fontibus*, Berlin and London, pp. 29–37; A. de La Borderie, *L'Hist. Brit. attribuée à Nennius*, Paris, 1883 (see later, bibliography, p. 51); Heeger, *Über die Trojanersage der Britten*, Munich, 1886; Zimmer, *Nennius Vindicatus*, Berlin, 1893; d'Arbois de Jubainville, *Rev. Celt.*, XV, 126–129; Mommsen, *Neues Archiv*, XIX, 285; Duchesne, *Nennius Retractatus*, *Rev. Celt.*, XV, 174–197; Zimmer, *Neues Archiv*, XIX, 436–443, 667–669; Heeger, *Gött. Gel. Anz.*, 1894, 399–406; Thurneysen, *Ztsch. f. deutsche Phil.*, XXVIII, 80–113; J. Loth, *Rev. Celt.*, XVI, 267–268; Duchesne, *Rev. Celt.*, XVII, 1–5; Thurneysen, *Ztsch. f. celt. Phil.*, I, 158–168; F. Lot, *Rom.*, XXVIII, 337–342. [1] Nennius, chaps. 57–66.

[2] Perhaps, however, the two documents had not at that time been combined.

[3] Of which the Harl. MS. 3859 is the type.

Either by Nennius or by some predecessor of his in South Wales, there was added to the book a list of *mirabilia* (or wonderful natural phenomena) of the South Country, on the model of two which evidently came with the manuscript from the North. Nennius was a disciple of St. Elbodug, Bishop of Bangor, who was the great representative of that party among the Britons which upheld the Roman views in the bitter ecclesiastical controversy over the Easter celebration and the tonsure. Some person (perhaps Nennius himself) who lived in Anglesey and was under the spiritual direction of a priest named Beulan, prepared an abridged version [1] of Nennius's work, at the desire or for the use of Beulan, or more likely for his son, in the first half of the ninth century. From these Nennian versions are derived all existing manuscripts of the *Historia Britonum* (including those of the Irish translation) with the very important exception of the incomplete Chartres manuscript, which in origin antedates the time of Nennius.

The following is an outline (in the important parts, almost a full translation) of the relevant sections of Nennius's story,[2] — that is, of the work which Mommsen has entitled *Historia Brittonum cum additamentis Nennii.*

In the prologue, after alluding to the neglect of the Britons to preserve records of their history, and after mentioning the Roman authorities who evidently supplied part of the facts of universal chronology and of the history of Britain to the end of the Roman period with which the work begins, Nennius names, as his other sources, *the annals of the Scots and Saxons* (which probably did not furnish information about anything here to be considered) and *British tradition*, which must evidently refer largely to the *Historia* itself in the form which it bore before his expansions.

His account of the Arthurian period commences baldly [3] with the statement that Guorthigirnus reigned in Britain and was in constant fear of the Picts and Scots, of the Romans, and of Ambrosius (whom, like Guorthigirnus, he has not before mentioned).

---

[1] Called by Zimmer "the version of North Wales."

[2] The comparatively small interpolations made after Nennius's day are here omitted.   [3] Chap. 31.

Meanwhile, there arrived from Germany three ships filled with men driven into exile, among them the brothers Hors and Hengist. Guorthigirnus received them kindly and gave them the island of Tanet. [Here is inserted a long narrative of the missionary visit and miracles of St. Germanus. Resuming the main story, Nennius says [1] that] Guorthigirnus promised to give the Saxons [here first specified by that name] food and clothing as they should need it, and in return they agreed to fight his enemies valiantly. But when the barbarians had multiplied, the Britons were not able to feed them, and asked them to depart, "since we do not need your aid." They took counsel also with their elders to break the peace. Hengist, however, was a politic man. Seeing the inefficiency of Guorthigirnus and the weakness of the Britons, he offered to send to his countrymen in Germany for more men to fight for the Britons. Guorthigirnus assented, and there came sixteen ships filled with picked warriors, who were accompanied by the beautiful daughter of Hengist. Hereupon Hengist made a feast for Guorthigirnus and his men and his interpreter, who was named [2] Ceretic, and bade the girl serve them with wine, and they became drunk. Then Satan entered into Guorthigirnus's heart, and he loved the girl and by his interpreter asked her from her father, saying, "All that you demand I will grant, to the half of my kingdom." [3] Hengist took counsel with his followers, and they all thought it best to ask in exchange for the girl the region which "in their language is called Canturguoralen, in ours Chent." This the king granted them, though Guoyrancgonus [4] was then reigning in Cantia and did not know that his kingdom was being given to the pagans. Here Nennius leaves the incident with a bare "and so the girl was given to him in marriage and he slept with her and loved her greatly."

After this [how soon Nennius does not state] Hengist said to Guorthigirnus: [5] "I am thy father and counsellor; and, that thou mayest not fear any man or race, I, since my race is strong, will invite my son with my brother's son, [6] to fight against the Scots. Give them the regions in the North, near the wall." Guorthigirnus assented, and Octha and Ebissa [who, of course, by direct implication are respectively Hengist's son and

---

[1] Chap. 36.

[2] *Vocatur ;* all the other verbs here are in the past tense.

[3] Evidently the writer had in mind Herod and Salome.

[4] Probably this is merely a title, meaning "governor" or "sub-king"; but the later chroniclers took it for a man's name.

[5] Chap. 38. [6] *Cum fratrueli suo.*

nephew] came with forty ships; and, when they had sailed round the country of the Picts, they devastated the Orkneys and came and occupied many regions beyond the Firth of Forth,[1] up to the boundaries of the Picts. And Hengist kept constantly summoning more ships to him, a few at a time; and when his race had grown strong they took possession of the city of the Kentishmen.[2]

Now Guorthigirnus added to all his sins by marrying his own daughter, who bore him a son. St. Germanus, hearing of this, called a great synod to consider appropriate measures. Guorthigirnus [as Nennius tells at some length] tried to face the matter out; but he was put to shame, fled before the face of Germanus, and was condemned by him and by all the council of the Britons.

Afterwards[3] the king called to him his magi and asked what he should do. They bade him go to the extreme limits of his kingdom and build[4] a strong tower (*arcem*), "because," they said, "the race which you have received into your kingdom will hate you and kill you by treachery and seize the whole country after your death." So, with the magi, he sought through many provinces, and at last in the region of North Wales (*Guined*), on one of the mountains of Snowdon (*Hereri*), they selected the place for the tower, which, they said, would be forever safe from the barbarians. But when he had assembled masons and got together the wood and stone, in one night all the material was carried off, and this happened three times. Then the magi replied to the king's inquiries, that the work could never be done unless he should find a child without a father, kill him, and sprinkle the ground about the tower with his blood. So Guorthigirnus sent some of the magi throughout all Britain, and after long journeying they came to the field Elleti,[5] in the region Gleguissing.[6] Here boys were playing at ball,

---

[1] *Mare Frenessicum.*

[2] *Venerunt ad supra dictam civitatem Cantorum.*

[3] Chap. 40.

[4] The Latin word is *invenies.*

[5] Supposed by Roberts (*Cambrian Popular Antiquities*, pp. 58–59) to be the village formerly called in Welsh Mæseleg, now Bassalig, in Monmouthshire, mentioned by Geoffrey of Monmouth, viii, 4, 11.

[6] Stevenson, *ad loc.*, says, the tract between the Usk and Rumney, named from Glivisus, father of the Welsh saint Gundlæus. Lot, *Rom.*, XXVIII, 338, says, the region between the Teivi [Teifi] and the Usk; and he refers to J. Loth, *Mab.*, II, 212, note. Phillimore (*Y Cymmrodor*, XI, 47) says only that Gleguissing certainly comprehended no region north of the Towy.

and one in anger at another addressed him [1] as a fellow (*homo*) without a father. Then the messengers sought out the boy's mother and asked if he had a father. She assured them with an oath that he had not; that she did not know how he had been conceived; and that she had never had intercourse with any man. When the boy had been taken to the king and was about to be killed, he inquired of Guorthigirnus why he had been brought. On mention of the magi, he asked that they be summoned; and when they came, he demanded who had revealed to them that his blood was necessary for the tower. " I, O king," he said, " will tell you the truth." Then he challenged the magi to say what was under the surface of the ground. They answered, " We do not know." " There is," he said, " a pond (*stagnum*) in the midst of the place. Dig, and you will find it." Men dug and came to water. Then successively, and each time after drawing from the magi an acknowledgment of ignorance, the boy revealed that the pond contained two vessels, the vessels a folded tent,[2] and the tent two sleeping snakes (*vermes*), one white and one red. Being uncovered, the snakes began to fight. At last the red seemed weaker, but again he became stronger and drove his adversary out of the tent; then the one followed the other across the pond,[3] and the tent vanished.[4] Hereupon the boy proceeded to interpret. " This mystery," he said, " is revealed to me. The tent signifies thy kingdom; the pond is this world; the red snake is thy dragon, and the white is the dragon of that race which has seized many parts of Britain. It will hold almost all the island from sea to sea, but afterwards our race will rise in might and manfully drive the race of the Angles across the sea. Do thou nevertheless depart from this tower, because thou art not able to build it, and seek through many provinces to find a safe tower, and I will remain here." [5] And the king asked the youth [6] his

---

[1] Here the narrative passes into direct discourse, and so it continues to the end of the incident. [2] *Tentorium complicatum.*

[3] *Alter alterum secutus.* This clause evidently has no significance as to the result of the fight; it merely means that the snakes disappeared.

[4] For a closely related dragon story, which reappears also in the *Brut Tysilio* (Roberts's translation, pp. 68–70), see the tale of Lludd and Llevelys, in the *Mabinogion* (Loth, I, 178–182; Lady Guest, III, 311–313).

[5] On the preservation of the name Dinas Emreis (Fortress of Ambrosius) in the mountains of Snowdon, see Lady Guest, *Mabinogion*, III, 317; F. Lot, *Rom.*, XXVIII, 338; cf. also Rhŷs, *Celtic Folklore*, Oxford, 1901, pp. 218, 469 ff., 487, 507.

[6] *Adolescentem. Puer* is the word applied to him up to this point, except in the single case already noted.

name, and he replied, " I am called Ambrosius." " That is," interprets Nennius, " he meant that he was Embreis the supreme prince."[1] The king inquired of his ancestry, and he replied, " My father is one of the consuls of the Roman race." Guorthigirnus gave him the tower, with all the kingdoms of the western part of Britain, and he himself with his magi went to the northern part, to the region called Guunnessi,[2] and built there the city which is called by his name Caer Guorthigirn.

Meanwhile,[3] Guorthemir, the son of Guorthigirnus, fought fiercely with Hengist and Horsus (*sic*) and their race and drove them from the isle of Tanet, and there three times reduced them to extremities.[4] They sent messengers to Germany and called in many shiploads of warriors, and afterwards they fought against the kings of " our race," sometimes extending their territories, sometimes having them circumscribed. Guorthemir fought valorously against them in four battles, the first by the river Derguentid ;[5] the second at the ford " which is called in their language Episford, in ours Rithergabail," and there fell Hors with the son of Guorthigirnus, whose name was Categirnus. The third battle was in a place near the " *lapidem tituli*," which is by the Gallic sea, and there the barbarians were completely defeated and fled to their ships. But after a short time, Guorthemir died. He had bidden his servants bury him in the port from which the barbarians had gone forth, on the shore of the sea, because, he said, " though they hold elsewhere a port in this region they will forever be unable to establish themselves." But his servants did not obey his command. And the barbarians came back in force, since Guorthigirnus was their friend because of his wife ; and no one dared to oppose them, since they seized Britain not by their valor, but by the will of God. " And who," asks Nennius, " can resist that ? "

After the return of Hengist, the barbarians made a plot, and sent legates to Guorthigirnus to propose perpetual peace. When Guorthigirnus and his counsellors assented, a conference was arranged, to which both parties were to come without arms. But Hengist instructed his men to bring each a knife concealed under his garment, and at his word of command (*eu Saxones eniminit saxas*) they killed all the counsellors of Guorthigirnus to the

---

[1] *Id est, Embreis Guletic ipse videbatur.*

[2] Lot (*Rom.*, XXVIII, 339, note) says that the place is unknown.

[3] Chap. 43.

[4] *Conclusit, obsedit, percussit, comminuit, terruit.*

[5] There is no agreement as to the exact location of the places here named ; but certainly they were all in the South.

number of three hundred. The king himself was allowed to redeem his life with the lands of the East Saxons, South Saxons, and Middle Saxons.[1]

Now[2] St. Germanus preached to Guorthigirnus that he should repent and abandon his incestuous life. Guorthigirnus fled to the region named from him Guorthigirniaun,[3] to hide himself there with his wives, and from there to the tower of Guorthigirnus in the region of the Demeti near the river Teibi.[4] St. Germanus with all the clergy of Britain followed, praying; and in the night fire from heaven destroyed the tower with Guorthigirnus and his wives. "This," says Nennius, "is the end of him, as I found it in the book of St. Germanus. But others report differently"; some that, as he wandered about, hated by all for his crime, his heart burst; others, that the earth opened and swallowed him in the night in which his tower was burned. He had three sons, Guorthemir and Categirnus; and a third, Pascent, who ruled in the two regions of Buelt[5] and Guorthigirniaun after the death of his father, under the favor of Ambrosius, who was king among all the kings of the British race. By his daughter also Guorthigirnus was the father of St. Faustus.

Here follow the genealogy of the "present" ruler of the regions named, back to and beyond Guorthigirnus, a mention of the return of St. Germanus to the continent, and a long account of the ministry of St. Patrick in Ireland, inserted as belonging chronologically at this point. Then the narrative resumes:[6]

At that time, the Saxons increased and grew strong in Britain. After the death of Hengist, Octha his son came from the northern part of the island to the kingdom of the men of Cantia, and from him are descended its kings. Then Arthur fought against them in those days, together with the kings of the Britons, but he himself was leader in the battles.[7] The first battle was at the mouth of the river Glein; the second, third, fourth, and fifth, on the river Dubglas, in the region Linnuis; the sixth on the

---

[1] I have supplied this last name from the Irish version. It is also given by some of the later chroniclers who follow Nennius, and evidently belongs to the authentic text. [2] Chap. 47. [3] Powis.

[4] The names *Demeti* (i.e., Demetians) and *Teibi* (i.e., Teifi) belong to the South; so the passage is in flat contradiction to the previous one which (correctly, according to Lot) located the city of Guorthigirn in the North.

[5] Brecknock-Radnor. [6] Chap. 56.

[7] *Dux bellorum.* The Vatican manuscript. which represents a late recension, of about 946, adds "although many were nobler by birth (*nobiliores*) than he."

river Bassas; the seventh in the wood of Celidon; the eighth at the
fortress Guinnion, when Arthur bore the image of the Virgin Mary on his
shoulders [1] and a great slaughter was made of the pagans; the ninth at Urbs
Legionis; the tenth on the shore of the river which is called Tribuit; the
eleventh on the mountain Agned; the twelfth on Mount Badon, when
Arthur alone in one day killed nine hundred and sixty men; [2] and in all the
battles he was victor.   But the enemy continually received aid from Germany, whence they brought kings to rule over those of them who were in
Britain up to the time of Ida, who was the first king in Beornicia.

Next [3] comes the section containing genealogies of the kings of
the invaders and dealing with wars and other affairs in the North
from the middle of the fifth to the end of the seventh century. [4]   In
a chronological computation at the end of this passage, mention is
made of a quarrel between Guitolinus and Ambrosius, said to have
occurred twelve years after the rule of Guorthigirnus.   Next comes
a list of the twenty-eight cities of Britain, and then the account of
its *mirabilia*.   Of these the tenth or eleventh [5] (according as one
reckons) is said to be in the region of Buelt.   In that province is a
heap of stones, and on the top is one stone bearing the print of a
dog's foot.   This mark was made by Cabal, who was the dog of
Arthur the warrior, [6] when he hunted the boar Troynt.   Arthur
afterwards collected the pile of stones under this one, and it was
called Carn Cabal.   Then the account adds that whenever the
stone is carried off, it reappears upon the heap the next day. [7]

There follows immediately the description of another wonder in
the region of Ercing. [8]   This is a tomb situated beside the stream

---

[1] *Super humeros suos.*

[2] The manuscripts, needless to say, do not agree exactly as to this number.

[3] Chaps. 57–66.

[4] And for Mercia to the end of the eighth.   This is the section which has
already been mentioned as constituting one of the originally distinct documents
at the basis of the whole composition.

[5] Chap. 73.

[6] *Arthuri militis.*

[7] This story contains the germ of that of the hunt of Twrch Trwyth, which
appears very fully in the tale of Kulhwch and Olwen (Loth, *Mabinogion*, I, 185–
283; see also especially Lady Guest, II, 360, and Rhŷs, *Celtic Folklore*, 1901,
p. 538).   [8] Hereford.

called "the Source of the Anir," and Anir was the name of the man who was buried there. He was the son of Arthur the warrior, who himself killed him there and buried him. After this we are told of the wonderful property of the tomb.[1] With the *mirabilia* the work of Nennius ends.

The *Historia Britonum*, then, not only contains the earliest known mention of Arthur, but presents a detailed story of the whole Arthurian period. It is natural, in the first place, to compare this story with that of Gildas.

In very general outline the two do not greatly differ, — that is, Gildas's narrative, apart from his expressions of personal feeling, might serve as a vague outline for the equally anti-Saxon narrative of Nennius.[2] Although Nennius, who lived some centuries later than Gildas, does not, like Gildas, exaggerate the Saxons' conquests and dwell upon their cruelty, he nevertheless substantially agrees with his predecessor in making it appear that the barbarians furnished no real aid against the Picts and Scots. The statement of Nennius that the Saxons conquered only by the will of God, corresponds to Gildas's prevailing idea that the invasion was a punishment for the sins of the Britons. Again, Nennius makes Ambrosius, in his rôle of *magus*, express the impassioned belief of the Britons that their overthrow was not final, while Gildas [3] had mentioned, doubtless in accordance with a popular tradition, a limited time — three hundred years — as the period assigned by prophecy to the Saxon occupation. At the beginning of his account and elsewhere, Nennius preserves, however vaguely, reminiscences of the civil wars between various factions for which Gildas so bitterly blames his countrymen. Indeed, it can be proved from resemblances in phraseology [4] that one of the pre-Nennian authors of the *Historia Britonum* had Gildas's work at hand when he wrote, and utilized it in some of his earlier chapters.

---

[1] For remaining local traces of this story, see Rees, *Liber Landavensis*, cited also by Zimmer, *Nennius Vindicatus*, p. 114.

[2] Their agreement as to the number of ships which brought the first invaders (three) can hardly be regarded as significant.

[3] Chap. 23.

[4] Almost all of these are cited by Mommsen, pp. 21 ff.

But the differences between the two accounts are far more important than the agreements. The most obvious is the general one
caused by the greater fullness of Nennius. He seems to include all
the statements of fact that appear in Gildas, except that of the
pestilence concomitant with the last invasion of the Picts, and
he adds all the following material: the name of Guorthigirnus;
entirely new characters and rôles in Hengist's daughter (whom he
does not name) and in St. Germanus, Hors, Hengist, Guorthigirnus's
interpreter Ceretic (who is of very little importance), Octha, Ebissa,
Guorthemir, Pascent, and above all Arthur, as well as his son Anir
and his dog Cabal; the specification of Tanet, and later of Kent,
as the first abode of the Saxons; the dissatisfaction of the Britons
with the Saxons before the latter had performed any overt acts of
hostility; all the stories of Hengist's plots (including the details of
his manner of securing reënforcements), the incidents of his feast
and the marriage of his daughter to Guorthigirnus and his treacherous slaughter of the Britons; the whole tale of Guorthigirnus's
tower, with all its incidentals; the wars of Guorthemir, which take
the place, with much more detail, of what Gildas says of those of
Ambrosius; the legend about Guorthemir's burial; the legends of
Guorthigirnus's death; the account of Arthur's wars *in toto*, except
for Gildas's mention of the siege of Mount Badon; and, finally, the
mirabilia relating to Arthur. Nennius also differs from Gildas in
making no allusion to Ambrosius's descendants and in saying that
the Saxons came to Britain by chance.

There is a very notable divergence in the fact that, with Nennius,
Guorthemir practically replaces the Ambrosius of Gildas. To be
sure, Nennius speaks of Ambrosius also, but in subordinate and
inconsistent notices. Three times Ambrosius appears dimly in the
story as a powerful leader: where it is said that Guorthigirnus was
in fear of him; where he is called chief king of the Britons after
the death of Guorthigirnus; and where his strife with Guitolinus is
mentioned. Evidently the conception of the child of supernatural
attainments in the tower episode was originally a very different one;
and confusion appears in that episode in that the child's mother
declares that he has no father, while he himself (agreeably, be it
observed, to Gildas's account) claims to be the son of a Roman

consul. From these facts it seems not unreasonable to surmise
that Nennius's story is that of the British faction in the island, as
opposed to the Roman faction of Gildas, — that Guorthemir crowds
out Ambrosius because he was the hero of this British faction, but
that Ambrosius's fame was too great to allow him to be passed over
without mention. The character of magician assigned to Ambrosius in Nennius is in harmony with this theory ; for it is an explanation of a great chief's successes very natural to the minds of a
hostile party, especially after the lapse of time has afforded opportunity for legends to arise.[1] Evidence will soon be given that this
whole incident of the tower is one of the later additions to the
Historia.

It is clear, therefore, that the entire section of Nennius's work
with which we are concerned is independent of Gildas in origin ; or,
if not, that in the process of expansion and alteration it has been
completely transformed in substance and largely in spirit.

The contributions of the *Historia* to the Arthurian story being
thus indicated, the next step is to consider their sources. Unfortunately, nothing more definite can be determined than that they rest
upon British traditions of uncertain age.

Nennius's own mention of British traditions may refer chiefly or
altogether to the version of the *Historia* which came down to him,
and the starting point of our investigation must therefore be the
unique Chartres manuscript, which alone represents the work at
a pre-Nennian stage of its development. The Chartres version is
unfortunately a fragment, ending at the point where Guorthigirnus
is falling in love with Hengist's daughter. As far as it goes, it
agrees closely, for our period, with Nennius's redaction, so that we
cannot assume that it lacked anything which appeared in the latter.
Its heading, however, is important for our present purpose :[2] *Inci-
piunt excerpta filii Urbgen de libro Sancti Germani inventa et origine et
genealogia Britonum.*

---

[1] Rhŷs, it may be observed, thinks that a mythical Ambrosius was already
known (*Hibbert Lectures on Celtic Heathendom*, pp. 151–152).

[2] I have adopted a number of corrections and have omitted *De aetatibus mundi*
(which is really the title of chap. 1). For the original, see *Rev. Celt.*, XV, 174 ff.

The sources indicated in the latter part of this heading evidently refer, not to the portion of the *Historia* which deals with our period, but to other portions of the work. It seems, therefore, as if the "son of Urbgen" meant to say that he took his account of our period from a Life of St. Germanus. Now only two or three of the incidents with which we are concerned have anything to do with St. Germanus. It follows, therefore, that the original "liber Sancti Germani" did not contain most of them, and that they were either inserted in the *Historia* by the son of Urbgen or had been added to the Germanus book before it came into his hands. The whole episode of Guorthigirnus's tower was either a specially late addition or else had an origin quite different from that of the other incidents in question.[1] The *mirabilia*, also, are pretty certainly accretions to the original.

This is all we know of the development of the text, and it does not really show that any part of the work is necessarily much older than any of the others: for (1) we cannot tell the date of the son of Urbgen, or of any version of the *Historia* previous to Nennius; (2) all additions (except for a clause or two) were made at least as early as the time of the latter, that is, by about the year 800; (3) even if the additions were made by Nennius himself, as seems unlikely in the case of most of them, they may have been taken from independent written records; and (4) the age of an oral tradition cannot be determined by the date at which that tradition happens to be committed to writing.

What is to be said, therefore, of Nennius's material is that it represents more or less inconsistent British traditions of uncertain age, some of which [2] had probably been written down about a century after the time of Gildas, and that the work was completed

---

[1] This is evident from the following considerations: (1) the episode represents Ambrosius in a character different from that in which he appears in the rest of the narrative; (2) it locates Caer Guorthigirn differently; (3) it is loosely connected with what precedes; (4) it calls the Saxons *Angli*, — a name which occurs nowhere else in Nennius except in the account of Northern affairs, which, as we have seen, may easily have come from a source different from that of the rest of the work.

[2] But not necessarily any of the portions with which we are here concerned.

about the year 800. The next question is. How far is the narrative historical?

It is not surprising that some writers have denied to Nennius any credibility whatever. The story of Germanus's miracles, of Guorthigirnus's tower, and of Guorthemir's burial, the *mirabilia*, and many other sections, are clearly altogether fabulous; the account of the Saxons' treachery in killing the British chiefs is a bit of continental tradition;[1] and the requirement of a boy's blood to mix with the mortar is only a motive from Celtic (or, indeed, from universal) folklore.[2] Then, again, Nennius is too much of a partisan. There is also external evidence which counts strongly against him, for we have in the Saxon *Chronicle* a very different and much more straightforward account of this same period. This testimony from the opposite party we must now briefly consider.

The early portion of the *Chronicle*, which here concerns us, though probably not written down before the eighth or ninth century, doubtless represents traditions which go back to a time not far removed from the events to which they refer. After mention of the coming of the Germans and of their establishment in the island (taken from Bede's account, which will soon be discussed), the succeeding entries of the *Chronicle*, as far as they relate to the present subject, are as follows:

455. In this year Hengest[3] and Horsa[3] fough· against Wyrtgeorn[3] the king, in the place called Agælsthrep (and his brother I. a was killed[4]), and after that, Hengest succeeded to the kingdom, and Æsc[3] nis son.

457. Hengest and Æsc fought against the Britons at Crecganford, killed four thousand of them, drove them to London, and won Kent.

465. In a fight of Hengest and Æsc with the Welsh near Wippedsfleet, the Welsh lost twelve leaders and the Saxons one, Wipped.

473. Hengest and Æsc conquered the Welsh.

----

[1] Widukind (*Mon. Germ. Hist., Script.*, III. ed. 1839, p. 419) recounts it as having been practised by the Saxons against the Thuringians.

[2] See Dr. Jamieson's *History of the Culdees*, pp. 20 ff., and Tylor, *Primitive Culture*, 3d ed., 1891, I, 104-108.

[3] These names may have been taken from Bede, though I do not think they were; see below, pp. 24, 25.

[4] Probably from Bede.

This is the last that is said of Hengest, and the next entry, at 477, tells of the arrival of Ælle and his three sons in three ships. Under 508 it is stated that Cerdic and Cynric (historically the founders of the kingdom of the West Saxons,[1] and represented as having come to Britain thirteen years before) slew a British king called Natanleod[2] with five thousand of his men, from whom that region was named *Natan leaga*.   Except for the statement of a fight of Cerdic and Cynric in 527, and the conquest of the Isle of Wight in 530, there is no mention of any further warfare with the Britons until 552, after the end of our period.

Now while this narrative agrees substantially, or at least does not disagree, with the much vaguer outline of Gildas, except that it does not speak of Ambrosius, it does stand in striking contrast to the story of Nennius.   And we can have no hesitation which to prefer.   The authors of the *Chronicle* were probably biased; they must be expected to omit British names and victories, and they have probably recorded here and there a purely legendary detail. Still, it is manifest that they tried to set down only what they supposed to be the plain truth.   On their testimony, as well as on *a priori* grounds, we are justified in rejecting Nennius's story of the alliance of Vortigern with the Saxons against his own people (which involves much of the narrative of Hengest's machinations), though we need not necessarily refuse to believe that Vortigern was at first very friendly to the Saxons and that he married a Saxon woman.

There is, however, in the outline of the *Chronicle* (apart from those details which it may have taken from Bede) one point of apparent contact with Nennius, — it specifies four battles as fought by Hengist against the Britons, which may perhaps correspond to the four assigned by Nennius to Guorthemir.   Even here, however, there is striking disagreement.   There is no certainty that the places mentioned in the *Chronicle* are to be identified with those of Nennius. Further, though the *Chronicle*, by not claiming a Saxon victory in the first fight, seems to admit a defeat,[3] it substantially contradicts

---

[1] As recorded in the *Chronicle*, ann. 519, in an interpolation.

[2] *Leod* = Welsh *llwyd*, "prince."

[3] In this part of the *Chronicle* a defeat is never recorded in plain terms.

Nennius as to the result of the others, giving very definite, though perhaps untrustworthy, details. Certainly the inherent probability is that the Saxons rather than the Britons were victorious. It looks, therefore, as if in Nennius the real facts had been inverted, and as if his laudation of Guorthemir (like Gildas's praise of Ambrosius) were, as we should expect, greatly exaggerated.

But it may reasonably be maintained that the *Chronicle* gives indirect confirmation of the most important of all Nennius's stories, that of the career of Arthur; for, during a long period beginning with the year 527 it records no advance of the Saxons. The most natural explanation, in which all historians agree, and which is in harmony with Gildas's account, is that the power of the invaders had been weakened by British successes. Even here there is a discrepancy, however, in that Nennius makes Arthur's victories end with the siege of Mount Badon, which must have occurred long before 527. Still, this variation is not a very serious matter, since both accounts are admitted to be highly inaccurate in details.

While, then, the Saxon *Chronicle* indicates that the narrative of Nennius is greatly distorted, it admits the conclusion that parts of his main outline may have a basis in fact. There are other considerations of like tendency. [In the first place, it must be remembered that, even though the *Historia Britonum* is only a record of popular traditions, the popular traditions of an unlettered time do not create something out of nothing, and are very tenacious of striking facts.) One may reasonably hold that Vortimer never thoroughly subdued the Saxons, and question whether Vortigern married Hengist's daughter; but it does not seem very reasonable to doubt that Vortigern, Vortimer, Ambrosius, and Arthur were real men who fought against the invaders.

In one point, indeed, — the remark that the Saxons first came to Britain by chance, — Nennius's story seems to be more nearly correct than that of Gildas; though Nennius is evidently wrong, like Gildas, in implying that none of them had ever come before the time of Vortigern. The *Historia* also appears to receive some confirmation in certain details from the *Ecclesiastical History* of Bede. Of this latter, therefore, something must now be said.

Bede composed his great work in his Northumbrian monastery in the year 731. He draws his brief account [1] of the period of the Saxon invasion chiefly from Gildas. For the most part he copies the latter's very words, making only slight alterations to improve the style. All that is here necessary, therefore, is to specify those points in which he departs from Gildas. In all of these which are really important,[2] he agrees with Nennius. He gives to the king who called in the Germans the name Vurtigernus; says that the leaders of the first comers are reported to have been two brothers, Hengist and Horsa; gives their genealogy, and adds that Horsa was afterwards killed by the Britons. Obviously, unless Bede was drawing from that form of the *Historia Britonum* which existed in his day, his evidence goes to substantiate at least these details of Nennius's narrative.

Now while, in the absence of proof to the contrary, the possibility that Bede used the *Historia* [3] must always be admitted, — and while it is perhaps still less improbable that he may have got information from the British population near his home,[4] — it is more natural to suppose that he drew wholly from Saxon tradition. From that source must have come his remark that a monument in the eastern

---

[1] Bk. i, chaps. 14–23.

[2] The less significant ones are the following: (1) Bede states directly, in marked divergence from Gildas, that the Saxons actually fought and conquered the Scots. This may have come to him from Saxon tradition, but it is an almost necessary inference from the general course of events as described by Gildas (and Nennius), though they themselves may deny it. (2) Bede's statement that, upon their break with the Britons, the Saxons allied themselves directly with the Picts (see the discussion of Fordun, p. 243, below), he takes from a Life of St. Germanus (*Acta Sanctorum*, July, VII, 213; see Thurneysen, *Englische Studien*, XXII, 166) upon which he is drawing for an account of the saint (as appears from an excerpt which he makes from it later, chap. 28). (3) Bede is the first of the historians to mention the fact that Lupus was associated with Germanus, — a detail which was taken into the story by Geoffrey of Monmouth. (4) Still more remote from the present subject is Bede's statement as to what parts of the country were occupied by the respective German tribes.

[3] Mommsen's argument to this effect (*Neues Archiv*, 1894, XIX, 291 ff.) from Bede's error in dating the fabulous story of King Lucius's conversion, has not been generally accepted.

[4] See Zimmer, *Nennius Vindicatus*, p. 61.

part of Kent still bears Horsa's name;[1] nor is it likely that the authors of the detailed notices of the early battles in the *Chronicle* were indebted to Bede for the names of Hengest and Horsa, the leaders in those battles.

A little later,[2] Bede gives, evidently from Saxon sources, information which seems to reappear, in an incomplete and greatly altered form, in Nennius. This consists of the genealogical table of the early kings of Kent, who are thus named in succession : Hengist, who with his son Oisc was first to come to Britain, invited by Vurtigernus ; Œric, called Oisc, from whom the Kentish kings are called Oiscings ; Octa ; Irminric ; Ædilberct. Now there can be no doubt that Nennius's Octha is identical with Bede's Octa, and it looks as if Nennius's Ebissa were really Bede's Oisc.[3] This suggestion assumes considerable corruption of the name, but Bede himself, it will be observed, gives an alternate form, *Œric*, and the Saxon *Chronicle* has *Æsc*. But if the supposition is correct, the authors of the *Historia Britonum* made Hengist's son into his nephew, and his grandson into his son ; for it must certainly be assumed that, in a point relating so directly to the Saxons, their own record is the more correct.[4] It follows that everything that Nennius says of Octha and Ebissa is distorted and fabulous. The narrative, indeed, is self-condemnatory when it states that these early Saxon leaders not only conquered the North but settled there.[5]

So far, therefore, Nennius seems to have preserved, amid a great deal of pure legend, some reminiscences of truth. It is now time

---

[1] Cf. on the French *Brut*, p. 218, below.   [2] Bk. ii, chap. 5.

[3] So far as I know, this suggestion has not been made before.

[4] Among the genealogies of North British origin which make up the last part of Nennius's work, that of the Kentish kings gives the succession as Hengist, Octha, Ossa, Eormoric (chap. 57).

[5] Why it does so is explained if we suppose that it was itself composed in that region. For each section of the British population might naturally tend to associate with its own locality the ravages of some of the first invaders of whom they had recollection ; and while the connection of the first settlement, under Hengist, with Kent, may easily have been too firmly established in every one's memory to be broken, the same need not have been true of all the exploits of succeeding kings. Nennius seems to return to the facts when he says that, upon the death of Hengist, Octha came back to Kent.

to consider directly that part of his story which is most vital to the present subject, namely, his account of Arthur.   On this small section is based practically our whole actual knowledge, real or supposed, of the facts about this hero, and an immense amount of ingenuity, mostly misdirected, has been devoted to its interpretation.   One must certainly reject, at the start, all such unsupported suggestions as that, for instance, which makes Arthur the son of Ambrosius, — an attractive idea which has been adopted by more than one writer.

Nennius's account of Arthur, with his similar catalogue of Guorthemir's battles, differs notably from most of the rest of his narrative in being concise and straightforward.   It has every appearance of having been originally set down by a man who was far more of an historian and less of a fabulist than the author of the stories about Guorthigirnus and Hengist.   Of course, in the statement that Arthur with his own hand in a single battle killed more than nine hundred men, a bit of legend has crept in ; but the only other notably suspicious features are the specification of the number of the engagements as twelve, and the statement that Arthur was always victorious.   While, therefore, we cannot accept the passage as absolute truth, we may reasonably conclude that it represents what was believed to be true by a Briton of a rather judicial mind some time before the end of the eighth century, and we may try to interpret it on that basis.   In the absence of evidence to the contrary, it must be allowed to indicate, in the first place, that Arthur was the hero of the battle of Badon, of the historicity of which Gildas's mention leaves no doubt.

The central point in the discussion of this account, — and that which has evoked most controversy, — is the attempt to fix the locality, or localities, in which Arthur performed his exploits.   This attempt is based, necessarily, on the identification of the names which Nennius connects with his twelve battles.   Now, as regards these, the whole debate has not brought us any nearer to actual certainty than were the students in the time of Henry of Huntingdon, who tells us,[1] summarily, that "all the places are now unknown," though we need not, perhaps, agree with the indolent archdeacon

---

[1] Ed. Arnold, Rolls Series, p. 49.

that this is due to the providence of God, who wished to show the worthlessness of earthly glory. This being the state of the case as regards the individual places, one must refuse assent to any of the efforts which have been made (many of them very elaborate) to trace strategically the course of Arthur's campaigns.[1] It may suffice here to say that there are two main theories, each supported by certain unconvincing arguments independent of Nennius. One of these theories is that Arthur belonged to the South and fought most of his battles in that region, though this does not necessarily imply that he may not have penetrated sometimes to other parts of the country. The other theory, which has been especially championed by Skene and Stuart-Glennie, is that his activity was limited chiefly or altogether to the neighborhood of the Roman walls in the North. Two facts are thought to favor this latter contention : (1) the names of Guinevere, Modred, and other personages of Arthurian story, and certain stories about them, are localized by popular tradition and the old romances, in southern Scotland exclusively, or almost exclusively[2]; and (2) the places mentioned in the Welsh Arthurian poetry likewise belong to the North.[3] But these

---

[1] The first of these attempts, as far as I know, was that of John Whitaker in his *History of Manchester*, 1771-1775, II, 35-58. After his time, minute reconstructions of the whole history of the Arthurian period, based often on an acceptance of everything said not only by Nennius, but by Geoffrey of Monmouth, and nearly every other of the mediæval English, Scottish, and French historical romancers, were not uncommon for fifty years, and they have not altogether ceased yet ; see, for example, John Milner, *Antiquities of Winchester*, 1839, I, chap. 5, especially pp. 55 ff. ; *Gentleman's Magazine*, 1842, a series of articles beginning Vol. XVII, p. 385, and continuing into XVIII (see index) ; Poste, especially pp. 103-108 ; Haigh, especially pp. 279-295 ; Babcock, pp. 142-177 ; W. H. Dickinson, *King Arthur in Cornwall*, London, etc., 1900. As less fanciful or otherwise more important, may be mentioned : Carte, *History of England*, 1747, I, 205 ; Gunn, *Historia Britonum*, pp. 173-183 ; Stevenson, *Nennius*, pp. 48-49 ; Todd, *Leabhar*, etc., pp. 109-111 ; Skene, *Four Ancient Books*, I, 50-60, and *Celtic Scotland*, I, 153-154 ; C. H. Pearson, in *Bishop Percy's Folio MS.*, ed. Hales and Furnivall, I, 403 ; Stuart-Glennie, *Arthurian Localities* in *Merlin*, ed. E.E.T.S., Part III, 1869 (also published separately, Edinburgh, 1869, with an argument by Pearson) ; Guest, *Origines Celticae*, II, 187-189.

[2] The fame of Arthur himself has of course left its traces also in the south of England and elsewhere.   [3] Cf. pp. 95 (note 1), 203, 242 ff., below.

arguments are by no means conclusive. The localization of names does not prove that they may not have been imported from elsewhere.[1] Moreover, if Arthur's victories were confined to the North, we can hardly understand the cessation of the Saxon advance after the battle of Badon. The *mirabilia* of Nennius prove that Arthur was already a traditional figure in the Southwest considerably before 800. And, finally, if Arthur were already famous in the North in the eighth century, it might perhaps be expected that Bede should at least allude to him. The matter is one which every student must decide for himself, and in any case it is of no great importance to the present subject.

That the author of the list of Arthur's battles knew nothing more about them than he records, is very probable. That he, or antecedent tradition, has obscured some of the facts, hardly needs to be stated. Either he has omitted the names of some engagements, or else he is quite wrong in saying that Arthur was victorious in all of those that he mentions. It is certainly possible that he does not name the battles in their proper order. There is nothing to show that he meant to represent them as following in rapid succession ; they may very well have stood in his mind for a whole lifetime of fighting.

The most important point of all, if we could only decide it, is perhaps that of Arthur's rank and office. Nennius says that he fought, together with the kings of the Britons, as *dux bellorum.* Now this is manifestly not equivalent to stating that Arthur was himself by birth one of the kings and was recognized by the others as overlord. Certainly the writer of the first of the Arthurian *mirabilia* cannot have had any such conception when he called Arthur simply *miles.* That Arthur was not of royal blood is directly asserted by the tenth-century Vatican version of the *Historia ;* but that is too late to have much authority. Taking everything together, it certainly looks as if Arthur owed his position of leader chiefly to his preëminent ability. It may be that his relation to the kings

---

[1] If we should choose to accept Professor Rhŷs's Arthur-Airem theory (*Studies in the Arthurian Legend*, pp. 45–47), we should have a sufficient explanation for the occurrence of some of the names in the North.

was simply something like that ascribed to Miltiades among the Athenian generals: they may all have given place to him voluntarily, as to the man most capable to command. It seems more likely, however, that there is truth in the theory advanced by Professor Rhŷs[1] and others, that Arthur owed some of his authority to the fact of holding the office which had belonged to one of the military chiefs under the Roman system of administration in the island. These offices may well have been kept up by the Britons, at least by the Romanizing party, after the departure of the Romans.

The idea of Arthur's position thus suggested is in harmony with the opinion of those writers who conclude that Nennius's record of Arthur's battles is not that of a series of campaigns systematically planned, but that he went from one place to another, wherever he was most needed for the help of his people. This would fit very well with the theory[2] (inherently reasonable and suggested by what Nennius says, though apparently by anticipation, of Octha and Ebissa) that the Saxons, during their conquest, made use of their fleets, as did the Danes later, in reaching points easy of attack, and did not always march overland through the enemy's country.

The picture of Arthur which we get from such considerations as these, is very different from that which was developed in later romance and which has passed from romance into modern literature. But if it has less splendor, it is at least as worthy of admiration. For it represents Arthur as a bold warrior and an energetic general, to whose preëminent abilities even jealous petty chieftains were obliged to bow, and who, standing firm in the midst of a period of distress and danger, for a long time, as William of Malmesbury was to observe,[3] sustained the falling fortunes of his country.

Yet, even after so reserved a concession as this to romance and enthusiasm, it is safer to end with a word of critical caution. There is always the possibility that Arthur never existed at all, and that even Nennius's comparatively modest eulogy has no firmer foundation than the persistent stories of ancient Celtic myth[4] or the patriotic figments of the ardent Celtic imagination.

---

[1] *Studies in the Arthurian Legend*, p. 7; *Welsh People*, p. 105.
[2] Advanced by Babcock.   [3] Cf. p. 40, below.   [4] Cf. pp. 96–97, below.

From all that has been said, it has appeared that the elements of probable definite fact which Nennius has added to Gildas's very meagre outline of the Arthurian period are scarcely more than these: (1) that the king [1] in whose territory the Saxons began their permanent conquest was Guorthigirnus (Vortigern),[2] and that his resistance to them, whether or not it was patriotic and determined, was unsuccessful; (2) that the earliest Saxon leaders were Hengist and Hors (Horsa), among whose contemporaries and immediate successors were Octa and Ebissa;[3] (3) that among the various British kings and leaders who fought against the invaders in the following decades, there was a certain Guorthemir (Vortimer), who may, or may not, have been the son of Vortigern;[4] (4) that the most important of these leaders, and one of the most efficient, was Arthur, the hero of the battle of Mount Badon, whose position as general (and perhaps as successor of one of the Roman officials) was probably due more to merit than to birth. These facts, with those which Gildas furnishes, are apparently the real historical basis for the whole Arthurian story as it appears in the chronicles.

But for that story Nennius's fables have equal importance with his facts. Geoffrey of Monmouth, as he was bound to do, adopted both without discrimination as the basis of his version, and it was Geoffrey who determined the form of the tradition. While it is true, therefore, that the subsequent magnification of the figure of Arthur vastly exceeds anything that was to be expected from Nennius's account, that it is chiefly due to other sources, and that it has thrown into the background, and in the romances has almost crowded out, the bulk of what he records, — nevertheless, in the works with which the present discussion is concerned, the *Historia* of Nennius is the chief source of Arthurian story in its main outlines. This will come out with sufficient clearness as we proceed.

---

[1] Perhaps only a tribal chief, though apparently the overlord of at least a considerable part of the country.

[2] Though some of the elements in his story may well enough be mythical, as Professor Rhŷs supposes (*Arthurian Legend*, p. 354).

[3] More properly, perhaps, *Oisc*.

[4] The resemblance between the names of the two is somewhat suspicious.

CHAPTER II

THE INTERMEDIATE STAGE

I. THE *ANNALES CAMBRIAE* AND *ANNALS OF ST. MICHAEL'S MOUNT*

NENNIUS, in his prologue, blames his countrymen for their failure to preserve the historical records of their race, and this reproach applies as well to the later Britons as to Nennius's predecessors. The only historical record of Welsh authorship which remains to us from a period of several centuries after Nennius is the brief series of annals known as the *Annales Cambriae*, jotted down in Latin by an anonymous writer in the second half of the tenth century.[1] This is the last important chronicle of British authorship with which we shall have to deal.

The entries of the *Annales Cambriae* are few and scattering, and there are only two which in any way concern the Arthurian tradition.

---

[1] The part of the *Annales* relating to the period before the Norman Conquest is printed in Petrie and Sharpe's *Mon. Hist. Brit.*, pp. 830 ff. (actually edited by Aneurin Owen; see Phillimore in *Y Cymmrodor*, XI, 140), with remarks by Hardy, pp. 92–95. The whole work is printed in a composite version from the three manuscripts, in the edition by J. Williams ab Ithel, Rolls Series, 1860. A review of this edition by L. Jones in *Archæologia Cambrensis*, 1861, p. 331, points out very serious blunders. The oldest (uninterpolated) version was properly printed by E. Phillimore, with discussion, in *Y Cymmrodor*, 1888, IX, 141–183. This is reproduced by J. Loth, *Mabinogion*, II, 345–357. For further discussions, see Ward, I, 431; J. Loth, *L'Emigration bretonne*, pp. 30–31; Schoell, *De Ecclesiae Britonum Scotorumque Historiae Fontibus*, pp. 37–39; and especially Phillimore in *Welsh Hist. Records, Y Cymmrodor*, XI, 134–148. There is a wrong argument by Franz Pütz in *Ztsch. f. franz. Spr.*, 1892, XIV, 186–192. The two later thirteenth-century versions of the *Annales* have more Arthurian material than the original version, but it is drawn from Geoffrey of Monmouth and therefore of no independent value.

Probably the writer had little or no more knowledge of the subject than he shows, since he begins his records with A.D. 444, and reckons all subsequent years from that date, as if he recognized the Saxon invasion as the commencement of a new era.

The two entries which concern us are the following:[1]

516. Battle of Badon, in which Arthur carried the cross of our Lord Jesus Christ for three days and three nights on his shoulders, and the Britons were victors.

537. Battle of Camlann, in which Arthur and Medraut fell.

The mention of the battle of Badon, and of Arthur as its hero, adds nothing to the information furnished by Gildas and Nennius. The statement about the cross is more significant. Its mere insertion in this connection can be explained, as will soon appear, from Nennius, but it points to a legendary conception which we have not yet encountered in so clear a form.

Nennius says that in Arthur's eighth battle he bore *the image of the Virgin* upon his shoulders. This looks like a clumsy or unintelligent repetition of a statement that Arthur bore the image as a device upon his armor. Geoffrey of Monmouth, in taking over this section of Nennius, changes (or restores) the sentence. He writes[2] that in the battle of Badon Arthur fastened to his shoulders his shield Pridwen,[3] on which was represented the image of the Holy Mary. William of Malmesbury also states[4] that Arthur had sewed the image on his arms.[5] Very much to the point, then, is the fact[6] that the Welsh word for "shield" (*ysgwydd*) differs only in a single letter from that for shoulder (*ysgwyd*). If the story was originally recorded or told in Welsh, as was doubtless the case, and contained

---

[1] Besides translating, I have given the dates according to our own system.

[2] ix, 4, 17–19. Possibly Geoffrey here preserves the genuine reading, which may have stood in his copy of Nennius.

[3] Cf. p. 95, below.

[4] See p. 40, below. Henry of Huntingdon (see p. 42, below), merely repeats Nennius.

[5] " Fretus imagine Dominicae matris, quam armis suis insuerat " (*Gesta Regum*, Rolls Series, I, 12).

[6] Pointed out by Williams (or rather, I suppose, by Aneurin Owen), p. xxiv; also by Skene, *Four Ancient Books*, I, 55.

the word for "shield," a later transcriber or narrator, whose influence manifests itself in the existing versions of Nennius, may easily have substituted "shoulder" by mistake. The theory is so probable that it may be accepted as a fact, and evidently it is equally good for the entry in the *Annales*, though there the mention is of the cross, not of the image.

Now clearly the statements of Nennius and of the *Annales* are so similar that we must assume that they are both derived from a common source, if we can only explain the differences : namely, — the substitution in the *Annales* of the cross for the image of the Virgin ; the addition of the mention of the three days and nights ; and the transference of the episode from the eighth battle of Arthur to that of Badon. An explanation is not hard to find. The Cambridge MS. of Nennius [1] adds at the end of the account of Arthur a legend which has been incorporated into the other manuscripts : " For Arthur went to Jerusalem, and there made a cross of the size of the true cross, and there it was consecrated, and for three whole days he fasted, watched, and prayed before the cross of the Lord that the Lord would give him victory over the pagans through this rood ; which was granted. And he took away with him the image of the Holy Mary, whose fragments are still kept at Wedel in great veneration." [2] The Cambridge MS. is of the thirteenth century, but, while the legend which it records may be developed from the very passage of the genuine Nennius which we are considering, it may, on the other hand, be older than the time of Nennius. [3] In any case, it seems probable that the compiler of the *Annales*, or some predecessor of his, finding, or thinking that he found, in his source (whether or not that source was Nennius) that Arthur carried the image of the Virgin on his shoulders, and finding also in the legend that victory over the pagans was granted him by virtue of the cross, concluded — perhaps with a suggestion from a Christian figure of speech — that it was more probable that what Arthur really carried

---

[1] See Mommsen, p. 200.

[2] Largely on the strength of this passage, Nennius's battle of the castle Guinnion has been located by Skene and others at Wedale (in Stow).

[3] There is no reason to suppose that the legend originated with the scribe of the Cambridge MS., or that it does not antedate the compilation of the *Annales*.

was the cross,[1] and wrote it so in his jottings. Then the mention of three days and nights might easily get in from the rest of the Jerusalem legend. The transference of the episode from the eighth battle to that of Badon, whenever it may have been made, is explained on the general principle by which all the details of lesser events tend to be attracted to greater ones.

There is no difficulty, then, in concluding that the statement in the *Annales* is merely an amplified version of that given by Nennius. The chief importance, in fine, of this first entry consists, as has already been hinted, in showing that at least as early as the tenth century Arthur had become for the Welsh an heroic legendary figure. With the whole subject hereby suggested it will be more convenient to deal later.[2]

For the same reason we may here pass over the second entry also, with the mere observation that it shows, already developed, the tradition of a battle at "Camlann" in which Arthur was killed, and together with him a warrior named Medraut. But special notice should be taken that this is absolutely all the information which it gives. Whatever the author may have had in mind, he does not say that Medraut was Arthur's nephew, or a traitor, or even that he fought on the opposite side.

This seems the natural place to mention a brief *Chronicle of St. Michael's Mount*[3] (similar in form to the *Annales Cambriae*), which was evidently composed by a Breton or some one with Breton sympathies, and (since it ends in 1056) possibly in the eleventh century. Its first entry, and that alone, relates to the Arthurian material:

CCCCXXI. Natus est S. Gildas. His diebus fuit Artus Rex Britannorum fortis, & facetus.[4]

---

[1] How the legend of Nennius and Geoffrey was later expanded is shown by Giraldus Cambrensis, who says (*De Prin. Instr.*, Rolls Series, VIII, 126–127) that Arthur had Mary's image painted on the inside of his shield, and that he used to kiss its feet in battle.   [2] See pp. 96 ff., below.

[3] Ed. Labbe, *Nova Bibliotheca Manuscriptorum Librorum*, Paris, 1657, I, 349. Delisle, in his edition of the *Chronique de Robert de Torigni* (*Soc. de l'Hist. de Normandie*, Rouen, 1872, II, 208, note), says that the manuscript is 213 of the library of Avranches. Migne reprints the chronicle, *Patrol. Lat.*, CCII, 1323.

[4] The two following entries are similar to statements in Geoffrey's history, but disagree with it in date and otherwise:

If this really precedes Geoffrey, it merely affords another bit of testimony, only slightly different in character from others that we possess [1] and less important than those already considered, of the fame of Arthur before Geoffrey's day.

II. ÆTHELWEARD

From the Britons, the task of preserving the historical records of what was thenceforth to be England, was destined to pass, with the possession of the island, to the Teutonic conquerors ; but with the exception of the authors of the Saxon *Chronicle* and of one comparatively insignificant Latin writer, the very few and unimportant English chroniclers of the first three hundred years after the death of Bede were silent about the Arthurian material. The same is true of the more ambitious annalists in whom the spirit of historical composition began to revive at the end of the eleventh and the beginning of the twelfth century, — Marianus Scotus, Florence of Worcester, Simeon of Durham, and the latter's authorities. It was not until the twelfth century was well under way that the tradition received any real enlargement. So to the twelfth century we may soon pass on. But some attention must first be given to Æthelweard, the exceptional writer to whom reference has just been made. [2]

Of Æthelweard's life we know with certainty nothing except that he was descended from King Æthelred, brother of Alfred the Great. It seems probable that he is identical with the powerful ealdorman of the end of the tenth century, [3] whose relations with the well-known ecclesiastic Ælfric were so close.

DXIII. Venerunt transmarini Britanni in Armoricam, id est minorem Britanniam.

DXXXIV. Occisus est Cauallonus Rex fortissimus majoris Britanniae.

[1] See pp. 98 ff. below.

[2] The text of Æthelweard is contained in *Mon. Hist. Brit.*, pp. 499–521, with discussions by Hardy, pp. 81–83, 122–123; see also Hardy, *Cat.*, I, 571–574, No. 1160.

[3] T. Wright (*Biog. Brit. Lit., A.-S. Period*) follows Nicolson in putting Æthelweard a century later.

In Æthelweard's very brief outline of the history of England from the creation to the year 975, he twice summarizes the story of the Saxon conquest. In the second instance he merely translates from the Saxon *Chronicle*, with an occasional insignificant explanation or divergence. In the first, he follows Bede, but with variations. He says that the Britons, hard pressed by the northern invaders, sent vast presents to the Saxons, of whose valor in piracy they had heard, and asked their aid. This was done especially by the advice of Vurthern, who was then held as king over all, and whose authority all the nobility allowed. Two youths, Hengist and Horsa, descendants of Woddan, came in three ships, were sent against the Scots, and conquered them. Honored by the king, they secretly sent home for their friends, informing them of the fertility of the land and the sluggishness of the people. The Saxons who came in answer to their summons were enthusiastically received by the Britons, who rewarded their services against the northern foes with gifts and honors. But at length the Britons, recognizing the ability of these allies, partly feared and partly despised them, broke the peace, and tried to drive them out. In the first battle which ensued, the Saxons were victorious, and now they sent openly to Germany for reënforcements, which came in great numbers. At length they entirely conquered the Britons.[1]

It seems probable that Æthelweard wrote with knowledge of the *Historia Britonum*. Bede does not say that the Britons were the first to break the peace, but Nennius distinctly asserts that they took counsel to do so. Very likely Æthelweard's remark that Hengist's first message to Germany for reënforcements was kept secret,[2] is an inference from Nennius's language, and there are also two minor coincidences of phraseology.[3] If it is asked why Æthelweard

---

[1] Here Æthelweard evidently notices that he has omitted a part of Bede's material which he meant to use, and so returns to it, thus interrupting the continuity of his narrative. In so doing he adds nothing to his original.

[2] Cf. p. 217, below.

[3] (1) Æthelweard says that the Saxons possessed *astutiam*, and Nennius (37) that Hengist was "doctus atque astutus et callidus"; while Bede does not characterize leader or people at all. (2) Nennius says (37) that Hengist found Guorthigirnus to be a *regem inertem*, and Æthelweard makes the message sent

should have taken so much from Nennius and no more, the answer must be that evidently, like many later writers, he regarded Nennius's narrative as fabulous, and preferred to draw, when possible, from Bede and the Saxon *Chronicle*.

We may infer, then, that Æthelweard took these details from Nennius. It remains to explain the others not traceable to Bede, — the mention of the vast presents which the Britons sent to Germany, and the conception of the relations between Vurthern and the nobility. Apparently these were due to Æthelweard's fancy, which, we may conclude, applied to the period of the conquest conditions with which he was familiar in his own time. This supposition is in harmony with the whole tone of his narrative and with the practice of later English chroniclers. It is possible, however, that Æthelweard found and used independent traditions, which may have been either vague or detailed, floating or written. This is a possibility which will have to be mentioned later in the discussion of Henry of Huntingdon and William of Malmesbury. But in any case Æthelweard adds nothing really significant to the Arthurian story, nothing at all which seems to have perpetuated itself in later versions ; and he does not even mention Arthur. His importance lies wholly in the fact that he serves as a kind of link between Bede and William of Malmesbury.

III. William of Malmesbury

We have now almost arrived at the period when the Arthurian story was to emerge, through the history of Geoffrey of Monmouth, from obscurity into world-wide popularity, which (increased by other influences) was to remove it in large measure from the field of history, real or supposed, to that of romance. This change, however, was not to be accomplished without intermediate steps, and we have still to consider the work of two chroniclers who, while allowing themselves a freedom of imagination and a very eclectic method in the choice of sources which dimly foreshadow,

---

to Germany speak of the *inertiam populi* as well as *fecundiam terrae*, while Bede's words are "insulae fertilitas ac segnitia Britonum."

and very likely actually suggested, the licentious procedure of Geoffrey, yet tried in the main to reconstruct the story of the Saxon invasion by judicial study of the existing authorities. One of these men was the writer who not unreasonably claimed [1] to be the first worthy successor of Bede in the line of English historians, — William of Malmesbury.

William of Malmesbury was born about 1095, probably in the south of England, from a marriage between members of the Norman and Saxon races. Brought up from childhood in Malmesbury Abbey, he soon rose to a prominent position among the monks. He was under the patronage of Earl Robert of Gloucester, brother of the Empress Matilda, and was acquainted with other powerful nobles. He had a special interest in Glastonbury Abbey, as is shown by his compilation *De Antiquitate Glastoniensis Ecclesiae*, but he never permanently removed from Malmesbury, where he died about 1143. The first version of his *Gesta Regum Anglorum* [2] — the only one among many works from his pen which concerns us at this point [3] — was finished in 1125, and the later recensions exhibit no changes in the Arthurian material. [4]

William's account of the Saxon Conquest [5] is based primarily on Bede, but he also uses the Saxon *Chronicle* and Nennius, and he has a touch or two which can be traced to Gildas. His general method, which is the most significant feature of his narrative, is to weave together as much as he finds convenient of the information which these writers afford. He aims to follow them closely, but it is evident that his compounded story must differ materially from that of any one of the originals. When they are contradictory, he is generally obliged to exclude the versions of all but one. Thus, he agrees with the *Chronicle* against Nennius in stating that the Angles had the advantage in the last three battles with Vortimer

---

[1] *Gesta Regum*, ed. Stubbs, II, 518, 567.

[2] The standard edition is that of Bishop Stubbs, Rolls Series, 2 vols., 1887–1889. For further discussion, see Morley, *English Writers*, III, 38–42.

[3] For the discussion of other evidence furnished by William, see pp. 98–99, 103–104, 191, below.

[4] As far as appears from the account given by Stubbs.

[5] Bk. i, §§ 4–8, pp. 7–12.

and in making Vortigern fight on the side of the Britons. These particular instances show that he writes with some critical discrimination, and this appears again in his omission of Nennius's fabulous story about Vortigern's tower and all the details of his marriage with his daughter.

Sometimes, however, William uses his sources carelessly and inconsistently. Their disagreement causes him to fall into complete confusion in regard to Octa and Ebissa and their relation to Hengist.[1] Moreover, he constantly adds, evidently from his own imagination, vivifying details, like the cavalry charge in the first fight of the Saxons with the Scots. Very likely it is on no other authority that he gives an entirely new version of the massacre of the British chiefs, according to which Hengist makes them drunk and then brings on a quarrel by taunting them. In the manner of Livy he introduces an account of the reasons which influenced the British council to call in the Saxons. Certain definite statements which he makes of the length of periods may be based on the Saxon *Chronicle*,[2] but some other variations from Bede and Nennius are deliberate changes made, as Stubbs says, in accordance with his "own impression about the fitness of things." Thus, in describing the resistance of the Britons, William, though he adds no new information, alters completely the order of events as given in his sources. He represents Ambrosius and Arthur as fighting in conjunction during the reign of Vortigern [3] and before the massacre of the chiefs, and he says that Ambrosius was king after Vortigern's death.[4] Clearly

---

[1] Cf. bk. i, chaps. 7, 8, and 44, and bk. iii, § 287 (II, 342) ; cf. below, p. 158, p. 214, note 4.

[2] This explanation involves the assumption of error or inaccuracy somewhere. Between the coming of the Saxons and their first battle with the Britons William makes an interval of seven years, and in this Henry of Huntingdon (bk. ii, chap. 3) agrees with him. Now the *Chronicle* says, six years ; but it is altogether possible that both William and Henry may have had copies which varied from those which have come down to us. Such errors as writing VI for V or *vice versa* (the dates are 455 and 456) are very common in manuscripts. Or, both William and Henry may have preferred to speak in round numbers, as William seems again to do when he assigns twenty years as the length of the war thus begun, though the *Chronicle* indicates eighteen (455–473). Cf. below, p. 159, with note 12.   [3] i, § 8.   [4] Here he is doubtless trying to follow Nennius.

William is attempting to construct a continuous, reasonable, and interesting narrative out of the fragmentary and inconsistent materials furnished by Bede and Nennius, and in so doing allows himself the utmost freedom.[1]

William does not add anything new to the definite substance of the Arthurian story, but certain points in his history of the period challenge our attention.   At his first mention of Vortigern he lays such emphasis on the wickedness and worthlessness of that tyrant as to make it seem probable that this conception was current in his time, apart from the works of Nennius and Bede.[2]   We shall later find evidence to the same effect in other chronicles.[3]   He also makes a very important statement in characterizing "the warlike Arthur": "This is the Arthur," he says, "concerning whom the idle tales of the Britons rave wildly even to-day, — a man certainly worthy to be celebrated, not in the foolish dreams of deceitful fables, but in truthful histories; since for a long time he sustained the declining fortunes of his native land and incited the uncrushed courage of the people to war" (p. 11).   He then goes on to speak of the battle of Badon, following the account of Nennius.   The passage just quoted is specially noteworthy.   It is one of several pieces of evidence, which will be discussed later,[4] that, before the time of Geoffrey of Monmouth, Arthur had attained in popular estimation (chiefly, it seems, among the Britons) a much greater importance than Nennius appears to ascribe to him.

William's significance, then, in the development of the Arthurian material in the chronicles, with reserve of certain contributions which remain to be mentioned,[5] comes from his characterizations of Vortigern and Arthur and especially from his method of using his sources.

---

[1] Cf. pp. 41, 261, 266, below.

[2] This current conception, however, may have originated from the accounts of these writers, at least in part.

[3] Cf. below, pp. 167, 183, 184, 200, 206, 213, 228, 251, 254.   Contrast pp. 232, note 1, 234, 257, 258, 261.

[4] See pp. 98 ff., below.

[5] See below, pp. 66 ff., 98-99, 103-104, 191.

IV. Henry of Huntingdon

The second of Geoffrey's more immediate predecessors, Henry of Huntingdon, was probably born about 1084 in Cambridgeshire or Huntingdonshire. His father was an ecclesiastic, apparently a Norman, and Henry seems to have been brought up in the household of Bishop Robert Bloet of Lincoln. About 1109 the bishop appointed him Archdeacon of Huntingdon, and he held this office till his death in (or about) 1155. The first edition of his *Historia Anglorum* [1] almost certainly appeared before 1133, and, though there were later recensions, these make no change in his account of the Arthurian period. [2] It will appear later [3] that, when Henry discovered in Geoffrey's *History* new material for the early part of his work, he preferred to put it into an appendix rather than to incorporate it into his original text.

For purposes of genuine history, Henry's work is far inferior to William's. He had good ability, but was too much of a worldling, too indolent and too careless, to be thoroughly well-informed or trustworthy, and he often involves himself in contradictions. He doubtless thought that his lack of scholarly method (if he was conscious of it) was compensated for by the rhetorical moralizing in which he often indulges.

In his account of the Arthurian period [4] Henry takes his material wholly from Nennius, Bede, and the Saxon *Chronicle*, sometimes adopting their very words, and (like William) often piecing together fragments from several of them in such a way as to produce a very complicated mosaic. He often enlarges upon his sources, and with more freedom than William, partly or chiefly, it is evident, from his own invention. His narrative is much longer than William's, and he utilizes far more of the material which his sources afforded [5]; but his general method is exactly the same, and it will therefore suffice to specify the most notable features of his version.

---

[1] Ed. Arnold, Rolls Series, 1879.
[2] See Arnold, p. xi.
[3] See pp. 119 ff., below.
[4] At the end of bk. i and beginning of bk. ii, pp. 36–49.
[5] Henry makes particular use of version E of the *Chronicle*.

Henry describes two of the battles with as much of vivid detail as if he himself had been an eyewitness. In this he is doubtless merely giving his imagination free play;[1] but it is just possible that he is following ancient Saxon tradition when he locates the fight of the Saxons against the Picts at Stamford. In one place he is more critical (or should we say less ingenious?) than William, since he rejects not only the tower story, but also the massacre of the British chiefs. Like William, when he comes to that part of the narrative which follows the death of Vortigern, he falls into hopeless confusion; but his rearrangement of the material is altogether different from that of William, — a fact which might have been enlightening to those modern enthusiasts who have thought it possible to reconcile the accounts of Gildas, Nennius, and the *Chronicle.* He inserts his mention of Arthur between two entries from the *Chronicle* of the dates of 527 and 530 respectively, while William, by introducing Arthur before the death of Hengist, seems to put him forty years earlier. In recounting Arthur's exploits, Henry follows Nennius almost word for word; but he calls him "dux militum et regum Britanniae," while Nennius said only *dux bellorum.* It is quite possible that Henry had no reason for making the change; but it is equally possible that he was influenced by popular tradition. If so, the case is interesting and significant, as showing that, before the time of Geoffrey, an Englishman could adopt an idea of Arthur which made him not only preëminent among Britons in his epoch, but actually supreme over the British kings.

---

[1] Guest (*Orig. Celt.*, II, 164) thinks that he may have drawn from old English war songs. But cf. Arnold, p. lx.

CHAPTER III

GEOFFREY OF MONMOUTH

AN endless succession of chroniclers like William of Malmesbury and Henry of Huntingdon would hardly have sufficed to give to the British story of the Saxon Conquest any real literary interest. But William and Henry had not ceased to work upon the revision of their histories when the subject was taken up by Geoffrey of Monmouth, who imparted to it a vastly greater popularity, and, for literature, a vastly greater importance.[1]

I. LIFE OF GEOFFREY

Little is known of Geoffrey of Monmouth except what can be gathered from a few incidental hints in his own writings.[2] He

---

[1] The standard edition of Geoffrey, though the text is poor, and the discussion, albeit of great merit, now largely out of date, is that of San-Marte (A. Schulz): *Gottfried's von Monmouth Historia Regum Britanniae mit lit.-hist. Einleitung und Brut Tysylio in deutscher Uebersetzung*, Halle, 1854. The text is merely reprinted from Giles, *Historia Britonum ex novem codd. MSS.*, Caxton Society, 1844. The *editio princeps* was by Ivo Cavellatus, *Britannie utriusque Regum*, etc., Paris, 1508 (here the text is divided into nine books instead of twelve); again, more accurately, Paris, 1517. Another edition by H. Commelinus in *Rerum Britannicarum Scriptores*, Heidelberg, 1587, pp. 1–92. An English translation by A. Thompson, *The British History*, etc., 1718; revised by Giles, 1842; also in Giles, *Six Old English Chronicles*, Bohn's Library, pp. 89–292. Lists of the manuscripts in Hardy, I, 341–350; and Ward, I, 222–250. I may note that I have found that the following manuscripts in the British Museum are mere abstracts or abbreviations of Geoffrey: Domit. A.x., No. 5; Nero, D.v., No. 3, fol. 393–395 (Hardy, I, 43, No. 108); Harl. 6069, No. 3.

[2] The latest and fullest discussion of Geoffrey's life, and of the general questions connected with his history, is that of Professor W. Lewis Jones, *Trans. of the Hon. Soc. of Cymmrodorion*, 1899, pp. 52–95; also reprinted in a separate pamphlet, 1899. All the known documents are here cited. Other important

was born, probably, not far from 1100, and doubtless the *Arturus*
which he himself joins to his name means that his father was
so called. The *Monumetensis* which he also adds must signify that,
as Welsh tradition asserts, he was either born or bred at Monmouth.
Undoubtedly Geoffrey was by race a Welshman. Yet it has been
held [1] that his writings show only a superficial acquaintance with
the Welsh language and that his education was chiefly in Latin and
French. This, it is maintained, is only what we should expect; for
Urban (who was made Bishop of Llandaff in 1107) and his archdeacon Uchtryd, Geoffrey's uncle and foster father, [2] must have
relied mainly upon Robert Earl of Gloucester and the Norman
interest, to which they owed their places. Perhaps Geoffrey was
actually brought up in the Benedictine priory founded by William I [3]
at Monmouth. Here he might well have come under the influence
of men who were specially versed in Breton traditions, since the
first head of the institution was a certain Wihenoc, evidently a
Breton, who brought over the monks from St. Florence, near Samur
in Anjou. Whether these suggestions are true or not, the mention
of a foster father shows, if the *Gwentian Brut* is to be trusted, that
Geoffrey lost his own father in his infancy. [4]

---

articles are those of Ward, I, 203–222, 278–286, and Madden (*Archæological
Journal*, 1858, XV, 299–312). Not now significant are those of Morley in *English
Writers*, III, 44 ff.; Ebeling, *Englands Geschichtschreiber*, p. 12; Fabricius, *Bibl.
med. et inf. Latinitatis*, VII, 28–33; P. Paris, *Mémoire sur l'anc. Chron.*, etc., *et sur
l'Hist. des Bretons de Gaufrei*, etc., Paris, 1865; *Quarterly Review*, June, 1826, No. 67,
pp. 285 ff.; San-Marte, *Zur Kritik der Hist. Reg. Brit.*, in *Neue Mittheilungen
aus dem Gebiet hist.-antiquar.*, etc., Halle, 1857, IX, 49–75; T. Wright, *Biog. Brit.
Lit.*, *Anglo-Norman Period*. Many of the books included in the general bibliography, pp. 2–3, above, speak of Geoffrey more or less directly. A bibliography of
more special books and articles will be given later (pp. 50–51).

[1] Ward, p. 205.

[2] According to the Welsh *Gwentian Brut* (*Brut y Tywysogion, the Gwentian
Chronicle of Caradoc of Llancarvan, with a translation by the late Aneurin Owen*,
printed for the Cambrian Archæological Association, 1863).

[3] As Jones guesses (p. 10).

[4] The supposition that Geoffrey was brought up in Normandy, though it has
been adopted by high authorities, rests on an almost certainly erroneous identification of the " William son of Robert " to whom the *Gwentian Brut* says that
Geoffrey was chaplain.

Geoffrey was an archdeacon, not at Monmouth, but probably at Llandaff. It is a necessary inference that he did not receive the appointment before 1140, the year in which his uncle Uchtryd was promoted to the bishopric. Geoffrey's advancement was probably due in part to the special favor of Earl Robert of Gloucester, to whom he dedicated his *Historia Regum Britanniae*, written about 1136.[1] This work soon attained immense popularity and doubtless brought Geoffrey considerable personal reputation. The *Gwentian Brut* (never to be greatly trusted) says that many scholars and chieftains sought his tuition. According to the same document, William, son of Earl Robert, appointed Geoffrey his family priest.

Geoffrey's real interest, as appears from the character of his writings, was in his own promotion rather than in the church. It was doubtless for this reason that he dedicated to Bishop Alexander of Lincoln his *Prophecy of Merlin*, published shortly before the *Historia* (in which it is also included); and it was probably about 1148, after the death of both the bishop and Earl Robert, that he put forth his poem the *Vita Merlini*, with a dedication addressed apparently to Alexander's successor, Bishop Robert, who had influence at the court of Stephen. At last, after long waiting, he was appointed bishop of the unimportant see of St. Asaph's. It is significant of Geoffrey's aims, again, that he was consecrated as a priest only eight days before receiving this office, and that (according to the *Gwentian Brut*) he did not even visit St. Asaph's before his death, which occurred in 1154.

As a writer, Geoffrey was highly endowed. The ingenuity and boldness, and in a very true sense the striking originality, with which he handled the materials of his *Historia*, will soon be made plain. As a master of elegant and rhetorical Latin style he had few superiors in the Middle Ages. It is a decided proof of his versatility that, in addition to his prose work, he should have composed

---

[1] All the indications go to show that it was not published, nor written, before 1135, and the latest date which can be assigned is 1137, or possibly the early part of 1138. See an article in *Publications of the Mod. Lang. Assoc. of America*, 1901, XVI, 461–469, where I have given my reasons for rejecting the opinion that Geoffrey ever made any regular revision of the *Historia*.

a poem like the *Vita Merlini*, which, whatever faults, according to modern taste, are entailed by its thoroughly mediæval plan, is nevertheless characterized by vigor, grace, and poetic feeling. It is no mere accident which has given Geoffrey his distinguished position as father of the real Arthurian tradition in English history and literature.

II. Outline of Geoffrey's *Historia*

In Geoffrey's *Historia*, as in the chronicles which we have already considered, and indeed in all that we shall deal with later, the Arthurian story is only one of many constituent elements. Geoffrey's book is so important, however, that even those portions which do not relate to the Saxon invasion must be considered in outline.

After a description of Britain, Geoffrey begins with the story of Brutus, the so-called eponymous founder of the British race. He tells of Brutus's wanderings, of his wars in Greece, and of his transportation to Britain of a colony of Trojans whom he finds in captivity among the Greeks, and to whom, as they are on the way, he joins another, with its leader Corineus. From Brutus, Geoffrey passes to an account of Brutus's descendants and later successors who ruled the island down to the Roman period. This account consists partly of mere lists of names; and, indeed, of most of the successive kings very little is said. The bulk of the narrative is made up of romantic tales of war, love, and adventure. It contains, for instance, the story of Sabrina (ii, 4–5), to which Milton alludes; of Bladud (ii, 10), magician as well as king; of Leir (ii, 11 ff.), immortalized by Shakspere; of Ferrex and Porrex (ii, 16); of Belinus and Brennius (iii, 1–10), who conquered Rome; and of Gorbonianus and his four brothers, who ruled in long-continuing succession (iii, 16–18).

Coming to the invasion of Cæsar (iv), Geoffrey recounts at length the campaigns against King Cassibellaunus (1–10). He mentions several kings of the next period, including Arviragus, who first fought against and then made alliance with the invading Emperor Claudius (13–16); Marius, in whose time the Picts came to Britain

(17) ; and Lucius, under whom the island was converted to Christianity (19 ff.). Then he tells of various Roman rulers of Britain, emperors and others, known to genuine history, including Constantine the Great (v, 6–8) and Maximianus. The latter, he tells us, invaded the continent, and gave the conquered province of Armorica to a British prince, Conan Meriadoc, who peopled it with Britons (v, 9–16).

This brings the story to the time of the Pictish invasions, which Geoffrey describes at length (vi, 1–3).

Relief from the barbarians is afforded to the Britons by the coming of Constantine (a descendant of Conan and brother of Aldroenus, King of Brittany) to rule over the island (vi, 4–5). Upon his death, Vortigern, Earl of the Gewissae, raises Constantine's son Constans from a monastery to the throne, has him assassinated by a Pictish body-guard which he has established ostensibly for Constans's defence and usurps the kingdom (vi, 6–9). Aurelius Ambrosius and Utherpendragon, the brothers of Constans, are taken for safety by their friends to Brittany. Now Geoffrey proceeds to give the story of the reign of Vortigern and the coming of the Saxons, practically in accordance with the account of Nennius, but with a great many additional details (vi, 10–viii, 2). Among the divergencies from Nennius need here be noted only the fact that the supernatural boy of the tower episode is called Ambrosius Merlinus, or simply Merlinus, and that book vii is made up of prophecies which Merlinus utters about events destined to happen in Britain from the then present moment to a period of indefinite futurity.

After this, Aurelius and Uther come from Brittany, and burn Vortigern in his last refuge, Aurelius having been crowned king by the nobles (viii, 1–2). Aurelius makes war on Hengist, who is captured in single combat by Eldol, Duke of Gloucester, the sole survivor (except Vortigern) of Hengist's massacre of the British chiefs, and executed by him in accordance with the sentence of Eldol's brother Eldadus, Bishop of Gloucester (viii, 3–7). Aurelius compels Octa and " Eosa " to surrender ; restores churches ; and, by the advice and with the indispensable aid of Merlin, has Uther bring from Ireland the circle of stones which Merlin sets up at Stonehenge for a sepulchral monument to the victims of Hengist's treachery (viii, 8–12). In another war Aurelius conquers Pascentius, son of Vortigern ; and when Aurelius falls sick, Pascentius and Gillomanius, King of Ireland, are overcome by Uther (viii, 13–14). Before the battle, Uther sees a wonderful comet, which Merlin interprets as portending the rule of his descendants.

Aurelius is poisoned by a treacherous Saxon, Eopa, an emissary of Pascentius and Gillomanius. Uther then becomes king. He conquers the Saxons under Octa and Eosa; strengthens the realm; falls in love with Igerna, wife of Gorlois, Duke of Cornwall; makes war on Gorlois; by the devices of Merlin gains admission to Igerna's castle in the form of Gorlois, and begets Arthur. After the death of Gorlois in a sally from his castle, Uther marries Igerna. He once more conquers Octa and Eosa, and is finally poisoned by the Saxons (viii, 15–24).

With book ix begins the reign of Arthur:

Anointed king at fifteen years of age, Arthur makes war on the Saxon leaders, Colgrin, Cheldrich, and Baldulph, and, with the help of Britons from Armorica led by his nephew Hoel, subdues them after several battles (not twelve), of which the last is that of *pagus Badonis* (1–4). Cador, Duke of Cornwall, destroys those of the enemy who escape from this final conflict, while Arthur marches north and crushes the Picts and Scots (5–7). After restoring his kingdom and dividing Scotland among its rightful monarchs (Lot, who has married Arthur's sister Anna, and Lot's brothers, Auguselus and Urianus), Arthur subdues Ireland and Iceland, and accepts the submission of Gothland and the Orkneys (8–10). To his court repair knights from all quarters of the world. All Europe fears him, and he resolves to conquer it. On behalf of Lot, rightful king of Norway, he invades that country, one of his young knights being Walvanus, son of Lot. He subdues Norway and Dacia (Denmark). Then he sails to Gaul, slays its tribune Flollo in single combat, is occupied for nine years in subduing it, and divides it among his lords (11). Returning to Britain, he assembles all his vassals on Pentecost at Urbs Legionum on the Usk, where he is crowned for the second time, amid scenes of the greatest splendor (12–14). On this occasion messengers come from Lucius of Rome, threatening Arthur (somewhat tardily, it should seem) for his invasion of the Empire. By the advice of his knights, he replies that he will come and conquer Rome (15–20).

He sails with his army to Brittany, where in single combat with a giant on Mont St. Michel he avenges the death of Helena, the niece of Hoel (x, 2–3). Walgainus and two other envoys whom Arthur sends to Lucius bring on a desperate partial engagement, in which Petreius Cotta, the Roman leader, is captured. Next day the convoy in whose charge Arthur is sending the prisoners to Paris, is attacked by a force of Romans, who are at last defeated. Lucius tries to retreat in order to get reinforcements. Arthur blocks his way, and in a last great conflict (in which Walgainus,

Hoel, and others of Arthur's knights, but especially Arthur himself, greatly distinguish themselves) Lucius is overthrown and killed. In this battle are slain Beduerus, Arthur's steward, and Cajus, his seneschal (4–13). Arthur is preparing to march to Rome when he learns that Modred, son of Lot, to whom he had entrusted Britain, has usurped the throne and made Ganhumara, Arthur's wife, his queen (13). Taking only his British and insular warriors, Arthur returns home. Modred has collected an army of Saxons, Scots, Picts, and Irish, and meets him as soon as he lands. In the battle that follows, Walgainus and many others are killed; but Modred is driven back, and Ganhumara, despairing of safety, becomes a nun. Arthur follows Modred into Cornwall, and in a great battle Modred and most of the leaders on both sides are killed. Arthur himself is wounded "letaliter," and is carried to the isle of Avallon to be healed (xi, 1–2).

To Arthur succeeds his kinsman Constantine, who conquers the sons of Modred and the Saxons (xi, 2–4). He is followed by Aurelius Conanus, Wortiporius, and Malgo. Malgo subdues the islands and countries of northern Europe (5–7).[1] In the reign of his successor, Careticus, the land is devastated by Gormund, King of Africa. There is a glorious revival of British power under Caduanus of North Wales, and especially under Caduanus's son Caduallo, who, after extreme reverses, conquers the Saxon kings and long rules at London as overlord of the whole island. Yet the recovery is only temporary. Caduallo's son, Cadualladrus, having fled to Armorica with many of the people, is forbidden by an angelic voice to return to the island, becomes a monk at Rome, and dies in the odor of sanctity. It is only the rule of Wales which he can delegate to his son Ivor and his nephew Iny. So ends the supremacy of the Britons.

III. GEOFFREY'S SOURCES: (A) THE "LIBER VETUSTISSIMUS."
GEOFFREY'S PURPOSE IN WRITING THE *HISTORIA*

Geoffrey's *Historia* was the first work in chronicle form to exalt the figure of Arthur above the other British leaders whom Nennius and Gildas had connected with the story of the Saxon invasion. It was the first to introduce into chronicle, from popular tradition and other sources, all those romantic features of the story of Arthur's reign which, in literature, have entirely superseded the

---

[1] " Sex comprovinciales Oceani insulas, Hyberniam videlicet, atque Islandiam, Godlandiam, Orcades, Norwegiam, Daciam, adjecit . . . potestati suae."

actual historical elements.   As far as can be made out, Geoffrey was also the first story-teller, whether popular or learned, to picture Arthur in the light of a great world conqueror.   It is abundantly evident, therefore, why in a study of the Arthurian material in the chronicles Geoffrey's work must occupy the most conspicuous place.

Geoffrey's creative genius manifested itself rather in development than in sheer invention.   Most of the raw materials already existed, and his distinction lay in gathering them together from all quarters and welding and transforming them into a unified whole whose total effect was very different from that of any of its parts.   The study of Geoffrey's sources, therefore, is a far more complicated matter than the mere demonstration of the details which he added to the accounts of Gildas and Nennius.

The investigation must begin with the much-debated problem raised by Geoffrey's own statements about his source.[1]

---

1 For the questions of the existence of the *liber*, the credibility of Geoffrey's *History*, and his own attitude in writing it, reference may be made to the books and articles in the following list, which is intended to be complete as regards important modern discussions (I have purposely omitted the chroniclers who are to be treated later): John Price, *Historiae Brytonum Defensio*, 1573; Leland, *Codrus sive Laus et Defensio Gallofridi Arturii*, published in his *Collectanea*, ed. 1774, V, 2; John Caius, *De Antiquitate Cantabrigiensis Academiae*, 1574, p. 53 (cf. Howes, *Historical Preface* to Stow's *Annales*, ed. 1631, and Stow's own *Brief Proof*, pp. 6, 7); Camden, *Britannia*, ed. 1586, p. 360 (cf. Holland's translation, ed. 1637, pp. 632–633); Ussher, *Britannicae Ecclesiae Antiquitates*, 1687, *Epist. Dedic.*; Sheringham, *De Anglorum Gentis Origine*, Cambridge, 1670, pp. 8, 124–134; Stillingfleet, *Origines Britannicae*, 1685, especially pp. 7, 77–78, 269, 278, 318, 329, 334–344; W. Nicolson, *The English Historical Library*, 1696, pp. 94 ff., ed. 1714, Part I, pp. 36 ff.; Aaron Thompson, *The British History of Geoffrey of Monmouth*, 1718, especially pp. vi–cxi; Wm. Wynne, *Introduction to the History of Wales written originally in British by Caradoc of Llancarvan, Englished by Dr. Powell*, 1774; Warton, *History of English Poetry*, 1774, ed. Hazlitt, 1871, I, 98 ff.; Sharon Turner, *History of the Anglo-Saxons*, 1799, I, ed. of 1840, pp. 168–176; Ritson, *Three Ancient English Metrical Romances*, 1803, I, c; W. Owen, *Cambrian Biography*, London, 1803, p. 145; de la Rue, *Recherches sur les Ouvrages des Bardes*, Caen, 1815 (cf. *Athenæum*, No. 425), and *Essais Historiques sur les Bardes*, Caen, 1834, II, 155–158; Price, in Preface to 1824 ed. of Warton (Hazlitt's ed., I, 69 ff.); Herbert, *Britannia after the Romans*, 1836, pp. xxiv–xxxii; P. Paris, *Romans de la Table Ronde*, Paris, 1838. Cf. Ward, I, 215–216; Wright, *On the Literary History of Geoffrey of Monmouth*, in *Essays on*

Geoffrey begins his *History* by saying that, when he had happened to turn his attention to the history of the British kings, he was led to wonder that Gildas and Bede had said nothing of the kings who held Britain before the incarnation of Christ, and nothing of Arthur and very many more who succeeded after that time, although their deeds were worthy of eternal fame and were celebrated by many peoples " just as if they had been written." [1] " While I was in this frame of mind," he goes on, " Walter, Archdeacon of Oxford, brought to me a certain very ancient book in the British tongue [2] which set forth, in unbroken order and in elegant style, the acts of all the kings from Brutus, the first king of the Britons, down to Cadwaladrus the son of Cadwalo. So, induced by his request, although I had not made a study of elegant language, nevertheless in my rude style I translated the book into Latin." Then he continues with his dedication to Robert of Gloucester.

Again, in the letter to Bishop Alexander with which he introduces the seventh book (Merlin's prophecies), he says that Alexander has caused him to translate the prophecies from British (*de Britannico*) into Latin.

After he has mentioned the treason of Modred and Ganhumara, he begins book xi thus: " About this, illustrious Earl (i.e. Robert

---

Archæological Subjects, 1861, I, 206–209; Stephens, *Literature of the Kymry*, 1849, 2d ed. by D. S. Evans, 1876, pp. 296–308; San-Marte, pp. xiii ff. ; Hardy's edition of Jehan de Wavrin, Rolls Series, 1864, I, lix ; de La Borderie, *L'Historia Britonum attribuée à Nennius et l'Historia*, etc., 1883, pp. 87 ff. (reviewed by Loth, *Rev. Celt.*, VI, 118–121 ; G. Paris, *Rom.*, XII, 367 ; Reynolds, *Y Cymmrodor*, VII, 155–165; Villemarqué, *Rev. de Bretagne et de Vendée*, January, 1884, pp. 23 ff.) ; Ward, I, 214–217, 425; Heeger, *Über die Trojanersage der Britten*, Munich, 1886, pp. 72–79 ; W. L. Jones, pp. 19–39. The following articles are concerned primarily with the significance of the words *Breton*, etc., but that discussion often involves Geoffrey's *liber :* G. Paris, *Hist. Litt. de la France*, XXX, 3–7 ; Zimmer, *Gött. Gel. Anz.*, 1890, pp. 785–832 ; id., *Ztsch. f. franz. Spr. u. Litt.*, 1890, XII, 231–256, especially pp. 255–256; and 1891, XIII, 1–117 ; Loth, *Rev. Celt.*, 1892, XIII, 488 ff.; Franz Pütz, *Ztsch. f. franz. Spr. u. Litt.*, 1892, XIV, 161–210, especially pp. 161–162, 208–209; Lot, *Rom.*, 1895, XXIV, 497–528, especially pp. 497–513; and 1896, XXV, 1–32 ; E. Brugger, *Ztsch. f. franz. Spr. u. Litt.*, 1898, XX, 79–162 ; Lot, *Rom.*, 1899, XXVIII, 1–48.

[1] " A multis populis quasi inscripta jucunde et memoriter praedicentur."
[2] " Quendam Britannici sermonis librum vetustissimum."

of Gloucester), Gaufridus Monemutensis will be silent.   But as he found in the before-mentioned British work[1] and as he heard from Walter of Oxford, he will briefly narrate in his humble style what battles Arthur fought with his nephew."

Finally, he ends his work with this chapter: "I leave the history of the kings of the people of Wales from that time (i.e. the time of Ivor and Iny) to Caradoc of Llancarvan; and that of the kings of the Saxons to William of Malmesbury and Henry of Huntingdon. But I advise them to be silent about the kings of the Britons, since they have not that book in the British tongue which Walter, Archdeacon of Oxford, brought out of Britain,[2] and which, as a history truthfully written in honor of those princes, I have translated into the present Latin version."

When these four passages are compared, the third seems to be not entirely consistent with the others; for, while they give no indication that Geoffrey drew from any source except the *liber vetustissimus*, this one mentions further information, apparently oral, derived from Archdeacon Walter.   Still, the discrepancy is not serious.   As a matter of fact, if there is any truth at all in what Geoffrey says about his sources, it is by no means the whole truth, as will soon appear, and perhaps he did not notice that his statements do not quite tally.   On the whole, Geoffrey gives us to understand that he translated his work from a British original, supplemented by oral communications from Walter.   His language as it stands, however, does not indicate that Walter told him about anything previous to the last battles of Arthur.

Now, to say nothing of the fact that the form and tone and conception of Geoffrey's *Historia* are altogether different from anything that we have any reason to suppose would have been written by a thorough Welshman or Breton either before his time or long after, his account of his sources is so incomplete, to say the least, as to be absolutely misleading.[3]   Unless we are to assume that Walter had independent knowledge about widely separated facts of the

---

[1] *Ut in Britannico praefato sermone invenit.*
[2] *Ex Britannia advexit.*
[3] This has been pointed out by many different scholars.

story (a very improbable assumption), it is evident that Geoffrey's *liber*, if that was his only other source, could not have been very old, as he says it was; for the *Historia* contains elements that could not have been put into any book very long before Geoffrey's own time. Such, for instance, is the mention of siege machines and Greek fire,[1] which were not known in Western Europe before the time of the Crusades; and such are certain apparent borrowings from William of Malmesbury and Henry of Huntingdon, which will here be discussed later. Again, if the *liber* had been very old, it could not have been written in an elegant style,[2] while Geoffrey protests emphatically that he has added nothing to the diction. It has been shown also, and will soon be pointed out here, that not only are the framework of the *Historia* and part of its substance taken from Nennius and Bede, but that in many places their words, and those of Gildas, reappear, sometimes with no change whatever. If, therefore, Geoffrey were following another original in these places, that original, which according to Geoffrey was in the British tongue, must have drawn from these sources; Geoffrey must have recognized the fact, and in translating from British into Latin he must have turned back to them and taken their language into his text. In that case he would have seen that the manner in which their accounts are combined in his own is absolutely destructive of the authority of any one of them and entirely incompatible with any consistent view of history. In short, it is impossible to doubt that Nennius, Bede, and Gildas were direct and important sources of Geoffrey's narrative. It is clear, then, that Geoffrey was guilty of what seems to be rather gross misrepresentation, whether intentional or not (a matter which must be considered later by itself), and the question arises whether there is any element of truth in his assertion, — whether he really had any British *liber* at all.

In the first place, if such a work ever existed, no investigator has been able to find it, or if he himself thinks that he has done so, to convince others that he is right.[3] Ever since the publication of

---

[1] i, 7.   [2] *Perpulcris orationibus* (i, 1, 14).

[3] De La Borderie's claim that he had discovered the source cannot be said to have been absolutely disproved, but it has gained very little credence. If established, it would have shown that Geoffrey's *liber* gave him, besides details not

the *Historia*, Geoffrey's statements have been the subject of much controversy. Some of the earlier critics, however, betray a not unnatural confusion of thought. They ask not so much *whether Geoffrey could have had such a book*, as *whether his narrative is historically true*, believing that an affirmative answer would establish, and a negative disprove, the existence of the *liber*. The more intelligent investigations of modern scholars have merely confirmed the opinion of Geoffrey's first outspoken opponent, William of Newburgh,[1] that the *Historia* consists largely of amplified British popular traditions and myths. Now there is no evidence that Geoffrey may not have taken these elements, and possibly some others, from some sort of book in the British tongue, to which his statements, however misleading, may refer. This question can be more easily decided after a detailed examination of the contents of the *Historia*.[2] Such an examination will make clear that the *liber* could not in any case have been a complete history, similar to that of Geoffrey in plan and conception; or that, if it was, Geoffrey did not follow it closely. Accordingly, the question of the *liber* is not of supreme moment in the study of Geoffrey's material, because the *liber*, if it ever existed, was only one of many sources from which he drew.[3]

Still, the question of the *liber* is of great importance in any consideration of Geoffrey's professional honesty and of the purpose with which he wrote. For we must either explain why he should have used such misleading statements, or look upon him as guilty of deliberate fraud. The latter view, which was that of William of Newburgh, has been very often held. As to the motives which might have actuated Geoffrey in addition to the ordinary desire for literary fame, it is quite possible, in the first place, that he was

---

belonging to the Arthurian part of his narrative, the idea of Arthur's conquests in France; how much more does not appear. I omit all discussion of Geoffrey Gaimar's obscure reference to "the good book of Oxford" of Walter the Archdeacon (*L'Estorie des Engles*, etc., ed. Hardy and Martin, Rolls Series, I, 275); for it is generally supposed that that really refers to Geoffrey's *History*, and in any case the reference affords no tangible proof.

[1] See pp. 101–102, below.

[2] See p. 115, below.

[3] Most modern scholars deny the existence of the British *liber*.

directly stimulated to envy by the success of William of Malmesbury and Henry of Huntingdon,[1] who were also *protégés* of Earl
Robert and Bishop Alexander, and whose histories certainly had
some influence on his work. William of Newburgh proposed as
efficient causes for Geoffrey's procedure, an inordinate love of lying
and a desire to please the Britons. This latter motive is intelligible enough in a born Welshman, who may have wished to make
other nations believe that the annals of his race were glorious. If
Geoffrey wrote particularly for Robert of Gloucéster[2] and the Normans, he may well have counted on their credulity about the past
history of their new home.

All these suggestions, however, are only explanations of a pre-
formed theory, and Geoffrey has never lacked defenders; though in
the present state of our knowledge most of their arguments must be
abandoned, and it can at most be held that in making false or incorrect statements Geoffrey was innocent of evil intent. This excuse
is more forcible than might at first appear. In the first place, if
we conclude that Geoffrey had access to a British book of some
kind, his assertions were no more careless or unfounded than those
which have been made by many other writers, — for instance, by the
certainly well-meaning Bishop Percy. The argument is somewhat
strengthened by the improbability that two ecclesiastics would
stoop to unqualified mendacity in a matter not involving substan-
tial benefit to themselves. Moreover, it is perhaps fair to say that
if there was deliberate deceit, Earl Robert, as the patron of the
book, must have been implicated, and that this is not likely to have
been the case. If we assume, on the other hand, that there was no
British *liber* at all, it may be urged[3] that in the twelfth century the

---

[1] Lot, *Rom.*, XXVII, 571.

[2] Cf. Lot, *Rom.*, XXVII, 570. See also p. 114, below. The idea seems perhaps
substantiated by a phrase in the part of the dedication addressed to Gloucester
in the peculiar Bern MS., "codicemque ad tuum oblectamentum editum." But
Ward seems to me right in rejecting Madden's suggestion that Gloucester com-
missioned the history, though I do not see adequate grounds for Ward's own
conclusion that Archdeacon Walter made a rough cast of the whole work and
handed it over to Geoffrey for elaboration.

[3] As Stephens suggests and Jones argues.

fiction of drawing from a non-existent source was a mere convention, and was so understood.   To be sure, Geoffrey lays reiterated emphasis upon his assertion, and for a long time it was very generally believed ; but he is not to be blamed for being unusually clever or successful in a warrantable literary artifice.

There is still another line of defense, more recent than the others, and not necessarily inconsistent with either, — namely, that Geoffrey's appeal to his *liber* is chiefly a joke.[1]   This would mean that his whole attitude, at times, was far from serious, and that he was willing that readers of penetration should understand that his so-called history was really a romance.   Once or twice, indeed, a humorous vein seems to appear through the polished surface of Geoffrey's rhetorical Latin ; especially in the first book, where he particularizes the number of Corineus's ribs broken in the wrestling match, — two on the right side and one on the left.[2]   In such humor there must have been a touch of irony, and Geoffrey may have intended to satirize other books which laid ridiculous claim to ancient sources.   If so, the mood was only temporary, and, indeed, almost everywhere it is evident that Geoffrey's artistic and patriotic instincts have crowded all others out of his mind.

Whatever we may think, then, Geoffrey cannot be actually convicted of intentional fraud, and his character must have the benefit of the doubt.   We cannot assert positively that unworthy motives mingled, at the inception of his history, with the natural and laudable ambition to produce a good piece of literature.   The moment was opportune and the plan and method were well adapted to their end.   For in his *History* Geoffrey did nothing less than to create the historical romance of Arthur for the mediæval world.   Indeed, considering the brilliancy of his idea and the immense success which he achieved, one might almost hold that, even had his intentions been other than honest, the result would excuse the means.

---

[1] Suggested by Ward and developed at greater length by Jones.

[2] i, 16, 34.   Just possibly also in the places where he mentions a lord from Oxford whom he calls *Boso*, which may be formed from the Latin word *bos = ox* (ix, 12 ; x, 4, etc.) ; very probably where he speaks of the *liber* as *veraciter editus* (xii, 20, 7).

From this digression, and from the whole doubtful question of the *liber*, we now pass naturally to the investigation of those sources of the *History* which can be definitely traced.

IV. GEOFFREY'S SOURCES : (B) NENNIUS, BEDE, AND GILDAS

The outline already given indicates in a general way that Geoffrey's work is closely related to those of Nennius, Bede, and Gildas. Ever since San-Marte published his edition of the *Historia*, it has been evident that these are Geoffrey's chief extant written sources, though he uses them very much less after the beginning of the Arthurian period (or, more exactly, after the end of book vi) than before. A systematic examination will show more definitely the nature and the great extent of his indebtedness. It will show that, starting with their accounts before him, Geoffrey either deliberately or unconsciously determined to follow the plan and order which, roughly speaking, is common to them all (at least in the Arthurian period); and furthermore, that he determined to make every possible use of the material which they offered, even to the most insignificant phrases.[1] He begins, as they do, with a description of Britain, borrowed from them, and he practically ends with Cadualladrus, who is the last king mentioned by Nennius [2] as ruling over all the Britons. That he should so have followed them is not strange ; for (whatever his object in writing) he must have wished to make his book appear as much like truth as possible, and they were the most widely recognized authorities. Besides, to invent the history of a race for several centuries is a task of no little difficulty.[3] That Geoffrey did not draw in the same way from the later chroniclers (especially from William of Malmesbury and Henry

---

[1] As to the phrases, cf. especially i, 2. The most striking case of Geoffrey's audacity in adopting his material is that in xii, 18, where, as has often been pointed out, he applies to his own wonderfully magnified Cadualladrus what Bede (v, 7) says of the death of the West Saxon Cadualla.

[2] Chap. 64.

[3] This idea, I observe, has already been expressed by C. H. Pearson in his excellent running summary of the probable sources of Geoffrey's narrative (*History of England during the Middle Ages*, London, 1867, pp. 619–625).

of Huntingdon) is equally natural, not only because they were his contemporaries and perhaps his rivals, but also because of their dependence upon Nennius, Bede, and Gildas in the Arthurian part of their histories, where alone their material would generally have been suited to his purpose.

Closely as Geoffrey followed these three authors, there were both small details and great sections of their histories which, from the nature of the case, he was obliged to omit, though chiefly in the non-Arthurian portion. When they were inconsistent, too, he had to choose among them, — for instance, in his inevitable adoption of Nennius's patriotic partisanship of the Britons as against Gildas's violent denunciation of them,[1] an attitude which with Geoffrey is exaggerated into a monstrous falsification of history. He intended, also, to produce a work of a very different character from that of Nennius, Bede, or Gildas, and he turned elsewhere for the great bulk of his material, which he proceeded to dovetail closely to the excerpts taken from them. The result is that such excerpts appear only occasionally in his completed fabric. This must be borne in mind in connection with what is now to be said of Geoffrey's manner in drawing from Bede, Gildas, and Nennius.[2]

Most often he takes from one of the three the general idea of an incident and expands it into a more vivid and minute account. In such cases, sooner or later, he is pretty sure to bring in a sentence or two almost verbatim, and sometimes, as in vi, 10 (the story of the first coming of the Saxons, from Nennius, 31), he scatters such sentences all through the episode. He very seldom copies a section without noticeable change, at least in phraseology, for he generally aims to improve the style; but a few such instances do occur, especially[3] when he is drawing from Gildas's lamentations.[4]

---

[1] But Geoffrey shows traces of Gildas's influence in his last two books.

[2] Illustrations of many of the following points are best found in the non-Arthurian portions of the *Historia*, because they are based so much more largely on these three authors. But it is important to make Geoffrey's method as a literary workman as clear as possible.

[3] Not, however, in the Arthurian portion of the narrative.

[4] The fact that Geoffrey ever copied verbatim, or nearly so, may seem at first sight somewhat strange, since such a course might then (as now) have laid the

Emphasis should be laid on the reconstructive skill and the capacity for selection which Geoffrey often displays in adapting and combining the statements of his sources. Sometimes, in particular, he recolors or rearranges for the sake of better motivation. Sometimes, also, he adds an explanation for an action which Bede, for instance, not having any more real knowledge on the subject than he, has felt obliged to leave in doubt.

This brief general description of Geoffrey's method in utilizing these three narratives prepares the way for a detailed exposition of his indebtedness to them in the Arthurian part of the story.

After drawing largely from Gildas's very words for an account of the Pictish invasions, Geoffrey (book vi) makes over from Bede (i, 11) the story of the reigns of Constantinus and Constans. Bede says that Constantinus (whose origin he does not indicate) was chosen emperor for the sake of his name; that he took his son Constans from the monastic life and gave him the title of Cæsar; that he made war in Europe and was killed there, and that his lieutenant Gerontius put Constans to death. Geoffrey introduces a new character, Archbishop Guethelinus, and gives an elaborate account of his mission to Brittany to fetch Constantinus, now represented as the brother of Aldroenus, king of Armorica. He also describes the coronation of Constantinus at Silchester, his victory, and his reign, and makes Aurelius Ambrosius and Uther [1] his sons, as well as Constans. He describes Vortigern as raising Constans from a monastery to the throne,[2] and adds the account of Vortigern's usurpation, with the flight of Aurelius and Uther to Brittany.

---

existence of his *liber* open to doubt. But if his attitude toward the *liber* was not one of dreadful seriousness, he may not have noticed (or may have been amused by) the inconsistency; or he may have counted on the fact that most of those whom his *Historia* reached would not have at hand copies of Nennius, Bede, or Gildas, or at any rate might not think of consulting them; or, finally, he may have been shrewd enough to see that verbal similarities to the standard authorities would excite respectful wonder rather than suspicion.

[1] Another new character.

[2] In representing Constans as crowned by Vortigern and not by an ecclesiastic, Geoffrey perhaps got a hint from the remark of Gildas (chap. 21) that kings were then anointed not *per deum* but for their crimes.

This latter detail explains the statement which Geoffrey now takes from Nennius (in whose narrative it was entirely enigmatical), that Vortigern was in fear of Ambrosius.

It is to Nennius that Geoffrey turns for the main ideas, many of the particulars, and even some of the language, in his account of the reign of Vortigern ; and in all the rest of the Arthurian period, apart from the general idea of the reign of Aurelius, he has only comparatively insignificant touches from Bede and Gildas, namely : (1) the name Aurelius, which they (in the form Aurelianus), but not Nennius, apply to Ambrosius ; (2) the mention (vi, 10, 54–56) of the Saxons' actual victory over the Picts, which seems to come from Bede (i, 5) ; (3) the statement that the Saxons were sent away from Germany by lot, which looks as if it might be suggested by Gildas (*secundo omine auguriisque*), but with which Geoffrey combines Nennius's idea that they were driven out as exiles ; (4) possibly the statement that, immediately upon the arrival of the Saxons, Vortigern agreed with them that they should fight against the northern barbarians in return for their living (Bede) ;[1] (5) the notice (chap. 13) of the mission of St. Germanus (Bede) ; (6) probably, in part, the suggestion of the animal figures in the prophecy of Merlin, from those which abound in the latter part of Gildas's work.[2] One particular detail in the prophecy also comes from Gildas. The latter said obscurely (chap. 23) that the Saxons came to Britain under a prediction that they should possess it three hundred years and devastate it for one hundred and fifty. Geoffrey drags this in inappropriately (vii, 3, 48 ff.) by stating in that part of the prophecy which immediately precedes the reference to the Norman invasion that the German snake shall be in trouble for a hundred and fifty years and bear sway for three hundred. In ix, 12, 12, also, Geoffrey uses language not unlike that which he copied from Gildas in i, 2, 16–17.[3]

To Nennius's story of the first part of Vortigern's reign, up to the wars of Vortimer (Geoffrey, vi, 10–13 ; Nennius, 31–38), Geoffrey

---

[1] This is Geoffrey's account, although he agrees with Nennius in saying that the Saxons came by chance, not by invitation.

[2] But cf. below, p. 87.

[3] For a possible further suggestion from Gildas, see below, p. 81.

adds: (1) the conversation of Vortigern and Hengist about the Saxons' gods;[1] (2) Hengist's pretence that he wished to send for more Germans because Vortigern's enemies were actually threatening Vortigern; (3) Hengist's stratagem of getting ground for a castle by the bull's hide trick; (4) The *drinc heil!* episode at Hengist's feast; (5) the name of Hengist's daughter, Rowen; (6) the figure of Childrich, with Geoffrey a subordinate Saxon leader.[2] He omits (1) the miracles of Germanus; (2) the mention of the Britons' requesting the Saxons to depart before any trouble had actually broken out; (3) the statement that Hengist perceived the cowardice of the British race; (4) the account, though not the suggestion (vi, 13, 15), of the expedition of Octa and Ebyssa against the Scots; and (5) all allusions to Vortigern's incest. Many of these variations are merely accidental, but that is not true of the omission of the Scottish expedition and of the reduction of the rôle of Germanus to one of absolute unimportance. These changes are evidently due to Geoffrey's desire to unify, and to produce a vivid and dramatic narrative. He takes pains also to develop the character of Vortigern and to bring out the craftiness of Hengist. He would have gained in unity if, for instance, he had left out St. Germanus altogether; but that was too material an alteration to be expected of a mediæval writer.

Geoffrey now changes the order of events, with excellent judgment, by postponing the story of Vortigern's tower.[3] He says that the Britons, in disgust at Vortigern's infatuation with his wife's kindred, chose Vortimer for king. He naturally omits the suggestion that there were other kings at this time. His account of Vortimer's four battles differs only in insignificant details from that of Nennius; but he adds a lively touch by saying that the Saxons, after their last defeat, sent Vortigern to Vortimer, asking permission to depart, and that, while the negotiations were going on, they

---

[1] Suggested by a passage in William of Malmesbury; see pp. 69–70, below.

[2] From the version in the Saxon *Chronicle*, probably through Henry of Huntingdon.

[3] Perhaps taking the suggestion from William of Malmesbury's postponement of the slaughter of the British chiefs.

made off and went to Germany. In this he affirms unmistakably (as neither Bede nor Nennius had done, though Gildas had said the same thing unplausibly) that the invaders were actually driven from the country. He inserts also a description of the prosperity of Vortimer's reign [1] and the story of his being poisoned by his stepmother. To the legend of his burial he adds that he was actually entombed in Trinovantum [2] (chap. 14). In the episode of the massacre of the British chiefs (chaps. 15–16) he enlarges greatly on Nennius (chaps. 45–46). He inserts at this place the statement which he had before omitted, that the Britons planned to expel the Saxons; specifies the number of the Saxons as 300,000; and adds the pretence of Hengist that he brought so many men because he thought that Vortimer was still alive. He inserts also the figure and the exploits of the valiant Eldol, who, before escaping, kills many Saxons with a stake which he happens to find. Geoffrey sets the number of Britons killed at "about 460," instead of 300, and does not indicate just what regions Vortigern gave up, though he does name some cities which the Saxons took.

Now comes the narrative of Vortigern's tower, with the finding of Merlin (whom Geoffrey substitutes for Nennius's Ambrosius Guletic) and the fight of the dragons (vi, 17–19; vii, 3). This follows the source much more closely than any other passage of considerable length in the whole *Historia*. But Geoffrey adds the name of the boy who was disputing with Merlin (Dinabutius), [3] and an account of how Merlin was conceived, with the philosophical explanation (suggested by a certain Maugantius) that the father might have been an incubus. [4] Geoffrey, more consistent than

---

[1] Nennius does not say definitely that Vortimer was king.   [2] I.e. London.

[3] The printed texts have *Dabutius*, but, though this name, like almost all the others, was much and variously corrupted in the various manuscripts and versions of Geoffrey, their forms leave no doubt that he wrote *Dinabutius*. *Dinabutius* appears, for example, in MSS. Tit., CXVII; Bibl. Reg. 13, D. v, and 14, C. i.; Arund. 10; Bodl. Rawl. 150. Inevitably, some manuscripts have *Dinabucius*, as Bibl. Reg. 4, C. xi; Cleop. A. i.; the metrical *Gesta Reg. Brit.* (see below, pp. 166 ff.). Wace reads *Dinabus* (nominative).

[4] This (San-Marte, p. 331) may have been drawn from Bede (*De Element. Philos.*, bk. i), who is drawing in turn from Plato and St. Augustine; or Geoffrey may have taken it from current superstition.

Nennius, is careful to omit the boy's claim to be the son of a Roman consul (which, however, he has taken pains to use before in speaking of the parentage of Ambrosius, vi, 5, 7). In general he heightens the reality and effectiveness of the scene, though in this passage Nennius is notably vivid. The rest of book vii consists of the prophecies of Merlin, which are entirely independent of Nennius. The account of the death of Vortigern (viii, 2) is suggested by Nennius's first version (chap. 47), since fire is the agent in both cases; but Geoffrey takes the incident out of the realm of the supernatural and speaks only of fire used by the men of Aurelius and Uther. For the story of the reigns of these two kings and the accession of Arthur (viii; ix, 1) Geoffrey is independent of Nennius as well as of Gildas and Bede, except for the mere names Aurelius, Pascentius (as Vortigern's son), Octa, Ebyssa, and Arthur. It is especially to be noted also that, in order to make a continuous narrative, he follows a single vague hint from Nennius instead of the more explicit indications of Gildas and Bede, and makes Aurelius succeed Vortigern. His transference of the activity of Octa and Ebyssa into the reigns of Aurelius and Uther is also a decided innovation.

Geoffrey utilizes Nennius's list of Arthur's battles as a basis, but merely as a basis, for his greatly expanded account of the first part of Arthur's reign, which is occupied with exploits against the Saxons. He introduces Colgrinus as leader of the Saxons, and, soon after, Baldulphus and Cheldricus, all of whom are unknown to Nennius. He omits Nennius's first battle, that of the Glein, and condenses into one (ix, 1) the four which Nennius put at the Duglas. Evidently he takes the river for the Duglas in Lancashire, for he makes Colgrinus flee from the battle into Eboracum. Then Geoffrey inserts many details, including a retreat of Arthur to London. For Nennius's sixth battle, at the river Bassas, he substitutes (ix, 3) one at Lincoln, after which he introduces Nennius's seventh, that of the Caledonian forest. In connection with this, he inserts an account of the Saxons' surrender; and then, passing by four of Nennius's battles, he comes (ix, 4) to that of Badon, which he identifies with Bath. Like William of Malmesbury, Geoffrey connects with the battle of Badon the mention of Arthur's wearing the image of the Virgin, which Nennius brought in earlier. Here Nennius terminates Arthur's campaigns, but with Geoffrey all this is only the beginning. He takes Arthur at once into Scotland, and there (ix, 6, 7) he brings in from Nennius's *mirabilia* the account of the two wonderful lakes and of the phenomena at the mouth of the Severn, which he represents as a lake. This is the last use which he makes of Nennius.

Just after the death of Arthur, in a section of which the first part is closely connected with the Arthurian story, Geoffrey returns to Gildas. Here we have a remarkable illustration of his freedom in treating his sources. Gildas, as has been said, utters violent diatribes against five Welsh chiefs (chaps. 28–30), whom he represents, evidently in deadly earnest, as being alive at the time when he writes, and therefore as all contemporaneous and mere tribal leaders. Geoffrey introduces four of these chiefs, but makes them successive rulers of the whole British population. The first of them, Constantinus, he calls the son of Cador, Duke of Cornwall, and has it that he owed his elevation to the throne to Arthur's appointment. He transforms (xi, 4) the two boys of royal blood whose sacrilegious slaughter (by Constantinus) Gildas denounces, into the sons of Modred, and says that they had continued the war against the Britons.[1]

Mention must be made also of the possibility that it was from Nennius's and Bede's inclusion of St. Germanus that Geoffrey took the idea of introducing into his story the figures of Welsh saints, some of whom appear in the Arthurian period.[2] For this procedure Nennius's use of biblical characters to fix the dates of some of his events may have been supplementarily suggestive. It is possible, moreover, that the name of Geoffrey's Archbishop Guethelinus, who goes to Brittany to get aid and brings back Constantinus, the father of Aurelius, was suggested by the Guitolinus whom Nennius mentions as an enemy of Ambrosius.

From what has been said it is evident that Geoffrey was far more deeply indebted for material to Nennius than to Gildas. If we consider the *Historia* as a whole, his obligation to Bede, also, was much greater than to Gildas; though this is not true of the

---

[1] Cf. below, p. 158.　　　　[2] See below, pp. 77 ff.

Arthurian period, where he could not have taken from Bede, with a very few slight exceptions, anything that is not also given by Gildas. This limitation in the use of Gildas was to be expected. What was available in Gildas, except for occasional phrases and a hint of the kings after Arthur, was almost entirely general description, which, though it lends itself especially well to verbatim adaptation, is comparatively unimportant in the development of the narrative. Probably that part of his *Historia* for which Geoffrey is indebted to Bede is about the same in bulk as that which he takes direct from Nennius; but this is by no means true of the Arthurian period. Further, he does not transfer nearly so much directly from Bede, while the significance of what he does take is far less than in the case of Nennius. To Bede Geoffrey owes little but the story of the Roman rulers from Cæsar to Constans, perhaps the suggestion of the story of Aurelius Ambrosius (which Bede copied from Gildas), and the accounts of the battles in the reign of Caduallo. From Nennius he takes the main data in the story of Brutus; the settlement of Brittany by Britons, which opened the way for all that he says about the Armoricans after the time of Constans; the outline of the whole account of the reign of Vortigern, with the tower and the supernatural boy; the basis for his narrative of Arthur's campaigns against the Saxons; and the description of the wonderful lakes.[1] In another sense Nennius must be called Geoffrey's chief ascertainable authority; for in every possible case except that of the Roman rulers, Geoffrey follows his story in preference to any other.

Besides showing just how much Arthurian material Geoffrey (and through him the later chroniclers) derived from Bede, Gildas, and Nennius, the examination just concluded makes it clear what processes — dismemberment, transference, adorning, and interpolation — we must suppose Geoffrey to have used in dealing with his other sources, many of which, if they were ever written, we no longer possess in the form in which he had them.[2]

---

[1] Possibly, also, the hint for Uther (see p. 89, below).

[2] Before leaving this subject, something must be said of the cases in which Geoffrey mentions Gildas by name. Besides three citations of Gildas as his

V. Geoffrey's Sources: (C) William of Malmesbury and Henry of Huntingdon

It has already been said that Geoffrey did not draw material from the works of William of Malmesbury and Henry of Huntingdon in any such way as he borrowed from Nennius and Gildas; but also that it may have been their histories which first gave him the idea of writing his own. This latter hypothesis is extremely probable on *a priori* grounds, since the works of William and Henry appeared only a few years before Geoffrey's, and he himself directly mentions them as historians,[1] — to say nothing of the possibility that William's remark about Arthur's being worthy of celebration in truthful histories may have struck Geoffrey's fancy.[2] But there are more definite arguments to the same effect.

In the first place, apart from the general resemblance which was sure to exist between any two twelfth-century chronicles, the literary

---

authority (i, 1, 3; vi, 13, 9; and xii, 6, 12: in the last two cases he probably means Nennius), Geoffrey asserts: (1) that Gildas wrote at length of the quarrel between Lud and Nennius about the change in the name of Trinovantum (i, 17, 14); (2) that he translated the Molmutian laws from British into Latin (ii, 17, 29; iii, 5, 20), adding that King Alfred translated them into Anglo-Saxon; and (3) that he wrote a book on the victory of Aurelius Ambrosius, which contained the names and acts of the holy men who came back to Britain with Faganus and Duvianus (iv, 20, 5) — a statement which passed current for centuries. Now, while it is impossible that Gildas wrote anything about the missionary legend (which did not exist in his day), and while it is unreasonable to suppose that he was the author of the other works mentioned, it is possible that such works were extant in Geoffrey's time and went under the name of Gildas. On the other hand, no previous author is known to have referred to them, and there is no evidence that any one before the etymologizing Geoffrey ever heard of a quarrel between Lud and Nennius, or even of this Nennius himself. In making two of these allusions Geoffrey adds a self-depreciatory remark about his own rude style (i, 17, 15–16; iv, 20, 6–7), which at once suggests that his mood is humorous. It seems most probable, then, that the works are creations of Geoffrey's playful imagination, and the same is probably true of a certain book on the exile of the Welsh saints (author unnamed) which he signifies his intention of translating (xi, 10, 12). Geoffrey names Bede in i, 1, 3 and xii, 14, 2, where he makes a very careless mistake (cf. Bede, iv, 15).   [1] In his last chapter.

[2] Suggested by Wright, *Essays on Archæological Subjects*, I, 224.

manner of Geoffrey's history as a whole is especially similar to that of William. The latter often digresses from the straight path of narrative to describe picturesque scenes, to quote letters and speeches, or to give information about famous cities and persons. Geoffrey does all of these things. He indulges his imagination to the utmost in writing of the coronation of Arthur, pauses to describe the city of Usk, repeats many speeches of the leaders in various battles, and gives at length the letters of Lucius, Cæsar, and Cassibellaunus. Even Geoffrey's bare lists of kings are only a little barer than some which William introduces,[1] and Geoffrey's supernatural incidents (such as Arthur's dream [2] and the appearance of Uther's comet) are of a piece with the dreams and celestial portents of which William's pages are full.

Moreover, there is one large section of Geoffrey's work which may be imitated more directly from both William and Henry. This is the account of the Saxon wars of Aurelius, Uther, and Arthur. Here some things are taken from Nennius, but the general character of the narrative is quite different from anything in his work, and exactly like that of the story of the Danish invasions as told by William and Henry.[3] The barbarians, driven off once, reappear at another time and place, now in the North, now in the South; the use of fleets is made especially prominent; the British kings have to march hastily from one part of the island to another to oppose the foe, and are forced to carry on continuous campaigns, now advancing and now retreating; the sieges of cities are mentioned, and the faithlessness of the invaders, which Henry emphasizes, is sometimes indicated. These wars are somewhat differently described, it is to be noted, from the later aggressive ones of Arthur, in which little is said of the strategic conduct of the campaigns, and which bear some resemblance to the wars of the Norman period as related by William and Henry. Thus, consciously or unconsciously, Geoffrey seems to have divided his history into

---

[1] For example, i, 72.　　　　[2] x, 2.

[3] Though the possibility ought to be mentioned that Geoffrey may have known the accounts of the Danish invasions in Asser, Æthelweard, Florence of Worcester, and Simeon of Durham.

periods which correspond to those described by his two immediate predecessors.

The influence exerted upon Geoffrey by William of Malmesbury and Henry of Huntingdon was not confined to the general features just mentioned. Certain particular episodes in their histories appear to have given him suggestions of method or to have furnished him with serviceable details. Especially important among these episodes is Cæsar's invasion, as described by Henry.[1] In the first place, Henry, so far as we know, is the only writer, before Geoffrey, who introduces Lud (or, as he calls him, Liud) as a relative of Cassibellaunus. Nennius, through a series of clumsy errors,[2] stated that Belinus, whom he puts in the place of the historical Cassibellaunus, was the son of Minnocaunus. Henry makes Belinus and Cassibella[u]nus brothers and substitutes Liud for Minnocaunus.[3] It is impossible to maintain that Geoffrey knew Lud first or chiefly from Henry, partly because Geoffrey makes Lud Cassibellaunus's brother instead of his father, but especially because, in introducing him, Henry must have been drawing, in some way or other, from a popular tradition which was equally accessible to Geoffrey. Lud is undoubtedly an ancient mythological figure,[4] identical with "Ludd of the Silver Hand" of Welsh literature. Henry may or may not have been following tradition when he substituted Lud for Minnocaunus. In either case, he had taken into his history a figure which Geoffrey, when he found it there, must have recognized as belonging to Welsh popular stories and very likely to fabulous Welsh historical traditions, — and Geoffrey introduced this same figure at the same point in *his* narrative.

More than this, Geoffrey's whole account of Cæsar's invasion resembles that of Henry in several respects. Henry indulges his fancy for expanding the dry data of his authorities into an animated narrative. He says that Cæsar saw that the Britons must be conquered by stratagem rather than by valor; he inserts a speech by

---

[1] i, 12–14.   [2] See Zimmer, *Nennius Vindicatus*, pp. 271–274.

[3] He gets the figure of Cassibellaunus from Bede, i, 2.

[4] This is certain, whether all Professor Rhŷs's speculations about him are correct or not (*Hibbert Lectures*, pp. 119–130; cf. Loth, *Mabinogion*, I, 252, note 2, 265).

Cæsar; and he quotes a line from Lucan. Geoffrey also expands greatly, gives a speech of Cæsar,[1] makes the Britons succumb only to treason,[2] and quotes a line from Lucan. This last point is especially significant. There is only one other place in which Geoffrey quotes[3] poetry, and that is only a few chapters farther on.[4] The parallel is prettily completed by the fact that the only other bit of poetry quoted in Henry's first book (the only other bit, indeed, which he quotes from any classical writer in books i–iv) comes in directly after this episode.[5] It looks very much as if Geoffrey saw Henry's account and was seized with the idea of bettering it, — as if he said to himself that he too could make a romance out of a few bald facts, could invent a Livian speech, and could quote Latin poetry.

Now there is certainly nothing impossible in the hypothesis that it was when Geoffrey first read this particular passage — the only very prominent one so imaginatively embellished in all Henry's work before the end of the Saxon Conquest — that he conceived the idea of writing a history of all the British kings in romantic form and with material from popular stories. The argument is strengthened by the fact that Geoffrey, though he adds details, agrees with Henry in introducing[6] King Coel of Colchester as the father of Helena, the mother of Constantine the Great. Here, as well as in the other case, he was doubtless acquainted with the same traditions which Henry utilized, but it is still true that to Henry belongs the priority, both in general method and in the use of these particular traditions.

We come now to cases where Geoffrey took over some more specific detail directly from William or Henry. The most certain instance of all is a borrowing from William. In his account of the coming of the Saxons, William, after mentioning Woden, says that to him the Angles "quartum diem septimanae, et sextum uxori suae

---

[1] Though, to be sure, the circumstances are different.

[2] Though this idea doubtless belonged to British tradition.

[3] He has also some lines (apparently original with himself) in the first book.

[4] iv, 16 (a line and a half from Juvenal).

[5] Chap. 16 (a line from Virgil). [6] v, 6.

Freae, perpetuo ad hoc tempus consecraverunt sacrilegio." Geoffrey
makes Hengist say to Vortigern that to Woden our ancestors "dica-
verunt quartam septimanae feriam, quae usque in hodiernum diem
nomen Wodensdai . . . sortita est. Post illum colimus deam inter
caeteras potentissimam, nomine Fream, cui etiam dedicaverunt
sextam feriam, quam de nomine ejus Fridai vocamus." Apart from
the mention of continuity, the fact that both authors select the
same two days, and those only, out of a possible six, seems a conclusive indication that Geoffrey drew from William.[1] Layamon
later[2] took the very natural step of adding the names of the other
days also.

A less certain case of apparent borrowing from William is this:
Both in the *Gesta Regum*[3] and in the *Gesta Pontificum*,[4] William
quotes a letter from Albinus (Alcuin) to king "Eielredus," in which
he refers to a heavenly warning in the shape of a shower of blood
(*pluvia sanguinis*) which has fallen at York. Geoffrey twice mentions such a shower. He says[5] that a *pluvia sanguinea* fell in the
time of King Rivallo, and he includes a *sanguineus imber*[6] among
Merlin's prophecies. Alcuin also mentions the change of a fountain from water into blood, — an idea which Geoffrey uses twice in
the *Prophecy*.[7] But it is theoretically possible that Geoffrey may
have drawn direct from Alcuin's letter ; or the episode may have
been preserved in popular tradition and apocalyptic writings ; or
Geoffrey may have known similar but not directly related stories.

It is possible that Geoffrey took from Henry the suggestion for
his statement[8] that when Uther was sick he made Lot commander
against the Saxons, and that Lot, after much fighting, was unsuccessful. For, while Henry has nothing of Lot, he does say (drawing
from the Saxon *Chronicle*) at a point about corresponding,[9] that the
British King Nazaleod was killed by the Saxons in a great battle.

---

[1] Geoffrey, vi, 10; William, i, 5.

[2] See p. 151, below.

[3] i, 70, ed. Stubbs, Rolls Series, I, 73.

[4] Prologue to bk. iii, p. 209, of Hamilton's edition, Rolls Series, 1870. The
whole letter is given in *Mon. Germ. Hist.*, *Epistolae*, IV, ed. Dümmler, 1895,
pp. 42–43.   [6] vii, 3, 29.   [8] viii, 21.

[5] ii, 16.   [7] vii, 3, 116, 140.   [9] ii, 13.

No other source of any kind for Geoffrey's episode is known,[1] and the resemblance between the last syllable in "Nazaleod" and "Lot" was quite enough to strike his active imagination.

In the other instances which can be mentioned, Geoffrey's debt to Henry consisted, if it is really a fact, in merely taking a hint for a phrase or episode and applying it at a different place, wherever it would prove most useful. In such cases it is not necessarily to be supposed that the borrowing was conscious.

One of the resemblances of this kind is between a particular sentence in Henry's account of Cæsar's invasion and something which Geoffrey says of the first battle between Arthur's men and those of Lucius.[2] Henry's words are: "Apparuitque virtus Romana, dum sagacius ordinati cautius pugnant, obstinatius perseverant. Fatigatis ergo Brittannis percutiendo, Romanisque studentibus in se protegendo, cum diu proelium durasset, fessis insulanis, Caesarei recentes videntur." Cf. Geoffrey: "At Britones toto affectu desiderabant militiam: sed nec multum curabant in quem eventum inciderent, dum eam incipiebant. Romani autem sapientius agebant, quos Petrejus Cotta, more boni ducis, nunc ad invadendum, nunc ad diffugiendum, sapienter edocebat: et ita maximum damnum caeteris impendebat."

Henry dates the death of Gortimerus in the reign of the emperor Leo (457–474), while Geoffrey later speaks of the same emperor[3] as ruling in Arthur's day, but has apparently the vaguest possible ideas about him and his rôle in the history.[4] Geoffrey may have taken the name from Henry and have known nothing else about the man. This seems the more likely since Henry has no other mention of Leo.[5]

It is possible also that Geoffrey[6] was influenced by Henry in reducing the number of men whom Arthur killed at the battle of Badon. For Henry says 440, and Geoffrey 460, while the manuscripts of Nennius (which vary) have about double those figures.

---

[1] There is no indication that he used or knew the Saxon *Chronicle*.
[2] Henry, i, 14; Geoffrey, x, 4, 60–65.
[3] Or at least of an emperor of the same name.
[4] Henry, ii, 4; Geoffrey, ix, 11; x, 6; xi, 1.
[5] Cf. below, pp. 82, 83.   [6] ix, 4.

But the idea of reducing their originals by half may have come to both Henry and Geoffrey independently.

There is a slight possibility that in telling how Vortimer's stepmother Rowen had him poisoned with a drink (vi, 14) Geoffrey has in mind Henry's story (v, 27, p. 167) of how St. Edward was stabbed by his stepmother as she gave him a cup of wine.[1] Again, while the idea of a dragon standard must have been familiar to Geoffrey as a Welshman, one may compare with the golden dragon which he assigns to Uther (viii, 17) that which Henry gives to the West Saxons (iv, 19). Henry speaks again of a dragon standard in vi, 13, without describing it. It may not be wrong to connect Cador's occupation of the ships of the Saxons (ix, 5, 7 ff.) with a naval fight of the time of Alfred described by Henry (p. 151).

Similar doubtful resemblances to episodes of William's history are as follows: Geoffrey says (vi, 8, 10-13) that Aurelius and Uther were taken across the Channel (to Brittany) on the assassination of their brother Constans, and William tells (ii, 179) how the English sent to Normandy for Ethelred on the death of Sweyn. Geoffrey describes (vi, 4) how at an earlier period Constantinus was summoned from Brittany, and William speaks (ii, 106) of Egbert's being recalled home by messengers. William says (v, 411) that when Henry I learned that the sellers refused to take broken pieces of good money, he ordered all to be broken; and Geoffrey includes the following sentence in that part of Merlin's prophecy which refers to the time of the same monarch (vii, 3, 67): " Findetur forma commercii: dimidium rotundum erit." But of course in a case like this Geoffrey may have learned the fact from some other source than William. William says (iii, 229) that before the birth of William the Conqueror his mother dreamed that "intestina sua per totam Normanniam et Angliam extendi et dilatari viderat," — which is much like what Geoffrey says (viii, 14, 48) of the comet which portended to Uther the career of Arthur: "Unus [radius] longitudinem suam ultra Gallicanum clima videbatur extendere." There is some resemblance also between William's account (iii, 281) of how the king of France jested at the Conqueror in his sickness

---

[1] William's account is more detailed (ii, 162).

and of the latter's threat in reply, which he fulfilled upon his recovery, and Geoffrey's story (viii, 21–23) of how Uther was sick for a long time, how the Saxons therefore regarded him as a contemptible opponent, and how he exulted over them when he had conquered them. But the parallel is slight, especially since it does not include the litter in which, according to Geoffrey, Uther had to be carried. For the sake of completeness, another case, not belonging to the Arthurian period, is to be recorded. William describes Normandy (v, 397) as a country troublesome to the neighboring provinces in something the same way in which Geoffrey speaks of Scotland (vi, 1, 18, etc.).

The most interesting of all these instances (also in the non-Arthurian portion) demands more extended discussion. One of the most surprising of Geoffrey's kings is Marius, who comes in (iv, 17) just after Arviragus, whom Geoffrey takes from ascertainable sources,[1] and before the Lucius who was famed in popular legend anterior to Geoffrey as the first Christian monarch of the island. What Geoffrey says of Marius is this: A certain king of the Picts, named Rodric, came from Scythia and devastated Albania; Marius met, defeated, and killed him, and in honor of the victory set up a stone (*lapidem*) in the province which was afterward called from his name Westimaria; afterwards the surviving Picts asked wives from the Britons, and, being scorned by them, went to Ireland, and brought wives from there. Geoffrey has taken the general idea of the Pictish immigration from Bede, altering the marriage feature so as to glorify the Britons, and adding the name of the leader, Rodric. Both these modifications are so much in his usual manner that they need no other explanation. The question is, where he got his king Marius, the triumphal monument, and the idea of connecting with both the Pictish immigration story, which properly belongs a good many hundred years earlier. Now in the *Gesta Pontificum*[2] William says, speaking of the desolate condition of the northern provinces of England,[3] that among the Roman ruins at Carlisle is a banquet

---

[1] See p. 86, below.   [2] Prologue to bk. iii, p. 208.

[3] It is perhaps from this passage of William that Geoffrey took his description of the devastated condition of northern England after the Saxon wars (ix, 8).

hall, — *triclinium lapideis fornicibus concameratum*, — over whose portal is inscribed *Marii Victoriae*. William observes that the region is called Cumbreland and the people Cumbri, and that he does not know the significance of the inscription unless it be that a part of the Cimbri came hither when they were driven by Marius from Italy.

It is within the range of possibility that a tradition about this stone, though unknown to William, was in existence in Geoffrey's time. But there is no evidence to that effect,[1] and no evidence that Geoffrey had ever seen the structure. He certainly characterizes it very differently from William, who, to judge from the minuteness of all his description in this section, had seen it. It is possible, then, that Geoffrey may have taken his whole idea from William, and the possibility becomes a strong probability when one considers that there is no apparent reason, except in William's silly guess, why Geoffrey, or any one before him, should connect the Pictish immigration story with the remains of a banquet hall in the midst of city ruins, with the Roman period, or with any Marius. It is true that the Cimbri had nothing to do with the Picts ; but, given the mere idea of *any* immigration, Geoffrey's imagination was quite sufficient for all the rest. The material came very opportunely to his hand, for he wanted a king to fill, however inadequately, half the time (after Arviragus) between the historical Claudius and the supposedly historical Lucius, and he had not yet made any use of Bede's and Nennius's accounts of the coming of the Picts. When everything else fitted together so well, the chance to etymologize the name *Westmoreland* was an additional piece of good luck for Geoffrey, and the transformation of a banqueting room into a triumphal *stele* a mere bagatelle.

To sum up, the natural presumption that Geoffrey derived the impulse to write his history, in part at least, from the histories of William and Henry, finds plausible confirmation in the following facts : (1) he imitates pretty closely the general manner of William ; (2) the general character of different parts of his narrative reproduces the varying tones of what may be called corresponding parts

---

[1] The expanded versions found in later chroniclers who drew from Geoffrey are of course not evidence.

of William's and Henry's; (3) he might well have got from Henry the suggestion for using two of the most important kinds of material which he employs, — namely, popular traditions and romantic fictions of his own based on the data of his written sources; and (4) he almost certainly took from William at least one or two definite details, and, it is very likely, adapted several more from both William and Henry. That both these historians are to be counted in some not insignificant degree as among his sources is therefore practically certain.

VI. GEOFFREY'S SOURCES: (D) CELTIC RECORDS

Since Geoffrey's work purports to be a history of Britain, we may expect to find that his sources include not merely the works of Gildas and Nennius, but also British documents and historical traditions. Examination shows that this is really the case. It shows, however, that here also Geoffrey followed his audaciously eclectic method, using whatever he found as raw material, and taking only a bit here and a bit there as he saw occasion.

We may first consider British historical and pseudo-historical tradition outside of Gildas and Nennius. From this source it is almost certain that Geoffrey drew much of what he says of the first few kings of the Roman epoch.[1] There can also be no doubt that he owes to such material something of his account of such a ruler as Dunvallo Molmutius,[2] the famous lawgiver, and, in the Arthurian period, his mention of Budecius of Brittany, to whom Aurelius and Uther are sent.[3] Again, though Geoffrey's ascription[4] of the death of both Aurelius and Uther to poison is one of a large number of parallelisms which constitute something of a literary fault in his work, and is of a piece also with the fact that in its most important part, that of the warfare against the Saxons, Uther's reign is necessarily only a doublet of Aurelius's, — nevertheless it is

---

[1] iv, 11–16; see Loth, *Mabinogion*, II, 283, note 2.
[2] ii, 17.
[3] vi, 8, 14; see San-Marte, p. 308.
[4] viii, 14 and 24.

quite possible that Geoffrey may have had in mind such a case as the poisoning, at a brief interval, of two Welsh chiefs, which is recorded in the *Annales Cambriae:*

943. Catel, son of Artmail, was poisoned, and Judgual and his son Elized were killed by the Saxons.

946. Cincenn, son of Elized, was poisoned.

It can be shown also that Geoffrey took from Welsh records the names of many of the less important personages which occur in certain of his bare lists,[1] — in spite of the constant corruption of names in manuscripts and although the only basis for comparison now accessible is found in the series of royal genealogies attached to the *Annales Cambriae.*[2] It should be distinctly understood in what follows that the genealogies of the *Annales* are to be regarded merely as representative of many similar ones which doubtless existed. There is no reason to suppose that Geoffrey ever saw these particular records, and, indeed, he disagrees with them elsewhere in dates and other respects.

Most of Geoffrey's lists above referred to pretend to record successive kings. The only list which refers to the Arthurian period[3] pretends instead to enumerate the persons attending Arthur's coronation feast, but it is evidently made up in large part in the same way. It includes among those who came Beduerus and Cajus (the famous Bedver and Kei of Welsh tradition), of whom Geoffrey has already spoken, and the three brother kings, also before mentioned,[4] Auguselus, Urianus, and Lot, who are regularly given in Welsh mythological genealogies[5] as sons of Cynvarch.[6] One of the British kings is Stater,[7] and in one of the genealogies[8] appears

---

[1] Especially ii, 8; ii, 16; iii, 19; xii, 6.

[2] Printed by Phillimore, *Y Cymmrodor*, IX, 176 ff., and thence by Loth, *Mabinogion*, II, 302–324.   [3] ix, 12.   [4] ix, 9.

[5] See, for example, Lady Guest, *Mabinogion*, I, 123; San-Marte, pp. 379–380.

[6] I have no hesitation in assuming that Auguselus is merely Geoffrey's Latinized form for *Arawn*, which *Brut Tysilio* restores. On Urien, see Thurneysen, *Ztsch. f. deutsche Phil.*, XXVIII, 83; and Rhŷs, *Arthurian Legend*, pp. 238 ff.

[7] Our printed texts read *Sater*, but *Stater* was evidently Geoffrey's spelling. It is so given in MSS. Bibl. Reg., 4. C. xi; Harl. 225 and 3773; Arund. 10; by Wace and Layamon; the French chronicle of MS. Harl. 636; etc.

[8] No. 2, Loth, II, 305–307.

a person of the same name. One of Geoffrey's *heroes* is Regin map Claut, and the same genealogy has Regin with Cloten as his great-grandfather. Kincar figures in both lists, and the genealogy has an Arthur.[1] Geoffrey names among the *heroes* Kimbelim map Trunat, Chatleus map Catel, and Kinlich map Neton ; and another of the genealogies [2] has Cinbelin map Teuhant,[3] Catlen map Catel, and Run map Neithon. A few of the other names which Geoffrey includes — distinctive names that could hardly have belonged to more than one person — reappear in the genealogies, and therefore were certainly figures of ancient tradition. This is the case, at least, with Danaut map Papo.[4] It is interesting to notice that Geoffrey has brought in Samuil-penissel, who, according to another genealogy, was a son of this same Danaut, as a king several hundred years before.[5] Not from these genealogies but evidently from some previous tradition, Geoffrey must have taken his Peredur, son of Eridur, since he has already (much earlier) [6] introduced these two names together, though in that case as those of brothers.[7]

A feature of Geoffrey's account of the Arthurian period which aids much in lending to it an appearance of historical fact is the introduction of the names of certain Welsh saints, some of whom without doubt, and all of them probably, were well known in Celtic legend in his time and long before.

Of these saints by far the most important is Dubricius. He is first mentioned as being made Bishop of Urbs Legionum, at the

---

[1] This Arthur is called the son of Petr, which is also the case in some of the lists of the *Liber Landavensis* (*Book of Llan Dâv*, ed. G. Evans, 1890) and in a quite different form of the genealogy in a Jesus Coll. MS. (Vaughan, *Y Cymmrodor*, X, 111). It is an interesting hypothesis that this Petr may be the original of Geoffrey's enigmatical Petreius Cotta, whom he puts in the time of his Arthur, although making him a commander of the hostile Roman army (x, 4).

[2] No. 16 (Loth, p. 313).

[3] The Tenuantius and Kymbelinus of Geoffrey (iv, 11 and 12).

[4] Genealogy No. 11 (Loth, p. 312). He appears also in the *Annales* at 595 (Loth, p. 236, note 4).

[5] Geoffrey, iii, 19, 24 ; genealogy No. 19 (Loth, p. 317).

[6] iii, 18 (Peredurus and Elidurus).

[7] For a theory about another of these names, see Phillimore, in *Y Cymmrodor*, IX, 176.

time when Aurelius is restoring the churches.[1] Geoffrey adds that divine providence had chosen him for the office. Later,[2] Geoffrey represents him as Primate of the island, and as most directly responsible for the elevation of Arthur to the kingship.[3] It is he, again, who exhorts the army before the battle of Badon.[4] He is also called Legate of the Pope,[2] and it is stated that he was so holy that his prayer would heal any sick person. The last act in his career is the second coronation of Arthur,[5] after which he voluntarily resigns his see and becomes a hermit.[6]

All this is directly taken or imitated from the Welsh traditions about Dubricius. They appear to be consistent in calling him the head (as a matter of fact, the first known head) of the British Church,[7] and the Lives of most of the saints of the fifth and sixth centuries[8] (some of which certainly antedate Geoffrey) are full of allusions to him. In especially close relation with Geoffrey's statements are those of the *Book of Llandaff*,[9] which was put together at about the time of Geoffrey, but in materials belongs very much earlier. Besides continual references to Dubricius, this document asserts[10] (falsely) that he was made archbishop, and gives a brief account of his life,[11] which includes the statements that he became a hermit and that the sick were healed by the laying on of his hands.[12] To what he learned from legend, therefore, Geoffrey has merely added, inevitably, the connection of Dubricius with Arthur. He has also, apparently, introduced one change which seems surprising at first sight, — namely, the transference of Dubricius from Llandaff, where the legends locate him, and which is said to have been Geoffrey's own town,[13] to Urbs Legionum. But this was a necessary consequence of Geoffrey's selection of Urbs Legionum as the capital of Arthurian Britain.

---

[1] viii, 12, 43. [3] ix, 1. [5] ix, 13, 3.

[2] ix, 12, 33. [4] ix, 4. [6] ix, 15.

[7] It is interesting, however, to note the chronological divergence from Geoffrey of the *Annales Cambriae*, which place the death of Dubricius at 612. On Dubricius, see Hardy, I, 40–44; and *Dict. Nat. Biog.*, XVI, 82.

[8] E.g. almost all those that are soon to be mentioned here.

[9] See Haddan and Stubbs, *Councils*, etc., I, 146–147, note.

[10] Ed. Evans, pp. 79, 81. [12] P. 81.

[11] Pp. 78–86. [13] Though possibly not at this time.

Another very famous saint whom Geoffrey mentions, though much more briefly, is Samson. He is characterized as being renowned for the greatest piety, and is said [1] to have been made by Aurelius Bishop of Eboracum, whence he is afterwards driven away by the devastations of the Picts.[2] Still later,[3] he is alluded to as having been archbishop of Dol (in Brittany). It is only the first and last of these statements that agree with the usual legends about Samson, as represented, for instance, in the sixth-century Life.[4] It seems most probable that Geoffrey took the association of the saint with York from some less common stories, since Giraldus Cambrensis,[5] at the end of the twelfth century, alludes to it as an erroneous opinion of the people of that city.[6]

Samson's successor at Dol, says Geoffrey,[7] was Thelianus,[8] — evidently the name of the famous St. Teilo in a Latinized form. The origin of this statement appears in the life of Teilo in the *Book of Llan Dâv*,[9] where it is said that when the Saxons were devastating the island Teilo went to Armorica and was joyfully received by Samson.

In the prophecies of Merlin, Geoffrey makes use of another legend about Samson, as is shown by an explanation of Alanus de Insulis. Geoffrey says,[10] "The pastor of Eboracum shall dwell with six others in the kingdom of Armorica." Alanus states [11] directly that this means Samson and that the reference is to the legend of the seven saints of Brittany, — whose popularity is shown by plenty of monumental testimonies still existing in that country.

---

[1] viii, 12, 42.   [2] ix, 8, 3.   [3] ix, 15, 4.

[4] Mabillon, *AA. SS. Ord. S. Bened.*, Venice, 1733, I, 154–173; see de La Borderie, *Hist. de la Bretagne*, I, 415 ff.; *Rev. Celt.*, VI, 4, note 3; Evans, *Book of Llan Dâv*, p. xxii; Haddan and Stubbs, *Councils*, I, 149; *Y Cymmrodor*, XI, 127.

[5] *De Invect.*, iv, 2, Rolls Series, III, 77.

[6] Of course, on the other hand, they may have taken it from Geoffrey.

[7] ix, 15, 5.

[8] The printed texts have *Chelianus*, but this is certainly incorrect. The corruption of *T* into *C* in the manuscripts is very easy, and forms with *T* appear, for instance, in MSS. Bibl. Reg. 4. C. xi, and 13. D. v.; Harl. 225 and 3773; and Arund. 10.   [9] Pp. 97–117.   [10] vii, 3, 26.

[11] *Prophetia Anglicana*, Frankfort, 1603, pp. 28–30 (pointed out by San-Marte, pp. 339–341; see San-Marte's discussion and his references; add, also, among others, Vincent de Beauvais, *Spec. Hist.*, xx, 30).

Similarly, a couple of lines later, Geoffrey makes use of a miraculous incident included in the *Life of Gildas* ascribed to Caradoc. Geoffrey says, "Praedicator Hyberniae propter infantem in utero crescentem obmutescet." The *Life of Gildas*[1] has it that one day when that saint attempted to preach, he found himself unable to speak, and that subsequently the impediment, as revealed by an angel, was discovered (the modern mind can hardly understand just why) to be the presence of Nonnita, the mother of St. David, with whom she was then pregnant.

Later,[2] Geoffrey introduces St. David by name, calling him the uncle of Arthur, an idea which seems to come from the statement of the legend[3] that David was of royal race. The Pyramus whom Geoffrey calls[4] Arthur's chaplain and Samson's successor at Eboracum, is perhaps the person of whose chapel at Cardiff Giraldus speaks.[5] Attention has already been drawn to the possibly significant similarity between the names of Geoffrey's important archbishop Guethelinus[6] and Nennius's Guitolinus, the opponent of Ambrosius.[7]

It may be mentioned that the Pope Sulpicius to whom, says Geoffrey,[8] Walwanus was sent by Arthur, is perhaps an historical personage, — Simplicius (A.D. 468–483).

VII. Geoffrey's Sources: (E) General History

Geoffrey, as his works show, was a true student. It is not surprising, therefore, that he did not confine his borrowings to Welsh material, but utilized the history of other peoples as well.[9]

---

[1] Mommsen, p. 107.   [2] ix, 15, 2; xi, 3, 8.

[3] See *Acta Sanctorum*, March, II, 38. The manuscripts of the Life of St. David are catalogued by Hardy, I, 118–124.

[4] ix, 8; cf. p. 187, below.

[5] *Itin. Kambriae*, i, 6, Rolls Series, VI, 64.   [6] vi, 2–6.

[7] I have not been able to trace the names of the other ecclesiastics whom Geoffrey introduces: Tremorinus (so MSS. Bibl. Reg. 4. C. xi; 13. D. v.; Arund. 10), viii, 10, 4; Eldadus, vi, 15, 44; viii, 9, 16; three other bishops, ix, 15, 8–9.

[8] ix, 11, 21.

[9] In connection with this source may also be consulted Section IX, pp. 108 ff., below.

The most unmistakable instance of such borrowing is perhaps his enlargement of Nennius's account of the parricide of Brutus from the actual facts of the death of William Rufus.[1] The most complicated and composite instance is his long narrative of the reigns of Belinus and Brennius.[2] But other cases occur in the Arthurian period.

Reference has already been made[3] to the fact that Geoffrey adopted from Bede the story of the death of Constantinus and Constans, assigning the part of the historical Gerontius to Vortigern. The combination is cleverly made. It not only produces a continuous narrative out of unrelated materials, but it accounts for Vortigern's succeeding to the throne, — a feature of the story which none of Geoffrey's predecessors had explained.

Perhaps the name Flollo, which Geoffrey gives to the prefect of Gaul,[4] comes in some way from the historical Rollo.

If the idea that Modred was Arthur's nephew and traitor to him had not been developed before the time of Geoffrey,[5] it may have been suggested to him[6] by the accusation which Gildas[7] brings against Maglocunus of oppressing the king his uncle with sword, spear, and fire. Possibly Geoffrey may also have had in mind one or two cases from the history of Roman Britain, — that of Constantinus and Gerontius, or that of Carausius. Concerning the latter, Geoffrey knew at least the bare statement of Bede[8] that he was killed by the treachery of his friend Allectus. In his own version of these two events[9] Geoffrey has misrepresented the facts, but he may nevertheless have been perfectly aware what they really were. Still another possible hint for the treason of Modred may have been taken from the conduct of Bishop Odo, brother of William the Conqueror. Odo, being left in charge of England, made all his

---

[1] i, 3, 19–21.
[2] See *Publ. of Mod. Lang. Assoc. of Amer.*, 1901, XVI, 469–474.
[3] Above, p. 59.
[4] ix, 11. See San-Marte, p. 386.
[5] A question which cannot be decided.
[6] Or to some less conscious maker of tradition who came before.
[7] 33. See Sayce in London *Academy*, 1884, XXVI, 139.
[8] i, 6.   [9] v, 4, 1–5.

preparations to set out for Italy with a great retinue, to secure the papacy for himself, so that the king had to return hastily and arrest him.[1]

Again, the part which Geoffrey assigns to the Armorican Britons under Hoel in Arthur's wars may have been suggested by the participation of many subjects of the historical Count Hoel of Brittany in William's conquest of England.[2]   The argument, however, is weakened by the fact that Geoffrey makes the military alliance of the Armoricans with the insular Britons go back to the beginning of the reign of Aurelius.[3]   Indeed, the point can hardly be determined without considering the other Breton elements in Geoffrey's history, — the emphasis which he lays on the usefulness of the Breton auxiliaries, who turn the tide in favor of Aurelius in an important battle; the Breton ancestry of Arthur's line; the bringing up of Aurelius and Uther in Brittany; the glorification of Hoel, especially in the battle with Lucius,[4] as equalled in prowess by Gawain only; the introduction of such a distinctly Breton tale as the battle with the giant on Mont St. Michel.   This problem of Geoffrey's Breton material is a very difficult one.   It is essentially connected with the question whether the *Britannia* which he names as the source of his *liber* means Wales or Brittany, and this in turn involves the whole controversy over the *matière de Bretagne*.   Perhaps, after all, in view of the close relations which had always existed between the Welsh and their Armorican kindred, it was only to be expected that Geoffrey would take pains to praise the latter.

For Arthur's invasions of France, whether or not they existed in tradition before Geoffrey, a source has been suggested in actual British history.   About 470, while Leo the Great was Emperor of the East, the Visigoths invaded Gaul, and the Emperor Anthemius sent for aid to Riothimir, "king of the Britons," as Jordanes calls him.   Riothimir with twelve thousand men sailed from some place

---

[1] See Ordericus Vitalis, vii, 8 (ed. Le Prévost, III, 188–192).

[2] Argued by Zimmer, *Gött. Gel. Anz.*, 1892, p. 824.   He goes into details which are not very convincing and have been partly refuted by Loth, *Rev. Celt.*, 1892, XIII, 491–493, and *Mabinogion*, I, 151, note 1; II, 241–242.

[3] viii, 2.

[4] x, 10, 10, etc.

not specified, and marched against the barbarians. The latter, however, surprised and defeated him.[1] Though the best recent opinion holds that Riothimir was probably settled in Gaul, not in Great Britain, so that his expedition does not make a real parallel with Arthur's, nevertheless the most natural *prima facie* interpretation of Jordanes's account [2] would be to the contrary, and several of the later chroniclers were puzzled by the apparent parallelism.[3] That Geoffrey did take an idea from this source is an attractive hypothesis, because it might help to explain why he so indefinitely introduces an Emperor Leo at the time of Arthur.[4]

But it is impossible to argue with any assurance for any single source for the episode of Arthur's attack on the Romans, or for the whole conception of him as a foreign conqueror, — whether or not it was original with Geoffrey, — because very likely several different influences may have contributed to it. Now that the subject is broached, it will be convenient to indicate these influences all together.

As the earliest, it appears most reasonable to count a mythical one.[5] A common incident in ancient Irish and Welsh tales is the visit of a (culture) hero to some country, sometimes, and probably originally, Hades, whence he brings back something which is of great benefit to his people. Taliessin's *Spoils of Annwynn* [6] tells how Arthur secured the cauldron of the monarch of Hades. Later,[7] Ireland, either because it was thought of as a land of mystery, or

---

[1] Jordanes, *De Rebus Geticis*, chap. 45 (ed. Closs, 1888, pp. 160–161). For discussions, see Lappenberg, *Geschichte Englands*, I, 106; Herbert, *Britannia after the Romans*, p. 20; San-Marte, pp. 398–400; de La Borderie, *Hist. de la Bretagne*, I, 251 ff.; Loth, *L'Emigration Bretonne*, p. 55, and *Rev. Celt.*, 1892, XIII, 482.

[2] Jordanes is our only authority here.

[3] Cf. p. 185, below.

[4] But cf. p. 71, above. Perhaps, also, if Geoffrey knew or remembered that it was really Justinian who was (Eastern) Emperor at the time when he placed Arthur (killed 542), he saw the difficulty of claiming European conquests for Arthur, and so substituted almost at random another name for the Emperor.

[5] For this theory, see Rhŷs, *Arthurian Legend*, pp. 10–11.

[6] Skene, *Four Ancient Books*, I, 265.

[7] As in the stories of Kulhwch and Olwen, and Branwen, daughter of Llyr (Lady Guest, *Mabinogion*, III, 123–124; II, 307–308).

because of the desire to rationalize the myth, takes the place of
Hades in the stories.   When such expeditions came to be associated with Arthur, they might naturally give the suggestion for a
definite conquest of Ireland, which, actually, in Geoffrey's account
does precede all Arthur's other conquests outside of Great Britain.
Then from one foreign land to others was an almost inevitable step.

For the conquests of the northern countries, however, there may
possibly have been [1] a special traditional suggestion in the application to Norway by the Welsh of their name for the other world; [2]
or more probably in the history of the Northern wars in the British
Isles, particularly those of the ninth century, between the Vikings on
the one hand and the British or Irish on the other. [3]

The attacks upon Rome, in turn, almost followed as a matter of
course from the elevation of Arthur to the position of the great
British national hero, whose exploits were to be compared with
those of the greatest monarchs of history.   For Rome was the only
world power in the time when he lived, and the supreme test of
his greatness was necessarily its overthrow.   And in the speeches of
Arthur and his knights in books nine and ten, Geoffrey shows that
he has in mind the idea of retaliation for the earlier subjugation of
the Britons by the Romans.   But more than this, attacks upon
Rome had formed a considerable part of the staple of history for
several centuries of the Christian era.   Geoffrey (or the previous
tradition maker) had the examples not only of all the barbarian
chiefs like Attila and Alaric and a dozen others, but of the British
Maximus and the first and second Constantinus, of whose exploits
he knew from Bede, and whom he had himself mentioned.   He
had also the examples of Pepin and Charlemagne, about whom
William of Malmesbury, as well as other chroniclers, had written.
Also he may have had in mind the Norman kings of England, who,
if they did not actually engage in vast foreign conquests, at least

---

[1] As Rhŷs suggests, *Arthurian Legend*, p. 11.

[2] For possible arguments that the tradition of conquests by Arthur in Scandi-
navia existed before Geoffrey, see below, pp. 126–127, 141–142.

[3] Zimmer argues for this theory, with much definiteness, in *Gött. Gel. Anz.*,
1890, pp. 820–821.

sometimes thought of doing so,[1] and were constantly making war in France.[2] For one incident of the campaign against Flollo he may have drawn upon the history of one of these kings. At all events, his remark[3] that Arthur's generosity (*largitas*) caused the greater part of the Gallic army to go over to him, reminds one of Roger of Hoveden's statement[4] that, when Henry I invaded Normandy in 1105, "almost all the chief men deserted their lord the duke and ran after the king's gold and silver."

VIII. Geoffrey's Sources: (F) Myths and Popular Stories. The Idea of Arthur before Geoffrey

The sources which have so far been mentioned account for much of Geoffrey's *History*, both in outline and in details; but other important sources remain to be considered. Among these the most significant are the myths and popular stories, chiefly of the Celts, but partly also of other races, from which Geoffrey drew. To illustrate from the non-Arthurian part of the *History*: it has been demonstrated with certainty, or with a very high degree of probability, that Geoffrey must have found in Celtic myth or tradition the characters, and at least in part the outlines, for his

---

[1] Cf. Freeman, *Reign of William Rufus*, I, 7.

[2] It is not possible to explain satisfactorily where Geoffrey got the name Lucius Hiberius (all seven of the manuscripts of Geoffrey which I examined have *Hiberius* or *Hiberus*; the printed texts read *Tiberius*) for the (Western) Roman Emperor whom he actually opposes to Arthur. Geoffrey speaks somewhat inconsistently of his office; for he not only calls him sometimes *Reipublicae procurator* (ix, 15, 14) and sometimes *imperator* (x, 4, 2, etc.), but sometimes implies or states that he acts under the orders of the senate (x, 1, 1; x, 13, 17), and sometimes says that he is a colleague of the Emperor Leo (ix, 20, 5; x, 6, 4), who is also stated (ix, 11, 33) to have been the superior of Flollo, procurator of Gaul. Probably this is a case of carelessness on Geoffrey's part, or of vagueness in his knowledge of history. Certainly his mention of two emperors at this time shows that he supposed, or assumed, that the Western Empire was still in existence. Cf. above, p. 83, note 1; and below, pp. 122, 133, note 10; 167, note 19; 156, 196, 200, 229, 231, note 4.

[3] ix, 11, 39–40.

[4] I, 162, Rolls Series.

stories of King Bladud,[1] Marganus,[2] Arviragus,[3] and Guanius and Melga,[4] as well as the figures of Caradocus and Conanus Meriadocus,[5] to say nothing of the eagle which he represents as having spoken at the foundation of Shaftesbury.[6]

At this point a cautionary observation may not be out of place. Our knowledge of the traditions current in Geoffrey's time is so slight that it is seldom possible to determine with certainty whether he found, already developed, stories which he took into his history without any great change, except that of adjusting them to his narrative; or whether he merely got the names and a few hints from popular tradition, fabricated the connection between the names and the episodes, and invented a large part of the detail. There is no clear evidence to show, for instance, whether he was the first to represent the Celtic gods Melwas and Gwynwas in the rôle of the foreign ravagers Melga and Guanius, though extant stories about Melwas prove that he had long before been made into a man. On the other hand, the tale of Bladud doubtless came to Geoffrey pretty straight from local tradition, and the question is chiefly whether he was the first to put Bladud into a definite line of kings. On the whole, considering what we know from other sources about Geoffrey's methods, it is safe to ascribe to him a very large share in the construction of his stories.

Again, from tradition not merely Celtic (or not Celtic at all) Geoffrey takes the Leir episode;[7] the eleven thousand virgins;[8]

---

[1] ii, 10. See Sayce, *Y Cymmrodor*, X, 207–221. It may be noted here that Sayce was certainly right in suggesting that Geoffrey's real form for the name of the king who appears in the printed texts as *Hudibras* was *Rudhudibras*. It is so written in all the MSS. of Geoffrey which I have examined and in many chronicles which draw from him. Many chronicles also have *Ludhudibras*.

[2] ii, 15. See Rhŷs, *Celtic Britain*, p. 118.

[3] iv, 13–16. See Schofield, *Publ. of the Mod. Lang. Assoc.*, 1901, XVI, 405 ff.

[4] v, 16; vi, 3. See Rhŷs, *Arthurian Legend*, pp. 342–347; Lot, *Rom.*, 1895, XXIV, 327–335; Paris, *Rom.*, XII, 502.

[5] v, 9–15. See San Marte, pp. 292 ff.; Edwards, *Y Cymmrodor*, XI, 72, note 3; Paris, *Hist. Litt.*, XXX, 245; Bruce, *Publ. Mod. Lang. Assoc.*, XV, 326 ff.

[6] ii, 9, 15; xii, 18, 1. See San Marte, p. 463.

[7] *Gesta Romanorum*, ed. Oesterley, No. 273, p. 672 (with references, p. 748); San Marte, pp. 221 ff.; Wright, *Essays on Archaeological Subjects*, I, 216.

[8] v, 16. Cf. Rhŷs's peculiar theory (*Celtic Heathendom*, pp. 165–166).

Gormundus, king of the Africans;[1] and probably occasional hints of Teutonic saga.[2] His giant Goemagot comes ultimately from the Bible, through the medium of widespread popular tradition.[3]

Elements from this miscellaneous body of tradition and story appear in a subordinate way in Geoffrey's account of the Arthurian period. There are apparently several reminiscences of the Bible. Besides Eldadus's citation of examples from the Books of Samuel and Joshua,[4] the valorous conduct of Eldol, who slew seventy Saxons with a stake and escaped from the massacre of the other British chiefs,[5] seems to be suggested by the exploit of Samson. We may compare also the insistence, in the narrative of Job's disasters, upon the escape of a single man from each company. The animal figures in Merlin's prophecy[6] have at least a resemblance to those in the Book of Daniel.[7] It is possible that the account of the murder of Constantinus by a Pict[8] reflects that of Eglon in Judges, iii, 15–22.

Geoffrey includes the twelve peers of France among Arthur's lords.[9] His long list of heathen kings who belong to the army of Lucius[10] is suggested by similar lists in mediæval poetry.[11] The age of fifteen years which he ascribes to Arthur at the time of his coronation[12] is the conventional one for the beginning of a hero's exploits in mediæval tales. The duel of Arthur and Flollo *in an island* reminds one strongly of the Norse custom of *hólm-ganga*.[13] The mention in the prophecy of Merlin of a snake encircling a

---

[1] xi, 8–10; San-Marte, pp. 439–443; Lot, *Rom.*, 1898, XXVII, 1–54; Zimmer, *Gött. Gel. Anz.*, 1890, p. 823.

[2] San-Marte, *Arthur-Sage*, pp. 17–18. The theory is carried to a still greater extent by F. Liebrecht, *Gervasius von Tilbury*, p. 96.

[3] i, 16. Cf. Bieling, *Zu den Sagen von Gog und Magog*, Berlin, 1882 (especially pp. 5, 21); Herrig's *Archiv*, LII, 89.

[4] viii, 7–8.   [5] vi, 16.   [6] vii, 3–4.
[7] But cf. p. 60, above.   [8] vi, 5, 15.

[9] ix, 12, 52; ix, 19, 11. He had already introduced them in i, 13, 18. On the peers, cf. Warton-Hazlitt, *History of English Poetry*, I, 108, and note 1. See also p. 187, below.   [10] x, 1.

[11] For example, in the *Chanson de Roland*, vv. 3215–3261.

[12] ix, 1, 10.

[13] ix, 11, 54 ff. We need not infer that Geoffrey was directly affected by Scandinavian tradition or custom at this point. The whole account of the duel is in the usual style of mediæval romance.

city[1] is evidently taken from the story motive which appears in the *Saga of Ragnar Loðbrók*. Another conventional literary episode is the prophetic dream which Geoffrey represents Arthur as having when he is on the voyage to France to fight Lucius.[2] It naturally reminds one of the ominous dream which the prose *Lancelot* (and from it Malory) assigns to Arthur at a later point in the story. The incident of Hengist tricking Vortigern into giving him for a castle as much land as he could enclose with a thong[3] is a very widespread folk tale, elsewhere applied to Dido and to Ragnar Loð-brók; but Geoffrey does not lay emphasis on the deception, because he is interested in an etymology which he is developing. From another folk tale, attached to both King Alfred and the Danish Anlaf, comes the story of Baldulph's getting access to his besieged brother in the guise of a harper.[4] Very hypothetical is Bugge's equation of Arthur's campaign against the Saxons, beginning at the siege of York and ending at the Battle of Badon,[5] with a story told by Saxo Grammaticus (*ca.* 1200), — an equation which would identify Cheldricus with Gelderus, Baldulphus with Balderus, and Cador with Hotherus.[6] But, in any case, Bugge's conclusion that Geoffrey invented the tale and that it reached Saxo very much distorted by oral repetition, seems less probable than that both Geoffrey and Saxo drew from a more ancient tradition.

The most important of all those among Geoffrey's characters for whom he did not certainly derive either the name or the rôle from Nennius or Bede — and one of the most important figures in his whole *History* — is Uther Pendragon, whom he makes the father of Arthur. An ingenious and attractive theory has been developed

---

[1] vii, 4, 69.

[2] x, 2, 9 ff.   It has some resemblance to the dream of King Ivar in the Norse *Sögubrot*, chap. 3.   Cf. R. Mentz, *Die Träume in den Karls- u. Artus-Epen, Ausg. u. Abh.*, LXXIII; W. Henzen, *Über die Träume in der altnord. Sagalitteratur*, Leipzig, 1890.   [4] ix, 1, 43 ff.

[3] vi, 11, 25 ff.   [5] ix, 1–4.

[6] Bugge, *Studier over de Nordiske Gude- og Heltesagens Oprindelse*, I, 185–188 (Brenner's translation, *Studien*, etc., pp. 192–196). See Holder's ed. of Saxo, Strassburg, 1886, pp. 71–74; Elton and Powell, *The First Nine Books of Saxo Grammaticus*, 1894, pp. 86–89.

by Rhŷs, that Uther was originally a god of death or a corpse god.[1]
If so, he belongs to the mythical element in the *History*. It still
remains to explain, however, why Geoffrey inserted Uther at this
particular point and connected him with Arthur. Here also there
is an enticing hypothesis.[2] Some texts of Nennius have at the
mention of Arthur (chap. 56) an interpolation which states that he
"was called *mab Uter* because he was cruel from his boyhood."
The proper interpretation of *mab Uter*, as the following clause
shows, is "terrible warrior"; but it might also be translated "son
of Uter." It is possible, then, that Geoffrey (or some one before
him) had a copy of the interpolated text, made the mistranslation,
whether by error or because it suited his purpose, and then equated
Uter with Uthr Ben. This procedure would have been just what
was needed to furnish Arthur with a father and to fill the gap which
Nennius's narrative implies between Arthur and the Aurelius Ambrosius of Gildas. The expansion of the name into Uther Pendragon[3]
presents no difficulty, since *Ben* and *Pen* are linguistically identical,
and *Pendragon* means "Head Leader."[4]

---

[1] *Arthurian Legend*, pp. 255–256; cf. *Celtic Heathendom*, pp. 93–94, 269, 567.
Taliessin has a poem (Skene, *Four Ancient Books*, II, 203–204) on Uthr Ben,
whose name means "the Wondrous Head." Rhŷs therefore equates Uthr with
Bran of the Venerable Head, and ultimately with Urien, whose head seems to
have been cut off; while the idea of a god whose head was the important or
only part of him was certainly common in European mythology. Taliessin's
poem applies to Uthr the adjective *arđu*, "black," "dusky," or "livid." Equally
ingenious. though still more doubtful, is Rhŷs's identification (pp. 161–162) of
Uther and Aurelius with the kings Ban and Bors of the romances; but it is true
that both Uther and Ban are represented as dying in consequence of drinking
from a poisoned well.

[2] Which has been several times advanced; for example, by Guest, *Origines
Celticae*, II, 159.

[3] Which occurs also in the twelfth-century *Black Book of Caermarthen* in
Arthur's dialogue with Glewlwyd Gavaelvawr.

[4] Rhŷs, *Celtic Britain*, p. 133; *Celtic Heathendom*, p. 568; *Welsh People*,
p. 106. Cf. Gildas, chap. 33. Similar is the story of the begetting of Sigmund,
father of Siegfried, and Professor Schofield has pointed out (*Publ. Mod. Lang.
Assoc.*, 1902, XVII, 284 ff.) striking similarities between the tales of Sigmund and
his sons and the career of Arthur as narrated in the prose romances.

The most important episode which Geoffrey assigns to Uther, his amour with Igerna, is certainly based upon a widespread folk tale, which appears in the classic story of Jupiter and Alcmena, and for which there is a close parallel in the *Kathāsaritsāgara*.[1]

In passing to the more decidedly Celtic elements, mythical and traditional, in Geoffrey's Arthurian story, it is important to remember that all the recent studies [2] concerning the mythical and Celtic traditional elements of the Arthurian cycle, have a real, though indirect, bearing on the argument. For, by showing that many parts of the very diverse Arthurian stories are of mythical or traditional origin, they establish a strong antecedent probability that the same is true of many other parts also. Apart from elements which can be traced to their sources, it is self-evident that very many of the details which appear, for instance, in the French Arthurian Romances, are not pure literary invention, but go back to popular traditions, so that Geoffrey, writing toward the middle of the twelfth century, must have had plenty of that sort of thing to draw from.[3]

The figure of Anna, whom Geoffrey represents as Arthur's sister and Gawain's mother, was certainly traditional, and perhaps originally mythological. She is prominently mentioned in the genealogies of the *Annales Cambriae* and elsewhere, though sometimes in very different relations from those in which Geoffrey puts her.[4]

It is especially unfortunate that we cannot tell whether or not Geoffrey was the first to connect with Arthur the very dramatic incident of the duel with the giant, Helena's ravisher, on Mont St. Michel. But the story is certainly much older than Geoffrey's time, and it is hard to see why any one should doubt that, with Helena in it, it goes back to very remote mythical antiquity; or that Arthur as hero has taken the place formerly occupied by the

---

[1] Tawney's translation, I, 300 ff. I owe this reference to Professor Kittredge.

[2] Such as Nutt's *Legend of the Holy Grail*, and Rhŷs's *Arthurian Legend*, so far as one cares to accept their conclusions.

[3] This is a safe proposition, whatever may be the outcome of the current discussions as to the *matière de Bretagne*.

[4] Loth, *Mabinogion*, II, 305; Rhŷs, *Arthurian Legend*, pp. 19, 336–337.

more early-famed Kei and Bedver, who are here retained in subordinate rôles and are still represented as principals in the similar
affair with Dillus Varvawc in the tale of Kulhwch and Olwen.[1]

Just at the close of the duel, Geoffrey alludes to the story of
another single combat between Arthur and the giant Ritho,— a
personage whom, with his very peculiar characteristics, Welsh and
Romance literature shows to have belonged to ancient tradition.[2]
The most significant thing to note here is the decisive evidence
which Geoffrey thus gives (though in fact we do not need it) that
he knew popular tales of which he made no extended use.

One of the most remarkable figures in Geoffrey's *History* is Merlin, and, while no conclusion seems likely to be reached as to his
real existence, or as to the origin of his name,[3] there is no doubt that
he was known in Celtic tradition before Geoffrey's time.[4] Though
this tradition (as it has come down to us) represents Merlin as a
great bard, and Geoffrey, on the other hand, makes him a prophet
and magician, it seems likely that the prophetic character, at least,
had already been associated with him before Geoffrey wrote.[5]

---

[1] For the whole incident, with parallels, see San-Marte, pp. 401–402; Rhŷs,
Celtic Heathendom, p. 161, with references; Rhŷs, *Arthurian Legend*, pp. 339 ff.;
Branscheid, *Quellen des Morte Arthure*, *Anglia*, 1885, VIII, *Anzeiger*, pp. 189–191,
etc.; Le Roux de Lincy, *Livre des Légendes*, 1836, p. 104, with references; Freymond, *Artus' Kampf mit dem Katzenungetüm* (in the *Festgabe für Gröber*, 1899);
Guil. de St. Paier, *Roman du Mt. St. Michel*, vv. 455 ff. (ed. Redlich and Stengel,
Ausg. u. Abhandl., 1894, XCII). P. Paris has pointed out, probably with too
much emphasis, resemblances to the story of Hercules and Cacus (Ovid, *Fasti*, i,
545–580; Virgil, *Æneid*, viii, 185–279; Livy, i, 7). Cf. also p. 163, below.

[2] See San-Marte, p. 402; Rhŷs, *Celtic Folklore*, pp. 560–562; Triads, Nos. 54,
55, in Loth, *Mabinogion*, II, Nos. 131–132, pp. 289–290; Malory, i, 24; *Li Chevaliers as Deus Espees*, ed. Foerster, 1877, vv. 199–312, 2081 ff. Cf. *Örvar-Odds
Saga*, chap. 23.

[3] For one theory, see d'Arbois de Jubainville, *Rev. des Questions Historiques*,
1868, V, 559–568; Phillimore, *Y Cymmrodor*, XI, 47.

[4] On Merlin in general, see Lot, *Les Sources de la Vita Merlini*, 1900, reprinted
from *Annales de Bretagne*, XV.

[5] Note also that Wace, only twenty years after Geoffrey, knew Taliessin as a
prophet, ascribing to him a prediction of the birth of Christ (*Brut*, ed. Le Roux
de Lincy, vv. 4972–4993). In Welsh tradition Taliessin and Merlin are exactly
similar figures.

That prophecies similar to these given by Geoffrey, to whomever they may have been ascribed, were current at an earlier day, Geoffrey himself indicates by twice referring [1] to the prophecy of the eagle at Shaftesbury; while Giraldus Cambrensis, who wrote only fifty or seventy-five years after Geoffrey, in mentioning prophecies of Merlin Silvestris, several times couples with them those of an Irishman callèd Melingus.[2] The previous connection of the idea with Merlin is suggested by the fact that Geoffrey himself mentions,[3] without reciting it, a prophecy of Merlin to Arthur, while William of Newburgh, in attacking Geoffrey's *History*,[4] especially includes the prophecies of Merlin among the things which Geoffrey took from the Britons and enlarged by additions of his own. Moreover, Giraldus Cambrensis quotes many prophecies of Merlin, taking it for granted that they are very old, and the majority of these do not correspond to anything which Geoffrey gives.[5]

Merlin's first appearance in Geoffrey is as the supernatural boy in the story of Vortigern's tower, which Geoffrey took from Nennius. In Nennius, however, the boy is called *Ambrosius*. The ch··ge, which does away with a confusing doublet of the warrior *Aurelius Ambrosius*, is a very happy one. There are at least two indications that it was made by Geoffrey himself: (1) in the book of prophecies and once in the last part of the preceding book Geoffrey calls Merlin *Ambrosius Merlinus;*[6] (2) Giraldus Cambrensis, who falls into the error of supposing that there were two different Merlins,[7] ascribes to *Merlin Ambrosius* only prophecies which he takes from Geoffrey, and to *Merlin Silvestris* (or *Celidonius*) only those which

---

[1] ii, 9, 15; xii, 18, 1.

[2] *Expug. Hib.*, i, 16, *Works*, Rolls Series, V, 254; i, 30, p. 276; i, 33, p. 279.

[3] xii, 17, 7.   [4] See pp. 101–102, below.   [5] See p. 93, note 1, below.

[6] vi, 19, 18 (in the passage that introduces the book of prophecies); vii, 3, 8. In all other places (vi, 17 and 18 and 19; vii, 1 and 2 and 3 and thenceforth) Geoffrey uses the form *Merlinus*. But in vi, 19, 13–14 he takes pains to explain: *Merlinus, qui et Ambrosius dicebatur*. It looks as if Geoffrey were making the identification precisely in order to appropriate the tower episode to his Merlin. Cf. G. Paris, *Rom.*, 1883, XII, 370, n. 5.

[7] *Itin. Kambriae*, ii, 8, *Works*, VI, 133; *Descr. Kambriae*, i, 16, p. 196. This error has been common ever since. It is a natural result of the great difference between Geoffrey's portrayal of Merlin in the *Historia* and that in his *Vita Merlini*.

do not appear in Geoffrey's work.[1] Giraldus says that (with difficulty, in a remote place) he found a copy of the predictions of
"Celidonius" in the British tongue.[2] But Geoffrey's Merlin is a
magician as well as a seer : he transports Stonehenge from Ireland,[3]
and he changes the shapes of Uther and his companions. It is
doubtful if this character had been ascribed to Merlin before Geoffrey wrote. Probably the exploits just mentioned (and other similar ones) belonged to Welsh tradition,[4] but there is no evidence
that Merlin had been associated with them.

On the whole, Geoffrey's extension of the rôle of Merlin beyond
that of the boy Ambrosius is not very considerable. Nennius
associates Ambrosius with Vortigern only ; Geoffrey carries Merlin

---

[1] The passages taken from Geoffrey are as follows: *De Invect.*, i, 4, p. 27
(Geoffrey, vii, 3, 58–59) ; id., ii, 1, p. 46, *De Jure*, ii, p. 171, and *Itin. Kambriae*,
i, 5, p. 56 (Geoffrey, vii, 3, 27) ; *De Prin. Inst.*, ii, p. 216, and *Expug. Hib.*, ii, 31,
p. 374 (Geoffrey, vii, 3, 84) ; *Top. Hib.*, iii, 52, p. 201, and *Expug. Hib.*, ii, 28,
p. 366 (Geoffrey, vii, 3, 89–90) ; *Expug. Hib.*, i, 33, p. 279 (Geoffrey, vii, 3, 87–88).
Cf. *Descr. Kambriae*, i, 16, p. 197, and ii, 7, p. 216. Ward (I, 293–294) speaks of
the passages ascribed to Silvestris, which are as follows : *Expug. Hib.*, i, 3,
p. 230 ; i, 16, p. 254 ; i, 20, pp. 261–262 ; i, 30, p. 276 ; i, 33, p. 279 ; i, 45, p. 300 ;
ii, 17, p. 339 ; ii, 31, p. 374 ; ii, 31, pp. 377–378 ; ii, 32, p. 381 ; *Itin. Kambriae*,
i, 6, p. 62 ; cf. *Expug. Hib.*, i, 38, p. 287. For instances not connected with the
Arthurian material, see p. 181, note 7, below.

[2] *Itin. Kambriae*, ii, 6, p. 124 ; ii, 8, p. 133 ; *Expug. Hib.*, iii, praef., pp. 401–403.

[3] viii, 10–12. That Geoffrey had any definite basis for most of the details
included in this episode no one has ever shown, though Rhŷs has a theory to
account for some of them (*Celtic Heathendom*, pp. 187–194). But evidently traditions about the origin of the stones must have been current from the time when
people first ceased to know the facts. The mention of Ireland as the place from
which they came is very likely due in part to the supernatural character attributed
to them ; but it is perhaps connected with an actual fact of Irish topography, which
may have been known to Geoffrey or some predecessor. Geoffrey says that the
stones stood originally on Mount Killaraus in Ireland, and Giraldus Cambrensis
(*Top. Hib.*, ii, 18, *Works*, V, 100) notes that similar stones are still to be seen in
Kildare, near Naas. Rhŷs (*Text of the Bruts from the Red Book,* p. xxxi) remarks
that Irish literature corroborates the supposition of the existence of a circle like
Stonehenge in Ireland.

[4] Cf. Schofield, *Publ. Mod. Language Assoc.*, 1901, XVI, 417 ff. The rationalizing Geoffrey suppresses the magic in this particular episode and represents Merlin
as employing special machinery.

on into the two following reigns, but does not have him appear after the time of Uther. Yet, here, as elsewhere, Geoffrey gives evidence of genuine literary skill. For some such figure, a being (whether supernatural or not) endowed with extraordinary wisdom, comes into prominence in most epic stories, — Nestor, for example, by the side of Agamemnon, and Naime de Bavière by the side of Charlemagne.[1] As the Arthurian legend developed, Aurelius and Uther sank into comparative insignificance, and Merlin was intimately associated with Arthur. In the prose romances especially he is constantly brought into the foreground, so that his importance to the tradition becomes as great as that of any character except the king himself.

Antecedent stories, originally mythic, may safely be inferred as the sources from which Geoffrey took the names of some of Arthur's knights who are celebrated in the later romances: Gawain;[2] Cador, whom he makes Duke of Cornwall,[3] a personage prominent in the triads and romances;[4] Eventus[5] (son of Urien), the Owain, or Yvain, of Welsh and French tales; Hiderus, son of Nu,[6] who is Yder, son of the god Nudd of the Celtic pantheon; and Er, son of Hiderus,[7] less well known to us. Geoffrey's very incidental manner of mentioning these heroes indicates that he knew more about them than the plan of his book allowed him to state, and took for granted the same knowledge in his readers. This is doubtless especially true in the case of Gawain, whose exploits as a warrior in Arthur's battles he magnifies as much as the romances exalt his prowess as knight-errant.

Certainly mythical in origin is the idea of Modred's abduction of Guenevere. In the romances, the abductor is generally Melwas, originally an infernal divinity, and there is no proof that any one before Geoffrey had substituted Modred for him. The antiquity

---

[1] Cf. Maugis as helper of Renaut in *Renaut de Montauban*, and cf. also the angels in *Chanson de Roland*, vv, 2452, 2525 ff., 2847–8, 3610 ff.

[2] Cf. pp. 104–105, below. See Miss Weston's *Legend of Sir Gawain*, 1897.

[3] ix, 1, 34, etc.

[4] Cf. Lot, *Rom.*, 1901, XXX, 11–12, and see p. 106, below.   [5] xi, 1, 28.

[6] x, 4, 56. The printed texts omit *filius Nu*, but it occurs in all the manuscripts of Geoffrey that I have examined (though the spelling of the latter name varies) and also in several chronicles which draw from Geoffrey. Cf. pp. 99, 103, below.

[7] x, 5, 32. The printed texts, but not the manuscripts, omit the proper name *Er*, which also occurs in various derivatives of Geoffrey's narrative.

of the episode as connected with Melwas is evidenced not only by its frequent occurrence but by its inclusion in the *Life of Gildas* ascribed to Caradoc.[1]

It is clear, then, that plenty of popular traditions (many of them, at least, of mythic origin) are worked into the Arthurian part of Geoffrey's *History*. It is equally evident that in their first stage these stories must have been entirely disconnected, and altogether possible that before the time of Geoffrey they had not been associated with Arthur at all. In other words, Geoffrey, unless he really had a comprehensive *liber*, must have brought together and combined names and incidents from many diverse quarters. It remains to point out the mythical and folklore elements in Geoffrey's conception of Arthur as an individual. It will be most convenient to present the facts first, and afterwards to discuss the theories as to their significance.

That Geoffrey removes Arthur from the story not by death[2] but by transportation to the isle of Avallon for the healing of his wounds, is manifestly the result of a mythical story which he knew, and of which more will soon be said.[3] Nor is any argument necessary to prove that Arthur's possession of weapons with special names,[4] — the shield Pridwen,[5] the sword Caliburnus, and the

---

[1] See p. 105, below. Cf. Lot, *Rom.*, XXIV, 327 ff., XXVII, 568; Rhŷs, *Arthurian Legend*, pp. 25–38. Here is to be mentioned what seems to be an unintentional preservation by Geoffrey of a fragment of an old story. He says (xi, 1, 39 ff.) that when Arthur won his first victory over Modred, Guenevere fled from Eboracum to Urbs Legionum, where she became a nun. He has not previously mentioned Eboracum in connection with Guenevere or the war, and there is nothing in his previous narrative to show why he thought of her being there. Supporters of the Northern theory of the Arthurian cycle certainly have a right to note this fact.

[2] He leaves this point doubtful, perhaps for political reasons.

[3] See pp. 100–101, below.

[4] ix, 4. Cf. Arthur's list of his treasured possessions in the tale of *Kulhwch and Olwen* (Lady Guest, *Mabinogion*, II, 258); what is said of the mantle in the *Dream of Rhonabwy* (II, 406); the sword of Leite in Irish story (*Rom.*, XXVII, 563); Taliessin's poem on the *Spoils of Hades* (Skene, *Four Ancient Books*, I, 264). See Brown, *The Round Table before Wace*, in *Studies and Notes*, 1900, VII, 199, note.

[5] The printed texts read *Priwen*, but all the manuscripts of Geoffrey that I have consulted have the *d*.

lance Ron, — is a remnant of mythical Celtic stories. In Geoffrey's narrative these arms are a mere traditional survival, in which he does not take much interest. In this same place he mentions Arthur's coat-of-mail and helmet without distinguishing them otherwise than by saying of the former that it was worthy of so great a king, and of the latter that it was adorned with the figure of a dragon; and later, in the fight with Flollo,[1] when he has special occasion to speak of Arthur's lance, he does not care or does not remember to name it. The name of the sword, however, was more thoroughly impressed upon him; for he gives it twice in other places.[2]

The theory of the mythical origin of Arthur as a foreign conqueror has already been stated.[3]

That Geoffrey's picture of Arthur, then, contains mythical and folklore elements, is certain. On the other hand, as has been shown, it has a definite historical or pseudo-historical basis. The discussion is brought, therefore, to this question: Were the mythical features added by Geoffrey, or by popular tradition before his time?

This question must be answered in accordance with one of two theories. The first holds that the mythical characteristics are only the *débris* of stories told originally about other figures, whether they were transferred to Arthur by Geoffrey, or were attracted to him by earlier and less deliberate development, after tradition had magnified his exploits. The second assumes that, besides the historical Arthur, there was an old Celtic god or " culture-hero " of the same name, who, in the breakdown of Celtic mythology, became confused with the famous warrior. This latter theory is by no means new. It was set forth or taken for granted in several works a century or more ago, and has since been upheld in various others.[4]

---

[1] ix, 11, 60.

[2] ix, 11, 75; x, 11, 16. On Arthur's arms, cf. p. 162, below.

[3] See p. 83, above.

[4] For example, the Rev. Edward Davies's fantastic *Mythology of the Druids ;* Owen, *Cambrian Biography,* 1803, pp. 13–18. Cf. also Poste, p. 129; Babcock, p. 135; Nicholson, *Academy,* 1895, XLVIII, 297; Herbert, *Britannia after the Romans,* II, 21.

Its chief exponent, however, is Professor Rhŷs, who has stated a general principle which is the foundation of the whole hypothesis: " In Irish and Welsh literature, the great figures of Celtic mythology usually assume the character of kings of Britain and the sister-island . . . and most of the myths of the modern Celts are to be found manipulated so as to form the opening chapters of what has been usually regarded as the early history of the British Isles." [1] This principle, in its general form, may pass without challenge, and its application has been illustrated more than once in the present investigation. The question is *whether it applies to Arthur*, for whose figure there is really an historical or pseudo-historical basis.

Professor Rhŷs's argument is somewhat extended.[2] It is based chiefly on an etymology of Arthur's name, and on the fact that the tasks which he gets performed for Kulhwch in the Welsh tale are largely such as would be suitable for a " culture-hero." But Professor Rhŷs himself admits that very likely Arthur ought to be regarded rather as a Celtic Zeus, and his theory certainly cannot be regarded as proved for either character. Fortunately its truth or falsity is of no great consequence in the present discussion. For the later development of the story it makes no difference whether the mythical characteristics were simply transferred to Arthur *en masse* from some other personage, or slowly grouped about his name one by one. Yet it is safer on the whole to proceed in accordance with the other theory, which is more in harmony with the facts in parallel cases. We may assume, then, that these characteristics of Arthur do not constitute the torso of a single colossal figure rescued from the wreck of the Celtic pantheon,[3] but rather that they are fragments of other figures brought together from many quarters and combined into a whole to which Arthur's name was given. The question remains, therefore, — Had they been assigned to Arthur before the time of Geoffrey? And with this is closely associated another question, — Had Arthur already been represented as the great national hero of the British race? The answer in both cases must certainly be in the affirmative.

---

[1] *Celtic Heathendom*, pp. 119–120.   [2] *Arthurian Legend*, pp. 23, 25–38.
[3] As Rhŷs expresses it (*Arthurian Legend*, p. 48).

That legends had begun to gather about the figure of Arthur long before Geoffrey, is shown by the *mirabilia* of Nennius and by entries in the *Annales Cambriae* and in the Vatican and Cambridge manuscripts of Nennius.[1] But there is other evidence of equal or even greater importance.

Not without significance, in the first place, is the space which Geoffrey allots to Arthur. The *Historia* covers a period, presumably, of over fifteen hundred years, but more than a fifth part of it [2] is devoted to Arthur's reign,[3] — more than twice as much as is given to the eponymous Brutus, who comes next to Arthur in this respect. Would Geoffrey ever have thought of exalting so highly a character no better known than Arthur would have been from the meagre account of Nennius?

Again, Geoffrey himself says flatly in his preface that the deeds of Arthur were celebrated in the memory of many peoples.[4] The force of this statement is decreased, not only because it is Geoffrey who makes it, but because he couples with Arthur "other kings after his time." Still, we have seen [5] that the language of Henry of Huntingdon allows the inference that he knew Arthur as a king supreme over the other kings of the island; and that William of Malmesbury, likewise writing before Geoffrey, testifies explicitly to the extravagance of the British ideas about him.[6] Still more striking evidence appears in the picture of Arthur as a king and knight-errant which William gives in his *De Antiquitate Glastoniensis Ecclesiae*,[7] though the authenticity of this episode has been questioned by high authority.[8] In the section *De Illustri Arturo*, William says:

---

[1] See pp. 15, note 7, 16, 28, 32–34, above.		[2] 38 printed pages out of 174.

[3] As much more to the period before the accession of Arthur, which I have here treated as belonging to the Arthurian story.

[4] See p. 51, above.		[5] See p. 42, above.		[6] See p. 40, above.

[7] Migne, *Patrol. Lat.*, CLXXIX, col. 1701; also in Gale, I, 307. The passage reappears in the enlarged version of William's work by John of Glastonbury (who flourished about 1400), ed. Hearne, 1726, I, 76.

[8] G. Paris, *Hist. Litt. de la France*, XXX, 199; cf. Holtzmann, *Germania*, XII, 276–277. On the date of the *De Antiquitate*, see Stubbs, *Introduction* to the *Gesta Regum*, pp. xxvii–xxviii. On the story in general, see Lot, *Rom.*, XXVII, 568.

It is narrated in the deeds of the most illustrious king Arthur [1] that when, at a celebration of the birthday of our Lord at Karlium, he had adorned a valiant youth, the son of King Nuth, called Ider, with military insignia, and, for the sake of proving him, had brought him to the mountain of the Ranae (now called Brentenol), where, as he had learned, there were three giants most distinguished for their misdeeds, to fight against them, — this same youth went ahead of Arthur and his companions without their knowledge, boldly attacked the giants, and killed them in a marvellous fight. When they had been slain, Arthur came up, found Ider overcome with the excessive exertion, and fallen into a swoon, and together with his attendants mourned him for dead. Therefore, returning home in the greatest sorrow, he left there the body which he supposed to be lifeless until he could send a vehicle to bring it away.

William (or the interpolator) then goes on to say that Arthur, thinking himself the cause of Ider's death, made an endowment at Glastonbury, when he arrived there, for twenty-four monks to pray for the youth's soul. Later on, Arthur is mentioned [2] at the head of the benefactors of Glastonbury Abbey.[3]

Besides these references previous to Geoffrey's time, quite as much importance ought to be assigned to a large number of passages in various works, written not long after his *History*, which represent Arthur as a great hero or king or refer to traditional stories so representing him.

Any one not blinded by preconceived contrary theories must admit the force of the fact that in all the French romances, like those of Crestien, which began to be written, to our knowledge, within less than thirty years after Geoffrey's *History* (and in fact probably earlier), Arthur appears in the characteristic romance position as the mere centre of a great court of knights-errant. In any romance cycle such a development requires a long time. It could not have come so soon from Geoffrey's story alone.

More direct is the evidence of Wace in observations which he inserts in his paraphrase of Geoffrey, observations which, though made about twenty years later than the *Historia*, clearly refer to

---

[1] Cf. p. 231, below.

[2] Migne, col. 1723; Gale, p. 326.

[3] For another somewhat similar story told by William, see pp. 103–104, below.

conditions which had long existed. After telling of Arthur's conquests in the North, he says [1] that, because his barons quarrelled about precedence at feasts he "made the Round Table, of which 'Bretons' tell many a fable." Here Wace introduces a popular tradition about Arthur as a great king, of which Geoffrey gives no hint whatever, and says that with the "Bretons" (whether Armoricans or Welsh) it is a subject of many fabulous stories. Later [2] he indicates that Arthur was in his time, and apparently had long been, the central figure of a whole cycle of romantic adventures: "In this great peace that I mention — I don't know whether you have heard of it — the marvels were proved and the adventures performed which are so much told about Arthur that they have been turned into fables. Not all of them are false and not all true; not all foolishness and not all sense; but the story-tellers have told so much and the writers of fables fabled so much to embellish their tales, that they have made the whole seem fables." Evidently Wace makes this remark because, knowing the stories, he thinks they should be mentioned in any complete account of Arthur's reign, and he is evidently relieved to find a period in Geoffrey's narrative to which they can plausibly and consistently be assigned. Again, in speaking of the coming of Arthur to Avalon,[3] Wace preserves the essential feature of the story, which Geoffrey omitted;[4] namely, that not only was his recovery there taken for granted by the "Bretons," but that they believed he would return to them at some later time. "He is still there; the 'Bretons' await him; they say that he will come back and live again."

The idea that Avalon as the refuge of Arthur was something more than an abode of mortals was fully expressed by Geoffrey himself in the *Vita Merlini*[5] some years after the publication of his *Historia*. His description, though written in a conventionally

---

[1] Ed. Le Roux de Lincy, vv. 9994 ff.; cf. p. 142, below.

[2] Vv. 10,032 ff.

[3] V. 13,685. For Layamon's paraphrases of these statements of Wace, see vv. 22,955 ff., 23,053 ff., 28,610 ff.

[4] Perhaps, as we have seen, for political reasons (see p. 95, note 2, above).

[5] Vv. 912 ff., ed. Michel and Wright, pp. 36–37.

poetical style, shows clearly enough the direct descent of the story from the general Celtic conception of the Happy Other World.

Even earlier, probably, than in Wace's *Brut*, the belief among the Britons that Arthur would return to vindicate their rights was alluded to by Geoffrey Gaimar,[1] and indeed by Henry of Huntingdon in his letter to Warinus (1139).[2] About 1190 Joseph of Exeter refers to it in his Troy poem.[3] It is also mentioned by Giraldus Cambrensis.[4] How strongly it was held among the Armoricans by 1175 appears in the often-quoted passage in which Alanus de Insulis says that denial of it in the country districts of Brittany would be likely to cost a man his life.[5] Most significant of all is the account of the begging journey of the monks of Laon to Cornwall, appended to the autobiography of Guibertus of Novigentum. This proves that as early as 1146 the Bretons (of Armorica) used to quarrel with the French about Arthur, and that as early as 1113 a belief in his return was a more sacred thing to the men of Cornwall and Devon than church, monks, or miracles.[6]

Evidence of the same general nature is furnished by William of Newburgh in the long and violent attack which he makes upon Geoffrey in the *Prooemium* to his own History of England, written about 1198.[7] Geoffrey, he says, "disguised under the honorable name of history, thanks to his Latinity, the fables about Arthur which he took from the ancient fictions of the Britons and increased out of his own head.[8] . . . I pass by all the things about the Britons before the time of Julius Cæsar which this fellow invented, or adopted after they had been invented by others, and wrote down for true. . . . It is manifest that everything which this person wrote about Arthur and his successors, and his predecessors after

---

[1] See pp. 125 ff., below.   [2] See p. 120, below.   [3] iii, 472–473.

[4] *De Prin. Instruct.*, i, *Works*, Rolls Series, VIII, 127; *Spec. Eccles.*, ii, 9, IV, 48 ff.   [5] *Prophetia Anglicana*, etc., Frankfort, 1603, bk. i, p. 17.

[6] For the fullest discussion of the affair, with references, see Zimmer, *Ztsch. f. franz. Spr.*, 1891, XIII, 106–112. On the expectation of Arthur's return to earth, cf. also below, pp. 145, 165, 167, 188, 190, 197, 202, 207, 230.

[7] The latest edition is that of Howlett, Vols. I and II of *Chronicles of Stephen*, etc., Rolls Series, 1884–1885. See his *Introduction*.

[8] *Fabulas de Arturo, ex priscis Britonum figmentis sumptas et ex proprio auctas.*

Vortigern, was made up partly by himself and partly by others; whether from an inordinate love of lying or for the sake of pleasing the Britons, of whom the majority are said to be so brutishly stupid that, according to report, they still look for Arthur as if he would return, and will not listen to any one who says that he is dead. . . ." He afterward says that the same Arthur, after he was mortally wounded in battle,[1] " disposed of his kingdom and went away to that island of Avallon which the British fables create; not daring, for fear of the Britons, to say that he is dead whose return the stupid Britons expect."

Even before the time of Geoffrey the fame of Arthur and some of his knights had made its way to Italy, as is pretty conclusively shown by the facts about Italian names brought forward by Rajna[2] and by the sculpture on the cathedral of Modena discussed by Foerster.[3]

Since, then, there can be no doubt that Geoffrey found the figure of Arthur already endowed by popular tradition with mythical attributes and exalted in some respects, at least, to the position of the national hero of the British race, it becomes important to determine how much of his conception he may have taken from this traditional source.

Now the evidence on this point is dubious. Almost none of the extant mediæval Welsh literature is free from the suspicion (often a certainty) of having been composed later than Geoffrey's time, and therefore, if it pretends to treat of Welsh historical figures, of having been influenced by him. Nevertheless, we may reason backward from this literature, much as we do from the French romances. All its indications point to the conclusion that Geoffrey's workmanship consisted in refining and magnifying the figure of Arthur which previously existed in the popular imagination. Though Skene's defense of the great antiquity of the poetry ascribed to

---

[1] *Letaliter vulneratum*, Geoffrey's own expression (xi, 2, 56).

[2] *Gli Eroi brettoni nell' Onomastica italiana*, etc. (*Rom.*, 1887, XVII, 161–185, 355 ff.).

[3] *Ztsch. f. Rom. Phil.*, 1898, XXII, 243 ff., 526–529. Villemarqué, *Romans de la Table Ronde*, 1860, pp. 23–24, mentions a bas-relief in a Breton church which may possibly give evidence for an Arthurian " cult " in Brittany about 1100.

bards of the sixth century has been disproved for most of the poems,[1] yet it seems to be agreed that some of them antedate Geoffrey; and in all of these which mention Arthur and his knights the pictures are chiefly those of brave warriors not distinguished above many other Celtic heroes, nor is Arthur himself always made to appear the superior of the rest.[2] We have already seen that the ninth- or tenth-century *mirabilia* of Nennius represent Arthur simply as a *miles*. Among the tales, only that of *Kulhwch and Olwen* can be used for evidence, and the Red Book of Hergest, the manuscript in which it occurs, is three or four centuries later than Geoffrey, so that the story may contain many late features, even if, as Rhŷs supposes,[3] it was mainly composed as early as the tenth century. Now, while it makes Arthur the head of an immense concourse and court of knights — comprising nearly all the figures of Welsh mythology — and speaks of his having conquered lands that seem to include the greater part of the known world, the very comprehensiveness of the lists of knights and countries indicates that many of them, at least, may have been added very late; and, in spite of Arthur's glory, the tale still represents him as performing (though generally by deputy) such trivial tasks as the collection of scattered grain or the winning of certain dogs, — folklore commonplaces which go back to the primitive condition of society reflected in all the Welsh mythology. It is doubtless easy to lay too much stress on the idea of primitiveness, because the Welsh imagination as revealed in its stories always continued so naïve, but the important point is that the stories which Geoffrey knew must have been pervaded with this element of what seems uncouthness to the modern Teutonic mind. Very similar is the evidence of the triads,[4] but their age is so doubtful that they must be left out of account.

The story of Ider in William of Malmesbury,[5] if it be authentic, shows that even before Geoffrey wrote, Arthur had been represented as the centre of a court of knights-errant. Elsewhere, in a passage

---

[1] See, for example, Lot, *Sources de la Vita Merlini.*

[2] See Skene, *Four Ancient Books;* Rhŷs, preface to the Dent edition of Malory, I (1893), xx–xxiv.   [4] Ed. Loth, *Mabinogion,* II.

[3] Dent Malory, p. xxxv.   [5] See p. 99, above.

of the *Gesta Regum* which is generally considered authentic,[1] William speaks of Gawain, giving various interesting details. In the province of Wales called Ros,[2] he says (some time not far from the year 1090, we must infer), was discovered the tomb of "Walwen, who, being the son of Arthur's sister, was not unworthy of him. He ruled in that part of Britain which is still called Walweitha,[3] — a very valiant knight, but he was driven from his kingdom by the brother and nephew of Hengist; first getting satisfaction, however, by inflicting great harm upon them. He shared deservedly in the glory of his uncle, because they deferred for many years the ruin of their falling country. The sepulchre of Arthur is nowhere known,[4] whence ancient songs[5] fable that he will come again. But the tomb of the other, as I have just said, was discovered in the time of King William upon the shore of the sea, fourteen feet in length;[6] where it is said by some that he was wounded by enemies, and shipwrecked; by others, that he was killed by his countrymen at a public feast. The truth, therefore, remains in doubt, but neither of them was unworthy of his fame."

Geoffrey, then, did not invent the tradition that Gawain was the son of Arthur's sister; he found it already in existence. He found also various tales about Gawain's death, — tales agreeing with his account in locating the event on the seashore, but differing widely as to the other circumstances.[7] Geoffrey's own version may very likely have been made over by him to suit his immediate purpose. William's account probably shows a trace of the earlier Welsh

---

[1] iii, 287, ed. Stubbs, II, 342.

[2] In Pembroke (see G. Paris, *Hist. Litt.*, XXX, 29).

[3] Galloway, according to Paris.

[4] *Nusquam visitur.*

[5] *Antiquitas naeniarum.*

[6] Probably this story rests on the actual fact of the discovery of some real tomb which either William or common popular opinion may have assumed (perhaps on the basis of the stories which he mentions) to be that of Gawain. Possibly, however, as Holtzmann suggested (*Germania*, 1867, XII, 277–278), the grave may really have been, or have been thought to be, that of the Welsh king Maelgwyn (Gildas's *Maglocunus*, Geoffrey's *Malgo*), and William may have confused the names.

[7] This is certainly true of one class of these tales.

conception in representing Gawain as an independent king.[1] And evidently the Welsh fancy before Geoffrey had associated Gawain with the pseudo-historical account of the Saxon invasion.[2]

In certain Latin lives of Welsh saints, written not much later than the time of Geoffrey, and based upon material which must have been current in his day and earlier, appear the same primitive or less exalted Welsh conceptions of Arthur and his knights which have been already remarked upon. One of the most important of these stories occurs in the *Life of Gildas* ascribed to Caradoc of Llancarvan, and therefore was recorded at just about the date of Geoffrey's *History*, whether before or after cannot be certainly determined.[3] Here it is said [4] that Gildas was contemporary with Arturus, King of all Great Britain, whom he loved as Arthur deserved, and tried to obey. But his twenty-three brothers resisted "this rebel king," being unwilling to acknowledge a master, and made war upon him, especially the eldest, Hueil, who often engaged in successful raids from Scotland, and who was looked upon with favor by the people as destined to be their future king. Arthur, however, met him in battle in the isle of Minau and killed him. Gildas, who was then in Ireland, heard of this, but he obeyed the scriptural precept and prayed for Arthur. On his return to Britain he granted Arthur the pardon which he sought.[5]

Here it is to be especially noted that, though Arthur is king of the whole island, he is so only by usurpation. Properly he has equals. He is not acceptable to all the people and appears, on the whole, in a rather unfavorable light. A little later the writer gives the Arthur-Melwas story:[6] When Gildas was driven from the island on which he had been living, he went to the abbey of Glastonia. This was at that time besieged by "Arturus tyrannus,"

---

[1] Cf. pp. 187, 251, below.

[2] For evidences of independent stories about Gawain or special praise of him, see pp. 139, 144, 163, 187, 197, 201, 207, 213, 218, 229, 258, below; contrast p. 123.

[3] Lot (*Rom.*, 1895, XXIV, 330) says about 1160. Cf. his remarks in *Rom.*, XXVII, 565–566.   [4] Mommsen's edition of Gildas, p. 108.

[5] The cause of Arthur's quarrel with Hueil is stated in *Kulhwch and Olwen* (Lady Guest, *Mabinogion*, II, 263), where Hueil is briefly characterized (p. 260).

[6] Cf. p. 95, above.

because the "wicked king Melvas" of "the summer region,"[1] after violating and carrying away Arthur's wife Guennvvar, had transported her thither for safer keeping.   Arthur had searched a year before discovering her place of concealment, and now he had collected the whole army of Cornubia and Dibnenia.   As the two kings are about to engage in battle, the abbot of Glastonia, with all the monks and Gildas, comes upon the field and advises Melwas to restore Arthur's wife.   This he does, with an apparent tameness which quite spoils the story.   Thus it seems that other kings were left in the island after all, and that in the mind of some one through whose hands the tale passed, Arthur was king only of a small region in the southwest of England.

Again, in the life of St. Carannog (preserved in a manuscript of about 1200)[2] Arthur appears, as in *Kulhwch and Olwen*, in the light of a destroyer of monsters.   Arthur and Cato (Cador) hold sway in the region of the Severn, and reside at Dindrarthon. Arthur, who is engaged in hunting a terrible serpent, gives information as to the whereabouts of a supernatural altar belonging to St. Carannog.   In return, he requires the saint to fetch the serpent, and the saint complies and tames him.[3]

A life of St. Iltutus in the same manuscript[4] gives a rather different picture of Arthur as a great conqueror and the centre of a rich court.   Iltutus, then a soldier, hearing of the magnificence of Arthur, his relative, visits his court, where he finds a great number of warriors (*militum*) and receives gifts to his heart's content.

Still other lives of saints, which, though now preserved only in later manuscripts, may go back in origin to a time anterior to Geoffrey, represent Arthur in homely, undignified, and unworthy

---

[1] Somerset.

[2] MS. Cott. Vesp. A. xiv. 4, fols. 90–91 *b*; Hardy, I, 46–47.   Printed by W. J. Rees, *Lives of Cambro British Saints*, pp. 97–101.   The date is given on the authority of Lot, *Nouvelles Études sur la provenance du cycle Arthurien*, *Rom.*, 1901, XXX, 1.   He says, following Phillimore, *Y Cymmrodor*, XI, 128, that the lives of this manuscript were *composed* about 1100.

[3] It is interesting to note that this life represents Arthur as wishing to make the altar into a table and as being miraculously prevented, — an idea which looks as if it might be connected with the Round Table.   Lot thinks this passage "clearly interpolated."

[4] Fols. 42 *b*–52; Hardy, I, 92, No. 282; printed by Rees, pp. 158 ff.

situations, — as punished like a naughty child for interfering with the saints;[1] as taking the part of a ravisher,[2] or even as wrangling over the color of cows.[3]

It is quite possible on the basis of the evidence to form an idea of the conception of Arthur which Geoffrey found current among the Welsh (and to a much less degree among the other peoples of his day) and which he took for the foundation of his own. The historical (or supposedly historical) tradition (partly represented by Nennius) had undergone considerable changes. In the popular estimation Arthur had become first a great king, and then a great conqueror, though foreign conquests[4] may not yet have been ascribed to him. He had been idealized as the national hero of the British race, and his destined return for the deliverance of his people was a matter of passionate faith both in Wales and in Brittany. Mythical traits and bits of folklore had become attached to him, and some at least of the earlier mythological figures of Celtic belief had been subordinated to him.[5] Further, he was sometimes regarded as the centre of a group of distinguished heroes, a *comitatus* or court,[6] and this court doubtless had some of those characteristics of knight-errantry[7] which appear in the French romances. Of course there was no firm consistency in such a body of miscellaneous popular material. Current stories differed widely, not only in details but in their general conception of Arthur. Some traditions survived which were only compatible with the idea

---

[1] *Life of St. Paternus*, published, for instance, by Rees, pp. 188–197; Hardy, I, 129, No. 387 (a misleading description). Cf., for the character of the story, MS. Cott. Cleop. D. viii, No. 2, fol. 2 *a*.

[2] Prologue to *Life of St. Cadoc* (Rees, pp. 23–24).

[3] *Life of St. Cadoc* (Rees, pp. 48–49).

[4] Particularly the conquest of Gaul and Rome.

[5] It is possible, but only possible, that these mythological traits were transferred to him (as Rhŷs thinks) *en masse* from some ancient divinity with whom he was identified.

[6] This is probable, whatever may be thought of the date of the Ider story in William of Malmesbury. Compare Conchobar and his court in the epic tradition of Ireland.

[7] In a rudimentary way, of course, without chivalric manners and French or Norman costuming. Here again the Irish epic sagas should be borne in mind.

of a petty prince, and the Welsh imagination, following its inerad-
icable tendency, had no doubt connected the king with many
anecdotes of an undignified or trivial character.[1]

We can form some opinion of the change which Geoffrey introduced into the story of Arthur's reign, as well as into all parts of
his narrative, from the astonishment with which his *History* was
received. It was doubtless Geoffrey who associated with Arthur
some of the traditional episodes and figures that were originally
unconnected with him. He may well have been the first to polish
away the naïveté of the Welsh conceptions, to draw Arthur in the
colors of a king of his own day, and to add the wars of conquest in
Gaul and against the Romans.[2] Certainly it was he who introduced
Arthur to the world as an important figure in universal history.

IX. Geoffrey's Sources: (G) Contemporary Manners and
the Romantic Idea

The general tone which Geoffrey substitutes in his *History* for
that of the earlier British tales about Arthur is the tone, somewhat idealized, of the chivalrous society of the Middle Ages. The
change is not only important in itself, but it differentiates this part
of Geoffrey's narrative from all the others. Wherever, indeed, he
writes with much detail (of Brutus, Belinus, Cassibellaunus, or Cad-
wallo), he draws to some extent, like all mediæval authors, from the
life of his own time; but it is only here that he fully portrays a
knightly court and knightly manners.

It would not be true to say that Geoffrey completely transformed
Arthur and his warriors into a Norman king with a Norman court
of nobles.[3] Not even the latest romances went quite so far as that.

---

[1] For further indications of independent stories about Arthur, see pp. 138, 145,
below.

[2] As already observed (p. 53, note 3), if De La Borderie's claim to have discovered Geoffrey's source should be admitted, the idea of conquests in France by
Arthur was long antecedent to Geoffrey. Zimmer gives a full statement of his
idea of the conception of Arthur before Geoffrey in *Gött. Gel. Anz.*, 1890, pp. 521 ff.

[3] For instance, the first seven chapters of bk. ix, besides being largely based
on Nennius, reflect mostly, as I have already said, the spirit of the period of the

Nevertheless, the strong influence of Anglo-Norman life on Geoffrey's story is sufficiently evident. When Arthur has established himself in his kingdom[1] he is represented as doing the things most characteristic of the Anglo-Norman kings; as ruling on a magnificent scale in the same general manner and in the same state as they. His first act is to hold a Christmas feast at York.[2] He is especially affected by the sight of the havoc that has been made of religion, and he calls together the clergy and people, appoints an archbishop,[3] and restores the churches. He also reinstates the nobles who have been expelled from their possessions; in particular,[4] the three brother kings of Scotland, who are thus represented as his feudal vassals. At a later period[5] he distributes to the deserving, lands and castles in Britain, and makes very important ecclesiastical changes. After conquering France he divides it[6] among various nobles. All this is exactly the sort of thing which William the Conqueror did when he had brought the country under control. Ordericus Vitalis tells[7] how in 1070 William convened a great assembly at Winchester and deposed unworthy churchmen; and earlier,[8] how he confirmed the chief Saxon nobles in their possessions after they had taken the oath of allegiance. He says also[7] that when order was restored the princes and bishops began to reëstablish the monasteries, whose monks had all been driven away. The division of a great part of the English lands among his own followers was one of William's chief actions.

In expanding the Celtic conception of Arthur's household and stating[9] that the bravest warriors from far-distant lands were invited to join it, Geoffrey is not copying exactly from what he

---

Danish and perhaps the historical Saxon invasions; the conquests of Northern lands in chap. 10 are unexampled in Anglo-Norman history (the conquest of England itself is not a real parallel); the list of heathen kings in x, 1, is from mediæval poetry; and the stories of the fights with the giants in x, 3, have lost little of their originally mythical-traditional character.

[1] Beginning with ix, 8.   [2] ix, 8, 1–2.

[3] Geoffrey has previously (viii, 12, 39 ff.) represented Aurelius as bestowing ecclesiastical honors, but Aurelius's reign as a whole is not greatly Normanized.

[4] Chap. 9.   [6] ix, 11, 90–94.   [8] iv, 1.

[5] ix, 14, 10 ff.; ix, 15, 1–9.   [7] iv, 6.   [9] ix, 11, 1 ff.

knew of the Norman courts, but he is doubtless giving an idealized and magnified picture of them, influenced somewhat by the romantic stories. One is reminded also of the host which William the Conqueror got together from all possible quarters in preparation for his invasion of England. The parallel is the more direct because Geoffrey makes Arthur set out on his foreign expeditions forthwith.

The account of the great Pentecostal feast and of Arthur's second coronation [1] could not have been written in England until after the time of the Norman conquest.[2] All the kings and lords of Arthur's realms are present, and the whole picture is one of extravagant courtly. and chivalrous splendor and elegance, such as was unknown among the Saxons and Britons.[3] The idea of having Arthur crowned a second time [4] may have been suggested by the custom which the Norman kings followed, of having the diadem placed on their heads in the minster on the occasion of a great feast; though perhaps Geoffrey intended rather to indicate that the second coronation was imperial, — a consequence of Arthur's conquests, — and the first, while his position was doubtful and far less glorious, only regal. But at any rate the ceremony in question used, with the Normans, to precede the passage to the banqueting hall, just as it does in Geoffrey's account.[5] Since Arthur has just returned from

---

[1] ix, 12–14.

[2] Although it also contains elements of a very different character: the mention of the gymnasium of two hundred philosophers who by means of the stars foretold to Arthur coming prodigies (chap. 12, ll. 20 ff.); the mention of the twelve peers of France (l. 52); the strange assertion that the Britons followed the Trojan custom of having men and women eat separately at feasts (chap. 13, l. 24); the introduction of games, including hurling of stones (chap. 14, l. 5). This last feature, though doubtless true to the habits of the lower classes, is hardly characteristic of Norman knights. It reminds one a good deal of the sports described by Virgil and other classic authors.

[3] Here Geoffrey may have been influenced as much by what he had seen at the castle of Robert of Gloucester or some other noble as by any particular ceremony at the royal court.

[4] Cf. p. 167, below.

[5] See Freeman's picture of a great festival of William Rufus (*Reign of William Rufus*, II, 264). It may be noted that Geoffrey also represents Aurelius as crowning himself a second time (viii, 12, 35).

his foreign conquests, there may be also a reminiscence of the coronation of William I as king of England. Certain definite historical events of the Anglo-Norman period which Geoffrey seems to have imitated in his *History* have been already noted.[1]

The most interesting adaptation of Norman history in Geoffrey's work is the process by which he makes over the old Celtic heroes Kei and Bedver into great Norman nobles.[2] After conquering France Arthur gives to Bedver his steward the province of "Neustria, now called Normandy," and to Cajus his seneschal the province of Anjou. Bedver is buried[3] at Bajocae (Bayeux), which Bedver the first, his great-grandfather,[4] had founded, and Cajus[5] at *Camus oppidum*, which he himself had built.

The chief historical facts to be here taken into account are as follows. The commonest Latin form of the name of the city Camus (now Caen) was *Cadomus*,[6] sometimes written[7] *Kaii Domus*. After 1132 the office of seneschal was one of the very highest at the Anglo-Norman court; and the seat of the Norman exchequer, probably as early as the time of Henry I, was at Caen. In France, the office of seneschal was at least equally important, and was hereditary in the house of Anjou. Norman documents not much later than Geoffrey's *History* identify the *praepositus* of Bayeux with the steward of the Anglo-Norman court; and, since all the great court offices were hereditary. there is no reason to doubt that the connection went back to a still earlier period. William the Conqueror was buried at Caen, a city which he had so extensively rebuilt that he might almost be called its founder.

---

[1] See pp. 81–82, 85, above.

[2] ix, 11, 90–92. The whole theory which follows was elaborated by Professor G. W. Benedict in his dissertation on *Sir Kay*, not yet published.

[3] x, 13, 4–12.   [4] *Proavus*.

[5] Geoffrey has here *Cheudo* (so all the manuscripts which I have examined except a poor one, Harl. 225, which reads *Kaius*). This may most satisfactorily be explained as a scribal error due to the fact that Eudo was the name of the seneschal of William the Conqueror (and also of William II) and that another Eudo, abbot of Caen, died in 1140.

[6] For earlier *Catomagus*. See Joret, *Bulletin de la Soc. des Antiquaires de Normandie*, 1895, XVII, as cited in *Rom.*, XXIV, 632.

[7] At least, after Geoffrey's day.

These facts in themselves, without comment, almost furnish the whole explanation. When Geoffrey wished, as in the development of his picture he naturally must have wished, to find some of Arthur's men to identify with the great lordships of his own time, he naturally thought first of Kei and Bedver, who were especially prominent in the old Celtic stories. The name *Kei*, or *Kai*, in Geoffrey's Latinized form *Cajus*, inevitably suggested *Cadomus;* Cadomus suggested the seneschalship, and the seneschalship (by an easy natural transition from the Anglo-Norman to the French court) suggested Anjou. This explains why Kei, the duke of Anjou, is connected with Caen, a city in Normandy. Kei being thus made a court officer, no other position more prominent than the stewardship remained [1] for Bedver, and the alliterative resemblance between *Bedver* and *Bajocae* was enough to clinch the association. Besides, it was almost a matter of course that either Kei or Bedver should be made duke of Normandy, the most important Anglo-Norman possession in France.

As to the burial of Cajus and Bedver, some other facts need to be brought out. Geoffrey says that Cajus was carried severely wounded *ad Camum oppidum*, where he soon died, and that he was buried in a cemetery of monks not far from the town.[2] William the Conqueror, after being fatally hurt, was carried to Rouen, and it soon became necessary, because of the noise of the city, to remove him to a monastery outside the walls. When he died he was buried at Caen in a church which he had founded.[3] The circumstances of his burial were so tragic as to fix the event firmly in people's minds. All this is in rather close parallel with what Geoffrey says of the death of Cajus. As for Bedver, his association with Cajus throughout the story involved, almost as a matter of course, their union in death. Geoffrey's gratuitous and rather surprising statement that one of Bedver's ancestors [4] had founded Bayeux is explained when we recall that, in contrast to Caen, Bayeux was an ancient city.

---

[1] Though the two identifications were more likely simultaneous.

[2] " In quodam nemore, in coenobio eremitarum ... humatus est " (x, 13, 10–12).

[3] Cf. Ordericus Vitalis, vii, 16 (ed. Le Prévost, III, 250).

[4] It may be noted that in the *Mabinogion* Bedver's grandfather is named Bedrag.

Geoffrey has not only Normanized the story of Arthur's reign; he has also surrounded it with an atmosphere of romance.[1] In the first place he has made of Arthur something not very different, in view of the great difference of his position, from the hero of a French Arthurian poem. Arthur's very existence, after a fashion very similar to that of the most approved knights of chivalrous stories, is due to the amour of a hero, using magic devices, with a noble lady.[2] In the romances, also, fifteen years is the usual age for the commencement of the hero's exploits. Whether by intention or by accident, Geoffrey has so treated the whole Nennian account of Arthur as to include it wholly at the very beginning of his career and thus to make it seem like the *enfances* of a biographical romance. After this, Arthur in all his wars is rather the valiant knight than the skilful general. He engages in a duel, fought in conventional romantic style, and is gloriously victorious only after having been almost overcome. His most romantic adventure, that of Mont St. Michel, may be a purely mythical survival, but it is none the less significant in this connection; for the same is true of many episodes in the romances, and Arthur's spirit in undertaking and prosecuting it is thoroughly characteristic of a knight-errant.

Geoffrey's Gawain, too, resembles a knight-errant (the Gawain of the romances) far more than he resembles a great feudal duke. His fame, like Arthur's, is measured by the slaughter he makes with his own hand in battle. The same is true of all the other lords. In the spirit of romance, also, is the requirement imposed by ladies of the court, that the warriors shall prove themselves valiant before they are esteemed worthy of love.[3] So is the description of the inspiration which the ladies give to youths who contend for honor in the sports.[4] The sports themselves, though seemingly reflecting other influences,[5] take the place of a regular tournament.

---

[1] Cf. also pp. 87–88, above.

[2] The whole idea goes back to older stories where the father was not a mortal, as in the lay of *Tydorel*. Cf. Bugge-Schofield, *The Home of the Eddic Poems*, pp. 74 ff., where are discussed the stories of Cormac, Wolfdietrich, Helgi, and others. Contrast p. 182, and note 1, below.   [4] ix, 14, 4.

[3] ix, 13, 40 ff.   [5] Cf. p. 110, note 2, above.

And Geoffrey stops to note that Guenevere was the most beautiful woman of the island.[1] Altogether, then, Geoffrey has brought an undeniably romantic element into his narrative, though in general he is, in form and style, rather a chronicler than a romancer. Here, again, it is not impossible that Geoffrey was only following an idea already prevalent in Arthurian stories. It is certain that his procedure was wholly in accord with the tendency of the times. We cannot tell how far the Breton or Welsh minstrels had gone in bringing the Arthurian story into harmony with the life and conceptions of mediæval chivalry. We cannot be sure that the French had not already adopted Arthur from them, and even begun to write metrical romances about his knights. But, however this may be, at least Geoffrey was the first to introduce the romantic atmosphere into the chronicles, and the first to connect it with Arthur in a work which won widespread and lasting popularity.

One important detail in Geoffrey's narrative of Arthur's reign is not to be explained in connection with any of the above categories. This is his choice of Caerleon-upon-Usk (*Urbs Legionum*) as Arthur's capital. There is no particular evidence that this association existed before Geoffrey's time, and it is generally assumed to be original with him.[2] There is some force in the argument that he may have been glad to connect Arthur with a city very near to the domain of his patron, Robert of Gloucester.[3] Further, the description which Giraldus Cambrensis gives of the Roman ruins of the city [4] shows that these may well have made a great impression on Geoffrey, or, for that matter, on any one who may have interested himself in Arthur before Geoffrey wrote.[5]

---

[1] ix, 9, 12.   [2] Cf. p. 163, below.

[3] Ward notes also (*Catalogue*, I, 206) that the daughter of Geoffrey's foster-father Uchtryd was married to the lord of Caerleon.

[4] *Itin. Kambriae*, i, 5 (*Works*, VI, 55).

[5] There is an article, still of some interest, on Caerleon, by T. Wakeman in *Archæologia Cambrensis*, 1848, III, 328–344. Wakeman states that, except for the legend of the martyrdom of Aaron and Julius, the local history of the city during the Roman period is a complete blank.

X. Final Words on the *LIBER VETUSTISSIMUS*

Having now completed our survey of the constituent elements of Geoffrey's *Historia*, we may give a final word to the *liber vetustissimus*. It is clear that any such work as Geoffrey describes, an "old book in the British tongue," cannot have included material from all the different categories which we have discussed. Such a book is not likely to have contained all Geoffrey's excerpts from Nennius, Bede, and Gildas; it certainly would not contain the ideas suggested by William of Malmesbury and Henry of Huntingdon, nor those taken from late Saxon and Norman history and Norman-English life. If there was any *liber* at all, these things must have been added by Geoffrey. On the other hand, such a book might conceivably have included pretty much all the Celtic material (except, perhaps, legends local in England); that from mediæval folklore and saga; the incidents suggested by ancient history; and — if we admit (what is possible enough) that the book may have existed even if Geoffrey's characterization of it as "very old" be false — it might have included the chivalrous and romantic ideas, so far as they were true to the life of France and Normandy before, say, the twelfth century.

But all this is merely conceivable, not probable or even reasonable. We cannot suppose that any such book recounted, as Geoffrey says of the *liber*, all the acts of the British kings consecutively from Brutus to Cadwaladrus. And if there is no evidence that before the twelfth century any Welshman or Breton had had the idea of writing a connected history of his race from its origin, there is scarcely a possibility that any Celt before Geoffrey had dreamed of using materials in any such audacious way as the *Historia* exhibits. If, then, the *liber* existed, Geoffrey has certainly exaggerated his obligations to it. It could not well have contained much more than a number of Celtic traditional stories, perhaps somewhat embellished in a manner suggestive of Geoffrey's, and it can hardly have been of greater importance to Geoffrey than his other chief sources. But as a matter of fact, there probably was no *liber* at all.

CHAPTER IV

THE ARTHURIAN STORY AFTER GEOFFREY: CERTAIN EARLY PROSE VERSIONS

THE history of the Arthurian material in the chronicles after Geoffrey is the history of the treatment to which Geoffrey's version of the story was subjected by later writers. However much these chroniclers have changed or curtailed his account, the *Historia* stood alone in purporting to treat the whole period (in fact, the entire history of Britain) at length, and it was almost universally accepted as true or partly true. Hence any author who did not choose to ignore the Arthurian tradition was almost compelled to consider Geoffrey's narrative first of all.

On its appearance the *Historia* naturally caused great astonishment, — how great may be judged from Henry of Huntingdon's often-quoted letter to his friend Warinus,[1] in which he says that he was amazed when he came across the work.[2] The immense popularity which it almost immediately achieved is shown by a passage, also frequently quoted, in the preface which Alfred of Beverley, writing apparently about 1150, prefixed to his *History*.[3] Alfred says that the *hystoria Britonum* (he never names Geoffrey) was such a universal subject for conversation that any one who did not know its stories was regarded as a clown.

---

[1] Printed in the chronicle of Robert de Torigni (*Chronicles of Stephen and Henry II*, ed. Howlett, Rolls Series, IV, 65 ff.).

[2] *Stupens inveni.*

[3] Alfred's history is, in the earlier part, practically a mere condensation of Geoffrey (see p. 171, below). The only edition is that of Hearne, *Aluredi Beverlacensis Annales*, etc., Oxford, 1716. For date, etc., see Ward, I, 211; Madden, *Archæological Journal*, 1858, XV, 305–308; Wright, *Biog. Brit., Anglo-Norman Period*, pp. 155–158; letter of Bp. Lloyd in *Gutch's Collectanea Curiosa*, 1781, 1, 263–269; Hardy, II, 169–174.

I. THE WELSH TRANSLATIONS OF GEOFFREY AND THE WELSH CHRONICLES

First among all the chronicles after Geoffrey it is natural to consider the Welsh translations of the *Historia*.[1] The date of these, indeed, is doubtful,[2] and their very misleading statements about their authorship afford no information as to the real facts; but by their language they stand in complete isolation from all other forms of the narrative, while in substance their agreement with the original is unusually close. Of the two classes into which the existing manuscripts are roughly divided, the so-called *Brut Gruffydd ab Arthur* may be dismissed at once, since, as its title indicates, it is a literal rendering of Geoffrey's work. The other, the *Brut Tysilio*,[3] follows Geoffrey rather closely, but with considerable condensation, with the addition of two or three distinct incidents in the non-Arthurian portion, and with some minor divergences. The following points deserve notice:

Eigr (Geoffrey's *Igerna*) is called the daughter of Amlawdd the Great;[4] Gwenhwyfar (Geoffrey's *Guanhamara*) is called the daughter of Goĝfran the hero;[5] and Cador, father of the Constantine to whom Arthur leaves the kingdom, is said to be the son of

---

[1] The text of *Gruffydd ab Arthur* is given in *The Text of the Bruts from the Red Book of Hergest*, ed. Rhŷs and J. Gwenogvryn Evans, Oxford, 1890, pp. 40–256. The text of both is included in the *Myvyrian Archaiology of Wales*, 1801–1807 (later ed., 1870), II, 81–390. Of *Tysilio* there is an English translation by the Rev. Peter Roberts, *The Chronicle of the Kings of Britain*, in *Collectanea Cambrica*, 1811, republished by M. Pope as *A History of the Kings of Ancient Britain*, 1862; there is also a German translation (from Roberts) by San-Marte in his edition of Geoffrey, pp. 475–619. See Ward, I, 254, 258; F. Zarncke, *Jahrb. f. rom. u. engl. Lit.*, 1864, V, 249–264; ten Brink, id., 1868, IX, 241–270, especially pp. 262–270, arguing against the hypothesis of du Méril (id., I, 1–43, reprinted in his *Études*, 1862, pp. 214–272); Skene, *Four Ancient Books*, I, 23–24; Heeger, *Trojanersage*, pp. 79–80.

[2] It can only be said that there is a manuscript of the Tysilio form written at the beginning of the thirteenth century (Rhŷs and Evans, *Text of the Bruts from the Red Book of Hergest*, p. xiii).

[3] So called from the legendary personage to whom its authorship was long ago erroneously attributed.   [4] San-Marte, p. 541.   [5] P. 549.

Gorlois.[1] All these statements may possibly be details of the old British tradition from which Geoffrey drew, but it is quite as likely that they are elaborations on his text.

It is stated that Arthur himself killed Medrod.[2] This is interesting because it coincides with what Henry of Huntingdon says in an account to which we shall presently come;[3] but it is so natural an enlargement of Geoffrey's account that no argument can be based on it. Indeed, it may very likely be taken from Henry. Otherwise the Welsh version of the last battle agrees substantially with Geoffrey's, except that it gives the number of Medrod's divisions as nine instead of three.[4]

A characteristic Welsh conception appears when Vortigern's magi are made into the twelve chief bards.[5] It is also said that, being ignorant of the real cause of the difficulty at the tower, they decided to prescribe an impossible remedy;[6] and Maygan, to explain Merlin's birth, mentions not Apuleius and Socrates, but the fall of man and the instrumentality of Lucifer and the devils.[7] These are points of agreement with the prose *Merlin*. They can be explained on various hypotheses. They may be, and most probably are, due to influence from the *Merlin*. Or they may be details of popular tradition which Geoffrey failed to insert, in which case they would be from the same source as the statement in the *Merlin*. Finally, since they are quite in the spirit of the Middle Ages, the coincidences may be due to independent elaboration of Geoffrey's narrative on the part of the Welsh author and of Robert de Borron.

Some of Geoffrey's rationalization disappears in the story of how the Great Circle was moved. Myrddin by his [magic] art alone draws the stones to the ships after the warriors have failed.[8]

It is said[9] that in Uther's battle with Octa and Eosa[10] the Saxons, not the Britons, were driven to a hill.[11] This again is noteworthy

---

[1] So Roberts; San-Marte (p. 567) omits.

[2] P. 567.   [4] P. 566; Geoffrey, xi, 2, 19.

[3] See p. 120, below.   [5] Pp. 532–533.

[6] Cf. p. 146, below, on Gottfried of Viterbo.

[7] Cf. pp. 144, 189, 195, note 4, below.

[8] Pp. 538–539. Cf. p. 140, below.

[9] P. 541.   [10] Geoffrey, viii, 18.

[11] Here called *Dannet;* Geoffrey has *Damen* (so MSS.).

as a correspondence with one or two later versions;[1] but it is also a natural alteration in the story, and may even be a rather stupid misunderstanding of Geoffrey.

Other changes probably due to the author himself are the statements that the Britons made Vortigern king the second time because they knew no other capable person;[2] that, in besieging Gorlois, Uther lost most of his men and divided the rest into three parts;[3] and that Lucius's final decision to retreat before Arthur was by the advice of his council.[4]

A bit of moralizing is introduced in the remark that Dubricius gave up his see because, after considering how long a preparation had been made for a three days' festival, he was struck with the perishable nature of worldly enjoyments.[5] Further, the barbarity of which Geoffrey makes Hirelgas guilty in cutting to pieces the body of Boccus, in revenge for the death of Bedver,[6] is qualified into a statement that Hirelgas (Hirlas) dragged Boccus to the body of Bedver and killed him there.[7]

Besides the *Brut Gruffydd ab Arthur* and the *Brut Tysilio*, there are various Welsh chronicle compilations, which, however, are brief and of no importance in this investigation.[8]

II. Henry of Huntingdon's Abridgment of Geoffrey's History in his Letter to Warinus

The letter of Henry of Huntingdon to Warinus[9] was written some time after January, 1139, when Henry, then on a journey to Rome, found a copy of Geoffrey's *History* at the monastery of Bec

---

[1] At least Robert of Gloucester; see p. 196, below.

[2] P. 530. [3] Omitted by San-Marte, p. 542.

[4] P. 562. [5] P. 554.

[6] x, 9, 39.

[7] P. 564. Cf. p. 139, note 1, below (Wace); p. 160, note 6 (Layamon).

[8] One of these, extending from Vortigern to King John, is printed by Rhŷs and Evans, *Text of the Bruts from the Red Book of Hergest*, pp. 104–106 (see p. xxiv). Another, coming down to 1639, is printed by Rees, *Lives of the Cambro British Saints*, pp. 612–622. It includes a brief summary of Geoffrey's narrative, but makes Modred Arthur's grandson, unless *nepos* is meant for "nephew."

[9] See p. 41, above.

in Normandy.[1] As Geoffrey's work seemed to convict his own chronicle of a serious omission, he made a summary of the *Historia* to serve as a supplement to his narrative and sent it to his otherwise unknown friend Warinus.

The summary has many minor divergences from Geoffrey's narrative, such as calling Uter Aurelius's son instead of his brother, and omitting the story of Vortigern's tower ; but they are all to be explained on the ground of condensation, Henry's general inexactness of method, his (much rarer) exercise of critical judgment, or the freedom of imagination which was characteristic of him. One of Henry's episodes, however, is important, — namely, his account of Arthur's last battle.

Henry disposes of the events just preceding, and of the beginning of the conflict itself, by saying that Arthur with a few men came upon Modred with many. [This is quite contrary to Geoffrey's account.] He then continues :

When Arthur saw that he could not retreat, he said, " Friends, let us avenge our dead. I will now smite off the head of that traitor my nephew ; after which, death will be welcome." So saying, he hewed a way through the host, seized Modred in the midst of his men by the helmet, and severed his armored neck as if it had been a straw. In the act he himself received so many wounds that he fell ; although his[2] kinsmen the Britons deny that he was mortally wounded, and seriously expect that he will yet come.[3] He was a hero surpassing all the men of his time in valor, generosity, and *facetia*.[4]

Geoffrey's own picture of this, the culminating scene of his whole work, is surprisingly bare and inartistic, especially after the spirited accounts of battles which he has just given at great length. It is easy to understand, therefore, why some of the chroniclers, even among those who otherwise followed Geoffrey closely, turned at this point to Henry's version in order to fill out their stories.[5]

---

[1] Cf. Fletcher, *Publ. of the Mod. Lang. Assoc.*, 1901, XVI, 461–463, and references there given.

[2] Henry, writing to Warinus, says *tui*. Robert de Torigni, in copying Henry, has *sui*.   [3] Cf. p. 101, above.   [4] P. 74.

[5] Cf. p. 118, above ; pp. 121, 175, below (MS. Cott. Cleop. A. i. 1), 188, 198, 202, 213, 230, 252. The prose *Lancelot* and the romances based upon it also have

There is, however, no reason to suppose that they knew the episode from any other source than Henry's work; and that Henry took the details merely from his own imagination is made altogether probable both by the great liberty of composition which he always allowed himself and by the fact that he had not inserted the scene in his own chronicle.

It appears, therefore, that to Henry belongs the distinction of making the first considerable addition to Geoffrey's Arthurian narrative, — or, at least, the first which was taken into later versions.

III. Benedict of Gloucester

Apparently the earliest writer to accept Henry's alteration in Geoffrey's narrative was Benedict, a monk of Gloucester. Sometime in the twelfth century he wrote a life of St. Dubricius,[1] in which he included (very briefly) what Geoffrey says of that saint, and an outline of Geoffrey's account of the whole Arthurian period, beginning with Aurelius. The borrowing from Henry is his only noticeable deviation from Geoffrey. He says: "After three battles . . . at last Arthur, measuring swords with Modred, was by him fatally wounded. But forthwith rushing more vigorously on Modred, he laid him low, and sent him with many of his men to Cocytus. Thus they perished with mutual wounds."

IV. The *Liber de Constructione Aliquorum Oppidorum Turonicae Regionis*, in the *Gesta Comitum Andegavensium* of Thomas de Loches [2]

The Arthurian portion of Geoffrey's *History* seems to be utilized to a certain extent, and his method seems to be imitated, by a certain

---

the incident of the personal conflict with Modred, though the account is much more elaborate. Derived from, or otherwise connected with that one, is the version in MS. Coll. Magd. Oxford, No. 72 (see p. 188, below); cf. *Publ. Mod. Lang. Assoc.*, 1903, XVIII, 85, note 3. Contrast p. 137, note 1, below.

[1] Ed. Wharton, *Anglia Sacra*, II, xxvi, 654 ff. Benedict begins to use Geoffrey with chap. 3. Cf. Hardy, I, 42, No. 105.

[2] I am under obligations to M. Ferdinand Lot for his kind assistance in this section, though he is in nowise responsible for any statements here made.

French author in the little book entitled *De Constructione Ali-
quorum Oppidorum seu Castrorum Turonicae Regionis*, which has been
incorporated into the *Gesta Comitum Andegavensium* of Thomas de
Loches.[1] The date of the original version of this little book is
1147, or not much later.[2]

After earlier fabulous material, mostly concerned with the foundation of Amboise but including also a short account, quite in harmony with Geoffrey, of the British conquest of Armorica, the
author gives a brief narrative of Arthur's invasion of Normandy,
with the foundation of "Chainon" by Cheudo (Kay),[3] the great
battle with Lucius, and the campaign against Modred. The narrative, though very summary and exhibiting some additions, has
every appearance of being based directly upon Geoffrey's *History*.[4]
The points of divergence are as follows:

There is incidental mention of the fact that in Arthur's time
Clodius was king in northern Germany, and he, it is added, "gladly
became very friendly with Arthur." Apropos of the division of
France, it is said that Oldinus was Arthur's standard bearer
(*signifer*) and Golfarius his sword bearer (*ensifer*).[5] Cheudo (Kay)
is made the founder, not of Caen, with which this work could not
concern itself, but of Chinon.[6] Like several later chroniclers, the
author combines Arthur's two invasions of France;[7] at least, he
says nothing of any movements between the feast at Paris and
the final battle against Lucius. The latter appears as a general of
the Emperor Honorius.[8] Arthur's losses in this conflict are said to

---

[1] Last published by Marchegay and Salmon, *Chroniques d'Anjou*, I, 1856
(*Introduction*, by Émile Mabille, Paris, 1871), Soc. de l'Hist. de France. I have
consulted also the earlier MS. mentioned by Mabille, Vol. XLVI of the *Mélanges
de Colbert*, in Bibl. Nat., fol. 165 ff., especially 200 ff.

[2] As shown by the mention (at the end) of the departure of King Louis for the
[Second] Crusade. Mabille (p. xliv) puts the work about ten years earlier, because
the MS. reads 1137, and he did not notice that this is an error, as appears from the
actual date of the Crusade.   [3] See p. 111, note 5, above.

[4] Geoffrey's *History* is referred to, and was evidently consulted, by the reviser
whose version is the one included in the composition printed by Marchegay and
Salmon.   [5] Cf. p. 184, below (Ralph de Diceto).

[6] Cf. p. 206, below.   [7] See p. 183, and note 11, below.

[8] Cf. pp. 83, 85, note 2, above.

have been due to the *impetus et stultitia* of Gawain.[1] The name of Cheudo's nephew is given not as Hirelgas but as Billeius. Arthur is said to have died in Avalon " in a certain wood."

Into this story are inserted several anecdotes which help to justify the title of the work by explaining the names of various towns in Touraine. It was for the same purpose, indeed, or at least on the same pretext, that the author brought in the story of Arthur, which is headed in the older manuscripts, *De Arturo Rege Britanniae & Castro Caynonis*. The first of these anecdotes informs us that Bliriacus (*Bléré*) was built by Billeius, to whom Cheudo had given Amboise, and who had married Fausta, daughter of Placidia, who in turn was daughter of Avicianus, a person later spoken of as Count of Tours. Another of the anecdotes explains the name Blesis (*Blois*) from the deceitful (*blesis*) words by means of which a certain British youth named Commodus (or Ivomadus) persuaded Boso Carnotensis[2] to give him the ground on which it was built. Later it is said that Billeius had a daughter, Lupa, who lived in Villa Lupa, and further details are given about her and her sons.

None of these above-mentioned characters can be proved to have been known before the composition of the chronicle,[3] though it is quite possible that they have their origin in ancient Celtic topographical heroes and divinities.[4] However that may be, it seems most reasonable to suppose that the author of the chronicle was stimulated by Geoffrey's success to follow his example in exploiting in a history (largely at least of his own invention) etymologies connected with his native region. After he had succeeded, by mistake[5] or by deliberate alteration, in connecting Kay with his narrative, the popularity of Geoffrey's story was reason enough for him to make as much use of it as he could. Neither the substitution

---

[1] Contrast p. 105, note 2, above.   [2] Cf. Geoffrey, ix, 12 ; x, 4, etc.

[3] So far as I have been able to find.

[4] As is argued by Alonso Péan in *Notice sur le Château d'Amboise*, Blois, 1860. He gives legendary details about Avicien that I have not discovered elsewhere, but does not mention his authorities.

[5] In the manuscript of Geoffrey that he used, the substitution of *Chinon* for *Caen* may already have been made by a scribe who thought that the Duke of Anjou would have resided more suitably there.

of the name *Billeius* for *Hirelgas* (even if it was not occasioned by corruption in the manuscript) nor any of his other alterations or additions need surprise us in a French author who was pursuing such a method, perhaps understood the fictitious nature of his original, and had an eye to the actual facts of history.

This chronicle is interesting, therefore, as an early and almost a unique case, not of direct copying of Geoffrey but of imitation of his method.[1]

---

[1] The readiness of local historians to accept Geoffrey as historical is illustrated by a chronicle preserved in a thirteenth-century manuscript at Arras. Here "Ligerus" comes first in the genealogy of the Counts of Boulogne-sur-Mer and he is said to have been appointed by Arthur (see Mone, *Anzeiger f. Kunde der teutschen Vorzeit*, IV, 346; Reiffenberg, *Philippe Mouskes*, II, lxii). "Ligerus" is probably the "Leodegarius" whom Geoffrey (ix, 12, 50) calls "consul Boloniae."

CHAPTER V

THE ARTHURIAN STORY AFTER GEOFFREY: POETICAL VERSIONS OF THE FIRST ONE HUNDRED AND FIFTY YEARS

I. Geoffrey Gaimar

At about the same time when Alfred of Beverley inaugurated the custom of inserting Geoffrey's narrative in serious prose chronicles,[1] the example was set for the metrical chronicles by an Anglo-Norman writer in the North of England, Geoffrey Gaimar.[2] The exact date of his work is uncertain, but it was probably a little before 1150.[3]

Gaimar's chronicle was in two parts: (1) a History of the Britons, which, as appears from statements at the beginning and at the end of the part preserved,[4] was a translation of Geoffrey's work; and (2) the History of the *Engles*. The History of the Britons, however, has been lost, crowded out of existence, probably, by the far superior version of Wace, which is substituted for it in all the manuscripts; and we can judge of its character as a translation only by the connecting introductory lines of the second part, which sum up its contents in a few clauses.[5] These lines are very meagre, but they perhaps indicate that Gaimar (as was certainly the case in

---

[1] See p. 116, note 3; above.

[2] *L'Estorie des Engles*, etc., ed. by Sir T. D. Hardy and T. C. Martin, Rolls Series, London, 1888–1889. See Ward, I, 423–446; Martin, in *Dict. Nat. Biog.*, XX, 360–361; P. Meyer, *Rom.*, XVIII, 314–318.

[3] See Vising, *Étude sur le Dialecte Anglo-normand du xiie Siècle*, pp. 33, 34; Meyer, *loc. cit.;* G. Paris, *La Littérature Française au Moyen Âge*, ed. 1890, p. 133; Gröber, *Grundriss*, II, i, 472; Suchier und Birch-Hirschfeld, *Geschichte der französischen Litteratur*, p. 113.

[4] Cf. p. 53, note 3, above.

[5] See the first 45 verses. Cf. also v. 3573, and the epilogue (according to MSS. LD), vv. 23, 125.

the second part) treated his original freely, at least to the extent of making additions. The *History of the English* itself, however, has a place in the present discussion. In this part of his work Gaimar has included a version of the Havelok story[1] which contains certain incidental statements about King Arthur.

Gaimar says that Arthur came to Denmark, conquered it, and killed the king, Gunter, because he withheld tribute.[2] This does not coincide exactly with anything which Geoffrey of Monmouth relates; but is akin to his bare statement that after the conquest of Norway, Denmark submitted to Arthur.[3] Gaimar's details are also practically identical with the brief account which Geoffrey gives of a much earlier conquest of Denmark by Gurgiunt Brabtruc,[4]— a conquest due to the refusal of tribute which had been paid to Gurgiunt's predecessor. Again, Gaimar, speaking[5] of the reigning monarch of Denmark, Odulf, who had treasonably become king by sending for Arthur and so bringing about the death of Gunter,[6] says that he was the brother of King Aschis, who " met his death for Arthur when Modret did him such wrong."[7] This latter statement agrees with Geoffrey's mention of Aschillius, king of Denmark, as among those killed on Arthur's side in his last battle.[8]

If we were to conclude that all these details are borrowed by the Havelok story from Geoffrey's *Historia*, we should have another striking testimony to the immediate vogue of the latter. It seems perhaps more probable, however, that the idea of Arthur's conquest formed a part of the Havelok tale before the time of Geoffrey.[9] For both the independent Anglo-Norman version of *Havelok* and the short version inserted in the Lambeth manuscript of Robert of Brunne's *Chronicle*[10] (both of which go back to a common original with Gaimar's form) agree with Gaimar in mentioning Arthur's interference in Denmark; though the Lambeth interpolation has it that Arthur had previously taken tribute, and that it was another

---

[1] On the versions of the Havelok story, see Max Kupferschmidt, *Die Havelok-sage bei Gaimar*, etc., Bonn, 1880; E. K. Putnam, *Publ. Mod. Lang. Assoc.*, 1900, XV, 1–16.　　[4] iii, 11.　　[7] Vv. 524–526.

[2] Vv. 410 ff.　　[5] V. 527.　　[8] xi, 2, 53.

[3] ix, 11.　　[6] Vv. 513–516.　　[9] Cf. p. 84, above.

[10] Printed by Madden, *Havelok*, pp. xvii–xix.

British king who attacked and killed "Gounter." Evidently the original of these two versions must have contained the idea of Arthur's interference, and one certainly cannot assume without further evidence that this original was of later date than Geoffrey's *History*. In any case, it is altogether probable that the mentions of Modred and Aschis are due to Gaimar and taken from Geoffrey of Monmouth, in which case, if Arthur already appeared in the story, they are quite insignificant. Gaimar's order of events cannot in any way be interpreted as consistent with Geoffrey's. He seems to have borrowed the names without considering whether his use of them was in accord with any rational system of chronology. It must be added that neither Aschis, Modred, nor Arthur is named in the English metrical romance of *Havelok*, which is supposed to be derived from a form of the story anterior to that from which the other extant versions come; but this English metrical romance is widely divergent from the others throughout.

II. Wace's *Brut* and other French Versions

One of the most interesting of all the reproductions of Geoffrey's *History* is the *Brut* of the Norman poet Wace.[1]

Wace's poem, with some of those which follow it in this chapter, differs from nearly all the chronicles in one important respect. These poems are only paraphrases of Geoffrey's *Historia*, and the authors, while doubtless supposing their original to be, at least in general, authentic, were in spirit poets rather than historians.[2]

---

[1] The only edition is that of Le Roux de Lincy, 2 vols., Rouen, 1836–1838.

[2] This is no less true because of a suggestion or two which Wace gives of a wish to have a good authority (vv. 4932, 10,038); or because of a trick of manner by which he occasionally expresses ignorance about the causes or means of things which he mentions, as when he says that he does not know where Eldol got the stake with which he defended himself against the Saxons (v. 7446); that he does not know where Merlin's fountain of Labenes (the *Galabes* of Geoffrey, viii, 10) was, and has never been there (v. 8219); or that he is not informed of the nature of Hoel's sickness (v. 9501). Cf. also vv. 8356, 9196, 9464, 10,572, 11,395, 11,438, 12,595, 13,151, 13,484.

The biography of Wace must be chiefly reconstructed from the information which he himself gives us in his poems.[1] He was born, apparently, about the same time as Geoffrey of Monmouth (not far from 1100), in the island of Jersey, whether of noble or of common parentage is uncertain. Educated partly at Paris, but chiefly at Caen, he lived for a long time in the latter city, studying and writing. He was *clerc lisant* (an office the exact nature of which remains unexplained) before 1135. In 1155 he finished the work which he called *Geste des Bretons*, but to which the scribes give the name *Brut*. Layamon says[2] that a dedication (lacking in the extant manuscripts) was addressed to Queen Eleanor, wife of Henry II. At any rate, Wace later had a regular position at the court while it remained in Normandy; and the composition of his *Roman de Rou*, begun in 1160, seems to have been due to the king's commission, the later withdrawal of which caused him to stop before the work was finished. He died, probably, not long after 1174.

In general Wace's *Brut* is merely a free paraphrase of Geoffrey's *History*. It follows exactly the same order and observes practically the same proportion; in brief, it closely reproduces, in the main, the substance of its original. But Wace was very far from being a servile translator, and the great differences which distinguish his race, character, occupation, aim, language, and literary form from those of Geoffrey reappear as fully as was to be expected in his work. They are manifested partly in certain general characteristics, partly in an infinitude of minutiæ which Wace adds merely as a poet and a literary artist. For any light upon the origins of

---

[1] On Wace's biography and the *Brut*, see Wace's *Roman de Rou*, ed. H. Andresen, 1877–1879, I, *Einleitung;* ed. Pluquet, Rouen, 1827, *Notice*, I, vii–xxii; Miss Kate Norgate, *Dict. Nat. Biog.*, LVIII, 404; G. Paris, *Rom.*, 1880, IX, 592 ff., especially 592–597, reviewing Andresen; Ward, I, 260; Gröber, *Grundriss*, II, i, 635; Morley, *English Writers*, III, 55; Bréquigny, *Notices et Extraits*, V, 21–78; De La Rue, *An Epistolary Dissertation upon the Life and Writings of Robert Wace* (*Archæologia*, 1796, XII, 50–79); id., *Essais Hist. sur les Bardes*, Caen, 1834, II, 158–165; E. du Méril, *Jahrb. f. rom. u. engl. Lit.*, 1859, I, 1–43, reprinted in his *Études*, 1862, pp. 214–272; *Wace the Trouvère, Retrospective Rev.*, 1853, II, 92–99; L. Abrahams, *De Roberti Wacii Carmine*, etc., Copenhagen, 1828; G. A. Kloppe, *Recherches sur le Dialecte de Guace*, Magdeburg, 1853.

[2] Ed. Madden, vv. 42–43 ("he *gave* it to Ælienor").

the organic material of the Arthurian tradition, such characteristics and details are of no consequence ; but in the literary study of the development of the tradition they assume significance. It is desirable, therefore, before taking up Wace's important changes and additions, to give attention to these others.[1]

In the first place, Geoffrey's *History* and Wace's *Brut* stand for very different literary styles. Geoffrey put his romance into the form of an ostensibly truthful Latin chronicle. Thus he had to preserve an appearance of veracity, to maintain dignity of style, and to cultivate rhetorical elegance. Wace, though he took the story seriously enough, and was doubtless willing to be believed, employs the form of the French metrical romance. Geoffrey's sympathy with his subject was not less keen than that of Wace, and his humor was probably greater ; yet the form of his work was sometimes a hindrance to him, while Wace had adopted a style and manner that were peculiarly well adapted to the material.

The most pervasive general contrast between the two styles is in vividness of narrative. Geoffrey had plenty of imagination, both dramatic and romantic, but Latin periods were not the aptest instruments for its expression. Besides, if his work was to have the air of truthful history, he could not, in general, lay claim to the detailed personal knowledge of an eyewitness or a contemporary. He could not venture to vivify and visualize the whole story. Perhaps a personal limitation entered into the case. What little we know of Geoffrey indicates that, while he was by no means a pedant, he was rather a student than a man of action ; he got his ideas rather from reading than from experience. Except for a case or two like his minute description of Arthur's second coronation (which may well be taken in large part from life), and even in his accounts of battles, where he most warms to the subject and seems to wish to be thoroughly dramatic, he writes almost always, not of details but in general terms. And he is not always convincingly practical.

---

[1] The discussion here, as in other cases, is chiefly based on that part of the narrative with which this study is directly concerned, — Geoffrey, vi, 6–xi, 2, and Wace, vv. 6615–13,706 ; but here, as elsewhere, the general results are true of the other portions as well.

His battle speeches, too, even when they are delivered in the thick of the fight, are ornate orations, which no general could really have delivered and no soldier would have stopped to listen to.

With Wace, on the other hand, the quick-moving conversational octosyllabic couplet scarcely allows the effect of dullness, even in the least interesting parts of the narrative. And Wace himself is never afraid of seeming to know too much, — rather of not seeming to know everything. He sees whatever he writes about, and for the most part makes his readers see it too. He does not content himself, for instance, with describing the course of a battle from the point of view of a pseudo-scientific strategist : he names the various parts of the equipments of the knights and soldiers, pictures how they crashed together in the shock of the charge, how they struck and fell. He gives the impression that he is not merely imitating other metrical romances, but is reproducing what he has himself witnessed and been fired by.[1]

One might illustrate this increase of vividness on the part of Wace by citing a large proportion of the fifteen thousand lines of his poem ; but a few instances must suffice. As to the more particular details of warfare, — he speaks of foragers ;[2] describes Arthur's smallest movements in the fight with the giant ;[3] and tells how Arthur had his men advance to battle slowly, not allowing them to straggle at all.[4] In beginning his account of Hengist's first treacherous proposals to Vortigern,[5] he gives a lifelike setting by observing that *one day* Hengist found the king disposed to listen. In the same passage he makes Hengist say that he will send to Germany for his wife and children. Geoffrey spoke only of the warriors who were important for the immediate purposes of his narrative and whose deeds were dignified enough for the pages of history ; but Wace's imagination was, or could afford to be, more practical. In telling of the escape of " Elduf " from the Saxons after his valiant

---

[1] For example, vv. 12,946 ff. But the difference is probably partly due to the difference of sources. Geoffrey presumably drew chiefly from comparatively crude Celtic stories, while Wace had the advantage of starting with Geoffrey's own far more suggestive narrative.

[2] V. 12,611.

[3] Vv. 11,921 ff.

[4] Vv. 9538–9539.

[5] V. 7009 (Geoffrey, vi, 11, 10).

defense, he takes pains to explain how it was possible: Elduf got away on his horse, which was very good.[1] When Merlin's mother was asked about her son, says Wace,[2] she held her head down and thought a little before answering. In describing the duel between Arthur and Flollo,[3] Wace expands Geoffrey's vague remark that the people were watching, by telling how the Parisians stood upon the walls and both sides prayed for the success of their respective champions. Longer passages of the same character occur. Thus in the account of the flight of the Saxons before Cador,[4] we are told how they went two by two or three by three as best they could, how they had thrown down their arms, and how Cador followed, shouting his battle cry. Most prominent, though not necessarily most important, in this connection, are certain notably extended passages of original details added by Wace. When Arthur's host is embarking for the campaign against the Romans, Wace inserts a splendid picture of the scene, with plenty of nautical terms,[5] — the memories of his boyhood serving him well. Not less spirited, though shorter, is the account [6] of the joy with which Arthur's soldiers are received on returning from their long sojourn in France.[7] A similar addition is the description of the bustling activity of the servants at Arthur's second coronation.[8]

Equally original, though perhaps with rather more direct suggestion from Geoffrey, is the account of the coming of Gawain and the other envoys to the army of the Emperor;[9] or again, that of

---

[1] Vv. 7455–7456 (Geoffrey, vi, 16, 8).

[2] Vv. 7598–7599; cf. vv. 11,056–11,057.

[3] Vv. 10,281 ff. (Geoffrey, ix, 11, 55).

[4] Vv. 9616–9627 (Geoffrey, ix, 5).

[5] Vv. 11,472–11,521.

[6] Vv. 10,431–10,452.

[7] Cf. p. 203, below. The interpolation of the statement that aunts kissed their nephews (as well as wives their husbands, etc.) in one of the manuscripts is surely due not to Wace but to some jocose cynic after him, and reminds one very much of the "world of kisses" which the First Folio makes Desdemona give to Othello.

[8] Vv. 10,610–10,634. The much longer addition (vv. 10,823–10,900) about the jugglers, music and musical instruments, dice playing, and the presents given by Arthur, is perhaps an interpolation in Wace's text.

[9] Vv. 12,092–12,109.

the pursuit of the envoys by the Romans after Gawain has killed Lucius's nephew,[1] beginning as it does with the extremely effective *es vous*, so useful to the mediæval French romancers.[2]

Another feature of Wace's style which contributes greatly to its vividness is his largely increased use of direct discourse. Sometimes he merely inserts an ejaculation or brief cry, as in Gawain's apposite exhortation to his companions when they have got into trouble in the Emperor's camp, — " alés monter ! "[3]   Such an undignified kind of naturalness was entirely out of the range of Geoffrey's aristocratic chronicle style.   More often, however, Wace gives a whole speech in the very words of the speaker.   Sometimes he enlarges a speech of Geoffrey's, as in Lucius's message to Arthur ;[4] sometimes he changes a piece of narrative into this form, as in the plea of the Scots for mercy ;[5] occasionally, as in Gawain's address after the message of Lucius, he invents the whole passage.[6]

Wace also manifests personal feeling about the events and characters of his story.   Sometimes he expresses sorrow or disgust, as at Vortigern's desire to marry Roven ;[7] he stops to curse the slayer of Bedver ;[8] he occasionally applies abusive epithets to the enemies of the Britons.   He makes appeals to the reader, not only by the device of employing the second person of the verb (especially *veissiés*) to introduce a description,[9] but more directly, as when he asks, speaking of Hengist's treachery, " Who would have feared a traitor ? "[10] or observes, "You never saw such a fight!"[11] or, of the death of Ambrosius,[12] "The gentle king wished to recover, as any of you would."

---

[1] Vv. 12,168–12,188 ; cf. also vv. 1111–1178, 6178 ff., 13,887–13,926.

[2] I have noticed only two or three cases in which Wace omits some of the details given by Geoffrey, with a consequent loss of vividness.   An example may be seen in p. 137, note 1, below.   Another is the account of the poisoning of Vortimer by Roven (Geoffrey, vi, 14, 5–7 ; Wace, v. 7340).   On the other hand, his version of the poisoning of Aurelius (Geoffrey, viii, 14 ; Wace, vv. 8459–8485), while it omits one or two of Geoffrey's statements, is on the whole rather more vivid than the corresponding passage in Geoffrey ; and perhaps the same may be said of his narrative of the poisoning of Uther (Geoffrey, viii, 24 ; Wace, vv. 9195–9232).

[3] V. 12,161.

[4] Vv. 10,919–10,988.

[5] Vv. 9712–9758.

[6] Vv. 11,043 ff.

[7] V. 7163.

[8] V. 13,034.

[9] V. 7953.

[10] V. 7401 ; Geoffrey, vi, 15.

[11] V. 13,192.

[12] Vv. 8475–8476.

How thoroughly representative Wace is of his environment appears in the fact that he applies to the narrative almost universally (while Geoffrey did so only partially and in the more vivid portions) the manners and customs of his own time. This is true, for instance, of his descriptions of battles and warlike operations. He makes Vortigern's fortress a feudal castle, which Aurelius destroys by filling the moat with wood and setting this on fire.[1] He says that Uter, on going away, intrusts the care of his army to a baron.[2] He speaks of particular duels in the course of a main battle.[3] He calls even the pagans "chevaliers." Mediæval customs which he inserts or emphasizes are the feudal submission of one man to another; the pledging of his land by a lord; the appointment of viscounts and provosts; the use of the dais for king and barons at a feast. He omits Geoffrey's statements about other chiefs than the principal one in Ireland,[4] evidently because he was familiar only with the idea of one king for one country. He calls Petreius a rich baron, instead of a senator,[5] and he regularly retranslates Geoffrey's archaic *consul* by *quens* or *conte*. When he does retain the antique customs mentioned by Geoffrey, he explains that manners were different in those days. Wace has also the mediæval bigotry towards pagans,[6] something which scarcely appears in Geoffrey. He introduces a few touches of the descriptions of love which are so pronounced a feature in a writer like Crestien de Troyes.[7] In one case he shows that his taste is less reserved (more Gallic, perhaps) than Geoffrey's.[8] Once or twice he manifests the disregard for the fact of time characteristic of romances.[9] His omissions or assumptions sometimes make it clear that he is less of a scholar than Geoffrey, or is writing for a less learned audience.

Wace was not destitute of the critical instinct. He amends certain vague or inconsistent statements;[10] he modifies his original

---

[1] Vv. 7837 ff.   [2] V. 8953.   [3] V. 13,133.

[4] V. 9938; Geoffrey, ix, 10, 8.   [5] V. 12,310; Geoffrey, x, 4.

[6] But he seldom expresses it, and then in a conventional way.

[7] Vv. 8882 ff., 11,050. Geoffrey just mentions the customs of chivalric love (ix, 13, 40).   [8] Vv. 11,690 ff., 11,814 ff.; Geoffrey, x, 3, 34 and 38.

[9] V. 10,439 (the army has been gone nine years).

[10] As follows: (1) He does away with all Geoffrey's confusion about the Roman commander Lucius (cf. p. 85, note 2, above) by calling him always "emperor"

for the sake of naturalness or probability;[1] and in one or two
details he contradicts Geoffrey flatly, merely to give variety to the
narrative.[2] Not infrequently Wace adds an explanation for some
action or fact which he thinks Geoffrey has not made perfectly

---

and omitting all mention of the superfluous Leo. (2) At the time of the message
from Lucius, Cador, according to Geoffrey (ix, 15, 45) states that five years have
now passed since the Britons have engaged in war; but from his previous narrative it appears that this is the very summer in which they have returned from
Gaul, where they have apparently been fighting all the time. Wace (v. 11,031)
makes Cador's remark altogether indefinite as to the length of the period
(cf. p. 231, note 4, below). (3) Wace drops out of the story Bedver's unplausible
ancestor, Bedver the first (x, 13, 5). Some other possible incidents might be
cited, but perhaps they are due to scribal errors in manuscripts of Geoffrey.
Wace fails to correct one of Geoffrey's inconsistencies in v. 10,729, and is guilty
of one of his own in vv. 9994 ff. (compared with vv. 10,739 ff.).

[1] (1) Geoffrey implies (vi, 10, 55) that the Saxons defeated the Picts without difficulty; Wace (vv. 6983–6994) describes the battle as hotly contested.
(2) Geoffrey seems to mean (vi, 17, 14) that the messengers sent for Merlin went
all together; Wace says (v. 7543) they " vunt ensamble doi et doi." (3) Geoffrey
says (viii, 20, 4) that Gorlois went out of his castle to fight the superior attacking
force; Wace says (v. 8979) that he defended himself, but mentions no sortie.
(4) Geoffrey says (ix, 5, 9) that Cador filled the captured ships of the Saxons
with some of his best soldiers; Wace substitutes (v. 9614) archers and peasants.
Geoffrey makes no use of the stratagem, but with Wace it bears good fruit in the
result. To this end Wace omits all suggestion that the Saxons fled in any other
direction than toward Totness, where the ships really were, while Geoffrey, for-
getful of the actual situation, says that their last stand was in Tanet. (5) In giving
the lament of Helena's nurse, Geoffrey (x, 3) forgets that he is not pronouncing
a funeral oration and has the woman pour forth her eloquence at great length;
Wace (v. 11,672) makes her speak more simply. (6) Geoffrey says (x, 4) that the
six thousand knights who came to the rescue of the envoys had heard of their
flight. This would have been impossible, for the envoys had been getting away
from Lucius's camp as fast as their horses would carry them. Wace says (v. 12,286)
that Arthur had sent the six thousand to reconnoitre, so that their arrival was
altogether accidental (cf. p. 144, below). It is possible also that Wace aimed in
general to reduce the extravagant numbers, whether vaguely or definitely stated,
which Geoffrey employs in reporting the strength of his armies. But Wace's usage
is not uniform in this respect.

[2] He says (vv. 8397–8398) that Aurelius quickly chased away the marauding
Pascent. Geoffrey (viii, 13, 10) settles the matter by the stock device of a battle.
Similar cases are Geoffrey, ii, 15, 22; Wace, vv. 2138 ff.; and Geoffrey ix, 6,
Wace, vv. 9650–9659.

clear.[1] Sometimes, to be sure, no such explanation is needed,
but more often it is desirable or suggestive. Thus: (1) Arthur
retreated to London because there he could get the help of his
commons.[2] (2) The Norwegians were unwilling to receive Lot as
their king because they thought that, being a foreigner, he would
give their lands to others.[3] (3) A reason is given for the fact that
Helaine's nurse remained on the giant's mountain when the giant
was not there.[4] (4) A reason is given (perhaps unnecessarily) for
the warlike advice of the youths to Gawain.[5] (5) Arthur sent
his prisoners to Paris because he was afraid that he might lose
them if he kept them in the camp. (6) The disappearance of
Roven from the narrative (which Geoffrey had taken as a matter
of course) Wace explains by saying that she, as well as all the
other women, was burned with Vortigern in his fortress.[6] (7) Wace
tells us that Yvain, Aguisel's nephew, to whom, on Aguisel's death,
Arthur gave the kingdom of Scotland, was Aguisel's rightful heir.[7]
This satisfies Wace's sense of feudal propriety and follows naturally from the fact that no son of Aguisel is named in the
narrative. (8) The statement that those Saxons of the army of
Octa and Ebissa who escaped to York chose for their king Colgrin,
a friend of Octa and his cousin,[8] is introduced to explain the
appearance of Colgrin as king soon after, which Geoffrey not
unreasonably leaves his readers to account for as they choose.

---

[1] Cf. pp. 183, 213, below.

[2] V. 9368.

[3] V. 10,070.

[4] Vv. 11,802 ff.

[5] Vv. 12,086–12,090.

[6] For similar explanations in other chronicles, see p. 183, below. Since Nennius
also says the same thing (see p. 15, above), it is just possible that it appeared also
in Geoffrey's original text. It does not appear in the manuscripts of Geoffrey
which I have examined. There are two or three other instances where one is
inclined to wonder at first if Wace may not have used Nennius; but the coincidences can easily be explained as due to chance, corruption, or something of the
sort, and are not enough to overthrow a strong antecedent probability to the
contrary.

[7] Vv. 13,597 ff.; Geoffrey, xi, 1, 28.

[8] Vv. 9151–9152.

Occasionally Wace makes changes merely in order to improve
the literary effect.[1]   Some of his additions are mere incidental bits
of "general information": for example, the mention of *Febus* as
one of the Saxons' gods;[2] the bizarre etymology of the name *Essex*
and the other *-sexes;*[3] the remark that Crete (or Egypt?) had power
over one hundred cities.[4]

Wace occasionally omits things which he does not understand
or does not care for.   This is true of certain legendary elements
which in Geoffrey's narrative have lost their significance.[5]   Thus,
in repeating Vortimer's directions about his burial, Wace says
nothing of the copper pyramid.[6]   He omits the details of the fight
of the dragons (which give Geoffrey an opportunity for mystical
interpretation), and also the prophecies of Merlin (except those
about Vortigern), since, he says, he does not comprehend them.[7]
In telling of Arthur's dream of the fight between the dragon and
the bear, Wace drops out some less important details.[8]   He also
omits Geoffrey's statement that Arthur imposed silence on all those
who looked on the head of the giant.[9]

Geoffrey sometimes tries to describe the order of armies in
battle, but he never succeeds in giving a consistent or comprehensible account.   Wace leaves out these statements[10] or greatly

---

[1] (1) Geoffrey says (viii, 2, 5) that after the election of Aurelius his men wished
to attack the Saxons first, and he dissuaded them.   This is a natural incident, but
Wace (v. 7792) preserves the continuity of the narrative by omitting it.   (2) To
the account of the Battle of Badon, Geoffrey (ix, 3) prefixes a short speech of
Arthur.   Wace (vv. 9552 ff.) reserves this until the critical moment of the fight,
and then inserts it with many expansions but without representing Arthur as stop-
ping in order to make it.   (3) In the episode of the Battle of the Convoy, Geoffrey
(x, 5, 24–36) does not proceed in direct chronological sequence; but Wace
(vv. 12,584–12,633) gains a great deal in vividness and force by so rearranging.

[2] V. 6931.   [3] Vv. 7477 ff.   [4] V. 11,377.

[5] For similar instances, cf. pp. 140, 155, 160, 196, 201, 216, 218, 227, below.

[6] Geoffrey, vi, 14; Wace, v. 7355.

[7] Geoffrey, vii, 3 ff.; Wace, vv. 7719 ff.   Cf. pp. 189, 194, 200, 208, 218, 225,
251, note 2, below.   [8] Vv. 11,528 ff.

[9] Geoffrey, x, 3, 73; Wace, v. 11,951.

[10] Geoffrey, xi, 1, 34–36; Wace, vv. 13,513 ff.   Geoffrey, xi, 2, 18–26; Wace,
v. 13,659.

changes them. He omits also various names or other geographical details relating to England, especially Welsh names, though he sometimes changes his method by explaining where a place is, his object being, of course, to be intelligible to his French-speaking readers. He regularly translates the Latin names, — almost always into French, but sometimes, in the case of a well-known town in the south of England, into English. This method, together with corruptions which have got into the manuscripts, often makes his lists of lands and countries look quite different from those of Geoffrey. On the other hand, he frequently inserts names where continental geography is concerned.[1]

We come now to Wace's more important alterations of Geoffrey's narrative.

In the first place, it is evident that he knew — and to some extent he introduces into his poem — a conception of Arthur, and in a less degree of his knights, which is essentially that of the chivalric romances, and which Geoffrey, while he felt or foreshadowed its influence, did not by any means fully represent.[2] Wace says nothing to necessitate the conclusion that he got from any other source than Geoffrey the idea of Arthur as a world conqueror and a great emperor; but he makes it as plain as possible that he knew plenty of other stories about the hero and his knights. He refers directly to these stories as having already assumed in his own time very extravagant proportions at the hands of *conteurs*,[3] and he refers to their substance again when he says that while Arthur was in France many marvels happened, and he overthrew many a proud man and kept in restraint many a felon.[4] This is added to Geoffrey's statement that Arthur spent nine years

---

[1] It ought to be mentioned that Wace omits Geoffrey's account of Aurelius's reputation in Gaul (Geoffrey, viii, 3, 1–11; Wace, vv. 7849 ff.; contrast p. 166, below); and more strangely, even the meagre details which give some color to Geoffrey's description of Arthur's last battle, saying, for instance, that he does not know the names of those who fell. As a result, Wace's account of the battle is exceedingly inadequate (Geoffrey, xi, 2; Wace, vv. 13,662–13,682). Contrast p. 120 (and note 5), above, and cf. pp. 180, 216, 232, 233, 247, below.

[2] Cf. for the general subject, pp. 108–114, above.

[3] Vv. 10,032 ff. See p. 100, above.   [4] Vv. 10,402–10,404.

in conquering France.[1] Reference has already been made to Wace's
allusion to the Breton expectation of Arthur's second coming,[2] on
the probability of which he refuses to pronounce.

The spirit of these independent stories has influenced the tone
of some of Wace's statements,[3] though for the most part he follows
Geoffrey's representation of Arthur closely enough. It sounds, for
instance, like the romances when Wace calls Arthur *li bons rois*,[4]
or says that his men remarked enthusiastically that never before
was there so valiant a king in Britain.[5] In almost every case
he takes pains to expunge from the story certain suggestions of
barbarity or lack of chivalrousness on the part of Arthur or his
knights which occur (survive ?) in Geoffrey's version. Thus Geoffrey says that, after driving back to Ireland the Irish invaders *sine
pietate laceratos*, Arthur turned again to destroying the Scots and
Picts, *incomparabili saevitiae indulgens;* Wace says merely that he conquered the Irish quickly and drove them back to Ireland.[6] Geoffrey states that after vanquishing the Norwegians in battle, Arthur's
army destroyed cities and did not cease to "indulge its cruelty"
till the country was subdued ; Wace uses not much milder terms,
but only in connection with what happened before the battle, when
such conduct might be excused as a necessity of war.[7] Geoffrey,
who, in his quiet study, thinks of war only as a scene of pomp, and
of conquest only as a thing of glory, delights in observing that
Hoel devastated Gascony with sword and flame; Wace, indeed,
suggests the same thing, but indirectly.[8] Geoffrey says that, in the
battle with Lucius, Arthur killed a man or a horse at every stroke ;
Wace omits all mention of injuring horses, which was not strictly
in accordance with the ideas of chivalry.[9] Wace says that Arthur

---

[1] ix, 11.
[2] Vv. 13,685–13,697. See p. 101 (and note 6), above.
[3] Cf. pp. 105, 107, above; pp. 163 ff., 167, 186 ff., 196, 199, 201, 206, below.
[4] V. 13,301.
[5] V. 9833.
[6] Geoffrey, ix, 6, 20–22 ; Wace, vv. 9695 ff.
[7] Geoffrey, ix, 11, 27 ; Wace, vv. 10,083–10,085.
[8] Geoffrey, ix, 11, 86; Wace, vv. 10,371 and 10,384–10,386.
[9] Geoffrey, x, 11, 26; Wace, v. 13,298.

had the body of the dead emperor cared for with great honor; Geoffrey merely mentions his scornful sending of it to Rome.[1]

That Wace knew Gawain from other sources than Geoffrey[2] is shown by the praise of him which he adds at the first mention of his name.[3] In one striking instance Wace introduces the characteristic romance conception of Gawain.[4] When, in the council of Arthur's lords, Cador has made his speech in favor of war, Gawain (according to Wace) replies, praising peace. The pleasures of love, he says, are good, and for the sake of his *amie* a young man performs feats of chivalry. Geoffrey mentions no speech by Gawain.[5]

Wace's idea of Merlin is more like that of the later romancers than is Geoffrey's.[6] Wace represents Merlin as a great magician of unique power and position, which are recognized as a matter of course by the other characters. He has no suggestion of Geoffrey's remark that, when Aurelius was advised to send for Merlin, he did not already know of him; and states that the king at once sought him at his fountain. Geoffrey represents messengers as dispatched to all parts of the country in quest of him.[7] According to Geoffrey, when Uther was perplexed at the appearance of the comet, he sent for wise men, among them Merlin; but Wace mentions Merlin alone, implying that, with him to rely on, no others were needed.[8] So much for Merlin's position. As to his power, Geoffrey hesitates to admit into his narrative a wholly supernatural figure; but Wace has no scruples of the sort. So when Geoffrey, doubtless following some old magical tale, tells how Merlin transformed his own appearance and that of Uther and Ulfin, he makes Merlin observe that

---

[1] Wace, v. 13,395; Geoffrey, x, 13, 17. The single exception which I have noted to this procedure of Wace, is that he follows Geoffrey in saying that, in revenge for the death of Bedver, Hirelgas mutilated the body of Bocu, king of the Medes (Geoffrey, x, 9, 39; Wace, v. 13,114). Contrast p. 119, above (*Brut Tysilio*), and p. 160, note 6, below (Layamon).

[2] Cf. p. 105 and note 2, above.

[3] Vv. 10,106–10,109.

[4] Vv. 11,043 ff.

[5] Cf. p. 161, below.

[6] Cf. pp. 118, 167, 180.

[7] With Geoffrey this means not mystery, as the same statement does later with Layamon, but merely that Merlin has relapsed into insignificance since his last exploit.

[8] Geoffrey, viii, 15, 4–5; Wace, v. 8515.

his arts are unknown to that time,— meaning, apparently, that they belong to the mysterious past. But Wace merely takes up the expression "new arts" (by which Geoffrey seems to intend, new *to Uther*) and employs it in a non-significant way, omitting all suggestion that it was strange that Merlin should have such power.[1] Again, when Merlin moves the great stones from Ireland, after all Uther's army have failed in the attempt, Geoffrey rationalizes the scene and makes Merlin a sixth-century Edison, who merely has far more ingenious mechanical devices than any one else. Wace, however, says that Merlin mutters something which enables the youths to handle the stones: "I do not know," observes Wace, "whether he said a prayer or not."[2]

It is quite possible that Wace developed these ideas from the material in Geoffrey alone, — that the conception of a thoroughly supernatural wizard was perhaps for any twelfth-century French romancer a necessary substitute for the anomalous Merlin of Geoffrey. If so, Wace's change is merely another instance of the natural development of Geoffrey's story in the hands of a man of Wace's race and time. But it is also possible that, as in the case of Arthur, Wace knew independent stories about Merlin.

In the second place, there are certain definite details added by Wace which either are, or may seem to be, derived from something else than Geoffrey's narrative. On closer consideration, however, most of them prove to be merely elaborations due to Wace himself. Such are several statements that one person was cousin to another;[3] the remark that the Emperor Lucius was born in Spain,[4] which is evidently an inference from his surname *Hiberius;* the statement that Arthur and Genievre could not have an heir,[5] which, indeed, is scarcely an enlargement on the mere fact that according to Geoffrey

---

[1] Geoffrey, viii, 19, 60; Wace, v. 8930.

[2] Geoffrey, viii, 12, 23–24; Wace, vv. 8354 ff.

[3] The knight Borel to Holdin (v. 10,422); Houdin to Gavain (v. 13,220); and Genievre to Cador, who brought her up (v. 9888). Cf. pp. 159, 218, 225, 251, 266, below. In the first cases the knights are very closely connected in the narrative.　　　　　[4] V. 12,852.

[5] V. 9895; cf. pp. 155, 215, below. Wace may have been influenced by similar incidents in Breton lays or other popular stories.

they did not have any. It is interesting, however, as showing that
Wace either did not know, or else disregarded, the Welsh traditions
which give Arthur a son.[1] More important in the history of the
story is Wace's seemingly superfluous addition,[2] in the episode of
the flight of the envoys from Lucius's camp, of a fifth Roman, a
cousin of Marcel, who is severely wounded by Gawain.

Certain other of Wace's additions are somewhat more doubtful.
Probably, however, his statement that Arthur's helm was that which
Uther had formerly worn, is derived from Geoffrey's observation
that it was adorned with the figure of a dragon.[3] One cannot be
at all sure that Wace has any authority for naming the mount of
Tenedic as the place where Cheldric was killed,[4] especially since he
implies that Cheldric was fleeing toward Totness, and Geoffrey that
it was toward Tanet. Wace's statement that Modred had already
loved the queen before he was left in charge of Britain[5] may be
from independent tradition, but may as easily be an inference of
his own.

Perhaps traditional (but not due to Wace) are certain interpolations in one of the early manuscripts: (1) the name *Dinabuc* for
the giant of Mont St. Michel; (2) the statement that Modred was
brother to Genievre,[6] which is interesting in comparison with the
idea which appears in the romances that Modred was the offspring
of incest between Arthur and his sister.[7]

But after all scrutiny there still remain a few real additions made
by Wace to Geoffrey's story, and certainly, or almost certainly, from
independent traditional sources.

In speaking of the northern kings who submitted to Arthur when
he assumed the rôle of a foreign conqueror, Wace introduces[8]
" Romarec de Guenelande " or " Venelande." It seems probable that
Romarec was a figure of popular saga, more especially because
Layamon says that it was his son who first began to quell the fight

---

[1] Sometimes called *Llacheu.* He appears in the triads (Loth, *Mabinogion*, II,
230); the *Dream of Rhonabwy* (id., I, 312); Ulrich's *Lanzelet ;* the prose *Perceval*, etc.

[2] Vv. 12,262–12,279; cf. pp. 144, 156, 213, 229, below.

[3] Geoffrey, ix, 4, 17; Wace, 9523.   [6] V. 11,458.

[4] V. 9628; Geoffrey, ix, 5, 17.   [7] Cf. p. 119, note 8, above; pp. 188, 242, below

[5] V. 11,460.   [8] V. 9947.

at Arthur's banquet.[1] There is no proof, however, that any one
before Wace had associated him with the Arthurian story.[2] Such
a previous association, if established, would be an important point,
as giving another indication[3] that probably before the time of
Geoffrey the idea of Arthur's conquest of lands outside the British
Isles, at least in the North, was in existence.

Much more significant are Wace's additions about the Round
Table. Into the passage which tells of the great prestige of Arthur
he inserts the statement that, because each of the barons thought
himself better than the others, Arthur made the Round Table, " of
which the ' Bretons ' tell many a fable," so that none could boast
of sitting higher than any other.[4] Twice afterwards[5] he speaks of
the table, saying once that the knights who were in the court and
formed the king's bodyguard belonged to it, and in the second case
that the praise of its knights was great throughout the world. This
certainly indicates that Wace knew previous stories about it, which
may be considered substantially proved by the nearly certain fact[6]
that round tables were a very ancient pan-Celtic institution. The
antiquity of the thing being admitted, there is no reason to doubt
that its close association with Arthur goes back to a stage of the
tradition anterior to Wace and Geoffrey.

What has been said of Wace's *Brut* may be briefly summarized
as follows. Wace paraphrases Geoffrey, but with all the freedom
natural to a mediæval French poet, a freedom which leads to the
insertion of plenty of mediæval local color, and the infusion of much
vividness into the style and the presentation. He almost always
corrects Geoffrey's inconsistencies and obscurities, and in general
he tries to make everything clear to his readers. Thus he adds a
great many minor details of various kinds, which are not substantially important but which contribute very largely to Wace's entire
change of the literary form. He introduces something of the

---

[1] Vv. 22,787 ff.

[2] Dr. A. C. L. Brown thinks that he had been thus associated; see his suggestions in *The Round Table before Wace, Studies and Notes*, 1900, VII, 201.

[3] Cf. p. 84, above.   [5] Vv. 10,555, 13,675.

[4] Vv. 9994–10,007.   [6] Demonstrated by Dr. Brown, *op. cit.*

chivalric idea of Arthur and his knights, and the conception of Merlin as a magician. This may be partly (or, in the case of Merlin, wholly) his own development from Geoffrey's story; but it is far more probable that he drew to some extent from other Celtic Arthurian stories. From such he almost or quite certainly took some additional touches about Gawain, the mention of the Britons' expectation of Arthur's return, and the institution of the Round Table. And from some source not traceable he brought in the very unimportant figure of Romarec of Guenelande.[1]

To be mentioned in connection with Wace's poem are certain other much less important French metrical works of about the same date, all of which are preserved only in part.

First may be mentioned the fragments of an anonymous version of Geoffrey in monorhymed *laisses* of alexandrines, in the style of a *chanson de geste*, of which about three quarters (some twenty-five hundred lines) belong to the Arthurian period.[2] Quite in the regular *chanson de geste* manner are its descriptions of battles; the praise given by Bors and Gerins to the stroke by which Gawain kills Marcel;[3] the descriptive formulas applied to some of the characters — *od la chere dorce* to Aurelius[4] and Bedver,[5] and *pleine de cortesie* to Goneoure;[6] and the frequent emphasis of the *felonie* of the

---

[1] For the later influence of Wace, see pp. 148, 195 (note 6), 203, 215, 226, below. One of the scribes who set out to copy Wace (MS. Bibl. Reg. 13, A. xxi., fols. 40 *b*–113, 13th century; see Hardy, II, 428, No. 584; Ward, I, 264) seems very soon to have conceived the idea of emulating or improving his original; for after the first fifty-two lines he begins to abridge and entirely alters the phraseology, making also, apparently, a little independent use of Geoffrey. Beginning with the begetting of Arthur, fol. 77b (Wace, v. 8963), he copies much more exactly, but even after this he abridges somewhat and alters the phraseology to a slight extent. He does not introduce any notable new features.

[2] MS. Harl. 1605, No. 1 (see Hardy, I, i, 357, No. 837; Ward, I, 272–274). 149 lines are printed by Michel and Wright, *Vita Merlini*, pp. lxxxv–xc. See O. Wendeburg, *Über die Bearbeitung von Gottfried von Monmouth's Historia Regum Britanniae in der Hs. Brit. Mus. Harl.* 1605; Gröber, *Grundriss*, II, i, 637. Michel gives about 115 lines in the *Collection des Documents inédits sur l'Hist. de France, Rapports au Ministre*, Paris, 1839, pp. 195 ff. Cf. also the fragment, likewise in alexandrines, published by I. Bekker in *Roman von Fierabras*, pp. 182–183, and reproduced in Le Roux de Lincy's edition of the *Brut*, I, 392–395.

[3] Fol. 40 *a*.   [4] Fol. 13 *a*.   [5] Fol. 36 *a*.   [6] Fol. 33 *a*.

Britons' enemies. Not organically significant is the long and apparently original description of the pictures (biblical scenes) worked on the pavilion of the ship which carried Arthur to fight against Lucius.[1] Of Constantine's assassination the author says only that it was committed by one of his knights.[2] The characterization[3] of Gauuan as "le hardi . . . meillor cheualer," etc., is probably not altogether derived from Geoffrey.[4] A possible connection with Wace is suggested by the fact that in two cases when he enlarges on Geoffrey, this version does the same, though what it says is different. Where Wace added the episode of the fifth Roman, Marcel's cousin, wounded by Arthur's envoys,[5] this version has instead five other Romans ;[6] and it explains[6] the coming of the six thousand Britons to the aid of the envoys[7] by saying that Arthur reflected that the Romans might say things that would provoke Gawain to violence. Aside from these points, the fragment follows Geoffrey pretty closely.

There remain also 258 lines of a French verse rendering of the story of Vortigern's tower,[8] covering only what was intended for the introduction, as far as the beginning of the prophecies. Its only noteworthy difference from Geoffrey is the statement that Merlin's father visited his mother in the form of a bird, which, when inside the chamber, became a man.[9]

The four thousand and more lines which are left of the so-called *Münchener Brut*,[10] another anonymous paraphrase of Geoffrey, bring the story down to a point in Geoffrey's second book, — not, therefore, to the Arthurian period. This *Brut* is more diffuse than Wace, and draws also from other sources than Geoffrey.[11]

---

[1] Fols. 35–36.   [2] Fol. 13 *a*.   [3] Fol. 33 *a*.   [4] Cf. p. 105 and note 2, above.
[5] Cf. p. 141 and note 2, above.   [6] Fol. 40 *b*.   [7] Cf. p. 134, note 1, above.

[8] Ed. La Villemarqué, *Archives des Missions Scientifiques et Littéraires*, 1st Ser., V, 90–96, also in his *Myrdhinn ou l'Enchanteur*, 1861, pp. 422 ff.; see Ward, I, 384; Gröber, *Grundriss*, II, i, 913.   [9] Cf. p. 118 and note 7, above.

[10] Edited by Hofmann and Vollmöller, Halle, 1877. About nine hundred lines are printed in Le Roux de Lincy's *Wace* (I, lxxxv–cxv). Gröber, *Grundriss*, II, i, 473, is inclined to identify the *Münchener Brut* with Gaimar's *History of the Britons*.

[11] P. Paris (*Hist. Litt. de la France*, XXV, 338; *Romans de la Table Ronde*, II, 36, note) notes that the author of the *Roman de Merlin* alludes to a translation of the story into French verse by "Martin of Roecestre." Of this nothing seems to be known.

III. *Draco Normannicus,* and Gottfried of Viterbo's
Pantheon

Two exceptions, perhaps the most striking of all, to the fidelity which generally marks the paraphrases of Geoffrey, are afforded by Latin metrical chronicles which appeared within about half a century after the *Historia.* These works may be briefly dismissed, because in the Arthurian portions they belong to the domain rather of romance than of history, and also because they exercised little or no influence upon later authors.

The first, written about 1170, and reasonably ascribed to the rather prolific Étienne, a monk of Bec, is a fragmentary and disordered record of Norman and French affairs, bearing the suitably fantastic title *Draco Normannicus.*[1] Apart from many references to that portion of Merlin's prophecies which applies to the first half of the twelfth century,[2] the relevant material concerns Arthur himself. The chronicle says[3] that when Henry II was fighting and conquering in Brittany, Count Rollandus[4] sent to Arthur, then staying in the antipodes,[5] a letter, as a result of which Arthur wrote to Henry describing himself as *fatorum lege perennis,* magnifying his own glory beyond measure, outlining his previous career as it is told by Geoffrey, and bidding Henry leave the Britons in peace. Arthur is already on the way to help them, he says, with his immortal and invincible army and fleet, resting, or intending to rest, his legions in Cornwall.[6] Henry is not at all disturbed by the message, and nothing ever comes of it.

Étienne's conception of Arthur is more exalted than would presumably follow from Geoffrey's account,[7] and this must apparently be set down to his knowledge of other stories of the king, — the more so (1) since Arthur is made to belong especially to the

---

[1] Ed. Howlett, *Chronicles of Stephen,* etc., Rolls Series, II.

[2] Chiefly in bk. i, vv. 172–428; others in bk. ii.

[3] ii, 945 ff.

[4] Possibly an historical character.

[5] Cf. pp. 167, 188, below.

[6] On Arthur's return to earth, cf. pp. 100 ff., above.

[7] Cf. pp. 98–108 (with note 1), above.

Armorican Bretons; (2) since the idea of his future return is not only mentioned but greatly emphasized; and (3) since Avalon is equated with the antipodes and becomes a typical Celtic earthly paradise, described with much poetic beauty. In this description Étienne apparently imitates Geoffrey's *Vita Merlini*.[1] Either from this latter (by misinterpretation of the name "sisters" which Geoffrey there applies to the nymphs of the island) or from independent tradition, Étienne takes the idea, which later appears regularly in the romances, that Morgana, the only one of the ladies whom he names, is Arthur's sister.

The second of the two poems is the no less jumbled *Pantheon* of universal history written about 1186 by the distinguished and conceited Italian courtier of the Hohenstaufen, Gottfried of Viterbo.[2] The relevant passage is Particula xviii, entitled *De Anglis et Saxonibus*, which gives in 564 lines an astonishing version (or rather metamorphosis) of that part of Geoffrey's story included between the beginning of the reign of Constans and the establishment of Aurelius and Uther, *plus* Uther's amour. The features original with Gottfried could be indicated only in a very full summary. It must suffice to mention the points which may perhaps be ascribed to something else than his imagination, working, whether directly or indirectly, upon Geoffrey's narrative.

The Saxons, according to the German story previously accepted by Gottfried,[3] are identified with the Macedonians. Acquaintance with the prose *Merlin*, or something akin to it, may possibly be implied in the statement[4] that the motive of the magicians in bidding Vortigern find a boy without a father was to hide their ignorance. Interesting in connection with a later version, the *Petit Brut* of Rauf de Bohun,[5] is the statement that one of the

---

[1] Cf. pp. 165, 188, 190, 230, below.

[2] Ed. Migne, *Patrol. Lat.*, CXCVIII, 871 ff. For the passage in question, with comments, see San-Marte, *Beiträge zur bret. u. celt.-germ. Heldensage*, 1847, pp. 189–209. On Gottfried and his works, see Waitz, in Pertz, *Mon. Germ. Hist.*, *Script.*, XXII, 1 ff.

[3] See his *Particula* xv (in San-Marte, l.c.).

[4] Which is like that in the *Brut Tysilio* (see p. 118, above).

[5] See pp. 210–211, below.

dragons of the tower flew away, and Uther fought and killed it. And apparently there is a relation to German etymological stories as to the name of the region where the Saxons had lived when this latter is called Angria,[1] though this certainly does not show that Gottfried was following any example in transferring this name to Geoffrey's Rowen.[2]

A striking feature of Gottfried's version is the fact that he quite loses sight of the distinction of race between the Britons and the Saxons. Geoffrey of Monmouth did not inveigh against the Saxons in anything like the manner of Gildas; but he did exalt the Britons at their expense, and his patriotic feeling was so pronounced that some critics have supposed that he wrote his *History* in exultation over the conquerors of his race, now themselves brought into subjection by the Normans. Gottfried, on the other hand, does not seem to realize that the Britons and the Saxons were different peoples, and he sometimes uses one name when he means the other.

IV. LAYAMON'S *BRUT*

This forgetfulness of the historical in the romantic elements of the Arthurian story was not confined to foreigners. It is equally characteristic of the English chroniclers and chronicler poets who, after an interval of about half a century, began in large numbers and in various manners to follow the example set by Henry of Huntingdon and Alfred of Beverley in copying from Geoffrey or Geoffrey's imitators. These chroniclers appropriated Arthur and the other British warriors as their own national heroes.

None of them takes more pride in the glorification of Arthur than the most thoroughly Saxon of them all, the priest-poet Layamon.[3]

---

[1] San-Marte, *Beiträge*, p. 192.

[2] For a coincidence of detail between Gottfried's version and Layamon's, see p. 152, note 13, below.

[3] Indeed, in v. 14,242 Layamon himself uses the name "Bruttes" where he seems to mean English, but this case is perhaps unique with him, and probably due to carelessness.

Of Layamon nothing more is known than the very scanty facts
which he himself gives in the first ten lines of his *Brut*.[1] He was
a priest, the son of Leovenath, and lived at the church of Ern-
ley, near Radestone (Arley Regis, or Lower Arley, in northern
Worcestershire), on the banks of the Severn. Here he "read
books," — that is, the church services, being evidently the parish
priest. Fortunately his duties left him plenty of time for indulging
his love of literature.

The language of Layamon's poem indicates that it was begun
not long before the end of the twelfth century, and its composition
may well have occupied him for several years. As to his sources,
he says that he journeyed widely among the people to find books
to help in writing of the deeds of the English. He names three
books which he found and used: (1) Wace's poem, on which his
own, in fact, is directly and almost entirely based;[2] (2) what must
be the English translation of Bede's *Ecclesiastical History;* and (3)
another which is evidently to be identified with Bede's Latin text.
Investigation has proved, however, that if Layamon made any use
at all of Bede, which is doubtful, it was only in a single (non-
Arthurian) episode. This does not indicate any attempt on his
part to deceive his readers. He wants them to know that he took
all possible pains to secure authorities; but evidently when he got
to work he found that details from Bede's story would not combine
well with Wace's, and so fell back upon the latter. The question
naturally arises whether Layamon made any use of Geoffrey. The
probability is that if he had done so he would have mentioned him
among his other sources; and most of his apparent agreements with

---

[1] The only edition of the *Brut* is that of Madden, 3 vols., 1847. Among critical articles only a few call for mention here: Wülker, *Ueber die Quellen Laya-
mons*, in Paul and Braune's *Beiträge*, 1876, III, 524–555; *Dict. Nat. Biog.*, under
Layamon; H. Krautwald, *Layamon's Brut verglichen mit Wace's Roman de Brut
in Bezug auf die Darstellung der Culturverhältnisse*, Breslau, 1887; M. Kolbe,
Schild, Helm, und Panzer, zur Zeit Laȝamons, Breslau, 1891. Interesting, but
sometimes over-sentimental, is Morley's appreciation (*English Writers*, III,
206–231). References to earlier notes are given in Madden's *Preface*. For
manuscripts, etc., see Hardy, I, 352–354.

[2] Cf. p. 143, note 1, above.

Geoffrey as against Wace can be explained away.[1] However, it is
possible that Layamon may have thought, or believed that his
readers would think, that Geoffrey was untrustworthy; and there
are some coincidences in details which lend a little support to the
idea that Layamon did directly or indirectly know Geoffrey's work,
or parts of it, or else had a manuscript of Wace which had been
altered by the scribe on comparison with Geoffrey.[2] However,
these agreements are very few and slight and may be due to chance
or corruption. Of course one is not justified in assuming that he
knew Gaimar's paraphrase of Geoffrey, or any other.

Layamon's treatment of Wace's narrative is freer than Wace's
treatment of Geoffrey's. Indeed, Layamon's poem is more than
twice as long as Wace's, — 32,241 lines[3] against 15,300. Layamon
is perhaps the greatest English poet between Cynewulf and Chaucer.
He enters fully into the spirit of the story, and when his imagination is fired he is ready enough to compose verses of his own.
Such are the mocking speech of Arthur on the occasion of the surrender of Childrich, in which he compares Childrich to a fox and
vividly describes a fox hunt;[4] the shorter but equally vivid speeches
a little later, in which Arthur likens Colgrim on Bath Hill to a goat
and himself to a wolf, and the Saxon warriors lying dead in the
Avon to bright-scaled fishes;[5] and again, his taunts at the bodies
of Baldulf and Colgrim, whom he has killed.[6] It is not only in
speeches, however, that such additions occur. Of the coronation
of Constans, Wace says substantially only this:[7] The people were
in doubt which of Constantine's sons to make king. Not daring to
take Constans from his monastery, they would have chosen one of
the others; but Vortigern leaped forward and said that Constans
was the rightful heir, and that he would take upon himself the sin
of his election. Thereupon he went to Winchester, easily persuaded
Constans to renounce his irksome life and agree to exalt Vortigern,

---

[1] As Wülker has shown.

[2] See Fletcher, *Publ. Mod. Lang. Assoc.*, 1903, XVIII, 91–94.

[3] To be sure, these are properly half lines, but they average nearly as long as
those of Wace.

[4] Vv. 20,827–20,898.

[5] Vv. 21,297–21,348.

[6] Vv. 21,431–21,456.

[7] Vv. 6623–6688.

took him back to London, and with his own hands crowned him, despite the horror of the other barons.   Layamon expands the whole passage and adds much lively detail.[1] The Britons, he says, had already chosen Ambrosius in a hustings at London, when Vortiger arose and advised them to wait for a fortnight, after which he would have good advice to give. They assented. Vortiger went to Winchester, where he got leave of the abbot to speak with Constans.   He persuaded Constans to agree to his plan, disguised him in a knight's cape and sent him away, while he himself remained behind, talking with a swain whom he had dressed in Constans's habit.   "Monks went upward, monks went downward," and finally came to the abbot and said they believed that Vortiger's long conversation with Constans meant mischief.   The abbot replied that Vortiger was advising Constans to continue a monk.   At last Vortiger went away.   The monks came up and found only the discarded clothes.   The abbot leaped on his horse, overtook Vortiger, and bade him restore Constans.   Vortiger threatened to hang the abbot if he would not release Constans from his vows.   The abbot dared not disobey, and he received twenty plow-lands as the price of submission.   Vortiger enjoined silence on his attendants and kept Constans secretly in London.   At the day set the council was about to choose Ambrosius, when Vortiger sprang to his feet, gave his own version of what he had done, produced Constans, and crowned him, no one daring to oppose.   In contrast to Wace, Layamon similarly expands the accounts of the assassination of Constans, Vortimer, and Uther.[2]

Perhaps more purely original than any of these latter episodes is Layamon's invention of the scene when Arthur is informed of the treachery of Modred.   Wace, after telling what Modred had done, merely states baldly, like Geoffrey, that Arthur heard of it.[3] Layamon begins the whole episode [4] by saying that a young knight came to Arthur from Modred.   Arthur welcomed him, thinking that he brought good tidings, but all night long could not find out

---

[1] Vv. 12,972–13,270.
[2] Vv. 13,511 ff., 14,898 ff., 19,660 ff.   Cf. p. 132, note 2, above.
[3] Vv. 13,437 ff.   [4] Vv. 27,992 ff.

from him how things were going. The next morning Arthur rose from bed as if exceeding sick. The knight asked him how he did, and he related a dream which vividly foretells for the reader all his subsequent misfortunes.[1] When he finished, the knight said, "Lord, if it had happened — and may God forbid ! — that Modred had taken thy queen and thy land, yet thou mightest avenge thee and slay all thine enemies." Arthur replied that he never supposed that Modred and Wenhaver would betray him, and then the knight stated the fact bluntly. Here Layamon's art fails him, and he makes no adequate use of the fine situation which he has prepared ; but up to this point his treatment is admirably dramatic.

Such long original passages are rare, however. The bulk of Layamon's additions to Wace consists of minor supplementary or modifying statements here and there throughout the poem.[2] Among these are the following :

The observation that Vortiger had half of Wales in his possession ;[3] his stipulation that in return for his services Constans should make him his steward ;[4] the definition of ·the "rich garments" in which, according to Wace,[5] Vortiger clothed Constans, as the cloak of one of his knights ;[6] Vortiger's statement to Constans that it is from chapmen that he has learned that enemies are going to come, and the mention among them of the kings of Rusie and Frise ;[7] Constans's reservation of the name of king when he puts everything into the hand of Vortiger ;[8] a speech of Vortiger to the Picts whom he called the king's bodyguard ;[9] the statement that the Saxons of Hengist and Horsa were the fairest men who ever came to Britain ;[10] Hengist's assertion that one out of every six is obliged to leave Germany ;[11] the addition,[12] in the account of the Saxon names of the days of the week, of those called after "þunre," "Saturnus," "the Sunne," the moon, and "Tidea" ;[13] Hengist's respectful characterization of his wife ;[14] the remark that it was a wise man who cut the bull's hide for Hengist, and that he made it as thin as twine ;[15] the expansion of Wace's vague remark that

---

[1] Cf. Arthur's similar dreams in the prose *Lancelot* and versions derived from it.
[2] Compare Wace's treatment of Geoffrey in this respect.
[3] V. 13,021.   [7] Vv. 13,313 ff. ; cf. Wace, vv. 6709 ff.
[4] V. 13,067.   [8] V. 13,360.   [11] V. 13,861.   [14] V. 14,144.
[5] V. 6678.   [9] Vv. 13,382 ff.   [12] Vv. 13,929 ff.   [15] Vv. 14,211 ff.
[6] V. 13,097.   [10] V. 13,797.   [13] Cf. pp. 69–70, above.

Wancastre (Layamon, *þwong-Chastre*) was later called Langcastre by men who did not know the etymology, into the explanation that the change was due to the Danes;[1] the invention of another feast, to which the Christians did not come, as the scene of Hengist's suggestion that he send for Octa and Ebissa;[2] the statement that Vortimer offered twelvepence for the head of each heathen;[3] the observation that after Vortimer drove out the Saxons, Vortiger wandered about the land for five years, reviled by all;[4] Vortimer's invitation to Germain and Leois to come to Britain;[5] details in the account of Rowenne's poisoning of Vortimer;[6] of Vortiger's message to Hengist upon the death of Vortimer;[7] a very vivid expansion of Wace's observation[8] that at the Stonehenge slaughter Hengist seized Vortiger by the mantle (apparently only to hold him), into a description of how Hengist pulled on the mantle with his "grim grip" until the strings broke, and how the Saxons set on the unhappy king and wished to kill him, but Hengist defended him and would not allow it;[9] the substitution (for Wace's profession of ignorance as to who brought Elduf his club)[10] of the statement that it had been brought by a sturdy churl of Salisbury;[11] the entirely new idea that after the massacre, Vortiger, by means of his treasure, got together sixty thousand Britons and Scots, who brought all West Wales under his sway;[12] Vortiger's agreement with Merlin that, if the story of the magi is proved false, they shall be killed, which, Layamon says, was carried out;[13] Merlin's explanation that the immediate cause of the fall of the tower was that the dragons attacked each other at midnight;[14] great improvement in

---

[1] Vv. 14,241 ff.   [3] V. 14,684.   [5] Vv. 14,806 ff.

[2] Vv. 14,423 ff.   [4] Vv. 14,792 ff.

[6] How she sent frequent messengers with presents, asking to be allowed to live with Vortiger, which Vortimer granted at Vortiger's request; how she came to Vortimer, pretending to be about to fulfill his condition and become a Christian; how he made a feast; how Rowenne got a cup of wine, drank half of it, wished him health, and put in the poison while he was laughing merrily at her strange Saxon speech (vv. 14,898 ff.); how at night she and her men had their horses saddled and stole away to Thwongchester.

[7] V. 15,082.   [10] V. 7446.

[8] Vv. 7430–7431.   [11] V. 15,290.

[9] Vv. 15,272 ff.   [12] Vv. 15,402 ff.

[13] The death of the magi is mentioned also by Gottfried of Viterbo, but by no other witness before Layamon. It is so natural an idea that it may easily be due to chance. Certainly no direct connection between Layamon and Gottfried is to be supposed. See vv. 15,858 ff., 15,988 ff.   [14] V. 15,942.

the description of the investigation at the tower;[1] the change to direct discourse (as a speech of Aurelius)[2] of Wace's account of how order and
religion were restored after the victory over the Saxons;[3] great gain in
vividness in the description of the Irish king's blustering and mocking rage,
emphasized with an oath by St. Brandan, when he hears that Aurelius wants
to take stones out of Ireland;[4] additional details in the story of the poisoning of Aurelius[5] (such, for instance, as Appas's assertion that Uther sent
him); the mention of the Irishmen's custom (at which Layamon cannot
refrain from expressing his wonder) of taking off their breeches before a
battle;[6] the statement that Uther put his spear, as well as the dragon
standard, in the church at Winchester;[7] the specification of churls among
those whom Uther summoned to his great feast at London;[8] the bold
defiance of Gorlois when Uther bids him return to court;[9] the characterization of Ulfin as an old man;[10] the substitution, for Wace's brief statement
that Uther's men attacked Gorlois's castle because he was not there to
restrain them,[11] of an account of how the king's barons took counsel and
planned the assault;[12] a change in the conclusion of the Ygerne episode;[13]
the transformation into effective direct discourse[14] of Wace's statement that
Octa and Eosa bribed their guards to let them escape;[15] the statement that
they went to Saxony[16] before making Uther trouble in Scotland; great expansion of the story of the elevation of Arthur to the throne[17] (including the
mention of Brittany as the place from which he was brought; the description of the effect of the summons upon Arthur, who becomes alternately
red and white; an assurance to the reader that his years had been well
employed; an account of the journey to Britain, with geographical names);
similar expansion in the first battle of Arthur (at the Duglas), with a speech
by Arthur and a simile comparing him with the howling wolf who comes
from the wood behung with snow and thinks to bite whatever beasts he
will;[18] the vivifying of the picture of Baldulf disguised as a harper, telling

---

[1] Layamon makes it clear that the whole episode occupied some time. He
also says that Vortiger took Merlin to his house to ask about the meaning of the
event, instead of their sitting down beside the pond (as in Wace, v. 7725).

[2] Vv. 16,916 ff.　　[3] Wace, vv. 8168 ff.　　[4] Vv. 17,307 ff.　　[5] Vv. 17,662 ff.

[6] Vv. 18,028, 18,059. For the custom, see Madden, III, 367, and his references.

[7] V. 18,220.　　[8] V. 18,503.　　[9] V. 18,584.　　[10] V. 18,707.

[11] Wace, vv. 8969 ff.　　[12] Vv. 19,082 ff.

[13] Vv. 19,220 ff. Uther sends tokens to Ygerne of what they had said to each
other. She still refuses to believe, and the knights surrender the castle without
her consent.　　[14] V. 19,306.　　[15] Wace, vv. 9065 ff.

[16] V. 19,355.　　[17] Vv. 19,826 ff.　　[18] Vv. 20,072 ff.

how all the Britons took him for a fool and struck him with wands;[1] the mention of Childrich's castle at Lincoln;[2] the very harrowing increase in definiteness in the description of the ravages committed by the perjured Saxons when they landed at Totness, with their boastful song of how, if Arthur dared to fight, they would make a door mat of his bones, binding them together with golden ties;[3] further details in the account of the battle of "Bath" (especially the remark that the Saxons fled across the Avon in getting to the hill);[4] a minute account of the bats or "clubben swiðe græte" with which Cador armed the churls whom he put in ambush in the Saxons' ships and of his directions to them how to lay on when the enemy should come;[5] the statement that Arthur held a hustings at Exeter before his invasion of Ireland;[6] the description of how the warriors got ready for the expedition, preparing their burnies, rubbing their horses, and making ready darts and shields and spears; the description of how Arthur entertained the captured Gillomar at a feast, with the specification of the amount of tribute which the latter agreed to pay, including the relics of St. Columkille, St. Brandan, and St. Bride;[7] the description of the tribute which the king of the Orkneys was to give, — sixty ship-loads of good fish brought every year at his own cost to London;[8] details about the surrender of Aeschil of Denmark and the tribute exacted from him;[9] a note of the number of warriors whom Arthur took to France from his various subject realms;[10] a detailed description of the first battle of Arthur against Frolle, with a speech by Arthur;[11] the statement of Frolle that he has lost fifty thousand men;[12] the observation that if Frolle had supposed Arthur would accept his challenge to a duel, he would not have made it for a ship full of gold; the statement that Arthur's shield was made of elephant's bone; the vivid description of how Arthur and Frolle came to the island in their boats;[13] emphasis on the great fear of Frolle throughout the episode; the envy of the women at Arthur's coronation feast;[14] the remark that when the king was at the banquet it was Dubriz who, for his convenience, changed his heavy state crown for a lighter one;[15] the alteration of Wace's statement that Arthur's knights reviled the ambassadors who brought the message from Lucius,[16] into a description of how the knights would have torn them

---

[1] Vv. 20,303 ff.

[2] V. 20,679.

[3] Vv. 20,955 ff.

[4] Vv. 21,266 ff.

[5] Vv. 21,504 ff.

[6] V. 22,255.

[7] Vv. 22,357 ff.

[8] Vv. 22,543 ff.

[9] Vv. 23,291 ff.

[10] Vv. 23,359 ff.

[11] Vv. 23,477 ff.

[12] V. 23,618.

[13] Vv. 23,845 ff.

[14] V. 24,534.

[15] V. 24,563.

[16] Wace, vv. 10,989 ff.

to pieces if Arthur had not interfered;[1] the limitation of the men whom Arthur called for his council (the boldest and wisest);[2] a number of changes in the episode of Arthur's fight with the giant on Mont St. Michel;[3] the statement that Arthur, in pity for the people, challenges Lucius to settle their quarrel by a duel;[4] the alteration of a good many comparatively insignificant details in the campaign against Lucius; the presence of Arthur's spies in the camp of Lucius;[5] the statement that Modred promised the people of Winchester "free law" evermore if they would fight for him;[6] the hanging of the citizens by Arthur when Winchester is taken.[7]

As was to be expected, Layamon not only adds details to Wace's story, but very often omits details which Wace mentions. Of these omitted features, which are generally of no importance to the substance of the narrative, the following are typical:

Aurelius's speech to Eldof, as he is going to attack Vortiger;[8] the citation of the case of the Gabionites as an analogy for sparing the conquered Saxons;[9] the statement that Uther had his men rest during the night before fighting the Irish;[10] the description of Igerne's beauty;[11] the statement that Gorlois expected help from the king of Ireland;[12] the observation that Arthur and Wenhaver could not have an heir;[13] the statement that at the time of Arthur's second coronation the queen was crowned in her chamber;[14] all description of Lucius;[15] all mention of Mount Giu in various places;[16] the statement of the deaths of several of Arthur's knights in the last battles (for instance, that of Aguisel on the landing in England).[17]

For the greater part of these omissions we need not assume any deliberate choice by Layamon; the details naturally fell out as he

---

[1] Vv. 24,842 ff.   [2] V. 24,880.

[3] Vv. 25,720 ff. (cf. p. 135, above). Layamon adds to Arthur's company the knight who brought the tidings, and six swains. The giant bears twelve swine on his back. His bestiality is emphasized. The incidents of the combat are altogether changed.   [8] V. 16,180; Wace, vv. 7823 ff.

[4] V. 26,263.   [9] Wace, v. 8153.   [12] V. 18,620.

[5] V. 27,148.   [10] V. 18,005.   [13] V. 22,244. Cf. p. 140, above.

[6] V. 28,392.   [11] V. 18,530.   [14] V. 24,455.

[7] V. 28,407; cf. vv. 28,442 ff.   [15] V. 27,338.

[16] Wace, vv. 11,152, etc. (cf. p. 137, above). Layamon does name it in v. 25,354.

[17] Wace, v. 13,509. Layamon also fails to make any clear discrimination between the Armoricans and the insular Britons: see vv. 16,474 ff.; Wace, vv. 7915-7916, 7990. Cf. p. 82, above.

made over the narrative. But occasionally the omission improves the literary effect. Thus, by dropping the illustration from the Gabionites Layamon does away with the repetition of one Biblical story immediately after another.[1] Again, he leaves out the account of Gawain's killing a second Roman, the cousin of the first, in the flight of the envoys from Lucius's camp.[2] He seems generally to avoid all mention of the Senate in connection with Lucius, apparently in order to make it clear that the Emperor was the supreme power at Rome.[3]

It is obviously unnecessary to add any prolonged exposition of Layamon's manner as contrasted with that of Wace.

One of Wace's chief gains over Geoffrey is in realism and vividness; yet it is in precisely the same respects that Layamon most improves upon Wace. There is perhaps nothing in Layamon more realistic than Wace's description of Arthur's embarkation for France[4]; but Wace seldom has a passage of just that sort. The difference is chiefly one of race and position. Wace is a mediæval French court poet; Layamon is a direct descendant of the men who wrote *Béowulf* and the ode on Athelstan's victory. Wace calls up clearly before his mind the things which he writes about, and describes them in as pleasing a way as possible; Layamon lives among them and takes his readers along with him. Wace is elegant and vivacious; Layamon is intense.

In all other respects, also, Layamon is a thorough Saxon, and he makes the story over into a Saxon epic. He is not afraid of homeliness and simplicity, and they appear often enough in his poem, but in the Homeric manner. His warriors are not only fearless and self-reliant, but of unrestrained impulses, emotional, boastful, and cruel. Arthur's grim irony has already been referred to.[5] So

---

[1] Here it may be noted that, in giving his version of the Agag incident, Layamon draws independently from his knowledge of Scripture; but in so doing he makes a blunder, calling Saul's city Jerusalem (vv. 16,629 ff.).

[2] Wace, vv. 12,262 ff.; Layamon, v. 26,591. Cf. p. 141, above.

[3] Cf. p. 85, note 2, above.

[4] See p. 131, above.

[5] P. 149, above. Cf. also what Arthur says to the captured Petreius (vv 26,831 ff.).

Aldolf, when he has captured Hengist, cries,[1] "It is not so merry for thee, Hengist, as it was at Amesbury, where thou slewest the Britons;"[2] and then to Aurelius, "Let thy men play with this hound, shoot him with their arrows."[3] Layamon refers not infrequently to the Germanic custom of singing songs in anticipation or celebration of a triumph, as in the exultant strains of Uther's men: "Her is Vder Pendragun, icume to Verolames tun."[4] He introduces the idea of *grið*;[5] defines Vortiger's place with Constans as that of steward;[6] makes Ebissa Octa's "wed-brother";[7] says that Octa and his men surrendered to Aurelie naked, in order to emphasize their humiliation;[8] and, in describing one of the wonderful lakes in Scotland,[9] invests it with that atmosphere of weird unearthliness which marks, for instance, a famous passage in *Béowulf*.[10] Once Layamon expresses incidentally a Saxon hatred for the Normans.[11]

Like Wace, Layamon is often subjective and breaks out into exclamations of personal feeling.[12] The mediæval priest in him often becomes apparent. All who are not Christians are idolaters, and worship Tervagant, Apollo, Mahun, and "the Worse," — all devils of essentially the same nature.[13] With his heroes, he exults in the thought that their fallen enemies are doomed to hell.[14] He says that Arthur has his men spend the night in prayer for him before his duel with Frolle.[15]

There are certain kinds of detail in which Layamon pretty regularly differs from Wace. The forms of his proper names are commonly not the same. Sometimes this is merely due to his nationality; sometimes he alters them on purpose. When he knows the English form he generally substitutes it; and he often brings the spelling nearer the native Welsh (as *Wenhaver* for

---

[1] V. 16,527.
[2] Cf. v. 21,623 (Cador to Childrich).
[3] V. 16,553.
[4] V. 19,576; cf. also vv. 22,077, 22,701.
[5] V. 13,803.
[6] V. 13,067.
[7] Vv. 14,469, 14,505, 18,236.
[8] V. 16,759.
[9] Vv. 21,739 ff. He peoples it with nickers and elves.

[10] Vv. 1357 ff.
[11] Vv. 7115–7116.
[12] In v. 28,333, for example.
[13] Vv. 1140, 5353, 5406, 13,909–13,911, 13,948, 14,585, 16,790, 27,321.
[14] V. 19,562, and often.
[15] Vv. 23,730–23,751.

Genievre).[1] Occasionally he inserts an English geographical name. In numbers, especially the numbers of men in armies, Layamon does not feel at all bound to keep to his original: he generally alters the numbers given by Wace,[2] and often inserts a number where Wace has none. In describing orders of battle, again, he commonly follows his own invention;[3] and he occasionally adds such descriptions without any suggestion from Wace.[4] He is equally free in his narratives of battles, as where he speaks of streams of blood dyeing the grass,[5] and the like.

Layamon is not infallible, and in one case, at least, he makes a mistake which affects the substance of the story. Wace, following Geoffrey, gives two forms of the name of Octa's relative — *Ebissa* and *Eossa*. Layamon takes them for different persons, and often introduces them together, — Octa, Ebissa, and "Osa."[6]

None of the alterations by Layamon which have so far been mentioned appear to be derived from independent traditions. The same is true of certain other additions which may seem at first sight more significant. His occasional insertion of additional names of foreign lands in the lists of kings (*Rusie*, for instance[7]) was easy enough for any independent paraphraser who knew a little geography. It is in all probability from his own invention that Layamon sometimes gives also the name of the king of such a country, — as when among the vassals who came to Arthur's great feast he includes[8] *Kinkailin of Frislonde.* The same explanation will account for the names which he assigns to characters previously nameless, as well as for some entirely new figures. Such cases are the following names: — *Cadal*, given to Constantin's assassin;[9] *Eli*, to the reeve of Merlin's city;[10] *Conaan*, to Merlin's grandfather;[11] *Meleon*,[12] to one of Modred's sons;[13] and *Ridwaðelan*,

---

1 This comes, of course, from his residence on the Welsh border.

2 For example, Layamon, v. 15,103; Wace, v. 7380; Layamon, v. 15,270; Wace, vv. 7438–7439.   6 Cf. p. 39 (and note 1), above.

3 Vv. 16,362 ff., 27,248 ff., etc.   7 V. 13,323.   10 V. 15,597.

4 V. 21,710, etc.   8 V. 24,383.   11 V. 15,678.

5 Vv. 16,411 ff.   9 V. 12,945.

12 A character bearing the name Melion is the hero of one of the Old French Lays.   13 Vv. 28,742, 28,753; cf. p. 64, above.

substituted[1] for *Hiresgas* as the name of Bedver's nephew.[2] New personages are *Maurin*, represented[3] as Arthur's relative and his informant about Baldolf's plan ; *Patrice*, a rich Scottish thane, who gives news of Childrich's arrival ;[4] *Borel*, one of the Saxon warriors ;[5] and *Esscol*[6] (the son of Aelcus, as Layamon calls[7] Geoffrey's Malverus of Iceland). In two instances it is with fine literary effect that Layamon supplies a new rôle : — when to the Picts who assassinated Constans he gives a leader and spokesman, whom he calls *Gille Callæt ;*[8] and when in the story of Vortigern's tower he introduces a chief magus, *Joram.*[9]

Similarly without significance is Layamon's expansion of Wace's statement that Guinevere was Cador's near cousin into the information that her *mother* was of Cador's kin.[10] So, doubtless, the entirely new idea (so easy to infer) that Kæi was Arthur's relative.[11] Whether or not the idea of assigning a definite length (twenty-five years) to Vortiger's reign was original with Layamon,[12] it is certainly of no importance. Most probably Layamon's citations of prophecies of Merlin, which, except in one or two cases, do not come from Wace, are based, whether directly or indirectly, on Geoffrey's version.[13]

The elimination of these minor details clears the way for the discussion of certain matters which are organically more important.

There is a fundamental difference between Wace's general conception of Arthur and his knights and that of Layamon, — a difference, again, dependent on the authors' nationality. For Layamon, Arthur is in no sense a hero of romance, the centre of a knight-errant court. He is a very real monarch, like the famous conquering

---

[1] V. 27,593.

[2] Cf. pp. 123–124, above.

[3] V. 20,241.

[4] V. 20,354.

[5] V. 21,233. Borel is the name of a Briton in vv. 26,862 and 27,004.

[6] V. 22,495.

[7] V. 22,471.

[8] Vv. 13,564 ff.

[9] Vv. 15,521 ff.

[10] Vv. 22,227 ff. ; Wace, v. 9888. Cf. p. 140, above.

[11] Vv. 25,710, 27,517. It is possible that the foster-brotherhood between Arthur and Kay in Malory indicates an old Celtic story of relationship between them.

[12] Cf. p. 39, above ; pp. 195, 217, 232, note 1, 233, 251, 254, 258, below.

[13] See Fletcher, *Publ. Mod. Lang. Assoc.*, 1903, XVIII, 93–94.

kings of history, although the greatest and most magnificent of them all.[1] It is doubtless for this reason that Layamon omits the improbable and rather undignified narrative of Arthur's fight with the giant Rito, merely alluding to the fact of such a contest.[2] On the other hand, he greatly emphasizes Arthur's power and glory by dwelling on the tribute and the hostages that he receives from the kings who submit to him.[3] Layamon felt no more compunction than Geoffrey in representing Arthur as cruel to his foes; as, for instance, where[4] he expands the statement which Wace[5] had put into the king's mouth, — that he would go and conquer Ireland, — into a description of how he would waste it with fire and steel and kill the people.[6] An entirely new element, integral to Layamon's conception, is that of Arthur's sternness to his own men. When the council is called together to consider Lucius's message, the nobles sit in great awe, and no one dares to speak, for fear the king will punish it.[7] When Arthur wishes his men to do anything, he issues orders, which sometimes must be obeyed on pain of death.[8] When he appears disturbed after his dream on the Channel, no one dares ask him what the trouble is before he speaks himself;[9] and after he has told the dream, no one dares give it other than a good interpretation lest he should lose his limbs.[10] The long delay of the messenger in reporting the treason of Modred must be due chiefly to fear.[11] The most conspicuous instance of Arthur's severity to his own subjects is the barbarous punishment which he inflicts on the whole kindred of the man who began a bloody brawl at one of his feasts: the men are put to death and the women's noses are cut off.[12] Likewise, according to Layamon, Arthur's valor is of a more

---

[1] V. 22,979.

[2] Wace, vv. 11,956–11,987; Layamon, vv. 26,121–26,122. Cf. p. 91, above.

[3] For example, vv. 22,375–22,676.   [4] Vv. 22,267 ff.   [5] V. 9901.

[6] Cf. vv. 22,615 ff. Layamon does omit (v. 27,660) the single instance of notable barbarity which Wace retained from Geoffrey, — namely the account of the mutilation of Boccus's body by Bedver's nephew (cf. p. 139, note 1, above); but this might easily seem to Layamon unworthy of a brave warrior, even though his sturdy Saxon nature was not shocked by the conventional cruelties of a campaign.

[7] Vv. 24,891 ff.   [9] V. 25,559.   [11] Vv. 27,992 ff.

[8] Vv. 25,461, 26,013.   [10] V. 25,631.   [12] Vv. 22,837 ff.

absolute, though a more natural, kind. He never suggests, like Geoffrey and Wace,[1] that Arthur is afraid in a fight, and he represents him as the most formidable of all warriors, the only one dreaded by the giant of Mont St. Michel;[2] but he omits all mention of Arthur's impossible exploits in the last battle with Lucius.[3] Wace, like Geoffrey, says that Arthur tried to take the giant of Mont St. Michel unawares, before he could get his club;[4] but Layamon says that Arthur woke him and gave him warning, lest he should afterwards be upbraided.[5] To Wace the giant was a monster outside the pale of chivalrous laws; but Layamon will not admit that his hero needed to take unfair advantage.

Layamon also changes the character of Arthur's reign completely. Wace, in a well-known passage already quoted,[6] speaks of the marvels and adventures performed during the peace which preceded Arthur's expedition to Norway and France. Layamon says nothing of marvels, and entirely rationalizes the passage. Arthur, he says,[7] lived in peace; no man fought with him; and greater prosperity cannot be imagined than that which he and his people enjoyed. Layamon omits also the romantic element in the pictures of Arthur's knights. He leaves out of Gawain's speech in answer to Cador[8] all the suggestion of romantic love which Wace had put into it. Similarly, in paraphrasing the account of the customs of Arthur's court which Wace, following Geoffrey, inserts in the description of the coronation feast, he speaks,[9] not of *amies*, but of brides, as the reward of approved prowess. In two or three places Layamon omits the names of knights who are more or less celebrated in the Arthurian cycle.[10] He alludes only incidentally to the death of Aguisel[11] and does not mention Ywain, his successor;[12] he leaves out Yder;[13] and while he records the death, in the

---

[1] Wace, v. 11,956; Layamon, vv. 26,025, 26,119. Cf. p. 232, below.

[2] Vv. 26,075 ff.   [4] V. 11,874.   [6] Vv. 10,032 ff.; see p. 100, above.

[3] Vv. 27,802 ff.   [5] V. 26,033.   [7] V. 22,723.

[8] Vv. 24,955 ff.; cf. above, p. 139.

[9] W., v. 10,791; L., v. 24,674. Cf. p. 205, below.

[10] Cf. p. 136, above, with note 5.   [11] V. 28,342.

[12] Contrast below, pp. 199, 201, 207, 225; cf. 219.

[13] W., v. 12,336; L., v. 26,655.

battle of the convoys, of the Borel insignificant in romance, he omits the names of the other knights killed with him (Er, son of Ider; Hiresgas, and Aliduc), merely referring to them as three other highborn Britons.[1]

Layamon's Saxonizing of the story does not, of course, imply its complete rationalization. To the picture of Arthur, especially, Layamon has added certain characteristically Teutonic touches of supernaturalism. As soon as Arthur was born, he says, elves took him and enchanted him with powerful magic. They gave him gifts, to be the best of all knights, to be a rich king, to live long, and to be the most generous of all men.[2] This naturally reminds one of the coming of the Norns at the birth of Helgi. Again Layamon says that elves dug one of the wonderful lakes in Scotland.[3] To Wace's statement that Arthur's sword Calibeorne was made in Avalun,[4] Layamon adds that his burnie was the work of Wygar, an elfish smith,[5] and his spear of the smith Griffin and made in Kairme[r]ðin [6] (Merlin's city). The similarity of these passages to what is told of the legendary Wayland is obvious.[7] Besides mentioning Pridwen and Ron, Layamon gives a name, *Goswhit*, to Arthur's helm,[8] whether he is here translating a British name or borrowing from Teutonic saga.

Layamon has a thoroughly supernatural conception of Merlin [9] which is at least as romantic [10] as it is Saxon and more pronouncedly so than Wace's. When Aurelius's messengers seek Merlin, he tells them [11] that on the preceding day he foreknew their coming, and that against his will they could not have found him. When Uther wishes to get Merlin's help in his affair with Ygerne, it is not merely, as with Wace,[12] a question of summoning him. No one knows where Merlin is except a hermit, whom Ulfin has to find. Then the hermit goes to a wilderness in the West, where he has long dwelt, and where he often receives visits from Merlin. There he finds

---

[1] W., v. 12,588; L., v. 27,008.   [9] Cf. p. 139, above.
[2] Vv. 19,254 ff.   Cf. p. 195, note 4, below.   [10] Cf. p. 140, above.
[3] V. 21,998.   [6] V. 23,783.   [11] Vv. 17,051 ff.
[4] V. 21,137.   [7] Cf. also p. 213, below.
[5] V. 21,133.   [8] V. 21,147.   [12] V. 8908.

Merlin, who tells by his miraculous power everything about the king's movements.[1] The mention of Merlin's life in the forest is altogether coincident with the idea in Geoffrey's *Vita Merlini*, and it is impossible not to suppose that Layamon was influenced by Welsh tales about Merlin Silvestris.

There are other instances (some of them certain, others highly probable) in which Layamon drew from traditional lore, Celtic in origin and romantic in nature. This is probably true of his exalta- tion of Gawain as the truest man on earth,[2] and may be of his observation[3] that Modred and Wenhaver became hateful in every land, so that no one would offer a good prayer for their souls.[4] It may be that in representing the giant on Mont St. Michel as having fallen asleep, Layamon is thinking of some mythical tale of the general type of that in *Kulhwch and Olwen* where Bedver and Kai take Dillus Varvawc.[5] Perhaps also his observation that some books say that Karlium was bewitched points back to popular stories (whether or not based on Geoffrey's[6]). The battle between Arthur and Lucius, he says, was the third greatest that ever was fought, as all the writings say that wise men made.[7] The mention of writings and of the number three suggests a Welsh triad. This impression is rather strengthened by the extravagant tone of the remark immediately following, — that at length no warrior knew where to strike, because of the quantity of blood, so that they moved the armies to another place. But as there is no evidence that the battle with Lucius was ever heard of before Geoffrey, no ultimate source earlier than his *History* can be assumed. Laya- mon's statement that Arthur was called from Brittany to be made king[8] implies (as nothing in Geoffrey or Wace does) that he was brought up there. But probably Layamon is here merely following the analogy of the cases of Constantine, Aurelius, and Uther; especially since he may well have wished to make good Wace's

---

[1] Vv. 18,762 ff.   [6] Cf. p. 114, above.
[2] V. 25,487.   [7] V. 27,481.
[3] V. 25,511.   [8] V. 19,834.
[4] Cf. pp. 175, 197, 198, 201, 207, 210, 219, 229, 252, 270, below.
[5] Cf. p. 91 (with note 1), above.

omission in failing, like Geoffrey, to say anything of Arthur from his birth to his accession.

Much the largest of all Layamon's additions is his account of how the Round Table was initiated:[1] At a Yule-tide feast of Arthur there were present seven kings' sons with seven hundred knights; and when the banquet was served, they began to quarrel about precedence. From words they passed to blows, until finally the son of Rumareth of Winetland, who was there as a hostage, advised Arthur to take his native knights and arm. Meanwhile he himself seized three knives and killed seven men, including the knight who began the disturbance. At this, bloodshed became general till Arthur returned with his knights and quelled the tumult, inflicting the punishment already referred to. After this, according to Layamon, "it says in the tale" that the king went to Cornwall. Here there came to him a carpenter, who stated that, having heard of the fight, he had come from beyond the sea and would make a table at which sixteen hundred men and more could sit without one being higher than another, but which Arthur could carry with him wherever he went. Timber was brought and the man completed the work in four weeks.

The thoroughly Celtic character of this episode is evident, and Dr. A. C. L. Brown has demonstrated that it must have had its origin in an ancient Celtic tale.[2] Very likely the story was not connected with Arthur at first, but there is no reason to suppose that it had not been associated with him long before Layamon.

Layamon localizes more definitely than either Geoffrey or Wace the scene of Arthur's overthrow; for while they merely said that it was on the Tambre,[3] he specifies Camelford as the particular spot.[4] The most natural inference is that he is following a local tradition.

Still more important is the fact that points of unquestionable contact in details with the *Morte Arthur* of the prose *Lancelot* occur in Layamon's version of the last battle, especially with regard to the disappearance of Arthur. When the conflict is over, says Layamon, Arthur has fifteen fearful wounds, into the least of

---

[1] Vv. 22,737 ff.   [2] *Studies and Notes*, VII, 184 ff.   [3] Cambula (Geoffrey, xi, 2); Camblan, *var.* Tanbre, Tamble (Wace, v. 13,659).   [4] V. 28,534.

which two gloves might have been thrust.[1]   Of all his two thousand
men, only two knights are left alive.   Probably in consequence of
this last statement, Layamon represents Constantine, Arthur's successor, as a boy who comes to him after the battle.[2]   Earlier in the
poem, in speaking of the "Bruttes'" belief in Arthur's return, Layamon has remarked by anticipation that Arthur himself said when
he was wounded in Cornwall that he should go to Avalon to
Argante the courteous,[3] doubtless the Morgante, queen of Avalon, of
Geoffrey's *Vita Merlini;*[4] that she would heal his wounds with herbs ;
and that when he should be well he would come again.   Layamon
repeats the statement,[5] putting it again into Arthur's mouth, and
adding to Argante the epithet "queen" and "elf."   "And upon the
word," he continues, "there came from the sea a little boat, driven
with the waves, and two women in it, wondrously fair, who took
Arthur and put him quickly in the boat and departed.   No man
born has ever been able to speak truthfully any more of Arthur,
though Merlin prophesied that he should return."[6]

The exact origin of the detailed story of Arthur's end, and the
precise relation which Layamon's version of it bears to those found
in the Prose *Lancelot* and cognate romances,[7] we shall never know.
We can say only this : — Shortly after Geoffrey's *History* was published (if not before) the story, sadly beautiful with the passionate,
hopeless aspiration of a conquered race, was widely current, with
constantly increasing variations, and Layamon drew his material
from one of its forms.

We may now sum up our examination of Layamon's *Brut*.   It
is for the most part a paraphrase of Wace's *Brut*, with possibly a
few insignificant touches from Geoffrey.   But Layamon treated
his original with the greatest freedom.   He doubled its bulk by
additions, mostly literary and original with himself.   These rarely

---

[1] V. 28,578.   [2] V. 28,590.   [3] V. 23,061.
[4] Cf. p. 167, below ; L. A. Paton, *Studies in the Fairy Mythology of Arthurian
Romance* (*Radcliffe Monographs*), Boston, 1903, pp. 26 ff.   [5] V. 28,610.
[6] Cf. pp. 101, above, 188, below.
[7] Cf. *Vita Merlini*, ed. Michel and Wright, p. 37.   See p. 146, above ; pp. 188,
230, below.   See also Fletcher, *Publ. Mod. Lang. Assoc.*, 1903, XVIII, 84 ff.

consist of entire episodes; they are almost always details. In his whole treatment he shows that he was a real poet of vivid imagination, and a thorough mediæval Saxon. For the courtly French tone of Wace's poem he substitutes the less elegant but more sturdy Saxon tone. To this general atmosphere corresponds his conception of Arthur and his warriors, from which is altogether eliminated the romantic knight-errant idea of Wace. Yet Layamon's Merlin is really more supernatural than Wace's, and he shows some other signs of slight influence from current romance or Welsh stories, besides certainly taking from them his important accounts of the institution of the Round Table and of Arthur's disappearance. From the general stock of Teutonic saga he adds the connection of Arthur and his arms with the elves.

Layamon's Saxon nationality, language, and conceptions prevented his work from attaining to any contemporary fame. Unlike Wace's it exercised little if any influence on the development of the Arthurian stories, whether in chronicle or in romance. But it is beyond question one of the most admirable members, ancient or modern, of the whole Arthurian cycle.

V. The Latin Metrical Versions of Geoffrey's History

The Latin metrical translations of Geoffrey's *History* are chiefly important as evidence of its popularity. The best known of these is the *Gesta Regum Britanniae*[1] formerly ascribed to Gildas. The author, who may have been a certain William of Rennes, wrote about the middle of the thirteenth century, for Cadiocus, Bishop of Vannes in Brittany,[2] and was certainly a loyal Briton (whether Breton or Welshman) with a very pronounced antipathy to the English.[3]

The poem has considerable literary merit. The author treats his original with some freedom,[4] understands the value of direct discourse,

---

[1] Edited by Michel for the Cambrian Archæological Association, 1862 (see Hardy, I, 177).   [2] Vv. 16, 4923; see pp. viii ff.

[3] He sometimes speaks of the Britons as "our" side. See also vv. 4912 ff., 4868–4884.

[4] See, for example, his expansion on Aurelius (vv. 2536 ff.); contrast Wace (p. 137, note 1, above).

and shows real dramatic instinct. For example, he makes effective use of the device of a reproachful personal address to one of his characters, — as to Vortigern on the occasion of his marriage with Rowen.[1]

He pictures strikingly the grief of the women and children as the Roman warriors set out against Arthur,[2] and gives an original description of the battle with Modred by the river "Cambula."[3]

Like Layamon the author is influenced by versions of the story more developed than that of Geoffrey.[4] He exalts Arthur to a loftier position, above all other earthly heroes;[5] Caliburn and Pridwen seem[6] to be more prominent in his mind than they were in Geoffrey's; he distinctly alludes to the belief that Arthur is not dead.[7] He follows romance ideas when he says[8] that it was according to his custom that Arthur assumed the crown at his feast in York,[9] and he mentions the mass as a regular part of the ceremonies. He has also a thoroughly supernatural conception of Merlin.[10] It is by magic songs that the bard makes the stones of the Great Circle manageable[11] and changes Uther's form.[12] Moreover, when Arthur is getting the worst of it in his duel with Frollo, Merlin inspires him with strength.[13] The author's mention[14] of the antipodes in connection with Arthur seems to point to the *Draco Normannicus* or something similar;[15] and he describes the earthly paradise, the *memorabilis insula*, to which Arthur passes, with its *regia virgo*,[16] in terms which correspond closely with the *Vita Merlini*.[17] Apparently from an entirely non-Celtic tradition (one which is best known, at any rate, in connection with Hercules) he adds[18] the idea that for the begetting of Arthur it was necessary that his father should remain with Ygerna three days and nights.[19]

---

[1] Vv. 2244 ff. Cf. p. 40, above.   [10] Cf. p. 139, above.

[2] Vv. 3561–3587.   [3] Vv. 4188 ff.   [11] Vv. 2746, 2772.   [12] V. 2918.

[4] Cf. p. 137, above.   [5] Vv. 2976 ff.   [13] V. 3339. Cf. p. 161, above.

[6] Vv. 3664–3665.   [14] V. 4155.   [15] Cf. p. 145, above.

[7] V. 4209. Cf. p. 101, above.   [16] Vv. 4213–4234.   [17] Cf. p. 165, above.

[8] Vv. 3249–3255.   [9] Cf. p. 110, above.   [18] Vv. 2923 ff.

[19] The author transfers the name of Brutus's soothsayer (Geoffrey, i, 11) to Arthur's (v. 3599; Geoffrey, x, 2). He calls Leo *princeps* (v. 3882; cf. p. 85, above). He inserts (v. 3928) a mention of an historical comet which is recorded in some of the Latin chronicles. Minor differences from Geoffrey occur in vv. 3354 and 3376 ff.

There is an anonymous unpublished *Epitome Historiae Britannicae* from Brutus through the reign of Henry III, in Latin rhythmic hexameter verses, arranged in couplets with feminine rhymes.[1] It follows Geoffrey as far as he goes, is very brief in the Arthurian period, and nowhere makes any changes in Geoffrey's story.[2]

---

[1] MSS. Harl. 1808, fols. 31*a*–44*a* and Cott. Claud. D. vii. 11, fols. 14*a*–20*a*. Hardy, III, 197, No. 322.

[2] There is a fragment of another twelfth-century rendering of Geoffrey into Latin hexameters in MS. Cott. Vesp. A. x, fols. 45*b*–52*a* (Hardy, I, 357, No. 836). But although it enlarges on Geoffrey, the six hundred and fifty lines which remain extend only to Ebraucus (bk. ii). MS. Harl. 1808, fols. 46*a*–55, contains an insignificant series of extracts from various Latin authors about the city of York (cf. p. 278, below), especially its ecclesiastical interests. The greater part is in heroic verses, and includes an adaptation from Geoffrey on the restorations of York by Aurelius and Arthur.

CHAPTER VI

THE STORY AFTER GEOFFREY: THE LATIN PROSE
CHRONICLES OF THE TWELFTH, THIRTEENTH,
AND FOURTEENTH CENTURIES

THE impulse toward the study and composition of chronicles which began to manifest itself in England early in the twelfth century was in full accord with the conditions which then prevailed in the scholastic portion of society; and when it had once got under way, it developed into one of the most important features in the literary history of the epoch. Many of the monasteries adopted before long the custom of collecting and preserving annals, and in course of time no small number of these compilations were put into definite shape and regularly published. Some individual writers, also, unconnected with monastic institutions, though in almost every case holding an ecclesiastical position, engaged in the same work. From the end of the twelfth century until well into the fourteenth, the number of Latin chronicles was very large, and they continued to be written after 1400.[1] These chronicles differ very considerably in character and in extent. Though almost all are arranged in the same annalistic form, some consist of a brief series of bare entries, while others narrate events in much detail and are of great bulk. Some make no pretence to originality, but merely copy from previous authorities; others are the productions of real historians, capable of weighing evidence and pronouncing shrewd judgments.

By the nature or limitation of their contents, some of these works have nothing to say of the Arthurian story, either because they treat only of a particular monastery, or because they begin with the Saxon kingdoms. Most of them, however, aim to trace either the

---

[1] For the more important of these chronicles reference may be made to Morley's *English Writers*, Vols. III ff., and for mention of more to Gross's *Sources and Literature of English History*, London, 1900.

history of the world from the Creation, or the history of England from the earliest times (one or two from the beginning of the Arthurian period) down to the date at which they were composed; and of these there are few that do not include something, at least a sentence or two, relating to the Arthurian tradition.   As a rule, they take their Arthurian material, and often their whole account of the Arthurian period, directly or indirectly, from Geoffrey. Those which have nothing to say of the Arthurian period (or draw what they say wholly from the Saxon, non-Arthurian account of it) must here be left out of account.   The others may be roughly divided into the following classes: [1]

1. Those which have only a few (sometimes but one or two) brief or comparatively brief entries relating to the Arthurian material, inserted at what the author takes to be the proper chronological point, in the midst of his other notices, or brought in incidentally.   Because of the very general character of these entries, it is not always evident whether the authors are drawing direct from Geoffrey or not; but what they say is almost invariably in harmony with his account except for dates.   This, the most numerous class, is represented by Ralph de Diceto.

2. Those which, while they break up the story and combine it with other material, include most of its essential substance as related by Geoffrey either:

a. In summary (represented by Sigebert of Gembloux, as interpolated by the monk of Ursicampum);

b. For the most part in rather full detail. (This is a small class. It is represented by the various versions of the *Flores Historiarum*, which, indeed, greatly condense and alter Geoffrey in the last part of the story, and to a less extent throughout.)

3. Those which take from Geoffrey everything (or almost everything) that they say about the whole period covered by his *History*,—

a. Giving a summary, long or short, of his narrative (a numerous class, represented by the *Memoriale* of Walter of Coventry);

---

[1] This classification (at best only approximately exact) relates merely to the treatment of the Arthurian material.   On almost any other basis a very different classification would have to be made.

b. Copying Geoffrey's narrative almost or quite verbatim (represented by Bartholomew de Cotton).

4. Those which draw from Geoffrey in much the same way as Class 3a, but make use also of other sources of comparison, substantiation, slight additions, or altogether new material. (A rather numerous class, represented by Alfred of Beverley.)

It should be distinctly stated that some writers in almost all these classes occasionally depart from Geoffrey, at least in slight details. We shall also meet with instances of omission and expansion, and even with some noteworthy additions.

For convenience, a list is here given of the chronicles which concern us in the present study, with an indication of the group to which each belongs according to the classification above.[1] When a chronicle can be dismissed with a brief note, such a note is appended. In other cases a reference is given to the page of this volume at which further treatment will be found.

Ca. 1135. Ordericus Vitalis (monk of St. Évroult in Normandy), *Historia Ecclesiastica.* Class 1. Ed. Le Prévost, 1838–55. Bk. xii, chap. 47 (IV, 486). An excerpt from the story of Vortigern's tower and the prophecies, taken probably from Geoffrey's earlier independent edition of the prophecies.[2]

Ca. 1150. Alfred of Beverley (treasurer of St. John's Church), *Annales sive Historia.* Class 4. Ed. Hearne, Oxford, 1716 (see Ward, I, 211). Alfred distrusts Geoffrey, prefers when he can to follow the authority of Bede and Gildas, and abandons Geoffrey altogether at the invasion of Gormund (Geoffrey, xi, 10). He often pauses (as at p. 76) to discuss the credibility of the account, and he omits things which, to use his own words (p. 2), exceed belief, — especially, the fight of the dragons, most of the prophecies, and the account of Arthur's coronation feast. See p. 183, below.

1162. Richardus Cluniacensis, in the second and third redactions of his Latin universal *Chronicle,* includes the prophecies of Merlin, which he had omitted in his first redaction. The first redaction ends with 1153, the second with 1162, the third with 1171. A fourth redaction, extending to 1174, is thought not to be Richard's own. See E. Berger, *Richard le Poitevin,* Paris, 1879, pp. 56, 80 (*Bibl. des Écoles franç. d'Athènes et de*

---

[1] The list includes also the few continental chroniclers who mention the Arthurian story.

[2] See Fletcher, *Publ. Mod. Lang. Assoc.,* 1901, XVI, 465–468.

Rome, VI). Portions of Richard's *Chronicle*, not including the portion in question, may be found in Martène et Durand, *Amplissima Collectio*, V, 1159 ff.; Muratori, *Antiquitates Italicae*, IV, 1080 ff.; Bouquet, *Recueil*, VII, 258–259; IX, 22–24; X, 263–264; XI, 285–286; XII, 411–417.

Ca. 1175 (between 1155 and 1200). The interpolated version of Sigebert of Gembloux's *Chronicon* of about 1111, made by a monk of Ursicampum. Class 2a. Ed. Gul. Parvus, Paris, 1513.[1] The genuine work of Sigebert, which naturally contains no Arthurian material, was soon and frequently altered and continued. The monk of Ursicampum used a text which had already been slightly interpolated (between 1138 and 1147) by a monk of Beauvais. His form became the standard, and hence " Sigebert " is sometimes quoted by later chroniclers as an authority for the Arthurian tradition. See L. C. Bethmann's edition in Pertz, *Mon. Germ. Hist.*, *Scriptores*, VI, 282, and especially 292, 461–3, 469–70. Cf. pp. 179, 182, 183 (note 11), 185, below.

Ca. 1175 (between 1160 and 1200). Ralph Niger. *Chronica.* Class I. Ed. Robert Anstruther, Caxton Soc., 1851.[2] In the second *Chronicon*, p. 137, in an addition perhaps by a later hand : — a mere reference to the *Historia Britonum* and Merlin's transportation of the Stones.

Ca. 1187. *Chronicle of the Abbey of Coggeshall*, arranged by Abbot Ralph. Class I. Ed. Joseph Stevenson (Rolls Series), 1875, p. 146. See pp. 189 (note 3), 190, below.

Ca. 1190. Ralph de Diceto (Dean of St. Paul's), *Opera Historica*, especially *Abbreviationes Chronicorum*. Class I. Ed. Stubbs (Rolls Series), 2 vols., 1876. Also, *Opuscula* (Class 3a), II, 222–31. Cf. pp. 184, 187, below.

Ca. 1192. *Gesta Regis Henrici II*, which goes under the name of Benedict, Abbot of Peterborough. Class I. Ed. Stubbs (Rolls Series), 1867, II, 159. Cf. p. 192, below.

Ca. 1187–1220. Giraldus Cambrensis, Archdeacon of Brecknock, courtier, and man of affairs. Class I. Works (Rolls Series), 8 vols., 1861–91 (I–IV, ed. by J. S. Brewer ; V–VII, by J. F. Dimock; VIII, by G. F. Warner). See pp. 92–93, above ; pp. 180–181, 185, 189–190, below.

Ca. 1195. Roger of Hoveden (courtier of Henry II), *Chronica.* Class I. Ed. Stubbs (Rolls Series), I, 64. Cf. pp. 186, 192, note 2, below.

Ca. 1195. A monk of Winchester, perhaps Richard of Devizes, Chronicle in MS. Corpus Christi, Cambridge, 339, partly embodied in *Annales de Wintonia* of ca. 1295, ed. Luard in *Annales Monastici* (Rolls Series),

---

[1] See sig. c iii to fol. 27b.   [2] See *Dict. Nat. Biog.*, XLI, 63–64.

II (1865). Class 1. See pp. xi ff. ; also *Dict. Nat. Biog.*, XLVIII, 197; Stevenson, *Chronicon Ric. Divisiensis*, 1838, *Preface;* Wright, *Biog. Brit. Lit.*, *Anglo-Norman Period*, pp. 360–2. Cf. pp. 183, 185, below.

Ca. 1200. Gervase of Canterbury (monk), *Gesta Regum Britanniae.* Classes 4 and 1. Ed. Stubbs (Rolls Series), 2 vols., 1879–80. See II, 106.

Ca. 1205. The same, *Actus Pontificum.* Class 1. See II, 334.

The same, *Mappa Mundi.* Class 1. See II, 414. See p. 191, note 2, below.

Ca. 1200. *Flores Historiarum*, compiled at St. Albans. Class 2b. Ed. Luard, *Matthaei Parisiensis Chronica Majora* (Rolls Series), I (1872). This edition reproduces Matthew Paris's form (*ca.* 1253), indicating also the readings of the almost identical older form. Practically identical (except as noted below) for the Arthurian period is the *Flores Historiarum* (the " Matthew of Westminster " version), ed. Luard (Rolls Series), 1890. For discussions of the complicated questions of the composition of this work, see Matth. Par., *Historia Anglorum*, ed. Madden (Rolls Series), 1866–69, I, xii ; III, xiii ff.; Hardy, III, xxxvi–lxxxv, 79–82, 114–116, 317–326, 399–445 ; Matth. Par., *Chron. Maj.*, ed. Luard, I, xxx–lxxxiv, especially xxxiii ; *The Flowers of History*, by Roger de Wendover (*ca.* 1236), ed. H. G. Hewlett, 1886–89, III, *Introduction; Flores Hist.*, ed. Luard, I, x–xi ; Coxe, Roger de Wendover, *Chronica*, etc., 1841–44, I, *Preface; Mon. Hist. Brit.*, ed. Petrie and Sharpe, 1848, *General Introd.*, p. 7 ; *Dict. Nat. Biog.*, under the names ; *English Writers*, III, 340–1, 346. Cf. pp. 183, 184, 185, 187, 189, 191 (note 2), below.

Ca. 1210. *Annales Prioratus de Dunstaplia*, compiled by Prior Richard de Morins. Class 1. Ed. Luard, *Annales Monastici* (Rolls Series), III (1866). Draws from Diceto ; see 392, 523, 535 (Diceto, 393, 523, 542).

Ca. 1211. Gervase of Tilbury (courtier of the Emperor Otto IV, though English by birth), *Otia Imperialia* (in strictness not to be called a chronicle). Classes 1 and 3a. Ed. (incompletely) by Leibnitz, *Scriptores Rerum Brunsvicensium*, Hanover, 1707 : I, 916–17, 921, 931–8. Also in Stevenson, *Radulphus de Coggeshall*, etc., pp. 419–441 ; see pp. xxiii–v. Selections, ed. Liebrecht, 1856. In the summary of Geoffrey, Gervase often inserts observations of his own about contemporary conditions or similar matters. See pp. 186–187, 188–189, below.

Ca. 1235. *Annals of Margan.* Class 1. Ed. Gale, *Hist. Angl. Script.*, II, 1–19, especially 10–11. See p. 191, below.

Ca. 1250. Albericus Trium Fontium. Class 1. Ed. P. Scheffer-Boichorst, in Pertz, *Mon. Hist. Germ.*, *Scriptores*, XXIII, 674–950 : see p. 669. See p. 191, below.

Ca. 1256.   Vincent of Beauvais (courtier of Louis IX), *Speculum Historiale* (part of his immense *Speculum Majus*).   Class 2a, as regards Merlin, Ambrosius, Uther, and Arthur ; merely copying the Arthurian entries from the version of Sigebert interpolated by the monk of Ursicampum.   Ed. 1474 ; also Venice, 1494 (the edition here referred to).   Bk. xvi, chaps. 5, 6 ; xx, 30, 55, 56 ; xxi, 74, covering Geoffrey vi, 17 ; xi, 2.   See John Ferguson, *Account of a Copy of Speculum Majus*, Glasgow, 1885, especially notes, pp. 1–6 ; Daunou, *Hist. Litt. de la France*, XVIII, 449–519.

Ca. 1258 (?).   Thomas Albus, *Chronicon* (MS. Harl. 3723).   Class 1. See fol. 45.   Cf. Hardy, III, 149, No. 253.

Ca. 1270.   Henricus de Silegrave (perhaps Abbot of Ramsay), *Chronicon*.   Class 1, with comparison of William of Malmesbury.   Ed. C. Hook, Caxton Soc., 1849 ; see p. 11.

Ca. 1275.   Martinus Polonus, Bishop of Gnesen, *Cronica Summorum Pontificum Imperatorumque*, etc.   Class 1.   Ed. Taurini, 1477.   A single entry under Emperor Leo, fol. 32b : " Per hec tempora fuerunt viri famosi milites tabule rotunde ut dicitur."   Cf. p. 142, above.

Ca. 1290.   Adam de Domerham.   *Historia de Rebus gestis Glastoniensibus*.   Class 1.   Ed. Hearne, 2 vols., 1727.   See p. 191, note 4, below.

Ca. 1290 (?).   Peter Ickham (?), *Chronicon de Regibus Angliae*.   Class 3a.   See *Dict. Nat. Biog.*, XXVIII, 411, and Hardy, III, 271–2, No. 488, with notes.   Makes a little use also of William of Malmesbury.   Also, in the Saxon part of the story, inserts from Geoffrey a brief outline of Hengist's career.   Cf. pp. 183, 185, 187, 188, below.

Ca. 1291.   *Annals of Waverley*.   Class 1.   Ed. Luard (Rolls Series), *Annales Monastici*, II, 129 ff. (see II, xxix ff.).   Entries under the years 543, 1278, 1283.   See pp. 191, note 4, 192, note 3, below.

Ca. 1292.   [" Martinus "] Minorita, a monk of Suabia, *Flores Temporum*. Class 1.   Edited in Eccard, *Corpus Hist. Medii Aevi*, 1723.   Ann. 458, col. 1590.

Ca. 1293.   *Chronica* ascribed to John of Oxnead.   Class 1.   Edited by Sir Henry Ellis (Rolls Series), 1859 ; see p. 2.

Ca. 1293.   Brother Walter of Coventry, *Memoriale*.   Class 3a.   Ed. Stubbs (Rolls Series), 1872–3 ; see I, Preface, especially pp. xix–xx.   See pp. 183, 187, 192, note 2, below.

Ca. 1298.   Bartholomew de Cotton, monk of Norwich, *Historia Anglicana*.   Class 3b.   Ed. Luard (Rolls Series), 1859.   Luard does not include the part dealing with the Arthurian period, but his statements (pp. xix, xxvi–vii) indicate that it does not deviate from Geoffrey. See also ann. 1294, p. 239.

Ca. 1298. Chronicle of MS. Cott. Cleop. A. i. 1, fols. 3–207. Class 4. Hardy, III, 258, No. 466. Gives Geoffrey's story very fully, sometimes almost *verbatim*, but sometimes substitutes and sometimes draws from Henry of Huntingdon (for example, the account of Arthur's last battle : cf. p. 120, above), Bede, Gildas, Nennius, and even Paulus Diaconus (who used Bede). See pp. 183, 186, note 5, below.

Ca. 1306. Johannes Beverus, monk of Westminster, *Chronica* (MSS. Harl. 641, no. 4, fols. 8a ff., and Cott. Titus D. xii., fols. 3 ff.). Class 3a. Hardy, III, 281, No. 507; II, 473, No. 621 ; I, 359, No. 842. The author sometimes employs his own judgment in making trivial additions, and he sometimes inserts Latin verses, especially on the faithlessness of women, apropos of Guenuara (Titus D. xii., fol. 21b). Cf. p. 163, above.

Ca. 1307. William Rishanger, *Annales Regum Angliae* (fragmentary). Class 1. See ann. 449, 516. Edited (together with the form of the *Chronica Monasterii S. Albani* ascribed to Rishanger, which also is of Class 1 ; see p. 107) by H. T. Riley (Rolls Series), 1865 ; see pp. xxv, xxxiv. Cf. pp. 182, 191, note 2, 192, note 4, below.

Ca. 1308 (originally). *Annales* of the Priory of Worcester. Class 1. Ed. Luard, *Annales Monastici*, IV, 353 ff. (see pp. xxxv ff.). Consult ann. 468, 1216, 1285. See p. 192, note 3, below.

Ca. 1314. *Chronicon Monasterii de Hales* (MS. Cott. Cleop. D. iii., fols. 1–56). Class 4. Hardy, III, 352, No. 580. Cf. pp. 182, 185, note 8, 187, note 8, 191, note 2, below.

Ca. 1352. Ralph Higden (monk of the Benedictine Abbey of St. Werburg's at Chester), *Polychronicon*. Class 4, chiefly. Edited (with Trevisa's English translation of 1387) in the Rolls Series, 1865–86 (I, II, by C. Babington, III–IX, by J. R. Lumby). Cf. pp. 181–182, 185–186, 191, note 2, below.

14th or 15th century (?). John Brompton (?), *Chronicon*. Class 1, but drawing wholly from Higden. Ed. Twysden, *Scriptores X*, 1652, I, cols. 1153, 1195. See *Dict. Nat. Biog.*, VI, 405 ; Gross, *Sources and Literature of English History*, p. 270, No. 1727.

Ca. 1350. Johannes Historiographus, *Chronicon*. Class 1. Ed. J. P. de Ludewig, *Reliquiae Manuscriptorum omnis Aevi*, Halae Salicae, 1741, vol. XII ; see chap. 38, p. 134.

Ca. 1350 (?). Canon of Lanercost in Northumberland, *Larga Angliae Historia* (MS. Cott. Claud. D. vii., no. 14). Class 4, making some use of William of Malmesbury and Henry of Huntingdon. Cf. pp. 180, 183, note 3, below.

Ca. 1350 (?). Nicolaus Gloucestriae, *Chronicon*, MS. Cott. Calig. A. iii., fols. 12–145b. Class 3b. Hardy, I, 512, No. 838. Cf. pp. 180, 189, note 5, below.

Ca. 1350. Entries, of uncertain authorship, in MSS. of Robert of Avesbury, *Historiae Edwardi III.* Class 1. Ed. Hearne, 1720; see p. 259. Cf. p. 189, below.

Ca. 1366. Thomas, monk at Malmesbury (?), *Eulogium Historiarum.* Classes 3a and 3b. Ed. F. S. Haydon (Rolls Series), 1858–63; see book v. Up to the beginning of the story of Vortigern's tower it follows substantially the version of the French *Brut* (cf. pp. 187, 191, note 2, below). The same author's *Chronicon brevius* is of Class 1.

Ca. 1395. Thomas Sprott, monk of St. Augustine's, Canterbury. Ed. Hearne, Oxford, 1719. The first, or annalistic, part is of Class 1 ; see ann. 469, 488, 1195. The second part is of Class 3a, but omits much of the important sections of the story. Cf. pp. 183, note 8, 187, 191, note 2, below.

Ca. 1400. Henry Knighton, *Chronicon.* Class 1, but drawing from Higden. Ed. Lumby (Rolls Series), 2 vols., 1889–95 ; see I, 149–50, 314. See p. 191, note 2, below.

Ca. 1400. Richard of Cirencester, *Speculum Historiale de Gestis Regum Angliae.* Class 4, but drawing chiefly from "Matthew of Westminster." Ed. J. E. B. Mayor (Rolls Series), 2 vols., 1863–9 ; see *Preface*, II, viii ff. Cf. pp. 179, note 3, 183, 184, below.

Ca. 1400. Thomas Otterbourne (?), *Chronica Regum Angliae.* Class 3a, but using also Higden to a slight extent. Ed. Hearne, *Duo Rerum Anglicarum Scriptores*, Oxford, 1732 ; see *Dict. Nat. Biog.*, XLII, 341.

Ca. 1400 (?). *Chronicon de Origine et Rebus Gestis Britanniae et Angliae* (MS. Coll. Magdalen, Oxford, No. 72). Class. 4, drawing largely from Higden. Hardy, II, 472, No. 620. Cf. p. 187, below.

Ca. 1414. Thomas of Elmham, monk and treasurer of the monastery (?), *Historia Monasterii S. Augustini Cantuariensis.* Class 1. Ed. Hardwick (Rolls Series), 1858 ; see pp. xix–xxiv. Consult ann. 1288, sec. 81, p. 265. See p. 191, note 4, below.

Ca. 1420. Thomas Walsingham, monk, *Historia Anglicana*, ed. H. T. Riley (Rolls Series), 1863–64. Class 1. Copying Rishanger. Also *Ypodigma Neustriae*, in Camden's *Anglica*, etc., 1603, p. 492 ; ed. Riley (Rolls Series), 1876, pp. 176, 220–221.

Ca. 1460.   Thomas Rudborne (monk of St. Swithun's, Winchester), *Historia Major Wintonensis.*   Class 1.   Ed. Wharton, *Anglia Sacra*, I, 187; see book ii, chap. 1; cf. *Dict. Nat. Biog.*, XLIX, 378.   See p. 185, note 9, below.[1]

---

[1] The following is a list, arranged in classes, of the less important (generally anonymous and altogether unimportant) unpublished chronicles which I have consulted: —

Class 1

Cotton MSS.: Jul. A. i., no. 1, fols. 2–42 (Hardy, III, 167, No. 287; III, 363, No. 599): see fol. 20a. — Jul. A. xi., fol. 23 (Hardy, III, 41, No. 67). — Cleop. D. ix., no. 3, fol. 35. — Galba E. iii., fols. 2–31b (Hardy, II, 533, No. 698): see fol. 2, ann. 524. — Vesp. B. xi., no. 4, fols. 72a–79a, *Chronica S. Martini de Dover* (Hardy, II, 263, No. 362). This does not contain the brief mention of Arthur which Leland (*Collectanea*, Hearne, 2d ed., III, 50) says that he took "ex chronico Dovarensis monasterii." — Dom. A. i., no. 10, fols. 138–155 (Hardy, III, 226, No. 397): see fol. 139b 2.

Brit. Mus. Bibl. Reg. MS. 13 D. i. (Hardy, III, 25, No. 33); see ann. 454.

Harl. MSS. — 1808, no. 1, fols. 1–8a (Hardy, II, 148, No. 213); also fols. 10a–17b, 98–105. — 37,251: see fol. 6b. — 7571, no. 1: see fol. 12b.

Class 2b

MS. Bodl. Rawl. B. 177, no. 1.

Class 3a

Cotton MSS. — Tib. A. ix., fols. 42–51. — Nero A. iv., no. 1. — Nero A. viii., no. 3. — Nero A. ix., fols. 25–73. — Faust. B. vi., fols. 38b–40b (Hardy, I, 575, No. 1161; see Ward, I, 374). — Vesp. E. iv., no. 5, fols. 104–107b (Hardy, I, 560, No. 1138).

Harl. MSS. — 902, fols. 14–46. — 1808, fols. 59–65 (Hardy, II, 264, No. 365). — 3860, no. 1 (Hardy, III, 196, No. 321). — 5418, fols. 1–77 (Hardy, II, 495, No. 647): see fols. 1 ff. Fols. 17 ff. are of class 2a.

Bodl. MS. 355, no. 3, fols. 32b ff.; but see fol. 45b.

Bodl. Rawl. MSS. — B. 150, no. 4, fols. 8 ff. (Hardy, III, 164, No. 281). Seems to resemble the chronicle of Johannes Beverus, and has Latin verses at intervals, some of them, at least, the same as his. — B. 167, no. 1 (Hardy, II, 38, No. 51).

Class 3b

Cott. MS. Dom. A. iv., no. 2, fols. 58–241.

Class 4

Cotton MSS. — Jul. D. iv., fols. 2–124 (Hardy, III, 387, No. 649). — Claud. D. vii., no. 11, fols. 9a–13b. — Titus D. iv., fols. 15–75 (Hardy, I, 674, No. 1275). A late composite account, making use of several chroniclers. — Dom. A. iv., no. 1, fols. 2–56.

Brit. Mus. Bibl. Reg. MS. 13. C. i., fols. 147–152.

In discussing more at large the works thus briefly catalogued, we may begin with the attitude of the chroniclers toward Geoffrey's

Manuscripts not belonging to the above classes: Harl. 6148, no. 18, fols. 67b–68a. Statements about Arthur from William of Malmesbury and others. — Harl. 7571, no. 2, fols. 85–89. A history of King Arthur, consisting of quotations from Gildas and Geoffrey, with interpolations.

My investigations have shown that the following do not contain Arthurian material : —

Cotton MSS. — Jul. A. i., no. 1 (Hardy, III, 167, No. 287) ; also fols. 44–50 (Hardy, III, 293, No. 526). — Jul. D. ii., fols. 3–20 (Hardy, III, 74, No. 142). — Jul. D. v., no. 2 (see Hardy, III, 351, No. 576). — Jul. D. vii., fol. 61 (Hardy, II, 84, No. 121). — Cleop. D. ix., no. 1, fols. 1–21 (Hardy, III, 233, No. 414). — Tiber. E. i., fols. 217–218b (Hardy, I, 84, No. 265). — Claud. C. ix., no. 1, fols. 1–14b (Hardy, II, 397, No. 538). — Claud. D. vii., nos. 2 and 13, fols. 20b–21b. — Nero A. iv., fols. 77–111 (Hardy, III, 199, No. 331). — Nero A. vi. — Nero A. viii., fols. 1–37 (Hardy, II, 280, No. 376). — Nero C. vii., fol. 215 (Hardy, II, 213, No. 295). — Vesp. A. xxii. — Vesp. D. iv., fol. 126 (Hardy, I, 667, No. 1265). — Vesp. D. xiii., fols. 1–58b (Hardy, II, 199, No. 271). — Vesp. D. xix., no. 6, fol. 53 (Hardy, III, 57, No. 110). — Vesp. E. iv., no. 8, fol. 139a–141b. — Domit. A. ii., fols. 130–143 (Hardy, III, 293, No. 527). — Domit. A. xv., fols. 1–7 (Hardy, II, 189, No. 252).

Harl. MSS. — 64, fol. 123. — 902, fols. 48–68 (Hardy, I, 674, No. 1273).

Brit. Mus. Bibl. Reg. MSS. — 4, B. vii., fols. 200–218 (Hardy, II, 448, No. 592). — Bibl. du Roi, 4932, no. 2, fols. 24 ff. (Hardy, III, 217, No. 375). — 4936, no. 1 (Hardy, III, 102, No. 199). — 6041. A, no. 2 (Hardy, II, 528, No. 687, and III, 124, No. 222).

Sloane MS. 289, no. 1 (Hardy, III, 61, No. 115).

Bodl. Rawl. MS. B. 177, fols. 192 ff. (Hardy, III, 277, No. 497).

Coll. Magd. Oxon. MS. 53, no. 10 (Hardy, III, 221, No. 385).

I have not consulted the following MSS. Perhaps of some importance are : — Marquis of Bath's MS., mentioned by Furnivall in his ed. of *Arthur*, etc., E.E.T.S., No. 2. — Marquis of Salisbury's MS., Hatfield House, B. d. 15 (Hardy, II, 167, No. 224). Probably of little or no importance are : — Cotton MSS. : Galba A. vii. 4, fols. 47–87 (Hardy, II, 64, No. 88) ; Faust. A. viii., fols. 119–212 (Hardy, III, 84, No. 157) ; Vitell. A. viii., fols. 113–132b (Hardy, II, 286, No. 389) ; Vitell. A. x., fols. 1–17 (Hardy, III, 382, No. 643) ; Vitell. A. xvii., fols. 1–16 (Hardy, II, 397, No. 539) ; Vitell. C. viii., fols. 1–17 (Hardy, II, 88, No. 124) ; Vitell. E. xvii., no. 4, fol. 189 (Hardy, III, 282, No. 508) ; Titus A. xiii., no. 1. — Titus D. xix., fols. 105–108 (Hardy, I, 623, No. 1225). — Harl. MS. 3775 (Hardy, III, 17, No. 19). — Arund. MSS. : 310, fol. 188 (Hardy, III, 200, No. 333) ; 326, fols. 10–22 (Hardy, III, 62, No. 118). — Sloane MS. 289, fols. 110–134 (Hardy, II, 474, No. 622). — Addit. MS. Bodl. II. D. 11 (Hardy, III, 150, No. 257). — Brit. Mus. Bibl. du Roi MSS. : 4861, no. 8 (Hardy, III, 223, No. 392) ; 4893 (Hardy, narrative. We have seen that Henry of Huntingdon accepted it almost without question, at least to the extent of copying it in abstract, and that Alfred of Beverley, more judicially minded in a timid way, regarded it as in great part true but as much exaggerated and needing to be checked by other authorities. By the year 1200, practically the whole substance of Geoffrey's story, in outline, had been adopted by one or two important writers; and from that time until the Latin chronicles ceased to be composed, it was generally accepted as a basis for British history to the end of the Arthurian period. Yet it was seldom accepted without reserve. Even the monk of Ursicampum three times remarks that the *Historia Britonum* does not agree with other authorities and is perhaps not to be credited.[1] The earlier compilers for the most part limited themselves[2] to taking from it a few brief notices. The same is true of a considerable number of chroniclers to the end. And even those who follow Geoffrey closely[3] often omit his most romantic and obviously fabulous episodes and many of his minute details. Sometimes a chronicler who makes much use of Geoffrey rejects his account of the coming of the Saxons in favor of that of

II, 402, No. 545); 4934, no. 1 (Hardy, II, 282, No. 381); 4938 (Hardy, III, 161, No. 272). — College of Arms, London, MSS.: X, fols. 39–114 (Hardy, III, 344, No. 567); Norfolk liii (Hardy, I, 555, No. 1129). — Lambeth MSS.: 371, no. 18 (Hardy, III, 43, No. 73); 527, fols. 1–43 (Hardy, III, 197, No. 324); 371, no. 16, fol. 32b (Hardy, III, 201, No. 337). — Pub. Record Office, London, MS. *Liber S. August. Cant.* (Hardy, III, 383, No. 644). — Univ. of Cambridge MSS.: I. i. 6. 24 (Hardy, III, 145, No. 243); Ll. 2. 14 (Hardy, III, 263, No. 471). — Corp. Christ. Coll. Cant. MSS.: 59. 14 (Hardy, III, 46, 291, Nos. 85, 520); 138 (Hardy, III, 145, No. 246); 194 (Hardy, III, 165, No. 282); 301, 7 (Hardy, III, 361, No. 596); 369, 3 (Hardy, III, 43, No. 75); 427, 3 (Hardy, III, 161, No. 273); 438, 4 (Hardy, III, 360, No. 595); 469, 4 (Hardy, I, 500, No. 1062). — Trin. Coll. Cant. MS. R. 14. 9. 1 (Hardy, III, 25, No. 34). — Coll. Emman. Cant. MS. serie 2a. 16 (Hardy, III, 207, No. 349). — Trin. Coll. Oxon. MS. X, fols. 1–182 (Hardy, III, 198, No. 326, and III, 283, No. 509); Coll. Jesu Oxon. 111. 10 (Red Book of Hergest), col. 516 (Hardy, III, 366, No. 605). — Other chronicles mentioned by Hardy. I, 360, No. 844; I, 585; III, 149, No. 254; III, 312, No. 555; III, 291, No. 518.

[1] Ann. 470, fol. 18a; ann. 491, fol. 21b; ann. 542, fols. 27b–28a.

[2] This, however, is often a necessary result of their plan and method.

[3] For example, Richard of Cirencester, though he happens to draw from "Matthew of Westminster" instead of directly from Geoffrey.

Bede.   Sometimes the narrative of Arthur's reign is abbreviated, —
particularly toward the end,[1] or (as in the *Chronicon* of Nicholas of
Gloucester[2]) in the story of the last battle.   Sometimes one of the
chroniclers even speaks contemptuously of Geoffrey with reference
to these sections, as is the case with the Canon of Lanercost.[3]

Moreover, even from the first, there were some writers who formed
a still juster estimate of the real character of Geoffrey's narrative.
Mention has already been made of the vehement denunciation of
Geoffrey by William of Newburgh, who seems to hit the truth very
nearly when he accuses him of inventing his history on the basis
of ancient fables.   Another outspoken opponent was Giraldus Cambrensis.   Once or twice he mentions the *Historia*, coupling it with
Geoffrey's name, as a thing of naught.[4]   One of these cases is famous.
Giraldus says that a certain Meilerius, of the region of Urbs Legionum, being possessed by devils, was by them endowed with the
capacity of discovering any falsehood with which he was brought
into contact.   When the Gospel of John was laid on his lap, the
devils vanished ; but when Geoffrey's *History* was substituted, they
returned in greater numbers than ever.[5]   In other places[6] Giraldus,
in referring to statements of his adversaries that the claim of
St. David's is among the fictions about Arthur, evidently does not
object to the implication against the Arthurian stories.

Nevertheless, Giraldus certainly accepts many of Geoffrey's statements, including : — the story of the begetting of Merlin by an
incubus and the naming of Kairmerdin from him (with a reference to the *Britannica historia*) ;[7] Merlin's removal of the Great

---

[1] This, indeed, sometimes happens in manuscripts of Geoffrey's *History* itself.

[2] Fols. 99b, 100a.   Cf. p. 137, note 1, above, and contrast p. 120.

[3] Fol. 27a, col. 1.

[4] Cf. *Descr. Kambriae*, i, 7, *Opera*, VI, 179.   But here he seems to do
Geoffrey injustice (cf. Geoffrey, xii, 19 ; ii, 4–6).

[5] *Itin. Kambriae*, i, 5, pp. 57–58.   This incident furnishes a parallel to what
Wace says about Merlin's spirits (cf. also pp. 139–140, above) ; for Giraldus states
that through the help of the devils the man could predict the future.

[6] *De Invect.*, iv, 2, p. 78 ; *De Jure et Statu M. E.*, dist. vii, p. 328 ; *Spec.
Eccles.*, dist. iii, p. 149.

[7] *Itin. Kambriae*, i, 10, p. 80 ; ii, 8, p. 133.

Circle from Kildare to Salisbury Plain;[1] Arthur's conquest of Ireland;[2] the famous court of Arthur at Urbs Legionum, with the coming of the Roman legates thither,[3] and the former ecclesiastical supremacy of the city;[4] Dubricius's transference of the primacy to St. David;[5] the idea that David was Arthur's uncle;[6] some prophecies of Merlin.[7] Still, there is no certainty how many of these incidents Geoffrey had from previous tradition, or, if he really invented them, how many had passed into general currency before Giraldus's time. In using some of them Giraldus may not have been drawing from Geoffrey, or may not have been aware that he was doing so. It is unfortunate that in the uncertain state of the question Giraldus's evidence cannot be certainly interpreted. Where, however, he cites the "Britannica historia" (namely, in the incident of the birth of Merlin, and in the account of the peopling of Ireland), there is no doubt that he is using Geoffrey.

It is not until a hundred and fifty years later, in the middle of the fourteenth century, that we find, in Ralph Higden, another historian who expresses great distrust of Geoffrey. Higden's attitude is similar to that which we shall meet in many of the sixteenth-century chroniclers who wrote in English. As he himself says,[8] it is only where Geoffrey's account appears extravagant that he questions it, — that is, from the beginning of the Arthurian period. That the less romantic earlier portion might be equally false seems not to have occurred to him. Accordingly, though he sometimes puts Geoffrey's statements side by side with contradictory ones

---

[1] *Top. Hib.*, ii, 18, p. 100. [2] *Top. Hib.*, iii, 8, p. 148.

[3] *Itin. Kambriae*, i, 5, p. 56; cf. *Descr. Kambriae*, i, 4, p. 169.

[4] *Itin. Kambriae*, i, 5, p. 56; *De Jure*, dist. ii, p. 170.

[5] *Itin. Kambriae*, ii, 1, p. 101, and places already cited; also *De Invect.*, ii, 1, p. 46. [6] *De Vita Sancti Davidis*, i, p. 378.

[7] See pp. 92–93, above. For instances not connected with the Arthurian material see: Geoffrey, i, 16, 13 and 21; Giraldus, *De Invect.*, ii, 1, pp. 44–45; *De Jure*, dist. ii, pp. 169–170; *Descr. Kambriae*, i, 1, p. 165; i, 7, p. 178. — Geoffrey, ii, 5; Giraldus, *Descr. Kambriae*, i, 5, p. 171. — Geoffrey, iii, 9; Giraldus, *Descr. Kambriae*, ii, 2, p. 207. — Geoffrey, iv, 17; Giraldus, *De Prin. Instruct.*, dist. i, p. 95. — Geoffrey, iii, 11; Giraldus, *Top. Hib.*, dist. iii, chap. 8, p. 148; *Expug. Hib.*, ii, 6, p. 319. [8] VI, 160.

from other authors, and often draws from Alfred of Beverley's summary rather than directly from Geoffrey, yet he includes almost all
the substance of Geoffrey's narrative up to the Arthurian period.
Indeed, he includes an outline of everything as far as the time of
Arthur himself, — discarding the story of Vortigern's tower as being
found (he says) only in "the British book," expressing doubts as
to the removal of the Stonehenge rocks from Ireland, and omitting
the magic elements from the account of Uther's amour, which he
converts into a lawful marriage.[1]   For Arthur's reign,[2] however, he
cites what is said by Henry of Huntingdon of the twelve battles,
William of Malmesbury's eulogy, and material from other sources ;
and then remarks that many wonder how the exploits which Geoffrey alone ascribes to Arthur can be true, since they are not
mentioned by Roman, French, or Saxon historians.   Probably, he
concludes, the British praise Arthur extravagantly, just as every
other nation exalts its particular hero.

Higden was perhaps the most popular of all the mediæval English
chroniclers ; but how impossible it was for such views to resist the
current of uncritical enthusiasm among the majority of his compatriots, is evidenced by the fact that Trevisa (who, after a quarter of
a century or more, translated his work into the vernacular) makes
vigorous objections.   Arthur is often over-praised, says Trevisa,[3]
but so are many others : "Soþ sawes beeþ nevere þe wors þey madde
men telle magel tales."[4]

Of the actual divergences from Geoffrey's story in chronicles
which for the most part follow it, some are evidently due to inexactness of statement in condensing, to carelessness, or to wilful
exaggeration.   There are a good many minor variations of this sort,
— such as the statement of the monk of Ursicampum[5] that it was
Constans whom the Romans persuaded to build a wall ; of Rishanger[6] that Arthur was crowned at Stonehenge; of the *Hales Chronicon*[7]

---

[1] Cf. pp. 184, 233, 242, 247, below.   [2] V, 328–338.   [3] V, 339.
[4] Stowe, in his "Briefe Proofe of Brute" (*Annales*, ed. Howes, 1631, pp. 6–7 ;
repeated by Howes in his *Historical Preface*), says that John of Whethamstede
opposed Geoffrey, but I cannot find anything to that effect in the editions of
Whethamstede's *Registrum Abbatiae* by Hearne and by Riley (Rolls Series, 1872).
[5] Fol. 9a.   [6] *Annales*, ann. 516.   [7] Fol. 7a.

that Hoel was son of Loth and Anna and brother of Walwanus and Modredus; of Walter of Coventry[1] that from the slaughter of the British chiefs Vortigern and Eldolf fled to Kambria, and that in *one battle* Arthur killed two giants and three hundred and seventy men.[2] MS. Cleop. A. i. 1. even confuses Vortimer with Vortigern. By a rather stupid blunder Frollo is called "Thomas Fullo," in several chronicles,[3] apparently[4] by a misreading of Geoffrey's *"Flolloni Romae tribuno."*[5] Evidently from Geoffrey's statement[6] that at the death of Constans, Aurelius and Uther were children and that Vortigern took the crown because he saw no one equal to himself, Richard of Cirencester unjustifiably concludes that Vortigern easily became king because almost all the other British chiefs were youths and children. Whether by error or by inference, the writer of one unimportant chronicle says that it was in Ireland that Arthur killed one of the giants.[7] Alfred of Beverley and others infer that, in order to marry Hengist's daughter, Vortigern put away his first wife.[8] It is a matter of course that some chronicles, like that ascribed to Peter Ickham,[9] blame Vortigern directly for the death of Constantine.[10]

More important is the confusion, which occurs in some of the early chronicles, between Arthur's two campaigns in France,[11] — a confusion which in the *Flores Historiarum* led to much greater condensation and more omissions than appear in other parts of its version of the story. With the compiler of the *Flores*, indeed, this must have been a deliberate emendation.

---

[1] Pp. 9, 10.   [2] Cf. p. 231, note 4, below.

[3] This error occurs in Peter Langtoft, in one of the French compilations (see p. 212, below) and in a few of the Latin chronicles (e.g., in that of the Canon of Lanercost, fol. 26b 2; also MS. Bodl. Rawl. 150, fol. 22b).

[4] As P. Paris pointed out in his discussion of Langtoft (see p. 199, note 8, below).

[5] ix, 11, 33.   [6] vi, 8 and 9.   [7] MS. Harl. 3860, no. 1.

[8] Sprott's surprising remark (p. 92) that the three ships which first came to Britain in the time of Vortigern were manned respectively by Angles, Saxons, and *Picts*, is doubtless due to a scribal error like that in Trevisa (v, 1; V, 265), where *Pictes* is written for *Iutes*, which is correctly given later in the same line.

[9] MS. Calig. A. x. 1, fol. 18b.   [10] Cf. p. 40, above.

[11] Monk of Ursicampum; monk of Winchester (Rich. of Devizes?), ann. 519; *Flores Hist.*, ann. 536–542 (I, 239–242). See also p. 122, above, p. 212, below.

The author of the *Flores* makes another emendation, seemingly on moral grounds,[1] when, by omitting all mention of Uther's getting into Igerna's castle before the death of Gorlois, he, like Higden later,[2] makes it appear that Arthur was a legitimate child.[3] In this, however, his example had little influence.

The desire to make the narrative clearer or supply better motivation[4] is the cause of occasional slight alterations of Geoffrey's story, like that in the *Flores* where it is said[5] that Vortigern tried to build his tower because the Britons had sent for Aurelius and Uther.

It is interesting to note in one of the earliest of these chroniclers, Ralph de Diceto, an extension, already practised by the French author of the work on the foundation of the towns in Touraine,[6] of Geoffrey's method of applying to the Arthurian period the conditions of his own time.   Ralph says[7] that Arthur gave Anjou and Touraine to Cheuno (Cajus), that he might have the double honor of being both seneschal and standard-bearer, an idea on which Ralph enlarges.

Very rarely one of the chroniclers adds a touch which appears to go back, whether directly or not, to some tradition older than Geoffrey. The character of extreme immorality which the author of the *Flores* gives to Vortigern at considerable length,[8] while it does not correspond verbally with the description by William of Malmesbury,[9] is so like it in effect that it seems to come from a similar source.   The same idea reappears in Richard of Cirencester. How rapidly some features of Geoffrey's own story passed into tradition, appears when the compiler of the *Flores* observes that some identify the fountain by whose means Uther was poisoned with one which St. Alban caused to spring out of the ground.[10]   The same author localizes another episode of the narrative when, in dividing the double battle in which Hengist is captured into two conflicts fought in different years, he locates the second on the river Don.[11]

---

[1] Cf. pp. 119, 161, above, pp. 196, 205, 233, 245, 270, below.

[2] See p. 182, above.   [6] Cf. p. 122, above.

[3] Ann. 498, pp. 228–229.   [7] *Opuscula*, II, 241, based on Geoffrey, ix, 11.

[4] Cf. p. 134, above.   [8] I, 185.

[5] Ann. 464.   [9] Cf. p. 40, above.   [10] Ann. 516, p. 233.

[11] Ann. 487–489, p. 220 ; Geoffrey, viii, 5–6. Cf. p. 261, below.

The localization of Arthur himself, which has left its traces over the whole of England, and certainly began before the time of Geoffrey,[1] is indicated by Giraldus when he mentions[2] Arthur's Chair in a mountain chain in the southeast of Wales.

It was inevitable that those chroniclers who combine Geoffrey's story with the statements of previous historians should modify Geoffrey in the process. Higden, recognizing the incompatibility of the accounts of Constantine, the father of Constans, as given respectively by Bede and by Geoffrey, was led to suppose that they referred to different persons, and therefore to make two Constantines out of one, a procedure which was to be followed by one or two of the later English chroniclers.[3] The author of the *Flores*, in introducing "Nathanliot" from the Saxon version of the story (through Henry of Huntingdon),[4] finds himself compelled to represent him as leader of Uther's army, taking the suggestion from what Geoffrey says of Lot,[5] which the *Flores*, however, reproduces after telling of the death of Nathanliot. The monk of Ursicampum suggests the possible identity of Arthur with Riothimir.[6] Geoffrey himself in his *Cherdicus*, and again apparently in his two *Cheldricus*es, probably preserves, though in disguise, the figure of the Saxon king Cerdic. The monk of Winchester seems to try to explain the successful establishment of the latter by the fact of Arthur's absence on the continent, and he says that during that time the Saxons made fortifications on all the high hills.[7] The *Chronicon* called Peter Ickham's[8] states summarily that Arthur made tributaries the Angles who remained. Other chronicles, including that of Higden,[9] make

---

[1] For example, Arthur's Chair in Cornwall is mentioned in the account of the journey of the Laon monks (see p. 101, above).

[2] *Itin. Kambriae*, i, 2 (*Opera*, VI, 36).

[3] Holinshed (see p. 268, below); contrast Stow (see p. 266, below).

[4] Ann. 508, p. 230.   [5] viii, 21.

[6] Ann. 470, fol. 18a; cf. pp. 82–83, above.

[7] *Annales de Wintonia*, ann. 519.

[8] MS. Calig. A. x., fol. 20a. Some other chronicles (for example, that of the Monastery of Hales, fol. 7b) make the statement, evidently following this *Chronicon*.

[9] The earliest that I have observed is that of MS. Cleop. A. i. 1. For Higden, whose version is a little abbreviated, see v, 6 (V, 330). He refers to previous

a more detailed attempt to reconcile the conflicting authorities, — an attempt which was later followed by some of the English writers. Cerdic, it is said, often fought with Arthur, and though frequently defeated, at last wearied him out, so that in the twenty-sixth year[1] after Cerdic's arrival, Arthur gave him Hampshire and Somerset and took his oath of allegiance.[2] "It is also said in chronicles of the Angles" that Mordred, wishing to reign, but fearing Cerdic alone, gave him certain districts, and Cerdic was crowned at Winchester and Mordred at London. This all seems to be suggested by Geoffrey's mention of the alliance between Modred and the (apparently) second Cheldrich.[3] The necessity which the annalistic form of almost all the chronicles imposed of assigning definite dates to every part of Geoffrey's narrative, forced their authors to apply to the *History* a standard to which it was never meant to conform, and naturally the results arrived at were diverse.[4] Some manuscripts[5] date the events by regnal years. Generally, however, this treatment was purely incidental; the Latin chroniclers seldom tried to make plain, as most of the English ones did later, how many years Arthur and the other kings ruled.

The chronicles, especially the later ones, show a slight tendency at times to enlarge on the romantic element of the story,[6] though this is perhaps less marked than was to be expected in an age when the Arthurian romances enjoyed such unbounded popularity. Probably the conceptions of the romances are in the mind of Roger of Hoveden when he adds[7] the name of Arthur (for the Britons) to the list of great national heroes to whom his source had compared King Edgar, and in that of Matthew Paris when, in his smaller work, the *Historia Anglorum*, he says, with reference to the greatness of the court of Henry II, that it seemed as if the times of Arthur were come again.[8] Gervase of Tilbury, speaking of Arthur's solemn and incomparable court at Caerleon, has it that there were present

---

works as his sources, and two of his manuscripts specify "in chronicis Dunensis." Rudborne also includes the account, book ii, chap. i.

[1] Cf. p. 159, above.
[2] Cf. pp. 251, 258, below.
[3] xi, 1, 12.
[4] Cf. p. 159, above.
[5] For example, Cleop. A. i. 1.
[6] Cf. p. 138, above.
[7] I, 64.
[8] Ann. 1176 (I, 397).

the Twelve Peers of France,[1] who, as he tells us just before, were instituted when Arthur was at Paris.[2] The natural tendency of tradition to associate famous names is illustrated when the chronicle ascribed to Peter Ickham[3] states that Gildas was Arthur's chaplain.[4] The scribe of one of the late manuscripts of the *Eulogium Historiarum* has inserted, at the mention of the twelve years' peaceful sojourn in Britain, a eulogy of Arthur, exalting him and the knights of the Round Table above all the others in the world. It was inevitable that some writers[5] should represent Arthur as having already crossed the Alps when Modred's treason called him home.[6] Gawain is often painted in much the same colors as in the romances. Walter of Coventry, for example, speaks of him as without a peer.[7] Not only does the *Flores Historiarum* copy from William of Malmesbury a mention of the discovery of Gawain's body,[8] but Matthew Paris adds,[9] evidently with reference to the same set of traditions, that Arthur gave Gawain his principality.[10] The Round Table is not infrequently mentioned, especially in the later chronicles. Gervase of Tilbury says[11] that Arthur established it *in insula Fatata*. More essentially in the spirit of the French romances are the statement of Sprott that when Arthur was in France he held the Round Table for forty days,[12] and the notice in the Magdalen College MS. 72, which says that Arthur established the Table by the advice of Merlin,[13] and gives at some length the laws which were prescribed for its members. As early as Ralph de Diceto there occurs an attempt to etymologize the name of Arthur's sword connecting it with a stream of magic properties in Western Britain;[14] and the name which Ralph gives to the stream, *Calibi,* suggests Merlin's

---

[1] ii, 17, Leibnitz, I, 936; cf. p. 87, above.   [2] Leibnitz, I, 936.

[3] So, at least, Wharton's copy (MS. Harl. 4323), at the end of the account of Arthur's reign.

[4] Contrast Geoffrey's Pyramus (see p. 80, above).

[5] Like the author of Brit. Mus. MS. Bibl. Reg. 13. D. i.

[6] Cf. pp. 202, 252, below.   [7] P. 11.   Cf. pp. 104–105, above.

[8] Ann. 1087 (II, 23).   It is mentioned also in the *Chronicon of the Monastery of Hales,* fol. 8a.   [9] *Hist. Angl.,* I, 33.

[10] Cf. p. 105, above.   [11] P. 936.   [12] P. 95.   [13] P. 47.

[14] I, 96.   See also the entry from the other MS. under the year 516.

fountain Galabes,[1] though possibly it may be connected with the Latin *chalybs*, because of the association with the sword. The chronicle ascribed to Peter Ickham, which devotes but one small page to Arthur's reign, gives a considerable part of that page to the account of Arthur's fights with the two giants.[2] The Magdalen College MS. says that Modred was Arthur's son by a concubine.[3] The idea of Arthur's second coming, mentioned not by Geoffrey but by Wace and Layamon, is not infrequently alluded to by the Latin chroniclers as a foolish British superstition.[4] A very interesting and decidedly extended story of Arthur's disappearance,[5] — quite different from anything related elsewhere, though having in parts an ultimate connection with versions like those of Layamon and the Prose *Lancelot*, — is given in the *Chronicon of the Monastery of Hales*. This tells how Arthur, as he sits weary and wounded after the battle, is treacherously stabbed with a poisoned spear by a warrior, whom he kills ; how he is carried to Venedotia and dies there ; and how, in a dark and violent storm which accompanies his obsequies, his body is inexplicably lost to sight.[6] The Hales *Chronicon* quotes also from Henry of Huntingdon's letter in describing the last battle and Arthur's personal conflict with Modred.[7] Seemingly from the version of this latter episode which appears in the Prose *Lancelot* is taken the account in the Magdalen College MS. As early as with Gervase of Tilbury,[8] and also in Thomas Sprott,[9] occurs that form of the story of Arthur's immortality which locates his resting place in the recesses of Mount Etna.[10] Gervase

---

[1] Geoffrey, viii, 10, 14.

[2] These are also made prominent in the brief abstract of Geoffrey in Cotton MS. Vesp. E. iv., no. 5, fol. 107b.

[3] Cf. p. 141, above.   [4] Cf. p. 101, above.

[5] Printed in *Publications of the Mod. Lang. Assoc.*, 1903, XVIII, 86–87.

[6] Cf. pp. 164–165, above.   [7] Cf. p. 120, above.

[8] *Otia Imperialia*, ii, 12, Leibnitz, I, 921 ; Liebrecht, p. 12.   [9] P. 96.

[10] Cf. p. 145 (with note 5), above. The story is repeated in a slightly different form, a few years after Gervase, by Cæsarius of Heisterbach (*Dialogus Miraculorum*, ed. Strange, 1851, xii, 12). Cæsarius refers again to Arthur as a subject of popular stories (iv, 36). Another fuller thirteenth-century form is found in Étienne de Bourbon ; see A. Graf, *Miti, leggende, e superstizioni del medio evo*, II, 303 ff., who discusses the story at length.

also states that members of what modern scholars call the Wild Hunt had told foresters in Britain and Brittany that they were of the household of Arthur.[1] The first indication of influence by the Grail story[2] appears in the jottings at the end of Robert of Avesbury, which trace Arthur's descent back to Joseph of Arimathea. They also carry back to *Petrus, consanguineus Joseph,* the race of Loth, husband of Arthur's sister, and name as their sons not only Walwanus, but also Agrauains, Gweheres, and Gaheries.

Skeptical as the chroniclers might show themselves about attributing supernatural exploits to laymen, most of them were credulous enough to a certain point when it came to the question of a prophet and professional magus. Hence the great majority of them accept Merlin, at least in his prophetic rôle. Many of them insert at the proper places mentions of parts of his predictions which they suppose to have been fulfilled, sometimes[3] predictions which are not given by Geoffrey and must probably be counted among the many which were composed and ascribed to Merlin after and in consequence of Geoffrey's *History*. While few of the chronicles include the prophecies as given by Geoffrey *in toto*,[4] the *Flores Historiarum* makes an exception,[5] and Matthew Paris adds a detailed interpretation of the first part.[6] The compiler of the *Flores* takes it for granted that Merlin is a thoroughly supernatural person; for he says that before giving Ambrosius advice about the Stonehenge monument, Merlin went into an ecstasy.[7]

Besides the account of the Arthurian period which they took from previous sources, the chroniclers record several interesting episodes testifying to the belief of their own contemporaries in the Arthurian tradition. Of these, the most important is the supposed discovery of Arthur's body at Glastonbury. Giraldus Cambrensis gives the longest account of this affair. In his *De Principis*

---

[1] ii, 12, Leibnitz, I, 921–922; Liebrecht, pp. 12–13.

[2] For later mentions, cf. pp. 211, 230, 252, below.

[3] For example, the Coggeshall Chronicle, p. 146.

[4] Cf. p. 136, above.

[5] I, 198 ff. Also Nicholas of Gloucester, fols. 80a ff. Cf. p. 220, note 3, below.

[6] As far as Geoffrey, vii, 3, 117. Cf. p. 225, below.

[7] Ann. 490, p. 222.

Instructione,[1] written about 1194, he tells how the body, which was of
gigantic size, was found in " our days " at Glastonbury between two
stone pyramids, buried deep in a hollow oak, with a cross of lead inscribed " Here lies buried the renowned king Arthur with Wenneve-
reia his second wife [2] in the isle of Avallonia." And in fact, the
body of a woman lay in the same tomb, with a lock of yellow hair
still well preserved, which crumbled away when a clumsy monk tried
to handle it, — a pretty incident which affords plenty of opportunity
for sentimental symbolistic fancies. The reasons for looking for the
body, says Giraldus, were partly visions which religious men had
had, and above all else the fact that Henry the Second had told the
monks, as he had heard from a British historical poet,[3] that they
would find the body there, interred at least sixteen feet deep; for
Arthur wished to be safely hidden from the Saxons. In his *Speculum
Ecclesiae*,[4] written twenty-five years later, Giraldus repeats the story
with additional details, some of which relate to Modred and may
have been drawn from Geoffrey. He also emphasizes the fact that
the search for the body was due to King Henry. It is interesting
to note how in these passages Giraldus rationalizes the story of
Arthur's disappearance. In the earlier account, he explains that
Morganis, a noble matron and the lady of those regions, a blood
relative of Arthur, took him to Glastonbury for the healing of his
wounds; and in the *Speculum Ecclesiae* he ridicules the Britons for
considering Morganis as *dea quaedam phantastica*.[5]

Different in important details is the account of the discovery
given in the Coggeshall Chronicle,[6] written at about the same time
as Giraldus's *De Principis Instructione*. This dates the event in 1191
(after the death of King Henry), and says that it was caused by
the burial of the body of a monk who had earnestly desired in his
lifetime to be placed in that particular spot. In later chronicles
there appear at least two still different versions, which need not

---

[1] VIII, 126–129.

[2] The idea that Arthur had two wives corresponds substantially with stories
which appear in the triads and seem to go back to the mythical part of the tradition. See Loth, *Mabinogion*, II, 227; Rhŷs, *Arthurian Legend*, pp. 35–37.

[3] *Ab historico cantore Britone antiquo.*   [5] Cf. pp. 101, 146, above.

[4] ii, 8–10; IV, 47–51.   [6] P. 203.

be seriously considered, since one (in the *Annals of Margan*) represents that Modred also was buried in the same tomb, and the other
(included by Albericus Trium Fontium) adds some Latin hexameters (inspired evidently by Joseph of Exeter) said to have been
found with the bodies.

The questions which of the two older accounts is correct and
how it is to be interpreted, are not important to the present subject.[1] But certainly, it is less difficult to believe that the whole
thing was a trick of King Henry, and that he had the bodies
discovered (and in all probability previously placed) under the
pyramids in order to persuade the Welsh that Arthur was really
dead, than to believe that bones buried at so great a depth were
really found by accident.[2] A passage in William of Malmesbury's
De Antiquitate Glastoniensis Ecclesiae[3] shows that as early as the first
half of the twelfth century the Glastonbury monks had invented the
story that Arthur and Guenevere were buried between the pyramids.

King Henry, Giraldus says, had the bodies magnificently rein-
terred. According to some of the later chroniclers, that other king
who found Welsh national sentiment so troublesome, Edward I, had
still another splendid monument erected for them.[4]

Not only was Arthur's body thought to have been found, but it
also was believed that some of his possessions were still in existence

---

[1] Cf. *Ztsch. f. franz. Spr.*, XII, 231–256; Rhŷs, *Arthurian Legend*, pp. 328–347;
Y Cymmrodor, IX, 180, note; Pearson, in Stuart-Glennie's *Arthurian Localities*,
pp. 135–136.

[2] See for the whole incident, San-Marte's *Gottfried*, pp. 417–430. Giraldus's
first version is copied by Higden (vii, 23; VIII, 60) and from Higden by Knighton
(chap. 12, I, 149–150). The Coggeshall version reappears in the *Flores* (ann.
1191; II, 379). The discovery, or the fact of the burial, is merely mentioned by
Matthew Paris (*Hist. Angl.*, at 1191; II, 27), Gervase of Canterbury (II, 19), Rishanger (*Annales*, ann. 516), Higden (V, 332), *Chron. Monast. de Hales* (fol. 8a),
Eulogium Historiarum (at mention of Arthur's death, II, 363, and again, III, 90),
Sprott (first part, ann. 1195), Leland (*Assertio Arturii*, fols. 22–23), and various
others. "Matthew of Westminster," ann. 542, I, 269, expands the statement that
Arthur wished his body to be hidden from the Saxons. Cf. p. 197, below.

[3] Gale, I, 306.

[4] Elmham, viii, 81, p. 265; Adam de Domerham, II, 588–589. *The Annals of
Waverley* (at 1277) disagree.

in the twelfth and following centuries. His sword Caliburn was said to have been given to Tancred by King Richard I when he was passing through Sicily on his way to the Holy Land. This statement was made by Benedict of Peterborough[1] only a year or two after the event, and is repeated in several of the later chronicles.[2] Others report[3] that one of the tokens of the complete conquest of Wales by Edward I was the surrender to him by the Welsh of Arthur's crown, which they had long kept in great honor. The same king Edward is associated in still a third way with the Arthurian story; for in 1301, when presenting to the Pope his claim to supremacy over Scotland, he cited from Geoffrey's narrative the cases of submission of kings of the Scots to those of England, prominent among which was that of Auguselus to Arthur.[4]

---

[1] Ann. 1191, II, 159.

[2] Roger of Hoveden, III, 97 ; Walter of Coventry, I, 433.

[3] " Matthew of Westminster," ann. 1283, I, 269 ; *Annals of Waverley*, ann. 1283; *Annals of Worcester*, ann. 1284.

[4] Rishanger's *Chronica*, p. 201, whence it is copied by Walsingham in his *Hist. Angl.* and *Ypodigma Neustriae*. Edward's whole letter is printed in Rymer's *Foedera*, ed. 1727, II, 883–884 (wrongly numbered 863–864).

CHAPTER VII

THE STORY AFTER GEOFFREY: THE MIDDLE ENGLISH AND CONTEMPORARY ANGLO-FRENCH METRICAL CHRONICLES

Down to the end of the thirteenth century, the knowledge of history was practically confined (in England, as elsewhere) to the religious and noble or wealthy classes; in England, that is, to those who could read works written in Latin or French. But the development of Norman-English nationality, and the reëmergence of the Saxon population and the English language, if slow were yet constant, and by the year 1300 there were many persons outside the monasteries who were glad to learn in the English tongue something about the past of their country and their race. It was perhaps a matter of course that the first chronicles written for them should be in verse rather than in prose.

In considering these works, it is necessary to remember always that while in form they resemble rather those of Layamon and Wace than the Latin prose chronicles, yet as regards substance they are to be classed with the latter, since they are complete histories of England reaching from Brutus down, generally, to the dates at which they were severally composed.

I. ROBERT OF GLOUCESTER

The earliest of these chronicles was written somewhere in the southwest of England probably a little before the end of the thirteenth century, and goes under the name of Robert of Gloucester.[1]

---

[1] Ed. W. A. Wright (Rolls), 2 vols., 1887; see Preface, especially pp. xv–xviii and xix–xxxiii. See also letters in the *Athenæum* for 1888 by W. H. Cooke, May 12, p. 600; June 30, p. 828; with replies by Wright, May 19, p. 630, and

As to the author and authorship, however, only this much is certain, that up to the death of Henry I the two recensions represented by existing manuscripts are substantially identical, except that there are considerable additions in the so-called second version, which, after Henry I, is much briefer than the other; and that the continuation in the first recension, from Henry I, was written after 1297 by a certain Robert, who was probably a monk, but whom there is no reason for connecting with Gloucester.

No one can claim for this first distinctively English chronicle a high degree of literary merit. It is composed in irregular doggerel couplets, and the author does not try to conceal the fact that he is addressing the common and little-lettered people, — as when he omits the greater part of the prophecies of Merlin, on the ground that they are not easily understood by the unlearned.[1] Yet his lack of inspiration may easily be exaggerated. He sometimes uses his own judgment in changing the order of events as given in his sources.[2] Once in a while he has a really poetic phrase.[3] Like Layamon, he is deeply interested in his subject, as he shows by occasional appeals to his readers[4] or outbursts of personal feeling.[5] He visualizes many scenes by expanding and vivifying the description[6] or adding a slight touch, — as when he says that the men of Merlin's town dared not refuse to give him to Vortigern's messengers,[7] or that, when Arthur had unhorsed " Fullon," he had to turn his own steed before he could begin the attack with the sword.[8] Occasionally he has a suggestion of dramatic power[9] or grim irony[10] that reminds one of Layamon. He is thoroughly patriotic, but, like Layamon, on the side of the Britons,[11] though he distinctly states

---

July 14, p. 64. See also, Hardy, III, 181, and Morley, *English Writers*, III, 337; and especially two German dissertations on Robert, *Über die Quellen*, etc., one by W. Ellmer (Halle, 1886, pp. 14–19, 27, 37), the other by K. Brossmann (Striegau, 1887, bibliography, and pp. 11, 44, 47).

[1] V. 2820; cf. p. 136, above.   [2] See instances noted by Ellmer.
[3] Cf. v. 2783 with Geoffrey, vi, 19, 26.   [4] For example, v. 2308.
[5] For example, on the massacre of the British chiefs, and vv. 2953, 4505.
[6] For example, vv. 2281 ff., 4221 ff.   [7] V. 2732.   [8] V. 3827.
[9] For example, vv. 2762 ff., Merlin's trial of skill with the magi.
[10] As vv. 4541–4542, on Guenevere's avoiding Arthur.
[11] Cf. vv. 2578, 3272.

that it is from the Saxons that the English of his own time are descended.[1]

As far as Geoffrey's *History* extends, this chronicle is chiefly a paraphrase of it. But in the first two thousand lines, before the Arthurian period, the author makes some use of the early Latin chronicles, of tradition, and of one or two other sources. In the Arthurian portion also,[2] he introduces similar slight additions from Henry of Huntingdon,[3] or from his own stock of general information.[4] He adds a few dates, as when he says[5] that Hengist had been in the land forty years when he was killed.[6] In forms of proper names,[7] slight misinterpretations and other instances of carelessness, abbreviations, expansions, and other minor changes natural in the recasting of the story, his chronicle exhibits variations from Geoffrey quite similar to those in the other paraphrases.[8]

---

[1] Vv. 2696–2697. On all these points cf. vv. 2264–2269, 3217.

[2] Vv. 2259–4596.

[3] As, the fight of Constantine with the Picts and Scots (v. 2260; cf. p. 42, above); the list of kings of the Saxons (vv. 3425 ff.); the seven years' period (v. 2577; cf. p. 39, note 2, above).

[4] As, the identification of " Frie " with Venus (vv. 2433–2434); the statement that Europe constitutes one third part of the world (vv. 3761–3762); or that the demons which have intercourse with women are called elves, and that sometimes they come to men in the form of women (v. 2753; cf. pp. 118, 162, above).

[5] V. 2995; cf. p. 159, above.

[6] The idea (see ten Brink, *Hist. Eng. Lit.*, Eng. transl., I, 276) that the author drew from Wace and Layamon is probably erroneous, as the few coincidences (Robert, vv. 3353 ff., Wace, vv. 8995 ff.; Robert, vv. 2522–2528, Layamon, vv. 14,339–14,353; Robert, vv. 2671–2672, Layamon, vv. 15,256–15,259) may easily be due to chance; though the author of the second continuation, beginning with Henry I, certainly made use of Layamon (see Wright, pp. 783 ff., xxxiii–xxxviii).

[7] Cf. Ellmer, pp. 23–26.

[8] Thus, he says that Vortiger in vain bade the ecclesiastics crown Constans (v. 2314) and that Vortiger had planned that all should happen as it did (vv. 2369 ff.). He inaptly changes Geoffrey's statement (vi, 13, 30) that the pagan newcomers had married daughters of the Britons, by saying that some fathers were Christian and the mothers heathen (v. 2563). For Maugantius he has "clerkes" (v. 2747). He says carelessly (v. 3080) that Ambrose was another name for Uther (but cf. the prose *Merlin*, where, at the beginning of chap. 2, it is said that Constans's sons are Moine, Pandragon, and Uter, — a case of complicated confusion which Paris, in the introduction to the *Huth Merlin*, says is

Worthy of mention as illustrating general tendencies in the history of the story are: his change in the account of Uther's fight with the Saxons, making it much more advantageous for the Britons;[1] his change, in the interests of morality, of Merlin's sympathy for Uther in his love for Ygerna, into regret for the king's folly;[2] his consistent application to Lucye of the title "senatour of Rome,"[3] and his elimination of Geoffrey's confusion about Leo.[4] He drops out some of the traditional elements of the narrative which for him have lost their meaning:[5] viz., Geoffrey's emphasis on the special help of the Armoricans in the wars; the description of the second and third wonderful lakes in Scotland;[6] the account of Arthur's feast at York, and the ecclesiastical promotions then and part of those at the coronation feast;[7] the statement that the duel with "Fullon" was on an island;[8] all mention of the fight with Ritho;[9] the coming of Hiderus's force to help the Britons, and the names of other warriors in later battles. He substitutes "an vatte barn"[10] for the pigs which Geoffrey said the giant was roasting — probably in the wish to remove a triviality; and says that it was because Arthur was weary that he commanded Bedwer to cut off the giant's head.[11] He calls Bedwer and Kay kings.[12]

Like Layamon and Wace, but to a greater extent, Robert is influenced by the conceptions of the Arthurian romances.[13] He thinks of Merlin altogether as an enchanter,[14] and takes pains to say several times that his prophecies were fulfilled.[15] Now and then his

---

original with the author of the *Merlin*). He adds checkers to the games which the youths played at Arthur's feast (v. 3965). He changes Geoffrey's account of Arthur's dream and the explanations, perhaps partly by misunderstanding (vv. 4146 ff.). He says that the German "Chelrik" brought Saxons to Britain (v. 4522).

[1] Vv. 3251 ff.; Geoffrey, viii, 18. Cf. p. 118, above.
[2] V. 3319; Geoffrey, viii, 19, 58–59. Cf. p. 184, above.
[3] V. 3988, etc.   [10] V. 4212.
[4] Vv. 4146 ff.; cf. p. 85, note 2, above.
[5] Cf. p. 136, above.   [11] V. 4243.
[6] Cf. p. 216, below.   [12] Vv. 4403–4405; cf. p. 105, above.
[7] V. 3980.   [13] Cf. p. 138, above.
[8] V. 3820.   [14] Vv. 3109, 3124–3125.
[9] V. 4345.   [15] Vv. 2816, 3461, 3849.

phraseology has something of a romance coloring, as when he says of Uther's feast,[1] "mony was þe vayre leuedi þat icome was þerto." He seems to assume that Gawain is well known,[2] and calls him "flour of corteysye."[3] He speaks several times of the Round Table.[4] He states directly that Guenevere was guilty and not a victim of Modred's violence.[5] Geoffrey had perhaps implied this by omitting any suggestion that Guenevere resisted Modred, and by speaking of her fear of Arthur and her flight from him when he returned to England; but Robert asserts, like a true mediæval monk, that it was at her advice that Modred committed treason.[6] Robert also greatly magnifies Arthur. He is the "beste bodi þat euere was in þis londe,[7] and never had any peer in prowess [8] or in courtesy."[9] He says [10] of "Calibourne," not that it was made in Avalon (that he omits,[11] doubtless as an incredible falsehood), but "nas nour no such ich wene." He even has a decided reverence for the sword, and calls it "sire."[12] It is a personal grief to Robert when Arthur's end approaches.[13] But he characterizes [14] the hope of Arthur's return,[15] which he ascribes to Britons and "Cornwallisse of is kunde," as unreasonable, because Arthur's bones have been found at Glastonbury and lie there in a fair tomb. Later, at the proper chronological point,[16] he mentions the discovery of the bones and assigns it, evidently erroneously, to the burning of the abbey.[17]

It is in the account of Arthur's last battle that Robert differs most significantly from Geoffrey. He says [18] that, with the possible exception of that of Troy, there was never any greater battle in the world, for there was scarcely any prince on earth who was not either there in person or else sent men. He declares that it was because Modred's men outnumbered Arthur's that most of the latter were

---

[1] V. 3280.
[2] V. 3773; cf. p. 104, above.
[3] V. 4351; cf. v. 4532.
[4] Vv. 3881, 3902, 3916.
[5] Cf. p. 163, above.
[6] V. 4503.
[7] V. 3334.
[8] V. 3480.
[9] Vv. 3747 ff.

[10] V. 3616.
[11] Contrast p. 162, above.
[12] V. 3841.
[13] Vv. 4528, 4552.
[14] Vv. 4585 ff.
[15] Cf. p. 101, above.
[16] Vv. 9852–9853.
[17] Cf. pp. 189–191, above.
[18] Vv. 4491 ff.

killed, and with this turns to the description given by Henry of
Huntingdon in his letter to Warinus,[1] which he follows closely.
After Arthur has smitten off Modred's head, Robert exclaims:
"þat was is laste chiualerye þat vaire endede ynou." A great poet
this simple Englishman is not, but certainly he is genuine and
intense.

II. THE ANONYMOUS SHORT CHRONICLE

As popular as possible in tone and method, like the English metrical romances of *Horn* and *Havelok*, is the chronicle, of the time of
Edward II, which summarizes the history of England from Brutus
to the death of Gaveston in about five hundred tetrameter couplets.[2]
The narrative down to the death of Arthur goes back ultimately
to Geoffrey, but the divergences are so considerable as to indicate,
even when allowance is made for the modifications certain to be
introduced by a strolling poet, that the direct source is some intermediate version. Occasionally the author expands an incident which
was likely to appeal to his audience; but much more distinguishing
features of his treatment are curtailment and omission. It is not
easy to see, however, why he should have left out such an episode
as Uther's amour, unless it was lacking in his source, as was the
case in some of the Latin chronicles. He makes very great alterations in the Arthurian period. He omits Aurelius altogether, and
dismisses Uther with six lines. He brings in Arthur before the
British Lucius and "Fortiger,"[3] evidently because his brief mention
of the latter makes a good transition to the account of the Saxon
period which follows. His narrative of Arthur's reign occupies
only forty-six lines, eight of which are taken up with a personal description of the king; and of definite events he merely
mentions the wars with Luces and Moddred, with the latter's violence to Genevre, not specifying whether or not it was against her

---

[1] Cf. p. 120, above.

[2] Ed. Ritson, *Anc. Eng. Met. Rom.*, 1802, II, 270, from MS. Bibl. Reg. 12. C.
xii., no. 8. Other manuscripts are Auchinleck, and Univ. of Camb. Ff. v. 20.
See Hardy, III, 310, 395, and Skeat, *Lay of Havelok*, E.E.T.S., p. ix.

[3] In this there is a slight resemblance (doubtless accidental) to William of
Malmesbury's account (cf. p. 39, above).

will.[1] He states that Arthur lived ten years after returning to England [2] and winning it back from Moddred, and that he, like Uther, was buried in Glastonbury.[3] His popularization of the story, then, has wrought a complete alteration of some of its most essential features, especially in the interest of the common notion that greatness is measured by success.

It was inevitable that this chronicle should reflect romance ideas.[4] The author's incidental mention of Merlin [5] assumes his current fame as a prophet, and he takes special pains to mention the prowess of Eweyn,[6] though he does not name Gawain or any of the other knights. He alludes also to the great adventures which happened, and magnifies Arthur as a king whose equal never has been known and never can be.

III. Peter Langtoft, and Other French Chronicles

Only a few years after the completion of the "Robert of Gloucester" *Chronicle*, another one of almost exactly the same plan and general character was prepared for the benefit of French-speaking people by a man who, like Gaimar, was a resident of the North of England, and who calls himself [7] "Peres de Langetoft." [8] Of his personal history nothing is known except for a statement made by his paraphraser, Robert Manning,[9] that he was a canon of (the Augustinian priory of) Bridlington, doubtless the village of that name not far from Langtoft in the East Riding of Yorkshire. His work, like many of the Latin chronicles, ends with the death of Edward I, in 1307, which may therefore be accepted as approximately the date of its composition.

As an historian, Langtoft is scarcely worthy of attention — though the number of manuscripts of his work attest its great, if

---

[1] Cf. p. 163, above. [2] Cf. p. 254, below.
[3] Contrast p. 254, below. [4] Cf. p. 138, above.
[5] V. 335. [6] Contrast p. 161, above.
[7] Ed. T. Wright (Rolls Series, 2 vols., 1866–68), I, 264.
[8] See especially I, xi–xii, xxi–xxii. Cf. Hardy, III, 298 ff.; P. Paris, *Hist. litt. de la France*, 1869, XXV, 337–350, especially pp. 339–341, 652–654 ; Morley, *English Writers*, III, 347.
[9] *Chronicle*, ed. Furnivall, vv. 16,703–16,704.

short-lived, popularity; every one who has studied him has specially remarked on the barbarousness of his language; and for
the history of the development of the Arthurian story his chronicle
affords few new facts. Nevertheless, it has some points of real
interest.

It begins with an abbreviated but close paraphrase of Geoffrey's
History, which, though commonplace enough, is not altogether destitute of poetical elements, — such as an effective use of direct
discourse;[1] occasional dramatic treatment[2] of a good scene; a
touch of vividness in narration,[3] or a sarcasm;[4] a good simile,[5] or
(rarely) an allusion to nature.[6] The only episodes entirely omitted
in the Arthurian period, are Vortimer's wars[7] and Merlin's prophecy.[8] No special notice need be taken of most of the inevitable
minor modifications and mistakes in the making over of the story;[9]
but Langtoft's treatment of details is freer than that of his predecessors and some of his alterations deserve mention. He says that
Vortiger was of the "false blood of the Welsh," that he in person
assassinated Constantine,[10] and that he recovered his kingdom by
war. He alters considerably Uther's use of his disguise[11] and the
details of the battle at Verolamium, so that Uther is made to have
a personal encounter with Octa.[12] He specifies "Kardoyl" as
destroyed by Octa and Eosa.[13] He confuses the actions of Arthur
and Cador;[14] says that Arthur had his dragon carried before him;[15]
changes Leo from an emperor into a pope, in connection with
which may be noted his constant mistranslation of *senatus* by "senatour" and his ascription of senatorial rank to Lucius.[16] Some
of Langtoft's emendations are anachronistic; as, — his constant
application of the title "sire" to his heroes; the invocation of the
aid of St. George for the Britons;[17] Arthur's appeal to the authority

---

[1] For instance, pp. 118, 194–196.
[2] As, Uther's conversation with Ulphin and Merlin, and p. 108.
[3] As pp. 172, 214.   [4] P. 216.   [5] Pp. 142, 208.
[6] P. 108.   [7] P. 106.   [8] P. 114; cf. p. 136, above, with note 7.
[9] Including the introduction of "Sir Thomas Frolloun" (cf. p. 183, above).
[10] P. 96. Cf. p. 183, above.   [11] P. 138.   [12] P. 144.
[13] P. 142.   [14] P. 154.   [15] P. 204.
[16] P. 176. He also calls Lucius Emperor (for example, p. 202).   [17] P. 204.

of Solomon for the statement that the Romans are proud and treacherous;[1] the specification of the arms of the barons and "raskayle " at the siege of Gorlois's castle;[2] the mention of laborers as being about their tasks when the Saxons came to Bath,[3] and of the provost of Paris as surrendering the keys;[4] the substitution for Geoffrey's names in the list of nobles at Arthur's feast of the names of lordships important in Langtoft's own day.[5] Interesting to note as a survival of the *chanson de geste* mannerisms is the characterization of two warriors as having flowing beards.[6] With Langtoft also appears the loss of originally mythic-traditional elements of the story in the omission of Ritho and in the statement that Arthur himself cut off the giant's head.[7] Possible borrowings from current popular versions of Geoffrey's story or its derivatives, are the statements that the white dragon had the better of the red one[8] and that Arthur founded the church of St. Aaron at Caerleon,[9] and, among the frequent specifications of the burial places of kings, that of Augusele at Wybre in Wales.[10]

Needless to say, Langtoft shows the influence of romance ideas.[11] He assumes Merlin's character as an enchanter,[12] although he expresses skepticism about the eagle's speaking at Shaftesbury.[13] He exalts Wawayn[14] as being courteous,[15] and especially well acquainted with Latin,[16] and says[17] that, though the history does not state who gave Lucius his death wound, it is attributed to Wawayn; he mentions Iwain in a manner which implies fuller knowledge of him;[18] spells the name of Arthur's queen, according to northern fashion, "Gaynore," and once pauses to curse her.[19]

---

[1] P. 204.   [2] P. 136.
[3] P. 150.   [4] P. 166.
[5] P. 170; cf. p. 205, below.   [6] Pp. 172, 184; cf. pp. 143–144, above.
[7] P. 192; cf. p. 136, above, and note 5.   [8] P. 114.
[9] P. 168; cf. Geoffrey, ix, 12, 18.   [10] P. 220.
[11] Cf. p. 138, above.   [12] P. 124.
[13] P. 32.   [14] Cf. p. 105, above.
[15] P. 198.   [16] P. 194.
[17] P. 216.   The same statement is made positively in the prose *Merlin*, p. 471 (ed. Sommer).   The *Morte Arthur* in the Thornton MS. ascribes the deed to Lancelot.
[18] Pp. 218–220; cf. p. 161, above.   [19] P. 218; cf. p. 163, above.

While he rationalizes Arthur's exploits at the battle of Badon[1] (reducing the number of men whom he kills from four hundred and seventy to seventy), he nevertheless thinks of Arthur as the greatest of all kings.[2] Caleburne, though he omits the reference to Avalon, is the best sword that was ever made in Britain.[3] He exaggerates the greatness of Arthur's feast,[4] and says that when the news of Modred's treason comes, he has already got across the Alps, and the horns are sounding for dinner in Pavia.[5] His account of Arthur's last battle is not only shorter than Geoffrey's, but very different, and evidently influenced by Henry of Huntingdon.[6] Langtoft says directly that Arthur struck Modred, and implies that it was Modred who gave him his death wound. He mentions the British belief in Arthur's return, and in surprising contrast to his usual rationalistic attitude, declares[7] that he does not know whether Arthur is really dead or not.[8]

IV. THOMAS CASTELFORD

In the early fourteenth century, the diversity of English dialects (to say nothing of other causes) was likely to restrict to a local reputation almost any literary work, however successful; and it is only a quarter of a century after Robert of Gloucester that we find another writer — from the North, like the French Gaimar and Langtoft — undertaking to do for the English-speaking people of his region what Robert had done for the South. The resulting chronicle exists in a single manuscript, which has never been printed, but has been described with considerable fullness.[9] It

---

[1] P. 152. [2] Pp. 188, 240, 246. [3] P. 152. [4] P. 174.

[5] P. 216; cf. p. 187, above. [6] Cf. p. 120, above. [7] P. 224; cf. p. 101, above.

[8] In connection with Langtoft may be noted the genealogy of the kings of England as far as Edward I in French verse which Hardy (III, 328, No. 560) mentions as existing in MS. Trin. Coll. Cant. R. 4. 26. I have not seen it. It may be added that the *Chronique rimée* attributed to Geoffrey of Paris, a writer of the early fourteenth century (Bouquet, *Recueil des Historiens de la France*, XXII), contains an incidental reference to Arthur as a typical royal hero of romance (v. 6641); and that several such occur in Guil. Guiart's *Branche des Royaus Lingnages*, published in the same volume (vv. 14, 12,386, 15,718).

[9] M. L. Perrin, *Ueber T. Castelford's Chronik von England* (Göttingen dissertation), Boston, 1891. The chronicle is mentioned by Miss L. Toulmin Smith, *Bibliographer*, March, 1882.

was written in the neighborhood of York, and apparently finished in the year 1327. At the beginning is inscribed the name of Thomas Castelford, who was probably the author, and who, according to Leland and later biographers, was a monk of Pontefract. It is more extended, comparatively, than the chronicle of Robert of Gloucester, as it consists of nearly forty thousand lines — about twenty-eight thousand on the period covered by Geoffrey.

According to Dr. Perrin, this earlier portion follows Geoffrey almost verbally. Yet its bulk is obviously much greater, and in the section which precedes the Arthurian period, as well as in that which follows it, the author makes various insertions, largely of legendary material, taken partly from known sources.[1] The same is true in the Arthurian period; but, as far as one can judge from Dr. Perrin's summary, the additions are of little importance for the question of traditions independent of Geoffrey. They consist partly of expansions of the incidents represented as taking place at York, — the sieges of that city by the Saxons[2] and by Arthur;[3] Arthur's feast there,[4] with a mention of the legend of Samson's going to Brittany, and an expanded account of the story of Queen Ginevra at York,[5] which Geoffrey only suggests.[6] This greater detail in regard to York is characteristic of the chronicle throughout, and is evidently due to the author's local interest. Probably, therefore, there is no new traditional material in his expansion of the story of the exploits of Uther in the North,[7] though several names not given by Geoffrey are introduced.[8] One may infer from the summary that the author knew Wace's *Brut*, since he mentions not only the Round Table,[9] but also the rejoicing of the people on Arthur's return from France.[10] In fact, the only traditional element which does not seem to be taken from Geoffrey or Wace is the inevitable statement that Arthur was buried at Glastonbury.[11]

---

[1] Perrin, pp. 36–39.   [2] Vv. 18,617–18,665.
[3] Vv. 19,850–19,856.   [4] Vv. 20,621 ff.
[5] Vv. 23,775–23,785.   [6] xi, 1, 39; cf. p. 168, note 2, above.   [7] Vv. 18,815 ff.
[8] Dr. Perrin does not tell what they are. That the order in which Vortimer's battles are named (vv. 14,457 ff.) is different from Geoffrey's may be due to Nennius (chap. 44).   [9] Vv. 21,125–21,140.
[10] Vv. 21,119–21,124; cf. p. 131, above.   [11] Vv. 24,011–24,012.

V. ROBERT MANNYNG OF BRUNNE

The third, and perhaps the last, of the more ambitious Middle English metrical chronicles is that of Robert Mannyng, often designated by the name of his birthplace, the village of Brunne in Lincolnshire.[1]

For the facts of his life no source of direct knowledge exists outside of his own writings, but in these he has given more information about himself than was usual with mediæval authors. In his *Handlyng Synne* he says that in 1303 he had been for fifteen years in the priory of [Gilbertine canons at] Sempringham, which was only six miles from his birthplace. It is possible that he was not himself a canon, but only a lay brother.[2] It was at another priory of the same order, however, — that of Sixhill in Lincolnshire, — that he composed his chronicle, which he wrote during the reign of Edward III and finished in 1338.[3]

Robert distinctly states that he writes, "not for the learned, but for the laymen "; not for story-tellers and harpers, but in as simple English as possible, for the love of simple men that cannot understand any other.[4] He wishes, he says, to furnish them with a means of amusement when they sit together in fellowship.[5] This human sympathy is the more noteworthy when one considers the austerities of the life which he had chosen.[6]

In the latter part of his work, Robert chiefly paraphrases Langtoft; but for the first part he uses Wace's *Brut*[7] as far as it extends,

---

[1] The first part of Robert's work, the paraphrase of Wace, has been edited by Furnivall, Rolls Series, 2 vols., 1887. It was previously printed as far as the birth of Christ by Zetsche in *Anglia*, 1886, IX, 43–194. The second part, the paraphrase of Langtoft from the end of Wace, was edited by Hearne, 2 vols., 1725 (2d ed., 1810). See Morley, *English Writers*, III, 356; Hardy, III, 304.

[2] As Dr. Furnivall thinks.

[3] See *Handlyng Synne*, ed. Furnivall, Roxburghe Club, 1862, p. 3, vv. 57–76 (quoted by Furnivall in his edition of the chronicle, p. iii) ; *Chronicle*, I, 1, 5, ed. Furnivall; II, 341, ed. Hearne, 1725; A. W. Zetsche, *Über den I. Teil der Bearbeitung des "roman de Brut" durch Robert Mannyng*, Reudnitz-Leipzig, 1887, pp. 1–3.

[4] Vv. 71–134.   [6] Described by Dr. Furnivall, pp. vi–xii.

[5] Vv. 9–10, 143–144.   [7] Cf. p. 143, note 1, above, and p. 226, below.

for the reason, as he himself says,[1] that Langtoft leaves out much
that Wace includes. He follows Wace very closely, though perhaps
with a little more freedom than Robert of Gloucester shows in han-
dling Geoffrey's narrative; but he obviously had Langtoft's version
at hand, since he occasionally draws a detail from it. There is no
evidence that for the Arthurian period he made use of any other
chronicle than those two, though he remarks that he knows Geoffrey's.[2] Of his general manner of treating Wace's account, little
more need be said. He shows himself a compatriot of Layamon
and Robert of Gloucester. His occasional expansions of Wace's
lines and his incidental slight additions prove that he clearly
pictures situations in his own mind, as, for instance, when he
describes the last fight with Lucius and other battles,[3] or Arthur's
armor,[4] gives verbatim Uther's lament for his brother,[5] or pictures
a game of "chekers."[6] His occasional touches of Saxon homeliness[7] and of mediæval bigotry,[8] and his partisanship for the ancient
Britons, whom he sometimes designates by first personal pronouns,[9]
may be mentioned in passing. There are inevitable additions in
unimportant details: such as, — the statement that Hengist took
an amount of land of which each side was equal in length to his
thong — a change, evidently, in the interest of plausibility;[10] the
statement that Merlin was only twelve years old at the time of
his first appearance;[11] his giving Arthur a horse at Mount Badon;[12]
his speaking of a legate distinct from Dubricius;[13] the substitution
of names of nations of his own time for those given by Wace.[14]
Robert shows a moral tendency in making over Wace's statement
about the love of knights for their *amies* so as to exclude those who

---

[1] Vv. 61–64.

[2] V. 10,595. It is evidently Geoffrey to whom he refers in vv. 58–59. On his
sources in general see Zetsche's dissertation, pp. 1–23; M. Thümmig, *Anglia*,
1891, XIV, 1–76, especially pp. 1–6; O. Preussner, *Robert Mannyng's Überset-
zung*, etc., Breslau, 1891. Zetsche's argument (pp. 10–37) that he used the
Münchener Brut scarcely deserves mention.

[3] Vv. 13,541 ff., 8465 ff.   [4] V. 10,027.   [5] Vv. 9071–9072.

[6] Vv. 11,397 ff.; cf. vv. 7018 ff., 8845 ff., 10,130, 10,291–10,292, 10,866, 11,025, etc.

[7] V. 13,182, etc.   [8] Vv. 11,971–11,974, etc.   [9] Vv. 9976, 13,581.

[10] Vv. 7510–7512.   [11] V. 8232.   [12] V. 10,099.

[13] V. 11,083.   [14] V. 10,549; cf. p. 201, above.

have wives.[1] Apparently by confusion, he identifies the castle which
Arthur built in France with Kay's tower, and calls it *Chymoun*.[2]

Robert identifies the wood of Calidon, where Arthur fought one of
his battles, with "ffsykertoun,"[3] possibly following a current interpretation of Geoffrey's story.　He expands an early mention of Vortigern,[4] ascribing to him the same very bad character that is insisted on
by several of the chroniclers from William of Malmesbury down.[5]

Robert gives rather more direct evidence of familiarity with the
romances than any of his predecessors.[6]　In describing the fight
of the dragons,[7] he introduces two alliterative lines in a metre altogether different from that which he ordinarily uses:

> Wyppyng wyþ wenges, ouer-wepen & went,
> Cracchyng wiþ clawes, rubbed & brent.[8]

This may be taken from some other poem, but if so, there is nothing
to show that that poem dealt with Arthurian material.　But the
"weye that he wiste gayn" by which Arthur gets ahead of Lucius[9]
is a characteristic romance "property."　In expressing his exalted
conception of Arthur he says:

> Þan of myrþe most was in halle,
> Glad-chered, louely, & lordlyest of alle . . .
> Ilka day come tydynges newe,
> Gestes of ioye, wyþ knyghtes trewe . . .
> Was no þyng so noble of þewes
> As men reden of hym & schewes.[10]

Caliburne, with Robert, has assumed, both literally and figura-
tively, wonderful proportions.　Its blade is ten feet long and more

---

[1] Vv. 11,347 ff. (cf. p. 184, above).　　[2] Vv. 14,007–14,012 (cf. p. 122, above).
[3] V. 9932.　　　　[4] Vv. 7032–7040.　　　[5] Cf. p. 40, above.

[6] It is interesting to note in this connection that for "Beus of Oxenford,"
whose name appears in the Petyt MS. (v. 12,536), the scribe of the Lambeth MS.
has been misled into writing "Beofs of Hamptone" (cf. p. 217, below).　The most
extended cases of use of romances occur in the non-Arthurian parts of Robert's
poem (cf. p. 138, above).

[7] He says that the sympathy of all the people was with the red dragon, which
was finally killed, though the white dragon languished on for only four days.

[8] Vv. 8197–8198.　　　[9] V. 13,309.　　　[10] Vv. 9751 ff.

than seven inches broad;[1] it "neuere for armes wolde scurne";[2] and its name is Irelgas's battle-cry.[3] But, instead of saying that it was made in Avalon, Robert observes: "In Ramesey & oþer stedes þe merke is ymade."[1] He refuses to believe the " Bretons lye " that Arthur is not dead and will return.[4] As a matter of course, his skepticism does not extend to Merlin, whose character as a wonder-worker he assumes from the outset, remarking, for instance, that it is by "coniurisouns" that he transported the Great Stones.[5] In saying of Merlin's fountain, "Baynes hit highte by olde tales, "[6] Robert may merely be thinking, across a scribal error, of Wace's name[7] for it, *Labenes*. That the Round Table had come to be as thoroughly associated with Arthur in his day as it is in ours, Robert shows when he says that it was to see the Table that some of the foreign barons came to Arthur's feast.[8]

The explanation that if Arthur had longer delayed following Modred into Cornwall the traitor would have been better prepared, looks like a reply to the emphasis laid in the prose romance on Arthur's refusal to wait for reënforcements. The statement that Modred's illicit relations with the queen preceded Arthur's campaign against Lucius[9] may easily have been inferred from Wace's account.[10] But the novel remark that when Arthur had been in France, Iweyn[11] had opposed Modred's treasonable practices, whether or not it is original with Robert, certainly rests on the popular fame of Iwain. Robert says that, after the death of Wawayn and Agusel, Arthur never gladly ate meat,[12] and of Wawayn he observes, " Mykel honur of hym euere men seys."[13] In mentioning "Rone-wen's " coming he makes an interesting allusion to other popular stories about the episode:

> But þis lewed men sey and singe
> & telle þat bit was mayden Inge.
> Wryten of Inge, no clerk may kenne,
> Bot of Hengiste doughter, Ronewenne.[14]

---

[1] Vv. 10,035 ff.   [6] V. 8752.   [9] Vv. 12,039 ff.

[2] V. 10,886.   [7] V. 8217.   [10] Cf. p. 163, above.

[3] V. 13,682.   [8] V. 11,361.   [11] Vv. 14,205 ff. Cf. p. 161, above.

[4] V. 14,301 ; cf. p. 101, note 6, above.   [12] Vv. 14,119–14,120.

[5] V. 8903 ; cf. vv. 8748 ff. (cf. Wace, vv. 8215–8216), 9386.

[13] V. 10,678 ; cf. p. 105, above.   [14] Vv. 7533 ff.

When explaining that he leaves out Merlin's prophecies because they are not comprehensible before the event,[1] he says that they are written in the books of Blase, Tolomer, and Sire Amytayn, who were Merlin's masters. His knowledge of Blase must have come directly or indirectly from the prose *Merlin*. Twice[2] in praising Arthur at length as the greatest of Christian kings, he expresses great dissatisfaction that, while his deeds have been celebrated in all foreign lands, especially in French books, little or nothing has been written about him in English.

---

[1] Vv. 8213 ff.; cf. p. 136, above.   [2] Vv. 10,589 ff., 10,967 ff.

CHAPTER VIII

THE STORY AFTER GEOFFREY: THE FRENCH PROSE CHRONICLES AND THEIR MORE DIRECT DERIVATIVES (WITH OTHER VERNACULAR CONTINENTAL CHRONICLES)

MORE important than the English metrical chronicles are those written in French prose, partly because they are much more numerous and extend over a much longer period, partly because they include the exceedingly popular *Brut*.

I. MINOR EARLY FRENCH CHRONICLES[1]

The earliest French chronicles that here concern us, all doubtless composed in England, were probably for the most part brief and insignificant. One,[2] written on a roll, which comes down to the time of Edward I, begins with an exceedingly concise outline of the whole of Geoffrey's *History*, accompanying it with an elaborate

---

[1] Some chronicles which probably or certainly belong here I have not seen. One occupies five leaves in Cambridge Univ. MS., Gg. i. 1, no. 50, fols. 484b ff. It is mentioned by Paul Meyer, in an article entitled *De quelques chroniques Anglo-Normandes qui ont porté le nom de Brut* (*Bull. de la Soc. des Anc. Textes français*, 1878, IV, 104–145). I have not here retained the classification adopted in that article because it seems to me that the question whether or not one of these chronicles has been called *Brut* is unimportant. Other manuscripts are Heralds' College MS. E. D. N., no. 14 (mentioned by Madden, *The Ancient English Romance of Havelok*, pp. xxiv, liv); Barberini 2689 (Hardy, III, 206, No. 348); Phillipps 1932 and 887 (Hardy, III, 373, No. 623). Neither the French chronicle of the Layamon MS. (Calig. A. ix. 3) nor the equally brief outline in Vesp. E. iv. 6, fols. 107b–112a, contains any account of the Arthurian period. Apparently the same is true of MS. Coll. Trin. Cant. R. 14. 7. 6. (Hardy, III, 251, No. 454). See also Meyer, *Bulletin*, 1879, V, 98; 1891, XVII, 70; Stengel, *Ztsch. f. rom. Phil.*, X, 278–285; Meyer, *Romania*, XVI, 154–155.

[2] Brit. MS. Addit. 11713.

but still less complete genealogical tree.   In the Arthurian period
it is rather less curtailed than elsewhere.   It has eight lines about
Arthur, including the common inference that "Wenheure" was
equally guilty with Modred,[1] and it states that Arthur was buried
at Glastonbury.

About 1300 or 1307, or more likely some twenty or twenty-five
years earlier,[2] was put together another very short chronicle.[3]   The
first part, *Le Livere de Reis de Brittanie*, begins with a series of
much-abbreviated excerpts from some of the more romantic portions
of Geoffrey's *History*.[4]   On the Arthurian period it has only a single
clause, — about Vortigern's "receiving" Horsus and Hengist.   The
second part, *Le Livere de Reis de Engleterre*, which originally ended
with 1274, is concerned only incidentally with the history before
the Saxon period.   Its brief account of the coming of the Saxons
partly follows that of Bede, since it represents the Britons as sending to the Saxons for aid; but it takes from Geoffrey's form of the
story a mention of Vortigern's marriage with Hengist's daughter
and the accompanying "waisseyl" incident.

The chronicle of MS. Bodl. Tanner, 195, fols. 129–138, is a slight
list of little more than names, coming down to the accession of
Edward II.   As far as Geoffrey goes, it follows him with practically
no difference.

Apparently based originally on the same work as the *Livere de
Reis de Brittanie*, is the very strange compilation[5] prepared in 1310
for Henry de Lacy, Earl of Lincoln, by Rauf de Boun, who called

---

[1] Cf. p. 163, above.

[2] See Meyer's article above (p. 209, note 1).

[3] Edited by John Glover, Rolls Series, 1865.   The work included in the Char-
tulary of Malmesbury Abbey (MS. Publ. Record Office, Incen's Records, Miscellaneous Books, no. 24; Hardy, III, 198, No. 325) is, as Meyer inferred, the same
in substance, though with differences in phraseology (see fol. 37b).   The first of
the two pieces printed by Glover has also been edited by John Koch, *Li Rei de
Engleterre*, Berlin, 1886, on the basis of MS. Cotton Calig. A. ix., which omits
the portion (regarded by Koch as an interpolation) dealing with the Britons and
begins at a place corresponding to p. 8, l. 17 of Glover's text.   See also Stengel,
Deutsche Litteraturzeitung, 1886, p. 994, and *Ztsch. f. rom. Phil.*, X, 278.

[4] Though with considerable differences in the story of Leir.

[5] MS. Harl. 902, fols. 1–11b.

it the *Petit Brut.* But in its present form it is altogether different and, at least in the first part, much fuller than the *Livere.* It has been well described as "a collection of historical notices chiefly derived from apocryphal sources, and put together in so confused and ignorant a manner, in defiance of chronology, as to baffle all ingenuity to reconcile them to each other."[1] Its account of the pre-Saxon period is based on Geoffrey's, but with various accretions, especially, as in some of the Latin chronicles, with regard to the foundation of various cities, and with most remarkable transformations; and it omits the whole of the actual Arthurian epoch. But after it has begun the story of the Saxon kings and has spoken of two Adelufs, father and son, it states that on the premature death of the latter, his younger brother Uter succeeded him.[2] Then, after telling how Uter fought with "le dragon serpent" in Westmoreland (the incident is perhaps suggested by Geoffrey's account of how Marius defeated and killed the Pictish Rodric there[3]), it relates at great length his amour with the wife of the Duke of Cornwall, calling the latter "Bodemound." Of Arthur it speaks in very general terms, naming Percival and Gawayne among his knights, referring to the romance of the Grail,[4] and mentioning Arthur's conquest of Wales, Ireland, and Scotland. It speaks at some length of his three sons, Adeluf III, Morgan le Noir, whom Arthur loved the best, and Patrike le Rous, and Arthur's division of the island among them. It apologizes for not recounting his exploits more at length on the ground that he owed them to his love, *la dame de faierie* (an evident allusion to Morgan the Fay or some similar lady of romance) and that it is not "amiable de mettre fayere en escripture." "But this king Arthur reigned twenty-one years, and he died at the castle of Kerlionus, and his body was carried to Glastinbery."

At several points in this unique narrative, the author refers for corroboration to "l'autre Brut." But as no other known document has anything similar to the stories here given, there seems to be no means of telling whether the worthy Rauf, determined to please his

---

[1] Madden, *Havelok*, p. xx.
[2] Fol. 4b.
[3] Cf. p. 73, above.
[4] Cf. p. 189, above.

patron at all hazards, amused himself by giving free rein to his imagination, or really had some authority now lost. His mention of Uter's killing the dragon is a point of resemblance to Gottfried of Viterbo's version of the story, especially since in both the term "serpent " is also applied to the dragon.[1]

Here, for convenience, may be mentioned the short manuals of English history which were drawn up during the period under consideration for many of the noble English families, sometimes in French, sometimes in Latin or English. In one of the few published specimens[2] the *résumé* of the Arthurian period exhibits the confusion already mentioned[3] between the campaigns against Flollo and against Lucius. In another,[4] which deals only with the relations between England and Scotland, is given an outline of Arthur's conquest of the latter country.

A very confused composite account of the Arthurian period with practically no new individual features occurs in another chronicle which comes down to Edward II.[5] In the early portion it is mostly an abbreviated paraphrase of Geoffrey combined with an increasing amount of material from other sources. In the Arthurian period, while it includes most of the substance of Geoffrey's account, it turns aside to speak of the Roman emperors, it draws much from Henry of Huntingdon (including some material which he took from the Saxon *Chronicle*), and it has points from Nennius. Thus it often repeats itself, and it presents one of the most hopeless and inconsistent *mélanges* conceivable. It has the "Thomas Fullo " absurdity.[6]

Much more interesting and important is the *Polistorie del Eglise de Christ de Caunterbyre*,[7] which comes down to the year 1313. For

---

[1] Cf. p. 147, above.

[2] Edited by Thomas Wright, *Feudal Manuals of English History*, 1872, No. 5, p. 125 (but Wright omits everything to the beginning of the reign of Arthur).

[3] Cf. p. 183, above.   [4] Wright, No. 6, p. 156.

[5] Brit. Mus. MS. Bibl. Reg. 20. A. xviii., no. 1 (Hardy, III, 393, No. 666).

[6] Fol. 65a. Cf. p. 183, above.

[7] Described by G. Paris, *Hist. Litt. de la France*, XXVIII, 480–486. It is worthy of note that in certain proper names where many copies and paraphrases of Geoffrey go astray, this chronicle generally has the correct forms. The MS. is Harl. 636; see Hardy, III, 350, No. 576.

the most part this chronicle follows Geoffrey, as far as he goes, rather closely, sometimes almost in a literal translation, with only an occasional slight omission or amplification. Points worthy of specification are: the author's animosity against Vortigern;[1] a conversation repeated between Ambrosius and Tremonnus, who is identified with St. David;[2] a mention of the Round Table;[3] the occasional introduction of a distinctively feudal or chivalrous touch, as when after mention of Arthur's distribution of honors it is said: "Mult li mercient cum per resun le devoyent disaunt: A teu seignur deyt humme biene servir, ke les seons ne veut oblier; mes avaunt requeste avauncer." Interesting is the introduction of a detail which seems to have originated with Wace, — the death of the fifth Roman, the cousin of Marcel, at the hands of Gawain, in the retreat of Arthur's envoys from the camp of Lucius.[4] The author adds that no one could resist Gawain's blows, and gives some verses which he says were inscribed on Gawain's sword to the effect that it was made by Gaban when Christ was fourteen years old.[5] Gaban is evidently a personage similar in character to Wayland the Smith and Layamon's Wygar and Griffin.[6] Beginning at this point, the author departs somewhat more than before from Geoffrey, once or twice trying to motivate better the details of the story.[7] He mentions the Round Table, and his praise of Gawain is not based altogether on Geoffrey.[8] The same is true of his account of the campaign against Modred, which has points of resemblance with the version in the famous *Brut*, to which we are about to come, — such, for example, as the mention of the ports Whytsand and Sandwych. But it does not agree with that version. It mentions Arthur's banner, and says that he killed Modred with his own hand.[9]

---

[1] Cf. p. 40, above.

[2] Fol. 16a 2.

[5] Printed in *Publications of the Mod. Lang. Assoc.*, 1903, XVIII, 90.

[6] Cf. p. 162, above.

[7] Cf. p. 134, above.

[3] Fol. 21b 2.

[4] Fol. 24a 2; cf. p. 141, above.

[8] Cf. p. 105, above.

[9] Cf. p. 120, n. 5, above.

II. The Large *Brut* and its English Translation (with the French and English Literal Translations of Geoffrey's *History*)

One of the books most widely circulated in England in the fourteenth and fifteenth centuries was the chronicle which came to be known, and still is known, as "the Brut"[1] *par excellence.* This work seems originally to have been composed about 1272, though most of the existing manuscripts continue the history for sixty years later. Its authorship is unknown, as some of the manuscripts expressly state; for one cannot take seriously the "Douglas of Glastonbury" named in one copy of the English translation[2] and by Caxton on the title-page of his edition. The manuscripts fall into two general classes,[3] but their differences occur almost altogether after the Galfridian section, and in the Arthurian period consist chiefly[4] of the insertion by the second redaction (in the

---

[1] On the *Brut* and its very numerous manuscripts should be consulted, besides the above-mentioned (p. 209, note 1) discussions of Meyer and Madden (the latter of which is largely repeated by Skeat in his *Lay of Havelok*, E.E.T.S., pp. xiii ff.), — the British Museum class catalogue (in the Manuscript Room) of works on the History of Great Britain and Ireland, Part II, pp. 505–517; Wm. Hardy, *Recueil des Croniques*, etc., *par Waurin*, Rolls Series, 1864, I, lxii, note 2; Madden, *Notes and Queries*, 1856, 2d Series, I, 1–4; F. S. Haydon, *Eulogium Historiarum*, Rolls Series, II, lxx–lxxi. Mention may be made of an article by the Abbé De La Rue in *Essais Historiques sur les Bardes*, Caen, 1834, II, 165.

[2] MS. Harl. 4690.

[3] The first redaction is represented, for example, by Harl. 200; Domit. A. x.; Addit. 18462, no. 2; Addit. 35113; Cleop. D. vii. The second, by Cleop. D. iii. 3; Addit. 18462, no. 1; Bibl. Reg. 20. D. iii.; Bibl. Reg. 20. A. iii. But sometimes manuscripts of the same class differ much in phraseology. For example, Addit. 18462, no. 1, is often curter in expression than Cleop. D. iii. 3. On the *Eulogium Historiarum*, which follows the *Brut* in the first part of the Arthurian story, see p. 176, above.

[4] Minor points of difference are the following: — The first redaction, in speaking of Uter's last victory, enlarges a little upon his joy over it. The second redaction has substituted Mont St. Bernard for Mont St. Michel in the adventure with the giant, — an alteration which may perhaps be due in part to influence from the romance story of Arthur's fight with the great cat, localized near a Swiss lake (see Freymond, *Artus' Kampf mit dem Katzenungetüm*). The second redaction makes Otta and Ossa brothers (cf. p. 39, above). Some MSS. of the second

midst of the account of Arthur's expedition into Scotland) of a prophecy made to him by Merlin about a lamb, a wolf, and other animals, in the usual style of the apocalyptic utterances which were popular for centuries after Geoffrey's successful use of them, if not before. Similarly, prophecies said to have been made by Merlin about Henry III, Edward I, and Edward II are inserted at the end of the accounts of their respective reigns.

To trace the exact pedigree of the *Brut* is probably impossible. Perhaps the work was influenced in some degree by Wace's version,[1] though I have noted only four or five seemingly or possibly significant cases of agreement: namely, — both mention Anna's marriage to Loth when she is first named;[2] both mention definitely the choice of Colgrin as leader of the Saxons on the death of Octa and Eosa; both observe at the first appearance of Guenevere[3] that she and Arthur had no heir; both speak of the institution of the Round Table and its cause;[4] and, after the end of the Arthurian period, both have the episode of the capture of Cirencester by the sparrow stratagem.[5] These coincidences may not prove much; but on the other hand, the *Brut* is so much more condensed than Wace's poem that many striking parallelisms could not be expected.

At any rate, after some introductory material, the *Brut* begins to follow the story of Geoffrey's *History* from the commencement, whether or not the writer is drawing directly from Geoffrey, and continues to paraphrase the story as far as Geoffrey carries it. The differences, in a general way, are similar to those which occur in other extended paraphrases, like Langtoft's for instance. But the

redaction (Addit. 18462, no. 1, fol. 39a; Bibl. Reg. 20. A. iii., fol. 160b) insert after the mention of Arthur's great feast a passage of considerable length which recounts in a manner far from clear how Arthur seated at the Round Table some knights for whom there seemed not to be room. By an interesting confusion or emendation, one manuscript (Addit. 18462, no. 1) says that after the last battle Arthur had himself carried to Salerne.

[1] Cf. p. 143, note 1, above.

[2] Geoffrey, viii, 20. The manuscripts of Geoffrey which I have examined agree with the printed text in not mentioning the fact here.

[3] Geoffrey, ix, 9; cf. p. 140, above. .

[4] At a point corresponding to Geoffrey, ix, 11.

[5] Wace, vv. 14,005 ff.; cf. Geoffrey, xi, 8.

narrative is much abridged in several places, — especially in the description of the battles of Bath and of those against Lucius, and in the actual duel with the giant.[1] Further, many incidents, etc., are omitted altogether. The chief omissions are the following: — the stratagem of "Bladulf" in getting into York;[2] the account of the second and third wonderful lakes in Scotland;[1] the expedition to Norway, and, indeed, all the previous foreign conquests except those of "Gutlande" and "Irland"; the account of the coronation festivities, except the banquet; practically all the speeches made by Arthur's men apropos of the Emperor's message; Arthur's dream on the Channel; the whole story of the embassy to the Emperor and the two first battles, which result therefrom; the battle with Modred at Winchester.

Constant characteristics of the French mediæval writers are vividness and liveliness of narration and lack of historical perspective. These qualities are even more strikingly evident in the author of the present chronicle than in Wace. He describes everything in terms appropriate to his own time. To him all warriors are feudal knights and men-at-arms, and all cities are walled towns of burghers, like Winchester and London. He conceives English geography in the age of Brutus as identical with that of the time of Edward I or Edward III, — regarding the land as divided into Northfolk and Southfolk and all the other Saxon counties fifteen hundred years before the Saxons set foot on it. To explain Arthur's great feast he says that he wished to be crowned king of Glamorgan, — being evidently unable to think of Caerleon as anything more than the capital of a Welsh county. With delightful naïveté he remarks that it was contrary to sacred law for Modred to take his uncle's wife. Neither can he adopt any other point of view than that of a Catholic Christian, looking for direct judgments of God in everything that happens, and feeling intense satisfaction when he thinks himself justified in declaring that a king was good and of good habits, or that the interests of the faith were advanced. He takes

---

[1] Cf. p. 202, above.

[2] This omission was necessitated by the statement that Colegryne left him in charge of the city and himself went to Cheldryk for aid.

pains to say that when Constantine came from Brittany, all the "Saracens" were killed except those who turned to God. He represents Arthur as encouraging his men on the ground that the Romans are allied with heathen, and that God will help the Britons because they have the right; and he observes that Lucius trusted more in his strength than in God Almighty, as appeared afterward.[1] He gives a prayer of Arthur before the battle. His national prejudices sometimes crop out, as when, after having said that the eagles in Loch Lomond gave warning whenever enemies attacked the land, he adds that it was because the Scots were great ravagers.

From the scientific point of view, this bias is disastrous enough, but literature and romance as evidently gain by it. For, as has already appeared in the case of Wace and others, it enables the author to enter with all his heart into his narrative, to call up the details to his mind's eye, to explain doubtful points, and to express the personal emotions aroused in him by events and characters. To this attitude, then, manifesting itself in these ways, are due the pervading difference of general effect and most of the very numerous differences in detail between the *Brut* and the original. But, in addition to the particular points already mentioned, certain others, generally explicable from these same considerations, ought to be noted.

Dates are added, both of the Christian era and of the respective reigns.[2] As a matter of course, the numbers given, in whatever connection, generally differ from those in the manuscripts of Geoffrey, and proper names, as in almost all versions of the story, are much corrupted. Constantine kills "Gowan," the oppressor, and Uter kills Pascent with his own hand.[3] Vortigern is called, as in some previous versions, Earl of Westsexe, which, however, amounts to the same thing as Geoffrey's description of him. It is definitely stated that Engist's first message to Germany for more Saxons was secret.[4] Engist's brother is Horn, — a case of scribal confusion with another romantic story.[5] It is said that he had built a fortress which he

---

[1] In his defeat. The author does not tell us whether the same reason is to be given for Arthur's overthrow. [2] Cf. p. 159, above. [3] Cf. p. 213, above.
[4] Cf. p. 36, above. [5] Cf. p. 206, note 6, above.

called Horncastle,[1] and that Vortimer, in wrath at the death of "Catagren," destroyed it. The scene of Vortigern's infatuation with Ronewen is made somewhat more vivid. The now thoroughly intrusive figure of St. Germanus is dropped out. Vortigern's restoration to the throne is on condition that he shall never allow Engist or any of his race to reënter the land.[2] When Vortigern is taken by the Saxons, some of them wish to burn him alive. Almost the whole of Merlin's prophecy is omitted.[3] It is Engist who divides the land into seven kingdoms, for purposes of defence against the Britons, it is said, — an idea quite different from that sometimes given in the chronicles; and the name *England* is derived from *Engist.* Merlin and the other " child " with whom he is quarrelling are said to be twenty-four years old. For moving the great stones Merlin receives whatever reward he will. "Aurilambros" is killed in the second year of his reign. Only one castle of Gorloys is mentioned, — "Tyntagell," — and it is not explained how he and Uter could both be in it at the same time and in the same form without trouble. Arthur is often said to act by the counsel of his men, — for instance, in allowing the Saxons to depart for Germany, in deciding to conquer France, and in being crowned king of Glamorgan. In the account of Arthur's distribution of fiefs, Auguselus and Urien are not mentioned,[4] but Gawen appears.[5] Aloth (Loth) is called son of Elyn, a feature which perhaps goes back to ancient Celtic mythology.[6] The Round Table is introduced, inevitably, but the reason for its construction is said to have been that all the knights were so good that none was worse than another.[7] Certain provinces of France are specified as given by Arthur to Holdinus, who is called his chamberlain, to Dorell his nephew, and to Richard his cousin, — the last, at least, a new character for the chronicles. It is after the banquet is finished that Arthur takes counsel as to his reply to Lucius. Both Key and Bedver are sent to explore the

---

[1] Presumably this idea was developed from the monument in Kent to which Horsa's name had been given, mentioned by Bede (cf. pp. 24–25, above).

[2] Cf. p. 244, below. [3] Cf. p. 136, above.

[4] Cf. p. 136, above. [5] Cf. p. 105, above.

[6] In Celtic mythology, no doubt, all the Helens, including the one of Mont St. Michel, were originally identical. [7] Cf. p. 142, above.

mountain where Arthur is to fight the giant, but before Arthur himself leaves the camp.   It is specified that the Emperor's departure
from Rome is in the month of August, — an idea which may be
developed from his previous demand that Arthur shall present
himself at Rome before the middle of that month, or may be due
to a misunderstanding of the name of the town *Augustodunum*,
which Geoffrey mentions in connection with the campaign.   To the
Emperor his messengers report that Arthur's state is greater than
his own or that of any other king in the world.   In the battle with
Lucius, Arthur kills five kings, besides a multitude of others.   Modred
is reported as sending to Cheldrik for aid, not as asking him to
get it.   In coming from France, the place of Arthur's embarkation
is specified as Whytsand, and that of his landing as Sandwych.
Arthur sends the body of Gawen, as well as that of Auguissel,
into Scotland, — an idea evidently connected with the Northern
set of stories of which Gawain was the hero.   No mention is made
of Eventus (Iwain).[1]   Gunnore is blamed by implication, and it
is said that after her flight to the nunnery (which is effected in
secret with four men) she was never seen among the people.[2]   It is
definitely stated that Arthur died, though mention is made of the
British hope.   The author's vividness of imagination sometimes
manifests itself in a practical touch, as when he says that on the
return to England of Childrick and his Saxons after their first defeat by Arthur they took all the armor that they could find, — a pre-
caution quite necessary at that stage of the story, since they had
given up all that they had ; or again, when he states that the men
of Bath defended themselves well.

In a more striking way, then, than most of the other chronicles,
the French *Brut* shows how in those centuries when the journal-
ist's imagination and the romancer's instinct for situations were
adjudged by the tacit vote of popular approval as no less valua-
ble for the historian than the scholar's judgment and conscience
and devotion, one of the most popular versions of a most popular
narrative, existing side by side with the original, could exhibit
variations great and small at every turn.   There was no standard

---

[1] Cf. p. 161, above.   [2] Cf. p. 163, above.

of comparison by which the unfelt complications could be simplified and the statements of the anonymous writers subjected to critical examination.

It was doubtless inevitable that prose chronicles in England should be written in French sooner than in English, and it was at least natural that what seems to be the earliest prose form should be a translation of a work so popular as the French *Brut*.[1] As to the date of this translation, to which frequent original additions were made, there is no definite evidence, but it probably belongs to the beginning of the fifteenth century.[2] It is frequently referred to by later writers as "the English Chronicle." It was made from the second redaction of the French, and followed its original very closely indeed, though various modifications crept into different manuscripts.[3] Its vogue and importance were vastly increased by the fact that Caxton selected it for publication. His edition, entitled *The Cronycles of Englond*,[4] appeared at Westminster in 1480. In all the early part (until after the Arthurian period) it follows the manuscripts of the usual type, and therefore corresponds almost exactly, except for unavoidable divergences in numbers and names, with the ordinary form of the second French redaction.[5] Accordingly, though it is a fine example of sturdy English, there is no reason to dwell upon it, nor do the later printed editions, as regards the Arthurian material, depart from the first in anything but trivial details.[6]

---

[1] For the MSS. of the English translation see the Brit. Mus. manuscript class catalogue, volume concerning the *Hist. of Great Brit. and Ireland*, Part II, pp. 449, 451. The chronicles from which extracts were printed by Böddeker in Herrig's *Archiv*, 1873, LII, 10–29, are merely copies of this English translation.

[2] So Madden; otherwise Wm. Hardy, ed. of Wavrin, I, lxii, note 2.

[3] Thus, MS. Galba E. viii. (fols. 29–148) differs in phraseology from the others which I have examined; and Harl. 63 abbreviates throughout and inserts occasional Latin verses, besides including Merlin's prophecies, in Latin.

[4] See Gross, *Sources and Literature of English History*, p. 272, No. 1733.

[5] Such as Cleop. D. iii. 3.

[6] Nearly an exact reprint is the edition of William de Mechlin, London, 1482, and only a little less close is that of Gerard de Leeu, Antwerp, 1493. The edition by the Schoolmaster of St. Albans, 1483, inserts at the beginning a *fructus temporum*, and, throughout the text, much material about other countries than

III. Philippe Mousket

In the extensive *Chronique rimée*[1] written before 1244[2] by the Fleming Philippe Mousket, there are occasional mentions of "Artus" as the type of a great king;[3] allusions to the Breton expectation of his return;[4] mention of Gawain;[3] and a few citations of Merlin, not always derived from Geoffrey.[5] Merlin is said to have been buried at "Malebierge."[6]

England; otherwise it also is very nearly a literal reprint. It was reproduced with very slight changes by Wynkyn de Worde at Westminster, 1497–8, by Julyan Notary, London, 1504, and by Richard Pynson, London, 1510.

In this connection may be mentioned two English prose chronicles catalogued by Hardy (I, 356–357, Nos. 834, 835), and said by him to be translations of Geoffrey. He notes of the first, which is the work of "Maister Gnaor," that it abounds in interpolations.

Reference may here be made, also, to the two known mere translations of Geoffrey's *History* into Old French. One is included in the vast historical compilation of MS. f. 17177 of the Bibliothèque Nationale, fol. 73a (see P. Meyer in *Bull. de la Soc. des Anc. Textes franç.*, 1895, pp. 83 ff.). This translation occasionally abbreviates a little (very greatly after the end of Arthur's reign), and it stops apparently unfinished, at the coming of St. Augustine. The other is that made in 1445 by a certain Wauquelin of Mons, in Hainault, for the Count of Chimay (Hardy, I, 358; Ward, I, 251–253), which appears to be a very free rendering, padded out in the usual French style of the period. The work mentioned by Ernest Langlois (*Notices et Extraits des MSS. de la Bibl. Nat.*, etc., 1890, XXXIII, Part II, p. 74) and by P. Meyer (as above, p. 90) is really a copy of part of Wavrin, beginning with book ii. It was used by Hardy (though he almost overlooked it) in his edition of Wavrin (see his *Introd.*, I, ccxvi, note, and *Notes and Emendations*, pp. 505 ff.).

As far as appears from the account of the *Fleur des Hystories* of Jehan Mansel de Hesdin (a writer of the end of the fourteenth century) given by P. Paris (*Les MSS. François de la Bibl. du Roi*, I, 61 ff.), the authentic manuscripts lack the British part, and I have found that the same is true of some, at least, of the copies of the work as abridged and rearranged (see II, 314 ff., 322 f.; V, 314 f., 418).

[1] Ed. Reiffenberg, 2 vols., Brussels, 1836–8, among the *Chroniques Belges* of the Belgian Royal Academy; also in part by Tobler (in Pertz, *Scriptores*, XXVI, 718 ff.) and in Bouquet, *Recueil*, XXII, 34 ff. See Gröber, *Grundriss*, II, i, 762–3; B. C. Du Mortier, *Compte-Rendu des Séances de la Commission royale d'Histoire*, 1st Series, IX, Brussels, 1845, pp. 112 ff.

[2] So Gröber, II, i, 763.

[3] V. 8862–8877, etc.

[4] Vv. 24,627–24,628, 25,201–25,204.

[5] Vv. 19,124 ff., 19,454 ff., 20,543 ff.

[6] Vv. 22,579–22,580.

IV. Jean des Preis

A work destined to be frequently referred to by the later English chroniclers was the immense *Mer des Histoires*, more properly *Ly Myreur des Histors*,[1] which covers the history of the world from the Deluge to 1340. It was composed, apparently near the end of the fourteenth century, by the Fleming Jean des Preis (or d'Outremeuse, born 1338), a bourgeois of aristocratic descent, who was clerk in the Court of Échevins at Liège.[2]   In this compilation Jean reduced into vernacular prose[3] a great number of chronicles, *chansons de geste*,[4] and romances. He includes a large amount of romantic Arthurian material, much of which was never admitted into any other extant chronicle.[5] He inserts it fragmentarily, after the fashion usual in works like his, wherever the various episodes seem to him to belong in his annalistic (though very extended) narrative. In substance this material is as follows: —

Merlin reigned as king in Great Britain, in great honor, about the year 478 A.D.[6]   Here the tower episode is mentioned. At the same time [apparently] and later, reigned Uter,[7] father of Artus. The mention of Uter's death introduces a summary outline (premature as regards Arthur's exploits) of Geoffrey's whole *Historia*, with slight variations.[8] Here it is said that the Round Table, which Merlin had made, had sixty seats,[9] and that in Artus's last battle he killed Mordret with his own hand, Mordret wounded him,

---

1 Edited by A. Borgnet and S. Bormans (among the *Chroniques Belges* of the Belgian Royal Academy), 6 vols., Brussels, 1864–1880, with an introductory volume by Bormans, *Chronique et Geste de Jean des Preis*, 1887.   This chronicle was later continued by Jean de Stavelot, but his work does not concern the present discussion.   See also Gröber, *Grundriss*, II, i, 1080–1081.

2 See Bormans, especially pp. xcii–xciii.

3 Without inventions of his own, according to Bormans.

4 G. Paris, *Mediæval French Literature*, p. 130.

5 This is not the place for any attempt at a study of his sources. Bormans, p. lvii, mentions as lost sources the early thirteenth-century *Chronique des Vavassours* (continued by Bishop Hugues de Pierrepont), the *Chronique* of Enguerrand de Bar, and the *Chronique* of Jean de Warnant.   See his discussion, pp. xcv ff.

6 Bk. i, vol. II, pp. 165, 171.   8 II, 188 ff.

7 II, 165, 182, 188.   9 II, 198.

and every knight of the Round Table was killed except two.[1] In the later and less incidental Arthurian passages Artus's conquests are made to extend far and wide. They include [2] the king of Persia, the Emperor Lucidar (Geoffrey's Lucius), the king of "Saynes" (who is killed, and his daughter and kingdom given to Artus's friend Paris of France), the Vandals, Syria, Jerusalem, and Egypt,[3] the Danes, who were devastating Saxony,[4] and Justin, son of the Emperor Anastaux, when he invades Britain.[5] There is special praise of Tristan, who is called king of Lonnois.[6] Several tournaments are described at some length, — one made by Uter at Carlon for knighting Artus and Paris,[7] and others at Lutesse (Paris) and London.[8] In connection with the tournaments are named various Arthurian ladies and knights, among the latter Ywain, Keux, Blioberis, and Erech. A second account of the end of Artus's reign, inconsistent enough with the first, is as follows : [9] — Tristan is assassinated by King March, who is therefore put to death by Artus's knights. March's natural son Galopes incites the Emperor of Rome to invade Britain. The Emperor is defeated and flees to Rome. Artus follows, and the Romans accept him as Emperor. Then comes the news of Mordrech's treason, and the last campaign. Artus, defeated and wounded in the final battle, goes with Gawain in a boat to the isle of Avalon, to the castle of his sister Morgaine, for the healing of his wounds : " et welt-ons dire que c'est feierie, et encors les ratendent les Brutons qui quident qu'ilh doie revenir." [10] All the knights of the Round Table are now dead except Lanchelot del Lac, who, assembling his people, and taking with him his vassal king Carados of Little Britain, besieges and captures London. He executes the guilty Genevre, and also Mordrech by shutting him up with the corpse of Genevre, which in his hunger he eats. Lanchelot bestows the crown on Constantin, son of Carados, and himself becomes a hermit.[11] Later there is mention of his coming to Paris at the age of one hundred and seventy-seven years and speaking of his former exploits.[12]

---

[1] II, 198–199. [4] II, 216. [7] II, 182. [10] II, 243.

[2] II, 203 ff. [5] II, 217–218. [8] II, 210 ff., 236–237. [11] II, 244.

[3] II, 214–215. [6] II, 181 ff. [9] II, 241 ff. [12] II, 357.

At much later points in his narrative Jean introduces the story of Ogier the Dane, drawing from his own *Geste d' Ogier*, and there he gives occasional Arthurian romance material, with exploits of Artus.[1]

V. The *Scalacronica* of Sir Thomas Gray

Another French chronicle is the *Scalacronica* of universal and British history put together about 1355 by the warlike Sir Thomas Gray while he was a prisoner at Edinburgh. This must here be judged from a few extracts only (which include the author's prologue) given by Stevenson in his edition of its last part[2] (beginning after the Arthurian period) and from a few notes included by Leland in his *Collectanea*.[3]

As to his immediate source, Sir Thomas states in his prologue that he translated out of rhyme, but this remark need hardly be accepted, since the whole prologue is of a fantastic character, and since Sir Thomas, as he says himself, based the later books on various prose historians. He mentions also Walter of Oxford (he says *Exeter*), but this doubtless means only that his source preserved Geoffrey's references to Walter.

Apparently the work follows the general course of Geoffrey's narrative, drawing from various versions of it, and with just such minor divergences and accretions (partly of a local nature, partly taken from romantic *rifacimenti*) as have already been so often noted here. Thus Leland quotes: "Sum Chroniques say that Uther vanquisshid Otta and Oza at Wyndegate by Coquet Ryver"; "Arthure was crouned at Wynchestre";[4] "Arthure gave to Loth, Anguisel, and Urien (the 3. Sunnes of Kahu) more Landes than their Auncetors had . . . to Loth Lownes and his eldest Sister."[5] (Geoffrey names only one sister of Arthur, though he implies

---

[1] Bk. ii, IV, 3, 20–21, 36–37, 50–51, 55–58; bk. iii, V, 125 ff.

[2] For the Maitland Club, 1836; *Prologue*, pp. 1–4; extracts, pp. 317–319 (on the author see pp. xii ff.).

[3] Ed. Lond., 1770, Part II, pp. 509–511; reprinted by Stevenson, pp. 259 ff. The manuscript of the *Scalacronica* is in the library of the University of Cambridge.

[4] Geoffrey, ix, 1, Cilcestria; cf. p. 229, below.   [5] Cf. pp. 232, 247, below.

another.)   "Arthure married Genouer, Cosin to Cador of Corne-
wail,[1] and Doughter to the King of Briscay,"—a monstrous romance
or ballad idea.[2]   According to Leland it was Hywain[3] who killed
Mordrede in the last battle, after which Arthur was "deadely
woundid, and cam to Avalon with Hiwayne."   The only narrative
passage printed by Stevenson, that relating to the battle of Bath
and Arthur's conquest of the Picts, is more abridged than Geoffrey's
text.[4]   There is inserted, however, a lively new detail, borrowed
from the author's acquaintance with actual warfare, of how Arthur
took archers to fight the Irish, mounting them behind his men-at-
arms.   The account of the wonderful lakes leads to the insertion of
other marvels, briefly described.   But Sir Thomas is not a lover of
the supernatural.   He leaves out Merlin's prophecies, because, he
says, they are not credible.[5]   Nevertheless, he defends the historicity of Arthur; to use Leland's words, in "a hole Chapitre spek-
ing agayne them that beleve not Arthure to have beene King of
Britaine."   Later, he mentions the discovery of Arthur's tomb and
Richard's gift of Calibourne to Tancred.[6]

VI. THE VERSION OF GEOFFREY'S STORY INCLUDED IN THE
RECUEIL OF SIRE JEHAN DE WAVRIN

At least as early as the first quarter of the fifteenth century, perhaps no later than 1390, there was composed in French and in
France, by a writer of whom nothing is known except that he may
have been a Bourbonnais, a version of Geoffrey's narrative which
was embodied, with only slight verbal changes, by Sire Jehan de
Wavrin in his voluminous *Recueil*, or complete history of Great
Britain,[7] begun about 1455, just a century after Gray's *Scalacronica*.
Of Wavrin himself it is enough to say that he was an illegitimate
son of a noble house, a brave warrior, who saw much service with
both the court and the Burgundian parties; that after the peace of

---

[1] Cf. p. 140, above.   [3] Cf. p. 161, above.   [5] Cf. p. 136, above.
[2] Cf. p. 266, below.   [4] ix, 3, 30–ix, 9, 7.   [6] Stevenson, pp. 37, 63.
[7] Edited by William Hardy, Rolls Series (see I, lxviii ff., 3).   My references
are all to the first volume of this edition.   On Wavrin see also Morley, *English
Writers*. VI. 154.

Arras in 1435 he settled at Lisle as lord of Forestel and Fontaine, and from that time chiefly devoted his energies to his history. As to the version of Geoffrey's story which he appropriates, there are, according to Hardy, certain features which clearly distinguish it from all others, but of these the only ones relevant to the present discussion are frequent allusions to the "Master of Histories" as an authority, and a commentary (inserted line by line) on the prophecies of Merlin.[1]

Examination proves beyond a doubt that this work is based directly upon Wace in the pre-Arthurian portion,[2] but that when it reaches Constantine, the father of Constans, it turns to Geoffrey, whom it thenceforth follows[3] with only occasional touches from Wace. The deviations from the sources, however, both in substance and in spirit, are decidedly greater than in any other of the real paraphrases of Geoffrey's story which have so far been considered.

In the first place, the whole manner of the narration illustrates in a still more marked degree all those characteristic mediæval French tendencies which have already been dwelt upon in the case of Wace and of the *Brut*. The style is that of the French prose romances. The author is prolix, vivaciously and delightfully garrulous and chatty, like a man who has all the time in the world himself and never imagines that his readers may be in a hurry. He abounds in figures and imaginative touches. Like a modern novelist, he takes us with him into the confidence of his characters, as when he says that Aurelien could not rest so long as he knew that there was any pagan left in the island;[4] or describes how Englist reflected on the easiest and safest way to deceive the Britons.[5] He shows great vividness in description, — he speaks of the pity and horror caused by the cries of the wounded and dying;[6] of the weeping of the women and children abandoned by the departing Saxons[7] and of

---

[1] Cf. p. 189, above.

[2] Cf. p. 143, above. Cf. also the treatment in the *Eulogium Historiarum* (p. 176, above) and Robert Mannyng (p. 204, above).

[3] Even to the inclusion (though with characteristic expansion) of Geoffrey's addresses to Bishop Alexander and Earl Robert (pp. 226, 436–438).

[4] Book iii, p. 305. [5] P. 212. [6] P. 302. [7] P. 207.

"Vorcimer's" people when they knew that he must die;[1] he dwells on the way in which the valiant knights fight;[2] he explains the stratagem by which the besiegers of Gorlois's castle entice him into issuing out;[3] he says that the giant, when mortally wounded by Arthur, roared so abominably that it seemed as if all the winds had got together into that place,[4] — and so on *ad infinitum*. He identifies the customs of the Arthurian period with those of his own time: — it is for artillery that Vortiger[5] and Gorlois[6] look when they wish to defend their castles; Greek fire is the cause of Vortiger's destruction;[7] "Vorcimer" is buried in St. Paul's at London, with his ancestors, the other kings of Britain;[8] Arthur is the heir of the royalty of the fleurs-de-lys;[9] all the battles are fought like those of the fourteenth century, with archers, men-at-arms, and knights.[10] Lucius has the men whom he sends out for an ambuscade choose their own leaders;[11] Arthur's war-cry is "Bretaigne";[12] his men are the "royalists";[13] and before engaging in any enterprise he takes counsel of his barons.[14] The speeches of the heroes are altogether modern,[15] and almost universally begin with the colloquial "Hee!" The desire to rationalize an old mythic element no longer understood appears when we are told that it was because "Vorcimer's" people respected him so much that they did not obey his directions about his burial,[16] or that Arthur himself cut off the giant's head.[17]

A marked characteristic of the author is his orthodox piety.[18] The Britons are always loyal Catholic chevaliers; Arthur's exaltation above other kings is especially due to his valiant enterprises in behalf of Catholic interests;[19] Vortigier's sins seem to be enhanced by the fact that they are fallings away from *la sainte foy catholicque*.[20] The author is also somewhat given to moralizing.[21] Altogether, it seems very probable that he was a churchman.

---

[1] P. 208.
[2] Pp. 408, 440, etc.
[3] Pp. 339–340.
[4] P. 399.
[5] P. 289.
[6] P. 335.
[7] P. 293.

[8] P. 211.
[9] P. 325.
[10] P. 348, etc.
[11] P. 410.
[12] P. 431.
[13] P. 445.
[14] Pp. 386 ff., 401, etc.

[15] Pp. 346, 425, etc.
[16] P. 210; cf. p. 136, above.
[17] P. 399.
[18] Pp. 205, 327, etc.
[19] P. 338.
[20] P. 220; cf. pp. 207, 324.
[21] Pp. 209, 299, 401, 434; cf. p. 208.

His personal interest in the story sometimes manifests itself in rather prolonged reproachful addresses [1] : — to Vortiger,[2] "Englist," Pascent, or Mordreth.   His abhorrence of the Saxons is extreme,[3] but he is as unconscious as Gottfried of Viterbo of racial differences, and even applies to the Britons the name *Anglois*.[4]

He characteristically introduces an element altogether new to the story by often referring to Dame Fortune as the arbiter of the affairs of men,[5] once or twice almost directly coupling her name with that of Jesus. Similarly, he introduces Cupid as the author of Uther's love, which he describes with the warmth and in the conventional language of amatory secular literature.[6]

The other points of interest can best be made apparent by running hastily through Wavrin's narrative of the Arthurian period and noting its chief variations from Geoffrey, so far as they have not been already mentioned.

Wavrin, or rather, his source, greatly expands the account of the first battle of the Saxons and Britons against the Picts, telling especially of Englist's valor ; Englist had long coveted the lofty rock on which he built his castle; his feast is described at greater length, and we are told that he has Ronixa repeat merry ballads in her own language for the entertainment of Vortigier.[7] By a strange confusion it is said that in the second of Vorcimer's battles, Pascent, fighting on the side of Vorcimer, and "Kartigern" on that of Vortigier, jousted against and pierced each other, but Pascent, it is added, recovered, through the excellent medical aid that he had. It is definitely stated that the third of these battles was least memorable.   Vorcimer gently rebukes Vortigier before the barons. Other Britons besides Eldol are made to escape from the massacre. It was the Saxons who had initiated Vortigier into the pernicious pagan error of augury to which he finally had recourse[8] — "and we ourselves," observes the author, "daily see the treachery of the *Anglois*, who are descended from the Saxons." On hearing Merlin's prophecy, Vortigier believes that in him is an angel of paradise, and

---

[1] Pp. 195, 197, 201, 216, 324, 436.
[2] Cf. p. 40, above.
[3] Pp. 301, 360.
[4] P. 204.
[5] Pp. 304, 324, 348, etc.
[6] Pp. 334, 336; cf. p. 258, below (Fabyan).
[7] Cf. p. 152, note 6, above (Layamon).
[8] Pp. 219–220.

repents that he consulted necromancers; similarly, later, Gavain's valor causes the enemy to believe that he is more than a human being.[1] Eldol asks and is allowed to lead the van in Aurelien's first battle against Hengist. It is the master-workman at Stonehenge, not Tremorien, who tells Aurelien of Merlin; Uther, by the advice of Merlin, sends messengers to Gillomith before proceeding to the Stones. There is great expansion in the narrative of Pascent's exploits in Germany, and somewhat less in the account of Uther's first battle against the Saxons. When Gorlois's men find Uther in the form of their master with Ygerna, they think that the real Gorlois, who was killed before their eyes, must have been a demon, sent to lead them to destruction.[2] Uther has a twelve years' interval of peace — apparently borrowed from the account of Arthur's reign. The manner in which Uther's well is poisoned is described. Misreading *Cilcestriae*, the author has made Arthur's coronation take place at "Cloucestre."[3] He misunderstands some of the details of the battle of Bath. He calls Duke Cador king;[4] says that Caerleon was on the Thames; that Quintilien had been made governor of Gaul by the Senate, not that he was the Emperor's nephew; makes Boso kill a second one of his pursuers, Cabellus.[5] Arthur, he says, had sent Gavain to Pope Sulpicius to be made a clerk, but the pope, foreseeing in the spirit of prophecy that he would be one of the most valorous knights in the world, sent him back. Leo is Lucius's companion, the Emperor of Italy.[6] There was hardly a Briton who was not wounded in the great battle with Lucius.

The author's source tries to explain why Geoffrey of Monmouth, whom, by a misunderstanding of Geoffrey's address to Earl Robert,[7] he makes an earl, said nothing (another mistake) about the campaign against Modred; and suggests that it was because Geoffrey himself was of the family of Modred. To this Wavrin adds that he thinks the reason was rather the abominable nature of the crime. It is especially noteworthy that the author tries to clear Queen

---

[1] P. 427; cf. p. 105, above.
[2] P. 341.
[3] Cf. p. 224, above.
[4] P. 446.
[5] Cf. p. 141, above.
[6] Cf. p. 85, note 2, above.
[7] Geoffrey, xi, 1.

Geneviere of all blame.[1] Her marriage with Modred, he says, was
due to his compulsion;[2] she hopes for aid from Arthur, and it is
because she is falsely informed that he was killed in the first battle
with Modred that she flees to Urbs Legionum to become a nun.
There she ends her days chastely and in great patience.[3]

In the account of Arthur's last battle and death, the author
clearly follows some current romance or traditional form. The
battle was the most terrible ever fought. Arthur himself pierces
Mordreth with his lance, so that a ray of light is clearly seen to
pass through the body of the disloyal traitor; but before falling
dead, Mordreth returns the blow and beats his uncle to the earth.
So far the resemblance to Henry of Huntingdon's account is obvious,[4] though the piercing, and that with a spear, and the wound by
Modred, are divergences, and points of similarity with the version
in the prose *Lancelot*. The rest of Wavrin's narrative, also, is much
like the *Lancelot*. At the end, he says, only Arthur and nine knights
are left alive. They go to a hermitage, where six of the knights die
forthwith of their wounds, and the seventh a little later, as Arthur
embraces him. Making his will, Arthur leaves the kingdom to Constantine, who is his nephew.[5] While the other two knights, Gifflet
and Constantine, are asleep, he vanishes mysteriously, but some say
that he was carried to the isle of Avalon. " But the history of the
Graal speaks otherwise, and some say that, Gifflet alone of his companions remaining, the two went to the sea-shore, where Arthur
gave Caliburne to Gifflet, entered into a boat which he found ready
there, and was borne away so rapidly that almost at once he was
out of Gifflet's sight."[6]

VII. Pierre Le Baud's *Histoire de Bretagne*

At about the beginning of the sixteenth century, Pierre Le Baud,
precentor and canon of Laval, composed, at the express command
of Anne of Brittany, a history of her native province.[7] In his
second chapter,[8] Le Baud begins a rather complete summary of

---

[1] Cf. p. 163, above.   [3] P. 441.   [5] Cf. p. 140, above, p. 252, below.
[2] P. 436.   [4] Cf. p. 120, above. [6] P. 447. Cf. pp. 101, 146, above.
[7] Edited by the Sieur d'Hazier, Paris, 1638.   [8] P. 20.

Geoffrey's work, which he follows closely, with occasional additional material, unrelated to the present discussion, drawn from other authors. The only point which need be noticed is that he often names, together with Geoffrey, "the author of the deeds of *Artur le Preux, autrement nommé le Grand*," which evidently must have been a work of a romantic nature.[1]

VIII. ALAIN BOUCHART'S *GRANDES CRONIQUES DE BRETAIGNE*

Another history of Brittany, composed at about the same time as Le Baud's, but much more notable as regards Arthurian material, is the *Grandes Croniques* of the Breton noble Alain Bouchart, published in 1514.[2] This begins with a somewhat condensed version of Geoffrey's whole story, largely interpolated in some places, but not in the Arthurian portion. The latter diverges from Geoffrey to a greater extent than the other sections, but the parallelism is generally very close, and the natural conclusion is that the author is chiefly following some work which in the main almost exactly reproduced Geoffrey's.[3] He occasionally draws (whether directly or indirectly) from the monk of Ursicampum's interpolated version of Sigebert, and to a slight extent from other authors, whom he names, principally, it seems, for ostentation. Many of his minor differences from Geoffrey are to be explained as mistakes in reading or interpretation, or as attempts to furnish an explanation;[4] and,

---

[1] Cf. what William of Malmesbury says of the source of his story about Ider (p. 99, above).

[2] Edited by H. Le Meignen, Nantes, 1886 (Société des Bibliophiles Bretons).

[3] The printed catalogue of books in the British Museum is certainly wrong in saying that Bouchart draws from Caxton.

[4] Such are: — the change of Saturnus into Neptune (fol. 41 a 1); the statement that Chedric was not present at the battle of Badon (49 a 2; cf. Geoffrey, ix, 4, 44) — doubtless to explain why he seems to appear again later (cf. p. 186, above, and p. 234, below); that Loth's province was London (49 b 2); that Arthur's coronation feast occurred five years after his return from France (51 b 1), — evidently to explain Cador's speech later (cf. p. 133, n. 10, above); that Lucius had been sent by Leo to reconquer France (52 a 1; cf. p. 85, note 2, above); that Arthur killed 476 Romans in the last battle with Lucius, — a remark resting evidently on confusion with the battle of Badon (cf. p. 183, above); that it was by

besides, there are the usual insignificant modifications in details.[1] Perhaps more important is the statement that the white dragon conquered the red.[2]

The author mentions the Round Table,[3] and expresses uncertainty as to whether Arthur is really alive or dead.[4] A decided change in the thread of the story appears when for the whole of Geoffrey's narrative of events between the duel with the giant and the last battle with Lucius is substituted an account of an embassy in the person of Guerin de Chartres, sent by Arthur to Lucius.[5] A still greater change is that which represents Arthur's victory over Flollo — who is called a giant [6] — as due to the interposition of the Virgin,[7] who blinds Flollo by covering Arthur's shield with her mantle.[8] As authority for this statement is adduced the *Memoriale hystoriarum*. Since the robe was furred with ermine, says Bouchart, Arthur, and after him the other kings of Britain, have worn the ermine in their arms.[9] A local French touch appears in the same place : because of this victory Arthur built a chapel to the Virgin in Paris on the site where Notre Dame now stands. A distinctly Breton twist is seen when we read that it was that one of Arthur's sisters whose name is mentioned by Geoffrey and others, namely Anna, here called Emine,[10] who is married to Budic and so becomes the mother of Hoel. She is also, very reasonably as regards some

---

the valor of Urianus that Modred was defeated in the first battle (55 b 1 ; cf. Geoffrey, xi, 1, 28) ; that Modred fled to Cornwall by sea (cf. Geoffrey, xi, 2, 10).

[1] Such are : — the statement that it was what the masons had built in eight days that fell down in one night (42 b 2) ; that Eldol wished to kill Hengist on the field, but Gorlois opposed (44 b 2) ; that the poisoning of Uther was effected by an embassy, which bribed his seneschal (48 a 1) ; the supplying of (inconsistent) dates, — 450 for Arthur's coronation (48 a 2), and 412 for his last war (52 a ; cf. p. 159, above) ; the statement that it is in the morning that Arthur goes against the giant (53 a 2). Not essentially more important is the assertion that at their death the assassins of Constans distinctly exonerated "Vortigerus" from having planned the crime (40 a 2 ; cf. p. 40, above).

[2] Fol. 43 b 2.   [4] Fol. 55 b 2.   [6] Fol. 50 b 2.
[3] Fol. 52 a 1, etc.   [5] Fol. 53 b 1.

[7] To whom also Arthur is made to appeal at Badon for the protection of the Catholic faith (fol. 49 a 2 ; contrast p. 161, above).

[8] Fol. 51 a 1.   [9] Referred to previously (fol. 5 b 2).
[10] Fols. 47 b 1, 48 a 1. Bouchard calls her "Anne ou Emine."

aspects of the story, represented as older than Arthur.[1] It is made
to appear, besides, that Uther did not get access to Ygerna until
after the death of her former husband and her marriage to Uther.
This in itself might have been due to the great condensation at this
point, but in effect it represents Arthur as of legitimate birth.[2]

IX. The *Cronica Cronicarum*

The compilation properly described by its title as *Cronica Cronicarum Abrege* was published at Paris in 1521.[3] Its history of Britain[4]
is a very brief and generally unmodified *résumé* of Geoffrey's. In
the Arthurian period it is especially abridged. It mentions the
Round Table, and expresses doubts of the possibility of Arthur's
expedition against " Flolon."

X. Jehan de Bourdigné's *Chroniques d'Anjou et du Maine*

Brittany was not the only province of France to find a native
historian in the beginning of the sixteenth century; for in 1529
Jehan de Bourdigné, an Angevin priest, published the *Hystorie agre-
gative des Annalles et cronicques Daniou*, etc.[5] The author is said to
have searched carefully for original documents, but naturally the
first part of his work, which extends fragmentarily from the Deluge
to Clovis, is almost entirely fabulous. After having spoken of
Julius Cæsar, he says[6] that, although he has heard of many notable
Angevins whose exploits as recounted seem sufficiently probable,
from then to the time of " Vortegrinus," king of Great Britain and
"occupateur du pays d'Anjou," he will omit them, for fear of arous-
ing incredulity. He then begins with Vortigern and recites the
Arthurian story, giving dates[7] which he has inferred, as he does
elsewhere, but otherwise for the most part following Bouchart's
version ; though he sometimes abbreviates (especially when he omits
all account of Arthur's first invasion of France)[8] and sometimes

---

[1] Cf. p. 224, with note 5, above; p. 242, below.   [3] For Jehan Petit.

[2] Cf. p. 184, above.   [4] Fol. 5 b.

[5] Ed. Angers, 1842, with an introduction by le Comte de Quatrebarbes and notes
by Godard-Faultrier.   [7] Cf. p. 159, above.

[6] Chap. 10, p. 45.   [8] Cf. p. 137, note 1, above.

inserts a bit of material irrelevant to this discussion, or makes an unimportant inference of his own. That he is ready to alter the narrative to suit his own ideas, appears[1] when, improving on Bouchart, he represents Childeric as escaping from the slaughter of the Saxons, evidently because he identifies him with the king of France of whom he speaks later.[2] He omits the story of Vortigern's tower, but he mentions it, with a "livre composé de la vie et faicts de Merlin le prophète anglois" and a prophecy of his which is evidently Geoffrey's. On the occasion of Arthur's wedding, he mentions[3] a tourney at which were present many knights, including "le paragon des hardis chevaliers, le très preux Lancelot du Lac, angevin, filz adoptif de la dame du Lac près Beaufort en Anjou, lequel y fist des proesses merveilleuses."

But the most original thing in Bourdigné's version of the story is the manner in which he connects it with Anjou and his own history.[4] It has already been stated that he incidentally speaks of Vortigern as "*occupateur* of Anjou." Where Bouchart says that Vortigern gave to Hengist possessions near London, Bourdigné asserts that the gift was "la ville d'Angiers et le consulat d'Anjou." An adequate reason for this alteration it is impossible to find, but the explanation is easy. Bourdigné was anxious to supply the lack of authentic history of his country as well and in as interesting a way as possible, and he has chosen to interpret the name *Angloys*, which Bouchart, like the other chroniclers, sometimes applies to Hengist's people, as meaning that they were Angevins. He has taken pains to prepare the way for this; for, where Bouchart[5] makes Hengist say to Vortigern "nous sommes Angloys de la terre de Saxonie, qui est une des régions de Germanie," Bourdigné puts it,[6] "Saxons de la région de Germanie." How Vortigern happened to be suzerain of Anjou, Bourdigné does not tell us.

The association of Hengist with Anjou naturally causes Bourdigné to look upon him with more favor than the other chroniclers. Thus, in speaking of Hengist's final treachery, he calls

---

[1] P. 60; cf. p. 231, note 4, above.   [2] Chap. 15, p. 70.   [3] Chap. 13.

[4] Of course this connection may have been made by some predecessor of Bourdigné's.

[5] Fol. 40b 2.   [6] P. 47.

it an act of vengeance for the ingratitude of the British nobles,[1] though he has previously followed Bouchart in saying that it was not seemly for the heathen Saxons to get so much power in a Christian land.

Bourdigné had the authority of the orthodox version of the Arthurian story for making Kay, whom he calls "Gayus," count — he says, *first* count — of Anjou. But he enlarges greatly the rôle of Gayus. He states, doubtless to establish a connection with his previous story, that Gayus was descended from the Dukes of Saxony, which race, however, as a true Christian, he held in great abhorrence. Bourdigné declares that he had greatly served Uter; ascribes to his arrival the victory in the battle of "Douglas," where he vainly tried to induce Colgrinus to stay and fight with him; associates him with Cador in the latter's ambush for "Badulcus" (which is made the direct cause of his elevation to the lordship of Anjou); says that he was the messenger whom Arthur sent to demand aid from Hoel; and otherwise magnifies his importance.

After speaking of Gayus's death, Bourdigné informs us that he was succeeded by his infant son Paul,[2] of whose subsequent brief history Bourdigné goes on to speak in a way which shows that he is drawing from a single obscure mention by Gregory of Tours[3] of a certain Count Paul of that period. Bourdigné can have no other reason for connecting this person with Kay than the desire to weave together the few bits of material which he was able to find. His whole method of composition is strikingly similar to that followed four hundred years earlier by his anonymous countryman who compiled the book on the building of the towns in Touraine.[4]

XI. Vernacular Spanish Chronicles

Of Arthurian material in vernacular chronicles of Europe other than those of France, I have found nothing except a single entry in a brief series of Spanish annals written at Toledo and extending

---

[1] Cf. p. 261, below. [2] Chap. 15, p. 70.
[3] Book ii, chap. 18 (*Recueil des Historiens de la France*, II, 170).
[4] See p. 123, above.

from the birth of Christ to 1219.[1] Here, under the year 542, it is recorded:

> Lidió el Rey Zitus con Modret su sobrino en Camblenc, Era DLXXX.

Menéndez y Pelayo states[2] that there is a passing allusion to the Round Table in the *Gran Conquista de Ultramar*, translated by order of Sancho IV, and that the prophecies of Merlin are mentioned in Ayala's *Crónica del Rey Don Pedro*.

---

[1] Published in the *España Sagrada* of Henrique Florez, Madrid, 1767, XXIII, 381–400.

[2] Fitzmaurice-Kelly, *Hist. de la Lit. Española*, Spanish translation by A. Bonilla y San Martín, Madrid, [1901,] p. xxvii.

CHAPTER IX

THE STORY AFTER GEOFFREY: CONTINENTAL LATIN CHRONICLES OF THE FIFTEENTH AND SIXTEENTH CENTURIES

EXCEPT for vernacular works in France, the Arthurian material seems to have received very little recognition from the Continental chronicles. As one looks over the universal histories written in Latin in Germany, France, and Italy, one is impressed with the fact that, for their compilers, the England of the middle ages was a distant corner of the world, whose affairs possessed but slight interest for them, — inhabitants as they were of those countries where the abrogation of the political system of the Roman Empire was accepted so slowly. For all the early part of English history, when they notice it at all, they often content themselves with a few brief sentences from Bede,[1] sometimes supplemented a little, however, from the stories, Arthurian or non-Arthurian, of Geoffrey.

The earliest of these writers [2] have already been included with the Englishmen in Chapter VI. And this was fitting, not only for convenience of classification, but also because of the universal and unnational character of the Latin culture of the period from the twelfth to the fourteenth century. Authors like Vincent of Beauvais, for instance, were for a long time well known and influential in England. But the decisive awakening of the modern spirit in the fifteenth century involved revolutions in literature as well as in all other phases of activity, so that while encyclopædic Latin histories

---

[1] As early as the eighth century, Paulus Diaconus (bk. xiii [xiv]) took from Bede the account of the summoning and the arrival of the Saxons (*Mon. Germ. Hist., Auct. Antiquissimi*, II, 200; Migne, *Patrol.*, XCV, 961).

[2] Ordericus Vitalis; Sigebert of Gembloux, as interpolated by the monk of Ursicampum; Gervase of Tilbury; Vincent of Beauvais; Albericus Trium Fontium; Martinus Polonus; "Martinus" Minorita; Johannes Historiographus.

continued to be produced as much as ever on the Continent, in England they almost came to an end, and the Continental ones can best be dealt with separately.

As regards the present subject, there is no particular change in the character of these chronicles. The following list, then, contains a sufficient account of those among them which I have found to contain Arthurian material.

Ca. 1422. Andreas, Presbyter of St. Magnus at Ratisbon, *Chronicon Generale.* This has merely the entry about Arthur which appears in Martinus Minorita (Pez, *Thesaurus,* 1721–1729, IV, iii, 362).

Ca. 1450. Antoninus (Forciglioni), saint and archbishop of Florence, *Chronica* (an immense universal history). He takes most of the Arthurian entries from Vincent of Beauvais, whom he cites. See Pt. II, tit. 10, chaps. 1 ff. (ed. 1543, *Chronica Antonini,* II, fols. xxxix a, b, xl a, xli b).

Ca. 1463. Flavius Blondus Forliviensis (antiquary, historian, and secretary to several popes), *Historiae ab Inclinatione Romanorum Imperii.* From Bede (or Gildas) is derived an entry with regard to the first coming of the Saxons at the invitation of " Vortigerius " (1st ed., Venice, 1483, fol. b. v. a). From the same source, though with free treatment, comes an entry of considerable length on the appearance of Ambrosius Aurelius, who, it is said, was finally killed, after many battles. The devastations of the Saxons compelled the Britons to emigrate. But Geoffrey, the writer continues, differs greatly from this, and he proceeds to give a summary of Geoffrey from Vortigern's marriage down to the accession of Arthur (fol. cii. b).

1474. W. Rolewinckius, *Fasciculus Temporum,* — an awkwardly composed summary of general history whose success was enormous. " Merlinus de incubo genitus claret in britannia spiritu prophecie, cuius instinctu Wortigonus rex britonum valde dilatauit fidem Christi. Huic successit Vterpandragon frater eius qui fuit pater arthuri " (ed. 1474, Coloniae, fol. [35a]). There are also three or four lines about Arthur (fol. [35b]).

Ca. 1474. *Magnum Chronicon Belgicum,* by an unknown Augustinian monk near Nussia (Pistorius, *Rerum Germanicarum Scriptores,* Ratisbon, 1726, vol. III ; see preface). This takes (pp. 17–18) from Vincent a brief summary of Arthur's reign to the battle of Bath, and another on Merlin and his prophecy, but as to Merlin's birth says : " Haec frater Bernhardus pene supra fidem." Bernhardus is unknown to me.

1486. Jacobus Philippus Foresti, Bergomensis (an Italian chronicler), *Supplementum Cronicarum.* On Merlin (1st ed., Venice, 1486, fol. 180b) there is an entry similar to that in the *Fasciculus Temporum*, but with more Galfridian details than occur in the first edition of the *Fasciculus*. There is also one short entry (fol. 183a) on Arthur, his arms, his aid to the church, his conquests, and the British expectation of his return.

Ca. 1486. Joannes Nauclerus (Chancellor of the University of Tübingen), *Memorabilium omnis Aetatis et omnium Gentium Chronici Commentarii*. After a line or two on the Saxon conquest (1st ed., 1516, II, 63a), the author observes (doubtless following Blondus) that Geoffrey writes otherwise, and gives a brief summary of Geoffrey's account from this point down to Merlin's prophecy. Under the year 478 (fol. 69a) he copies from Blondus the passage about Ambrosius, etc. Then he gives from Geoffrey an outline of Arthur's reign, but expresses doubts about the chronology, and after more from Geoffrey, and after quoting Foresti on Arthur's arms, etc., he ends with another expression of doubt.

Ca. 1500. Johannes Trithemius (Abbot of Spanheim), *Compendium, sive Breviarium . . . de Origine Gentis et Regum Francorum* (in his *Opera Historica*, Frankfort, 1601). In book i (p. 39) occurs a general entry of some length about Arthur and his conquests in the North of Europe, with an expression of distrust. There is also mention of Merlin and Utherpendragon.

1506. Raphael Maffei, Volaterranus (Italian cyclopædist), *Commentarii Rerum Urbanicarum libri xxxviii*, Rome, 1506. In the section on Geography (book iii, fol. 29) Maffei gives in two and a half pages an outline of the whole of Geoffrey's *History*, including the Arthurian period. He mentions the Round Table.

1521. Frater Laziardus, *Epitomata a Primęva Mundi Origine*, Paris, 1521. The author takes his Àrthurian material chiefly from Vincent of Beauvais, but shows independent knowledge. At fol. 103b he gives the story of "Vuertigerius'" tower, and a little about the prophecies, Aurelius, and Uter. He names as an authority a certain Ricardus. He omits the exploits of Arthur, "quia prolixę sunt et alibi inveniuntur ad plenum." At fol. 118a he has another brief mention of "Vertigerius."

1534. The Dutch Amand de Zierickzee in his *Chronica compendiosissima ab Exordio Mundi usque ad Annum Domini 1534*, published at Antwerp in 1534, gives a brief summary of the Arthurian section of Geoffrey's *Historia*, questioning its reliability.[1]

---

[1] See the extract printed by Reiffenberg, *Chronique rimée de Philippe Mouskes*, II, lxiii–lxiv. I am not sure that Reiffenberg is right in saying that Amand takes this material from Gervase of Tilbury.

1548.   For Paulus Jovius, *Descriptio Britanniae*, see p. 262, below.

Ca. 1564.   *Chronicon Monasterii Mellicensis*, in Pez, *Scriptores Rerum Austriacarum*, vol. I, Leipzig, 1721.   Under the year 464 (p. 191) occurs the entry about Arthur which appeared in Martinus Minorita.

? Robertus, canon of S. Marianus Altissidorensis, *Chronologia . . . Historiam Rerum in Orbe Gestarum continens . . . ad 1200*, Trecis, 1608.   Fol. 61 mentions Ambrosius Merlinus " sub Vorciguo rege."

For convenience of classification, mention may here be made of the late fifteenth-century rendering of Geoffrey into Latin prose by the Italian Ponticus Virunnius.[1]   This is a mere condensation, with no significant variations from its original, up to the beginning of the Arthurian period.   After this there are only a very few lines of incoherent jottings, based upon Geoffrey, except for the statement that from Bedver's son is descended the Venetian family of " Beduara," — for which family the book was written.[2]

---

[1] Edited by Commelinus in *Rerum Britannicarum Scriptores*, 1587, pp. 93–112 (see Hardy, I, 57–58, No. 163).

[2] Examination shows that there is no Arthurian material in the following chronicles, which on *a priori* considerations might be expected to contain something of the kind : —

Aeneas Sylvius, *Historia Rerum ubique Gestarum*, Venice, 1477.

Albertus Stadensis, *Annales*, 1256 (Pertz, XVI, 283 ff.).

Benedictus, monachus S. Andreae, *Chronicon* (Migne, CXXXIX).

Chronicon Incerti Auctoris, 1167 (in Pet. Stevart, *Insignes Auctores*, 1616, p. 717).

Hermannus Corner, *Chronica Novella*, 1435 (in Eccard, *Corpus Hist. Medii Aevi*, II, 431–1344).

Joannes Enenkl, or Einenkel, *Universal-Chronik* (in Pez, *Scriptores Rerum Austriacarum*, II, 537).

Theod. Engelhusius, *Chronicon*, 1420 (ed. J. J. Maderus, 1671 ; also Leibnitz, II, 977 ff.).

Johannes Marignola, *Chronica*, 1362.

Martinus Fuldensis, *Chronicon*, 1378 (Eccard, I, 1641–1732).

Otto Frisingensis, *Chronicon*, 1146 (Argentorati, 1515).

Romualdus II, archiepisc. Salernitanus, *Chronicon*, 1178 (in Muratori, *Rerum Italicarum Scriptores*, VII, 8 ff.).

Hartmann Schedel, *Chronicon*, 1493.

Sicardus, episcopus Cremonensis, *Chronicon*, 1213 (Muratori, VII, 530 ff.).

Siffridus, presbyter Misnensis, *Epitome*, 1307 (Pistorius, 3d ed., I, 1022 ff.).

CHAPTER X

THE STORY AFTER GEOFFREY: THE SCOTTISH VERSIONS

An altogether new phase in the history of the Arthurian tradition appears in the Scottish chronicles, which, in extant forms, began to be composed toward the end of the fourteenth century. Heretofore we have been concerned almost altogether with versions of the story told by those who in fact or in sympathy were countrymen of the heroes whom the tradition celebrates, and who were usually ready to exalt their fame. But in the Scots, we come to the traditional enemies of the races among which the Arthurian story arose and chiefly flourished, — a nation which, like the Saxons, were represented as contributing only by their defeats to the glory of Arthur and his predecessors, and which, unlike the Saxons, had not found opportunity or desire to forget that the defeats were theirs by going over to the side of the victors. We might naturally expect, therefore, to find the tone of the Scottish accounts different from that of all the others, and we must of course expect to find the record of British affairs subordinated to the Scottish history; but we could hardly have looked for the striking change in the attitude toward Arthur which has actually taken place.

The change is this: Loth and his son Modred have been regularly adopted as Scottish heroes; Arthur's illegitimacy[1] is emphasized; Modred is declared to have been the lawful heir to the British throne, so that in the war with Arthur (when that is not omitted) he is in the right, at least by implication, and Arthur, instead of being a paragon, is sometimes represented as one of the worst of kings.[2]

---

[1] Cf. p. 184, above.

[2] It must be noted that the *Brut* ascribed to Barbour by Wyntown is not known to exist. Cf. J. Nichol in Murray's *Minor Poems of Sir David Lyndesay*, E.E.T.S., Part V., 1871, p. xiii; Bradshaw, *Trans. of Cambridge Antiquarian Soc.*, 1866,

I. WYNTOWN AND FORDUN

It is true that these ideas do not appear at all in the interminable work on universal history entitled *The Orygynale Cronykil of Scotland*,[1] which was composed in the Scottish dialect about 1420 by Andrew of Wyntown, Prior of St. Serf's Inch. Wyntown, though distrusting such features as Merlin's prophecies,[2] takes from Geoffrey (immediately, as it seems) his outlining allusion to Arthur's conquests and last campaign.[3] He departs from Geoffrey only in mentioning the Round Table and in laying emphasis on the " Dowchsperys." But the ideas mentioned had already appeared in germ in the Latin narrative of the discriminating father of systematic Scottish history, John of Fordun, a work written about 1385, and properly to be entitled *Chronica Gentis Scotorum*.[4]

Of Arthur's reign Fordun says almost nothing, doubtless because it was not directly connected with Scottish affairs. But he does say distinctly that the succession to the kingdom belonged by right to Anna, the sister of Arthur and the wife of Loth, and to her children, because of Arthur's illegitimacy;[5] and he explains that the Britons actually chose Arthur for fear of the Saxons. He also notes the obvious but thitherto neglected fact that Geoffrey's statements about the relationship between Anna and Arthur are not consistent.[6] He explains Loth's connection with Scotland by saying that he was descended from Geoffrey's (pre-Arthurian) Fulgentius.[5] He takes pains to dispute the romance idea, which he records as existing,[7] that Modred was illegitimate.

---

reprinted in his *Collected Papers*, 1889, pp. 58 ff. The *Chronica of Mailros*, ed. Stevenson, Bannatyne Club, Edinburgh, 1835, aims primarily to continue Bede, and begins only with the year 731.

[1] Ed. by David Laing, 3 vols., Edinburgh, 1872–79; for date, see p. xxxiv.

[2] II, 9.

[3] II, 11–13. The direct use of Geoffrey seems to be shown by the occasional brief outlines of sections of Geoffrey's story in earlier parts of the work. Wyntown refers his readers for a full account of Arthur to the work of Huchown, now lost; and for the stories of Vortygerne, Utere, and Awrelius, to the *Brut*.

[4] Ed. W. F. Skene, Edinburgh, 1871–2 (vol. I, text; vol. II, translation); for date, see p. xiv. It is better known as the *Scotichronicon*, from the name given to its later (much enlarged) form. [6] Chap. 25; cf. p. 233, above.

[5] Bk. iii, chap. 24, p. 109. [7] Cf. p. 141, above.

Fordun's account of the rest of the Arthurian period shows, like the earlier part of his work, that the fabulous stories which he took,[1] doubtless from current traditions, as the genuine history of Scotland, had been largely built up, for the period extending from the time of Cæsar to that of Arthur, on the basis of those parts of Geoffrey's narrative which could be connected with Scotland, or at least that those sections of Geoffrey had been intimately combined with Scottish stories, with perhaps an occasional hint from Bede. What Fordun relates (always incidentally to the main thread of his narrative) of the British kings from Vortigern to Uther, is simply an often-interrupted story of wars and alliances entered into between them and the Scots. Practically, he represents that during the whole epoch the Britons and Scots fought in union against the Saxons and Picts. According to him, both Vortimer and Aurelius concluded special treaties with the Scottish sovereigns,[2] and this was finally true of Uther also, though at first he made war on the Scots and tried to take Westmeria from them. Evidently this is all based ultimately on Geoffrey, — who says nothing (at least explicitly) of any conflict carried on by Vortimer or Aurelius against the Scots, while he does say that Uther made an expedition against Alclud,[3] — with a suggestion, probably, from Bede's statement of a direct alliance between the Saxons and the Picts.[4]

II. JOHN MAJOR

The Latin *History of Great Britain* by John Major, or Mair,[5] differs from the work of Fordun in its treatment of the Arthurian period as a result partly of its combination of much material taken direct from Geoffrey's story with that of the Scottish version represented by Fordun, partly of differences of temperament in the two authors and of aim in their books, and partly of changes in judgment which the passage of a century and a half had brought about in the Scottish scholastic mind. As to form, it should be added also that, instead

---

[1] While also making as much use as possible of Bede.

[2] Pp. 99, 102, 103.   [3] viii, 19, 1 ff.   [4] See p. 24, note 2, above.

[5] Published in 1521. It is this first edition to which references are here made. On Major, see *Dict. Nat. Biog.*, XXXV, 386; Morley, *English Writers*, VII, 264.

of combining British with Scottish affairs in one continuous narrative,
Major separates them, giving for every period, first a section about
the southern part of the island, then one on the Scots.

It is Geoffrey whom Major takes as his main authority, and he
gives in brief outline practically the whole of Geoffrey's story, with
occasional slight differences suggested by sources which cannot be
definitely determined: as, for instance, in the details about Ronouen;[1]
in saying that Arthur conquered the Germans as well as the Gauls,[2]
and, like the *Brut*, that Vortiger's restoration to the throne was made
conditional on his not recalling Hengist.[3] The influence of the
Fordun version is evident in the mention of alliances of the British
kings with the Scots, and of Arthur's illegitimacy and Modred's right
to the throne.[4] Other Scottish elements not adopted by Fordun
appear in the statement that the alliance included the Christian
Picts; that Loth was also father of Thametes, who was mother of
St. Kentigern; and that Arthur's royal seat was at Edinburgh; and
in the account[5] of how Arthur returned the body of the slain
Anguischel with honor to his country (which, however, is summarily
stated by Geoffrey). The mention[2] of Arthur's holding the Round
Table in Cornwall reminds one of the southern elements of the story,
and the reference to Arthur's inclusion among the Nine Worthies is
a decidedly popular touch.[6] But ideas identical or related with some
which we have already encountered are : — the excuse which Hengist
gives to Vortiger for coming back;[7] the statements that after the
massacre of the British chiefs the Saxons took possession of all the
kingdom except Wales, that Hengist bade that it be thenceforth
called by his name, and that he divided it into seven kingdoms, and
destroyed all the churches and other signs of Christianity.

The personal element in Major's work consists in his comments
on the more fabulous portions of Geoffrey's narrative. This learned
scholar and divine does not reject the magic incidents, but tries
instead to explain them. He does, indeed, disbelieve the story of
the moving of the great stones[8] and Merlin's prophecy;[9] but he suggests two supernatural explanations for the birth of Merlin, besides

---

[1] Fol. 24.   [4] Fol. 28b.   [7] Fol. 24b.
[2] Fol. 29a.   [5] Fol. 29b.   [8] Fol. 27a.
[3] Fol. 24b; cf. p. 218, above. [6] Cf. p. 253, below.   [9] Fols. 27a and 28a.

the rationalizing one that his mother's account was false; and his criticism of Uther's amour takes the moralistic turn of condemning Merlin for his part therein.[1] Major expresses the opinion[2] that the exploits of Arthur, Gawain, and others are mere figments, if not performed by demoniacal art. But in the case of so great a king, he says, "I cannot assent to the belief of Bergomensis[3] that he was himself a magus."

III. Hector Boece and his Translators

A few years after Major's history, appeared one naturally to be grouped with Fordun's, to which it bears in character and effect[4] something the same relation which the work of Geoffrey of Monmouth bears to that of Nennius. This is the *Scotorum Historia* of the learned Hector Boece, first Principal of the University of Aberdeen, published in 1527. To discuss fully its extended treatment of the Arthurian material would demand much more space than the importance of the result would warrant. The main fact to be noted is that it is Boece who carries to an extreme the peculiar tendencies suggested by Fordun.

Boece differs from Fordun in that he makes no direct use of Geoffrey's *History*, but draws, evidently, from some later and expanded form of the story. But in the Arthurian period he approaches more closely than elsewhere to Geoffrey, doubtless because the Galfridian tradition was fuller at this point than any tales which he could find about his own country. In dwelling, like Fordun, on the alliances contracted by Aurelius and his successors with the Scottish kings, he lays emphasis on the utility of the assistance rendered to the former by the latter. He differs from Fordun's version, and to a certain extent agrees with Major's, in that during the earlier years he represents the Picts as parties to the alliance, not as opposing it. He is thoroughly patriotic, in mediæval fashion, and on almost all possible occasions makes it appear that it is the Scots who distinguish themselves and the Britons who are cowardly and treacherous.

---

[1] Fol. 28a; cf. p. 184, above. [2] Fol. 30a.

[3] I have not found this idea in Foresti's work, which Major here cites by the proper title.

[4] I do not know that Boece made any use of Fordun.

Boece's divergence from all previous recorded versions is scarcely less marked in details than in general spirit, and a rapid enumeration of some of the more striking points of divergence from Geoffrey seems necessary.

Vortimer is first introduced as a colleague of Hengist in an expedition against the Scots. The first settlement of the Saxons is said to have been in the North,[1] and Vortigern does not give them Kent until he begins to fear an attack from Aurelius. Vodinus, bishop of London,[2] reproves Vortigern for his marriage with Roxiena, and is therefore seized and put to death by Hengist. Hengist's excuses for his return after the death of Vortimer are that he wishes to help to avenge the latter's death, that he ought to look after Roxiena's son, and (as in Major) that he and his men want their lawful possessions in Kent. When Vortigern has fallen into the hands of the Saxons, he and all the Britons are compelled to leave England and go to Wales, on pain of death; and the same is later said of Uther when he has been conquered. The incidents in Aurelius's Saxon and Scottish wars, while most of them are included, are utterly disarranged and recolored, and the same is true of those in the wars of Uther and of Arthur. Uther is sick at the beginning of his reign; he makes Nathaliodus, a man without birth or fame, his commander, and this leads to the defection of Gothlois of Cornwall and the cession of half of the island to the Saxons. Another element from the original Saxon *Chronicle* version is the introduction of Cerdic and Cynric in their proper persons. Bede's Hallelujah Victory is associated with Uther.[3]

We come now to those details which touch the heart of the matter. Most significant of all is the treatment of Arthur's reputation. His revels in York are described in a most hostile spirit, and the opinion is cited that he was the first to celebrate Christmas with disgraceful orgies. Nothing whatever is said of any conquests of his outside the island. One of the main motives of Boece's narrative is the idea which appears so fully in the prose romances, — the hostility of Loth

---

[1] Cf. p. 25, above.
[2] Cf. p. 266, below.
[3] Cf. pp. 257, 261, 270, below.

to the Britons; but this is represented by Boece as being due to the faithlessness of the latter. Loth is portrayed as king of the Picts. His wife is called elder sister of Aurelius, not (as in Fordun and Major, and in the orthodox version generally) the [younger] sister of Arthur.[1] Uther's refusal to acknowledge Modred as rightful heir to the throne leads to wars between the Picts and the Britons, — wars which give way to an alliance when Arthur recognizes Modred as his future successor. It is because Arthur's barons persuade him to annul this agreement that Modred renews hostilities, and the (single) battle between the two kings, in which both are killed, is fought on the Humber. The Scottish king, Eugenius, an ally of Modred, remains master of the field and takes prisoner Queen Guanora (here first mentioned in Boece), whom the Picts hold in lifelong captivity. A local tradition about her tomb is mentioned.

Boece's work met with an enthusiastic reception, partly, no doubt, because it was the first Scottish history to be put into print. King James soon ordered two translations into Scottish to be made, — one in prose, by John Bellenden, which appeared in 1536,[2] the other by William Stewart,[3] in metre. Bellenden treated his original so freely that the result is almost an independent work; but with regard to the Arthurian period it is enough to note his tendency to supply reasons for the actions of his characters, to soften the records of cruelty, by whomever committed, and occasionally, — as in the account of Arthur's last battle,[4] — to abbreviate and condense.

Stewart's version, likewise, differs somewhat in details from its original, in the fact of condensation and otherwise, but demands no extended discussion. The author's final comment about Arthur,[5] however, is more extreme in tone than any single passage in Boece. He classes the fables which exalt Arthur's fame more than he himself

---

[1] Cf. p. 224, above.

[2] A new edition, Edinburgh, 1821, by Thomas Maitland, *The History and Chronicles of Scotland*. An English translation by Harrison was included in Holinshed's *Chronicles* (see p. 267, below).

[3] *The Buik of the Croniclis of Scotland*, ed. W. B. Turnbull, Rolls Series, 3 vols., 1858.

[4] Cf. p. 137, note 1, above.

[5] II, 261–262.

has done with those of " Fyn-Mak-coull " and " Robene Hude," and
concludes : [1]

> Considdering all his infelicitie,
> Haif e to richt and lat affectioun bé,
> I hald him for the maist vnhappie king
> Off all the Britis that did in Britane ring.
> For-quhy he wes so faithles and wntrew
> To king Modred, befoir as I ȝow schew,
> And manesworne als, the hand of God thairfore,
> As ressone wald, it tuechit him full soir.
> Britis bifore quhilk wes of sic renoun,
> Sensyne tha tynt baith thair kinrik and croun ;
> As plesis God, till all men weill is kend,
> Falsheid come neuir till ane better end.

IV. Other Versions (including Leslie and Buchanan)

The short chronicle of Scotland written in Scottish prose of about
1500 which appears in the Royal MS. of Wyntown [2] contains a single
Arthurian entry, [3] stating that Arthur was supported against the
Saxons by King Conrane of Scotland, whose nephew aided Modred,
King of the Picts, against Arthur in the battle where Arthur was
slain with all his nobility. This information is related to the assertions of Boece, and its importance is in about direct ratio to its
length. But there are still one or two more significant histories of
Scotland to be mentioned.

In 1578, to support the cause of Queen Mary and the Catholic
religion, John Leslie, Bishop of Ross, published at Rome his Latin
history *De Origine, Moribus, et Rebus Gestis Scotorum,* [4] which was
somewhat inaccurately translated into Scottish in 1596 by Father
James Dalrymple, who describes himself as a monk in the Scottish
cloister at Regensburg. [5] Leslie merely follows Boece until after the

---

[1] Vv. 27,977–27,988.

[2] Printed in Laing's edition of Wyntown, III, 321–338.

[3] P. 323.   [4] Reprinted in 1675.

[5] *The Historie of Scotland*, etc., ed. by Father E. G. Cody, Edinburgh, 1888–95,
2 vols.

end of the Arthurian period, but he abbreviates greatly. He does not even mention Vortimer, and as regards Arthur he does little more than repeat Boece's expressions of incredulity at the stories about him. But it is interesting to notice that he expresses the opinion that Arthur was the builder of a stone house formerly existing not far from the river Carron,[1] which Boece, while mentioning a vulgar ascription of it to Cæsar, was inclined to assign to Vespasian. He adds also a popular idea or two about Arthur,[2] saying that the number of his knights was twenty-four, and that he himself has seen what, "unless our ancestors have erred," is the veritable Round Table at Winchester (where we of the twentieth century may see it too if we choose).

Of the important and very popular *Rerum Scoticarum Historia* of George Buchanan, published in 1582, it is enough to say, at this stage of the discussion, that its account of the Arthurian period chiefly follows Boece, but with great condensation and some omissions and other changes of details due to the author's independence of judgment in comparing authorities and to his attempt to reason for himself as to the causes of actions.

---

[1] Ed. 1578, p. 95. [2] P. 146.

CHAPTER XI

THE STORY AFTER GEOFFREY: THE ENGLISH AND LATIN CHRONICLES OF ENGLAND IN THE FIFTEENTH AND SIXTEENTH CENTURIES

WITH the passing away of the interest in the rude rhymes of the early fourteenth-century chroniclers, English writers seem to have lost for a time all ambition to record the history of their country in their own language. Doubtless the reading public of the period following was satisfied for the most part with the translation of the *Brut*. Nevertheless, in the first half of the fifteenth century we again encounter English compilations, and at the end of that century begins a series of English historians whose works (thanks, in great measure, to the printing press) did far more to popularize English history among the people at large than those of all their predecessors put together.

I. JOHN CAPGRAVE

Decidedly significant from the historian's point of view is the chronicle of John Capgrave, the learned head of the Augustinians in England, who, using the annalistic form, made an attempt, sometime in the first half of the fifteenth century, to compose in English prose a really critical history of the island.[1] But among his two or three notices of the Galfridian story he includes for the Arthurian period only a single summary sentence about Arthur.[2] Later, under the proper dates, he mentions the discovery of Arthur's body and Edward's letter to the Pope.[3]

---

[1] *The Chronicle of England*, edited by Rev. F. C. Hingeston, Rolls Series, 1858.
[2] P. 87, ann. 5651–453.　　　　[3] Pp. 140, 172.

II. John Hardyng's Chronicle; and an Anonymous Chronicle in Metre

The chronicle of England which was composed in rough seven-line stanzas, probably about the year 1436, by the sturdy Northern squire John Hardyng,[1] shows, more than any other, direct influence from the romances.

The first part of this work consists in a condensed and interpolated version of Geoffrey's story. Most of Geoffrey's incidents, with the exception of several of the least credible ones, are reproduced or mentioned;[2] but the divergences in details, in some of which Hardyng agrees with the *Brut*, show that the source is not primarily Geoffrey's narrative. As points of difference from Geoffrey, the following may be especially mentioned : —

The assassination of Constantine is ascribed to Vortiger's instigation.[3] The whole account of the career of Constaunce[4] is confused, disagrees with Geoffrey in particulars (as in saying that Constaunce was a fool[5]), and is clumsily put together from two different versions, one of which represents Constaunce as being deposed. Vortiger is made to marry Rowan lawfully. Dates are given.[6] Uter's first victory over Occa and Oysa is put "beside Dane hill." Arthur is said to be especially tall.[7] Uter's arms,[8] called those of St. George, and Arthur's banners[9] are described. Cador is called Arthur's brother " of his mother's syde."[10] Loth is said to live at Dunbar,[11] — a Scottish touch. Arthur is said to have given Westsex to Cordryk after the battle of Bath ;[12] Arthur is said to have made Gawayne lord of Lowthyan ;[13] and is made to conquer almost all Western Europe.[14] Arthur's campaign between the fight at Mont St. Michel and the great battle with Lucius

---

[1] Edited by Sir Henry Ellis, 4to, Lond., 1812. See *Dict. Nat. Biog.*, and Morley, *Eng. Writers*, VI, 156.

[2] The chief exceptions in the Arthurian portion are: the story of Eldol's exploit (p. 113); the account of Vortigern's tower and Merlin's prophecy (p. 114), to which Hardyng alludes, but with a doubt of its authenticity (cf. p. 136, above); the story of the bringing of Stonehenge from Ireland (p. 116), as to which Hardyng merely says that it was erected at Merlin's advice.

[3] Cf. pp. 40, 184, above. [7] P. 121. [11] P. 124.
[4] Pp. 106–108. [8] P. 117. [12] Cf. p. 186, above.
[5] Cf. p. 257, below. [9] P. 122. [13] P. 126; cf. p. 105, above.
[6] Cf. p. 159 and note 12, above. [10] Cf. p. 140, above. [14] Cf. p. 223, above.

is omitted;[1] the latter is made to take place in "Romany," after Arthur has actually crossed the Alps and passed through Tuscany;[2] and the author distinctly states that Arthur himself killed Lucius.[3] Arthur gets to Rome and is crowned Emperor in the Capitol. Arthur in person kills Modred and receives his death wound from him.[4] Caliburn is said to have been of such virtue that it killed whomever it struck.[5] It is with a wise maiden that Gwaynour flees to Carlion.[6] Constantine is definitely represented as Arthur's nephew.[7] There is a categorical statement of Arthur's death and burial. In the final eulogy of Arthur, Gwaynour, whose beauty has previously been greatly lauded,[8] is especially blamed,[9] and with her "fals Fallas" or Deceit.

But the most significant changes consist in the insertion (briefly, in two sections) of practically the whole outline of those facts of the Grail legend[10] which are most closely connected with Joseph of Arimathea and Arthur's knights.[11] In connection with this are given the names of many of the knights of the Arthurian romances,[12] and, in various places, there is much detail about the Round Table. Hardyng says[13] that it was to comfort Ygerne that Uter[14] set the Table at Wynchester, which Joseph of Arimathea made for the brethren of the St. Graal only; that Loth was the first knight of the Table[15] (another Scottish touch); that, upon his marriage with Gwaynore, Arthur filled up the depleted ranks of the knights, upon which the laws of the order are given at length;[16] that Arthur's feast lasted forty days;[17] that in the battle at Winchester were killed all the knights of the Table except Launcelot[18] (for at Winchester, says Hardyng, the Round Table began and ended, and there it hangeth yet); that when Arthur had been buried, Launcelot and others came

---

[1] Cf. p. 136, above.

[2] Cf. p. 187, above.

[3] P. 144; cf. p. 201, and note 17, above.

[4] P. 146; cf. p. 120, above.

[5] P. 146; cf. p. 162, above.

[6] Cf. p. 219, above.

[7] Cf. p. 230, above.

[8] P. 124.

[9] P. 149; cf. p. 163, above.

[10] Cf. above, p. 189, and note 2.

[11] Pp. 83, 131–136.

[12] P. 137.   [13] P. 120.

[14] As far as is known, and as is said by Paris in his introduction to the *Huth Merlin*, Borron was the first to connect Uther with the Table. See chap. 3 of the ordinary *Merlin*, ed. Sommer.

[15] P. 120.

[16] Pp. 124–125; see above, p. 187.

[17] P. 128.

[18] P. 146.

to his tomb. And the names are given of more than a score of towns where Arthur sometimes held the Table.[1]

Together with Hardyng's *Chronicle* may be mentioned a fragmentary one of probably about the same period, also written in seven-line stanzas, which in its present form extends only from Gurgunt to Stephen.[2] The style is that of the old mystery plays; each king speaks in the first person. Arthur occupies twelve stanzas, beginning, "The first worthy I am of the faith cristian."[3] Most of the exploits attributed to him by Geoffrey are briefly outlined, and many of the late popular details, some of them drawn from Hardyng, are included.

III. The Metrical Version of the Story of Arthur's Reign in the Marquis of Bath's Manuscript

This manuscript is written for the most part in Latin and is unpublished, but the story of Arthur's reign is recounted in vigorous short-lined English verse.[4] It is based chiefly, with condensation, on the "frensch boke," that is, the *Brut*. There are some poetical touches, such as the observation (enlarging a little on the *Brut*) that the head of the giant whom Arthur killed was more horrible and great than that of any horse,[5] and the vivid description of the battle against Lucius.[6] The poet's religious feeling takes the form of occasional exhortations to his readers (or hearers) to pause and say a paternoster. Frollo is said to fight with an axe,[7] and the mortal wound which Arthur gives him is from the shoulder down, not in the head. Arthur's tomb at Glastyngbury is mentioned. For his sword, the name "brounsteelle," which appears also in romances, is given.[8] The Round Table is mentioned, with the cause of its institution.

---

[1] P. 126.

[2] In the sixteenth-century MS. Bodl. Douce, 341 (see Hardy, II, 197, No. 265).

[3] Cf. p. 244, above.

[4] Ed. Furnivall, *Arthur; a Short Sketch*, etc., E.E.T.S., 1864.

[5] Vv. 393–394.   [6] Vv. 457 ff.   [7] V. 85.

[8] In the English translation of the *Brut* it is written, by corruption, *Tabourne*.

IV. The Short English Chronicle of MS. Lambeth 306[1]

The two-page version of the Arthurian period here given is comparable to nothing but that of the short anonymous Middle English metrical chronicle. " Urtager " is called Earl of " Esex." The length of Constaunce's reign is given as three years.[2] No mention is made of any treachery on Urtager's part, and it is said that after he became king, he and Coslyn, the Bishop of London, sent Aurylambros and Uter into Litell Brettayne.   Engest is represented as having conquered all the land except Wales and as dividing it into eight kingdoms.   " Ingrene " was of the lineage of " Cornebyus of Troye,"—evidently an inference from the fact of her residence in Cornwall, — and it was from her name that Uter took that of England.[3]   There is no allusion to Modred, and it appears that Arthur ended his life in prosperity.[4]   " Where he is beryed the story make no mencion." [5]

V. John Ross and Nicholaus Cantaloupus

A belated Latin work, which certainly does not deserve to be included among the serious Latin chronicles, is the *Historia Regum Angliae* of John Ross of Warwick, written about 1485.[6] Its first part is based directly on Geoffrey's narrative, or more likely on incomplete excerpts therefrom; but nothing could be more discursive or fuller of interpolations of all sorts, great and small; and Ross is interested more in the stories of the foundation of his own city and in Greek philosophers than in the history of Britain.   His fragmentary notices of the Arthurian period are vague and inaccurate.   His laudation of Arthur,[7] who, he says, freed Britain from the Romans, is unqualified, at the opposite extreme from his brief characterization of Vortigern.[8]   He illustrates strikingly the popular tendency to connect heroes of the story with definite places

---

[1] Ed. James Gairdner, *Three Fifteenth-Century Chronicles*, Camden Soc., 1880, pp. 9–11.

[2] Cf. p. 159, above, with note 12.

[3] Contrast p. 218, above.

[4] Cf. p. 199, above.

[5] Contrast p. 199, above.

[6] Ed. Hearne, Oxford, 1716, 1745.

[7] P. 58.

[8] P. 56.   Cf. p. 40, above.

in the island. He states that Welsh records say that Constantine rebuilt Caerleon,[1] and asserts that Uter founded "castrum Pendragon" in the North.[2] He includes a Glastonbury fabrication which had been noticed by William of Malmesbury, to the effect that Arthur had given to that abbey the territory of Bremmerch.[3]

In this connection may be noticed the tradition, recorded earlier in the century by Nicholaus Cantaloupus, in his *De Antiquitate et Origine Universitatis Cantabrigiae*, that Vortumerus defended the scholars of Cambridge from the Saxons, — a statement accompanied by a transcript of the charter said to have been given to the university by Arthur.[4]

VI. ROBERT FABYAN

Coincident, roughly speaking, with the beginning of the sixteenth century, and a direct result of the new national consciousness and of the whole set of influences which the Renaissance exerted in England, is the appearance of that last and most important class of English chronicles to which reference has already been made, — those prose works, usually of considerable extent, whose authors, setting out, almost all of them, in an essentially modern, though not fully developed, spirit of judicial criticism, such as had characterized some of the Latinists like Higden, attempted to get together what seemed to be the credible facts, — in the later portion, from their own knowledge; in the earlier, from all the best previous authorities.

In one respect, however, the passage of time since Higden's day had made the task of these later historians more difficult, as regards the period here considered. There was no methodical criticism — and indeed no opportunity for it — to demonstrate that the now manifold series of chronicles which dealt with the Arthurian tradition in its post-Galfridian form really drew ultimately from a single source. Consequently most of these writers, unlike Higden, treated

---

[1] P. 53. [2] P. 58.
[3] P. 65. Cf. pp. 98–99, above. William's form of the name is Brentimaris.
[4] Edited in Hearne's *Thomae Sprotti Chronica*, 1719, pp. 267–269.

Geoffrey's book not as practically the sole authority for this current form of the tradition, but as only one (although the chief) among many or several authorities. But this fact may be over-emphasized ; for as a rule these chroniclers tend, even if not always on the best grounds, to look with some distrust on the incidents which are not mentioned by Nennius or one of the other pre-Galfridian historians.

The first work of this class, written about 1493, though not published until 1516, was the *New Chronicles of England and France*,[1] by Robert Fabyan, an opulent draper and very prominent citizen of London.[2]

Fabyan does not entertain a high opinion of Geoffrey's trustworthiness. He more than once speaks of him[3] as among the unauthentic historians whose testimony cannot be accepted without corroboration, and he shows no particular respect for his statements in the frequent discussions which he introduces as to the respective weight of conflicting evidence. Nevertheless, up to the end of the reign of Vortigern, he includes, sometimes with changes in details due to his collateral employment of other versions, most of the essential substance of Geoffrey's work. From the death of Vortigern the case becomes very different. As possible sources for Fabyan's divergences from Geoffrey in the Arthurian period, aside from indeterminable ideas, we need mention, from among the large number of authorities to which he constantly refers, only Bede, William of Malmesbury, Higden,[4] "the English Chronicle" (doubtless the translation of the *Brut*), "Guydo de Columpna"[5] (by whose name, Fabyan, following a long persistent error, probably means to indicate a form of the *Mer des Histoires*), and "an old chronicle of

---

[1] Ed. Sir Henry Ellis, London, 1811 ; see Morley, *English Writers*, VII, 267. The French material is given in occasional distinct sections.

[2] It ought to be remarked, by way of caution, that the following brief accounts of Fabyan and some of his successors, as well as those above given of some of his predecessors, are necessarily in a sense inadequate, even as regards the limited aspect of their work here under consideration ; because, with their somewhat prolix style, these writers sometimes elaborate details in a manner which is often quaint and interesting, but which must here pass without notice.

[3] For example, p. 75.   [4] In Trevisa's translation, according to Ellis.

[5] Cited, p. 18.

unknown author," which may be assumed to have been related to the *Brut*.

Up to the death of Vortiger, the following points deserve mention. Fabyan inserts [1] the Bede version of the prosperity of the Britons in the early part of Vortigern's reign, of the consequent sin of the land, and of the summoning of the Saxons. Like Boece, he connects Bede's Hallelujah Victory with Vortimer.[2] He gives as alternative to the other [3] an expanded version of William of Malmesbury's story of the Stonehenge massacre ; and in greatly abbreviating the narrative of Hengist's earlier machinations [4] he evidently draws partly from the same source. He presents in more detail an idea included by Hardyng, saying that Constant was put into a monastery because of his stupidity,[5] though others assert (he remarks) that it was of his own choice, from pure devotion. He adds that, according to most writers, Constant reigned five years ; [6] that, on the usurpation of Vortiger, many Britons went to Armorica to the help of Aurelius and Uther ; [6] that, after the Saxons had grown strong, Vortiger had to side with them, because the Britons forsook him ; [7] and that in his last extremity he victualled his castle well, knowing that he had not enough strength of knights to trust to.[8] The inconsistency of Fabyan's sources leads him to ascribe to Vortimer other battles besides the four.

The most important changes are due to Fabyan's critical attempt to make the narrative plausible. He merely refers to the story of Vortigern's tower and Merlin,[8] and later he omits all suggestion of magic in mentioning the transportation of the great Stones,[9] while he alludes to the story that Uther won his lady by Merlin's enchantment, only to say that it " is nat comely to any Cristen Relygyon to gyue to any suche fantastycall illusions any mynde or credence." [10] He modifies Vortimer's success, saying that he took from the Saxons most of their territory, and then often grieved them with such navy as he had. From this he passes on, alleging as his source "the olde cronycle," to an attempt at explaining Vortiger's restoration to the

---

[1] P. 59.
[2] P. 65 ; see p. 246, above.
[3] P. 66.
[4] P. 60.
[5] P. 58.
[6] P. 59.
[7] P. 62 ; cf. p. 40, above.
[8] P. 68.
[9] P. 69 ; but cf. p. 75.
[10] P. 75.

throne.   During Vortimer's reign, he says, Vortiger had been kept
in Chester under "tutors," but he demeaned himself so well that he
won the favor of the Britons.[1]

Beginning with Aurelius, Fabyan very largely rejects the Galfridian
story in favor of that of the Saxon sources.   He gives the outline of
most of Geoffrey's account of Aurelius and Uther, but sometimes
with entire confusion of details.[2]   Just as he had mentioned Hengist's division of the land into three parts (he supposes that the Saxon
conquest of the whole country was achieved, temporarily, at a single
stroke), he insists that the Saxons were never thoroughly crushed
nor driven away,[3] and that Hengist died in his bed after ruling
twenty-four years,[4] in spite of the British books.

Coming to Arthur,[5] Fabyan expresses his regret that he cannot
speak at length on credible authority of the hero's great exploits, half
apologizing to the Welshmen for his brevity of treatment.[6]   So he
gives only a summary, mostly from Higden, of Arthur's early wars,
alluding to the statement of some authors that the Saxons were trib-
utary to Arthur for the lands which they succeeded in holding.[7]
He goes on to remark that Arthur long fought against them, especially against Cerdic.[8]   He then mentions Arthur's expedition against
the Romans, refusing to accept it.   He gives without question the
story of Modred's union with Cerdic, and a brief outline of the usual
(Galfridian) narrative of Arthur's campaign against him; but he localizes the last battle at Glastonbury, and insists on Arthur's death and
his burial in "the vale of Aualon, besyde Glastynbury."[9]   His inclusion of the mention of Gawyn's death may be taken as indirect testimony to the vogue of the Gawain stories.[10]

Fabyan's attitude is so relentlessly that of the searcher for truth that
it is pleasant to mention, in leaving him, the single instance of poetic
feeling that he evinces in all this first part of his work.   Just before
stating that it was at the instigation of the devil that Vortiger asked for
Ronowen from his father, he observes, in the very manner of Wavrin,
that the king was wounded with the dart of the blind god Cupid.[11]

---

[1] Pp. 65–66.

[2] Pp. 68–70, 74–75.

[3] Pp. 68, 69, 79.

[4] P. 69.   Cf. p. 159, above.

[5] P. 79.

[6] Pp. 79, 81.

[7] Cf. p. 186, above.

[8] P. 80.

[9] Cf. p. 189 ff., above.

[10] Cf. p. 105, above.

[11] P. 61; cf. p. 228, above.

VII. John Rastell

The seriousness and real merit of Fabyan's chronicle did not pass without recognition, and it became a standard model for almost all those of the following century. Indeed, though the succeeding historians adopted Fabyan's method of careful independent investigation of sources, yet, for the early period of the history, several of them based their works directly upon his. Of these more immediate followers, the earliest is John Rastell, who in 1529 published *The Pastime of People, or The Chronicles of Divers Realms, and especially England.*[1]

Rastell's adherence to Fabyan's version of the Arthurian story is very close, but in some places he is a little less critical. For if he omits (very likely by accident) the story of Vortiger's tower, he mentions the statement that Hengist died in his bed only as an alternative account after saying that he was killed in battle against Aurelius. Fabyan did just the reverse of this. Rastell represents that it was after Arthur heard of Cerdic's death that he returned to oppose Modred, — as if Arthur had been afraid to do so earlier. He also gives considerable discussion to the print of what was supposed to have been Arthur's seal (which had been previously mentioned in the chronicles), then kept at St. Edward's shrine in Westminster, about the border of which, he says, was written, *Arthurus patricius Brittanie Gallie et Dacie imperator.* As to the credibility of the whole account of Arthur's exploits, after observing that Geoffrey's "long story" does not agree with other writers, so that some think he composed it "for affeccion," he expresses himself thus: — "But yet, all this not withstandyng, I wyl nother denye the seyd story of Arthur, nor exort no man presysly to affyrme it; but to let euery man be at his lyberte to beleue ther in what he lyste."[2]

VIII. Polydore Virgil

However sincere may have been the efforts of Fabyan to arrive at historical truth, he labored under one disadvantage, which his contemporary compatriots certainly would not have admitted as such,

---

[1] Ed. Dibdin, 1811, in the same large quarto series with Hardyng and Fabyan.
[2] P. 107.

namely, that of being an Englishman. To attain an attitude of still
more deliberate skepticism was reserved for a scholar of Italian birth,
the well-known Polydore Virgil. Polydore's foreign origin is the cause
of another fact which differentiates his work still more, externally,
from the other great English chronicles of the century, — the fact
that it is written in Latin.

Polydore Virgil held, for most of his life. various ecclesiastical and
other offices in England under the fickle favor of Henry VIII. It
was at the suggestion of that monarch that he prepared his *Anglicae
Historiae Libri XXVI*, which occupied him for many years, and
appeared in 1534.[1]

The most significant thing about Polydore's work, for the present
discussion, is his general attitude toward the Arthurian story and
the whole Galfridian narrative. This is often misrepresented. The
vigorous defence of Geoffrey which was undertaken by Leland,[2]
Price,[3] Stow,[4] Howes,[5] and others,[6] in the first century following the
appearance of Polydore's history, was originally called forth by him,
and was largely directed against him in a spirit of spiteful national
prejudice and in neglect of the fact that he was by no means the
first to deny Geoffrey's authority. As a matter of fact, Polydore
not only merely followed the lead of Fabyan and his successors in
this regard, but he does not flatly reject Geoffrey's narrative, though,
to be sure, this seems to be chiefly from unwillingness to speak out
too boldly. He does not attack Geoffrey by name, but quotes, with
disguised approval, part of William of Newburgh's arraignment of
him,[7] taking care to say that he does not endorse William's opinion
but merely repeats what has been said before. He even thinks it
wise to refer to Merlin, at the proper place,[8] though naming him only
as a figure of the belief of the "vulgus." While he states plainly

---

[1] At Basle. The edition to which references are here made was published in
the same city in 1570.

[2] *Assertio Inclytissimi Arturii*, 1544, and *Codrus, sive Laus Arthuri* (see p. 50,
note 1, above).

[3] *Historiae Brytannicae Defensio*, 1573.

[4] *A Briefe Proofe of Brute*, in his *Annales*, ed. 1631, pp. 6–7.

[5] Editing Stow (see *Historicall Preface*).

[6] See, for example, John Caius's animadversions against Polydore in *De Antiquitate Cantebrigiensis Academiae*, ed. 1574, p. 52.   [7] P. 17.   [8] P. 57.

that nothing is more obscure than the early affairs of Britain, he begins his historical narrative with an outline of the Galfridian account of the pre-Roman kings, expressing his unwillingness to do so and his belief that the story is full of errors,[1] and making as he proceeds frequent additions and corrections. For the Roman period, he draws mostly from classical historians, and once or twice notes the evident incredibility of the "historia nova."[2]

For the first part of the Arthurian period,[3] Polydore follows Nennius (minus his supernatural incidents), Bede, and Gildas; but with interpretation and descriptive expansion of his own which sounds at first to a modern reader scarcely less ridiculous than the fables which he rejected, — rationalization on an irrational basis, it might be called. Thus, he tells how "Vortigerius" was chosen king by the Britons because he was chief of all in authority, birth, and valor,[4] and says that the Saxons, when hard pressed by the Picts in their first battle, redoubled their efforts on reflecting that their success would determine their reputation with the Britons. It is notable that Polydore represents Vortigern as thoroughly patriotic,[5] at least in the beginning of his reign, and excuses his partiality for the Saxons on the ground of their services to him.[6] His moral bias[7] becomes evident occasionally, as when, accepting the story of Vortigern's union with Hengist's daughter, he characterizes it as setting the worst example within the history of mankind. His account of Aurelius and Vortimer, whom he seems to make contemporary (Aurelius as general, and Vortimer as king), is entirely confused, — a natural result of the effort to harmonize Gildas, Nennius, and other authorities.[8] He makes Ambrosius kill Hengist in the battle of the Don[9] and himself fall in battle shortly after. He includes Uther, but the chief works that he ascribes to his reign are the Hallelujah Victory[10] and the Battle of Badon.

When he comes to Arthur, Polydore makes it clear that he accepts, in a modified form, the current idea of his greatness. For although,

---

[1] Pp. 18–19.
[2] See p. 32.
[3] Pp. 54 ff.
[4] Cf. p. 266, below.
[5] Contrast p. 40, above.
[6] Cf. p. 234, above.
[7] Cf. p. 183, above.
[8] Cf. p. 40, above.
[9] Cf. p. 184, above.
[10] Cf. p. 246, above.

in giving a brief outline of the Galfridian story of Arthur's reign,[1] he specially observes that it is only a tradition of the common people, remarkably exaggerated, yet he decides that the king was "noe doubte suche a mann as, if hee hadd lived longe, hee surelie woulde have restored the whole somme beeing almoste loste to his Britons."[2]

IX. ARTHUR KELTON

One of the most indignant replies to Polydore was that of Arthur Kelton[3] in his little *Chronycle with a Genealogie declaryng that the Brittons and Welshemen are lineallye dyscended from Brute*, printed in London in 1547, and now exceedingly rare. Kelton, whose energetic patriotism can scarcely be over-emphasized, resolves the question into a dispute between the Romans, with "Polidorus" for their leader, on one side, and "us Welshmen" on the other. Nothing could be more unimportant than his wildly rambling doggerel tetrameter stanzas. He cites as authorities Geoffrey and other chroniclers (some of whom I have not been able to find), but has only two or three casual mentions of Arthur, though he describes, at a length of several lines, the discovery of his body. The genealogy at the end has, for the two extremes, Osiris and Edward VI, but it includes by name only the most important of the intermediate monarchs, following Geoffrey's list for the period which it covers.

X. GEORGE LILY

A work popular in its time, as numerous editions show, but now insignificant, written, by the accidents of the author's life, in Latin, is the *Chronicon* of George Lily, Roman Catholic divine, and son of the famous grammarian William Lily. It appeared first at Venice in 1548, in the same volume with a *Descriptio Britanniae, Scotiae, Hyberniae, et Orchadum, ex Libro Pauli Jovii Episcopi Nucer. De Imperiis, et Gentibus Cogniti Orbis*, etc. The *Descriptio Britanniae*[4]

---

[1] P. 60.

[2] I quote from the English translation made soon after the appearance of Polydore's history (ed. Sir Henry Ellis, Camden Soc., 1846, I, 121).

[3] See *Dict. Nat. Biog.*, XXX, 359.   [4] Fols. 5, 6.

gives in brief outline the Galfridian account of Vortigern's reign and of the wars of Arthur against the Saxons, and mentions the discovery of his tomb. Lily's part begins with a few pages[1] about English and Scottish names, and a eulogy, addressed to Paulus Jovius, of various English scholars of the sixteenth century.[2] His chronicle[3] is entitled *A Bruto . . . omnium in quos . . . Britanniae Imperium translatum Brevis Enumeratio.*[4] Lily perhaps shares Polydore's skepticism about Geoffrey's story, though, in view of the brevity of his treatment, this is not a certain inference. At any rate, he omits everything from Brutus to Julius Cæsar, and in the very summary and much curtailed outline of the story with which he begins his list of monarchs, he has scarcely more than a mention of Vortigern, Arthur, and the intermediate British and Saxon kings.

XI. Bishop Cooper

Polydore Virgil was the last of the significant Latin chroniclers. In the year following the appearance of Lily's book, was published another of those English works which go back directly to Fabyan, — the widely-circulated *Epitome of Chronicles* begun and carried down to the birth of Christ by Thomas Lanquet, and completed by Bishop Thomas Cooper of Winchester. The entries that concern the Arthurian period are few and brief, and they are almost entirely taken from Fabyan.[5] There is a marked tendency to omit all magic elements, to which the bishop sometimes refers as being of the common voice of the people. Cooper, indeed, distrusts the whole Galfridian story; and, in beginning the early history of Britain,[6] Lanquet, also, warns his readers that it is very doubtful, adding that he will not dissent from the common opinion, but will follow Geoffrey as nearly as possible.

---

[1] Fols. 42b ff.   [2] Fols. 45–54.   [3] Fols. 57–125.

[4] The later independent editions are called *Chronicon sive Brevis Enumeratio*, etc. It is reprinted in Gruter's *Chronicon Chronicorum politicum*, 1614, vol. I.

[5] Perhaps the only exception is the remark that the histories of the Scots say that the Picts and Scots were allied with the Britons (fol. 143b).

[6] Fol. 27b.

XII. RICHARD GRAFTON AND JOHN STOW

Among all the English historians from the beginning, there are scarcely any two who would have been more reluctant to have their names associated than the well-known printer Richard Grafton and his professional and personal antagonist, the antiquarian tailor John Stow. But in effect their rivalry has proved a reason for conjoining them hardly less sufficient than active collaboration would have been.

The most popular historical books in England in the last part of the sixteenth century were the brief outlines prepared first by Grafton, and afterward, when their success suggested imitation, by Stow. Grafton's little *Abridgement of the Chronicles of England* first appeared in 1562 or 1563, and was frequently reissued. It is essentially a series of dated annals, generally brief, extending from Brute to the year of publication. Each edition was newly revised, and differs from the others in many minor details. In all the early portions, at least, the book is based primarily on Fabyan, though it sometimes borrows from other chroniclers, ancient or recent.

Stow first put forth his *Abridgement of the English Chronicle* in 1565. It ultimately surpassed its rival in favor, and was often republished during a period of fifty years. The various editions are not always identical, nor even in agreement in all details.[1] They are seldom at variance with Geoffrey.

It is interesting to note that the personal hostility of Grafton and Stow does not prevent them from borrowing occasionally each from the other.

Not many particular features of these abridgments need to be registered. Toward Arthur, Grafton adopts an attitude of moderate skepticism similar to that of Fabyan, while Stow gives only a very scanty outline of the whole of Arthur's reign. Both are interested in the establishment of the Round Table and in the question whether it was held at Windsor or at Winchester.[2]

---

[1] The second, that of 1567, represents a somewhat shorter redaction, but the other editions which I have examined all belong to the earlier and larger form.

[2] In the edition of 1571 Grafton refers to and makes use (fol. 12a) of what seems to be an interesting lost chronicle "written by a Monke of Saint Albons, but his name by some indiscreete persons is torne out of the booke." Comparison shows that he does not mean the St. Albans edition of Caxton.

Less important is Grafton's minute *Manuell of the Chronicles of Englande from the Creacion of the Worlde to this Yere . . . 1565*, which in the really English portion (down to the Norman Conquest) is scarcely more than a list of kings, with a note of the length of each reign. Through the period covered by Geoffrey, it agrees almost entirely with him.

Neither Grafton nor Stow was willing to stop with these minor works, and, in the preparation of a more extensive history, Grafton again had the start. His *Chronicle at Large* appeared in 1569. For the most part it agrees substantially with his *Abridgement* in whatever that includes, and it is almost as dependent upon Fabyan for the Arthurian part of the story as was Cooper. For while, in the earlier portions, Grafton makes use of Cooper and others of the many authorities whom he names, when he comes to our period[1] he takes almost his whole account from Fabyan, often nearly verbally. The only points of divergence are: — the insertion (with slight changes) of Geoffrey's narrative of the death of Vortimer, of Vortiger's surrendering his land, and of Pascent's deeds, — these as alternatives to Fabyan's versions; the omission of Fabyan's rejecting allusion to the story of the building of Stonehenge; the use of Nennius (from whom Fabyan differs slightly) for the names of Arthur's twelve battles; the statement that Arthur built Windsor and there founded the Round Table, with mention of " Frosard " as authority, and the observation that some think it was rather Winchester,[2] because " there is the Table "; the mention, from Hardyng, of Arthgall of Warwick, with the addition of the names of two of his successors in his lordship, and one or two other local details.

Stow's larger work, *The Chronicles* (later called *Annales*[3]) *of England*, was issued in 1580. It generally agrees in dates and otherwise with his *Abridgement*. He bases his account of the Arthurian period on Cooper, but he draws also from many others of his predecessors — the Saxon *Chronicle*, Bede (from whom he takes a good deal), William of Malmesbury, Geoffrey, Hardyng, Fabyan, Grafton, and

---

[1] Ellis's ed., 1809, I, 73 ff.

[2] An opinion which he himself adopts in later versions of his *Abridgement*.

[3] This is the title in Howes's ed. of 1631, to which references are here made.

Ross, as well as some others who cannot be identified. The result is one of the most heterogeneous narratives in the whole history of the tradition. It will suffice to pass over most of the details and mention some of the especially notable features.

Stow omits [1] all mention of Geoffrey's story of Constantinus and Constans, because he follows the historical narrative represented by Bede. Of Vortiger's accession he says only that the Britons thought good to appoint some king, and so unanimously elected Vortiger.[2] He includes, briefly, most of the events of the reigns of Vortiger and Vortimer as they appear in the Galfridian story, but in the whole narrative he omits supernatural incidents, so that he has nothing, for instance, about Vortiger's tower. Whenever he has occasion to mention a place (Thong Castle, Stonehenge, or another), he shows his antiquarian instinct by entering into a digression upon it. He includes the incident of Vodine, Bishop of London,[3] which appeared first in Boece. After giving, with some confusion, Bede's account of Aurelius Ambrosius, he introduces from William of Malmesbury, though professedly only on William's authority, the statement that Aurelius and Arthur fought together against the Saxons.[4] He mentions the story in *The Chronicles of the Britaines* of the removal of the Stonehenge circle from Ireland "by the industrious meanes of Merlin."[5] On Uther he gives only a ten-line summary.[6] Like Sir Thomas Gray,[7] he says that Guinever was Cador's cousin and daughter to the king of Biscay. At the beginning of Arthur's reign he makes a statement[8] of the relations with Scotland not identical with anything in the extant Scottish histories, — namely, that Lotho and Conradus, Arthur's allies, envying his prosperity, made war upon him, but he conquered them and put Anguisel over them. He mentions the establishment of the Round Table, and says that it was held at Winchester (like Grafton) and at Camalet (here first appearing in the chronicles). He stops to discuss the remains of Camalet and to speak of a silver horseshoe found there, and of Arthur's Table in Denbigh. He speaks of the greater part of Arthur's doings at

---

[1] Contrast Higden (p. 185, above) and Holinshed (p. 269, below).
[2] P. 50 ; cf. 261, above.   [3] P. 51.   [4] P. 53.   [5] P. 53.
[6] P. 53.   [7] See p. 225, above.   [8] P. 54.

home, but for his foreign conquests merely alludes to his "warres beyond the seas (where he wrought many wonders, as some haue written, but farre vnlike to be true)." Then he passes to a summary statement of Modred's alliance with Cerdic, and Arthur's last campaign. He definitely dates Arthur's death on May 21, 542.

XIII. Raphael Holinshed and William Harrison

In 1577, three years earlier than Stow's large history, appeared an even more ambitious work, the *Chronicles of England, Scotland, and Ireland*, by Raphael Holinshed, which formed a part of an immense compilation of universal history planned, but never completed, by the publishers.

Some of the material of the work as printed was prepared by the industrious chronologer William Harrison.[1] Besides the account of the Arthurian period in his translation of Bellenden's translation of Boece,[2] he gives in the preliminary *Description of Britain*[3] a very brief outline of the succession of early British kings, intended to show that they had been supreme over Scotland. The Arthurian section of this outline shows in an interesting way how strange a version could now be compounded, especially by one who was inclined to give heed to the various Scottish stories. Constantine, it is said, kills Dongard, and subdues all Scotland. There is no mention of Constans. Vortiger gives various regions in Scotland to Hengist, who, desiring the whole kingdom, is banished, and conspires with the Scots against Aurilambrose, the right heir. He is taken prisoner in battle by Eldulph de Samor, and his head is struck off at the command of Aurilambrose. The Scots are vanquished, but Octa, son of Hengest, is spared, and receives Gallowaie. Uter conquers the Saxons and Scots. Arthur succeeds. His noble acts, says Harrison, have been stained by vulgar fables, but he subdued the Saxons with the help of the Scots and Picts. When the Scots rebel

---

[1] Harrison wrote also a *Great Chronology*, never published. See Morley, *English Writers*, VIII, 368.

[2] V, 136–162, of the six-volume quarto ed. of Holinshed, 1807–1808.

[3] I, 201–202. The *Description* was also edited, in part, by Furnivall for the New Shakspere Society, 1877–8.

and besiege Howell in York, Arthur defeats them and establishes Angusian and his brothers. At Arthur's royal feast Angusian (as in Geoffrey) bears his sword. It is strikingly illustrative of the difference between the spirit of the sixteenth century and that of the twentieth that this outline of the Arthurian period could appear without explanation in the same work with Holinshed's version of the history of that time.

Of Holinshed's life little is known except that he began his literary career as a translator in a printing office and describes himself in his will as steward to Thomas Burlet of Bramcote. His personality is attractive, — none the less so because one of his prominent characteristics is credulity. It was not possible for a writer at the end of the sixteenth century to accept *in toto* traditions like that of Arthur without question, but Holinshed was very far from possessing the temperament of Polydore Virgil, and often seems to take pains (not so much in our period as elsewhere) to record impossible marvels.

Among the long list of authorities cited by Holinshed[1] occur the names of Alfred of Beverley, Bede, the *Chronica Chronicorum*, the *Chroniques de Britaine*, Caxton's *Chronicles*, Fabyan, Gildas, Geoffrey, William of Malmesbury, Henry of Huntingdon, Boece, Hardyng, Fordun, Stow, Nennius, Polydore Virgil, and Cooper. As borrowings from most of these sources occur in the narrative of the Arthurian period, and as this covers about thirty printed pages (six or eight times as much space as the corresponding section of Stow), we must confine our attention to the more important features. First, as to Holinshed's attitude toward Geoffrey.

In a good deal of the pre-Arthurian story, Holinshed follows Geoffrey, sometimes rather closely, but in the Arthurian period he does so only very little. Several times he expresses directly an unfavorable opinion of Geoffrey's book. In a confused passage[2] in which he tries unsuccessfully to say (following the erroneous version in Higden[3]) that the Constantine of Bede is a different person from Geoffrey's, he observes that "there is not so much credit to be yeelded to them that haue written the British histories, but that in some part men may with iust cause doubt of sundrie matters

---

[1] I, ix.   [2] P. 552.   [3] See p. 185, above.

conteined in the same." Geoffrey's statement that the Saxons were driven from the land he characterizes as unlikely,[1] referring his readers to William of Malmesbury and other old authentic historiographers to whom we "maie vndoubtedlie and safelie giue most credit." Though he follows Fabyan in speaking of Hengist's return,[2] he glosses in the margin : " He might easilie returne, for except I be deceiued he was neuer driuen out after he had once set foot within this Ile." He alludes to the story of Vortigern's tower as "not of such credit as deserueth to be registred in anie sound historie,"[3] and, in mentioning[4] Uther's expedition to Ireland, he omits Merlin and the magic element. After noticing the story of Arthur's wars in France, he concludes :[5] " For so much as there is not anie approoued author who dooth speake of anie such dooings, the Britains are thought to haue registered meere fables in sted of true matters."

Geoffrey is not the only author whom Holinshed views with suspicion. He rejects Henry of Huntingdon's story of the destruction of Vortigern by fire from heaven,[6] and he occasionally notes and discusses the inconsistencies in his other sources. Evidently he desired to be critical; but how little that quality accorded with his natural mental disposition appears from his introductory observations about Arthur,[7] whom he calls, at his accession, " a yoong towardlie gentleman, of the age of 15 yeeres or thereabouts." " Of this Arthur," he goes on, " manie things are written beyond credit, for that there is no ancient author of authoritie that confirmeth the same : but surelie as may be thought he was some woorthie man, and by all likelihood a great enimie to the Saxons, by reason whereof the Welshmen . . . haue him in famous remembrance."

The other more notable points in Holinshed's narrative are as follows. He includes, drawing, it should be borne in mind, from many sources, chiefly not from Geoffrey : the story of Constantinus and Constantius ; Vortigern's scheming and accession, — with the statement that he garrisoned the Tower of London ; the coming of the Saxons, summoned by the council " after they [the council] had throughlie pondered all things " ; the early plotting of Hengist, with

---

[1] P. 559.   [3] P. 564.   [5] P. 576.   [7] P. 574.
[2] P. 560.   [4] P. 565.   [6] P. 564.

the wassail incident ; the story of Vortimer ; Vortigern's restoration and the massacre ; a long statement of the establishment of the Saxon kingdoms ; some material about St. Germanus, with the Hallelujah Victory ;[1] the coming of Aurelius and Uther ; more Germanus legend : Aurelius's whole reign, in very brief summary ; some account of Saxon affairs ; most of the story of Uther, following Fabyan's version of Arthur's birth, which makes him legitimate ;[2] an outline of Arthur's reign, through the northern conquests ; Arthur's last campaign chiefly according to Geoffrey ; the discovery of Arthur's body. Near the end, Holinshed makes a rationalizing observation which illustrates the Elizabethan manliness of feeling which attracts one strongly to him. He says of Gawain that, "like a faithfull gentleman, regarding more his honour and loiall truth than neerenesse of bloud and coosenage, [he] chose rather to fight in the quarell of his liege king and louing maister, than to take part with his naturall brother in an vniust cause."[3] With true knightly sentiment he defends the reputation of "Guenhera,"[4] mentioning the Melwas myth as we know it in the *Life of Gildas*

XIV. William Warner, Michael Drayton, and the End of the Chronicles

Holinshed and Stow are the last writers who have any strong claim on our attention. The only later works which need even be mentioned are two poems partly and incidentally of chronicle character, the *Albion's England* of the London attorney William Warner, published in 1586, and the *Polyolbion* of Michael Drayton, which appeared, with prose annotations by the learned John Selden, in 1613.[5] Different as these productions are in nature, each includes an outline (divided, in the *Polyolbion*, into widely scattered fragments) of a large part of the Galfridian narrative, not based altogether upon Geoffrey, but too brief or too poetical to differ very notably from him

---

[1] Cf. p. 246, above.   [3] P. 576.

[2] Cf. p. 184, above.   [4] P. 580; cf. p. 163, above.

[5] *Albions England*, ed. 1612, chap. 19, pp. 88–91. The book contains also a prose epitome of the history of England (see pp. 357–358). *Polyolbion*, ed. of 1622, reprinted by the Spenser Society, 1889–1890.

or to have any special importance. As to prose, there was no break in historical composition at the end of the sixteenth century, but the succeeding works have ceased to be chronicles and have become histories. The spirit of criticism, besides, was developing, and in these histories the pre-Saxon period of the story sank into a still less prominent place than with Grafton and Stow. Geoffrey's credibility was attacked by some and defended by others, but even those who maintained it adopted his narrative only in very condensed outlines.[1] The Arthurian tradition had ceased forever to have any large importance outside its legitimate sphere of romance and poetry.

---

[1] Here it may be noted that the fabulous English compilation of MS. Harl. 2414 and the slight summary of the Arthurian story in MS. Sloane 1090 are both of the seventeenth century and therefore too late to have any value.

CHAPTER XII

CONCLUSION

THE history of the Arthurian tradition in the chronicles, as it has been traced in the foregoing pages, may be briefly summarized as follows : —

About the middle of the sixth century, Gildas, a British ecclesiastic who had fled to Armorica, wrote, as introduction to a violent denunciatory epistle, a very brief sketch of the history of Britain. Though entirely incidental in character and warped by extreme prejudice, this sketch gives the only nearly contemporary account of the Arthurian period. It outlines in a few words the general course of events, —the coming, devastations, and conquests of the Saxons, the paralysis of the Britons at first, their subsequent uprising and resistance, which ultimately (when Gildas wrote) had checked the invader, and their continuance in civil wars. It names Ambrosius Aurelianus and the Battle of Badon.

During a long period which began, perhaps, not very much after the time of Gildas, there was gradually put together by other British authors, — of whom the last important one, at the end of the eighth century, was Nennius, — the very composite *Historia Britonum*. This work practically includes in a general way all the facts of the Arthurian period mentioned by Gildas, and it supplies also the name Vortigern for the unlucky prince whom Gildas represented as ruling when the Saxon invasion commenced, and the characters and names of Vortimer, Hengist, Horsa, Octha, and Ebyssa. For the last four of these, as well as for the first, some corroborative testimony is furnished by the Saxon accounts of the period given by Bede and the *Chronicle*, — accounts which are otherwise altogether at variance with Nennius. The bulk of the *Historia Britonum*, so far as it concerns our discussion, is made up of fabulous tales about Hengist's treacherous plots and his marriage of his daughter to Vortigern, and of

272

the story of Vortigern's tower and the supernatural boy Ambrosius. Much more straightforward and plausible is the summary catalogue of the twelve victories of Arthur, *dux bellorum*, of which the last is identified with the battle of Mount Badon. Legendary stories about Arthur are also briefly recorded in two *mirabilia*.

Among the few Saxon chroniclers of the next three hundred years, Æthelweard briefly retold the story of Bede, with perhaps a few touches from Nennius and a few from his own imagination. William of Malmesbury and Henry of Huntingdon, with whom the chronicles of England reëmerged into real importance in the first quarter of the twelfth century, employed much the same method as Æthelweard, but with far more license, — combining and rearranging at will the narratives of Nennius, Gildas, Bede, and the *Chronicle*. Their significance is mostly limited to the fact that they may have given the first stimulus and some general suggestions to Geoffrey of Monmouth.

With Geoffrey, a literary artist of great genius and remarkable good fortune, there came into being, a few years later, the romance which passed for centuries as the History of the Kings of Britain, and which determined — and indeed largely created — the form of the Arthurian story found in the chronicles. Geoffrey based his narrative as much as possible on the work of Nennius, and necessarily to a far smaller extent on Bede and Gildas; but he utilized the whole stock of his reading and knowledge wherever and however he thought most convenient. He drew especially from Celtic myths and traditions, including those which he found connected with Arthur, and which as connected with him had been already mentioned in the *Annales Cambriae* at the end of the tenth century and by William of Malmesbury. Geoffrey drew also from Celtic records, lay and ecclesiastical; from his knowledge of general history (sometimes borrowing directly from William of Malmesbury and Henry of Huntingdon), and from the life, manners, and romantic literature of contemporary Norman England and France. He wrought together all these diverse elements into a consistent and continuous narrative. To begin the Arthurian period, he appropriated from Bede the figures of the Roman Constantinus and Constans as the founders of the royal line in which he placed Aurelius (Gildas's "Ambrosius Aurelianus") and Arthur. Nennius furnished him with nearly the complete outline for his account of Vortigern's reign, and he added (or developed) Merlin and his prophecies. He invented (or took from sources now unknown) the whole history (consisting chiefly of successful wars against the Saxons) of Aurelius and the Uther whom he adapted as the brother of Aurelius and father of Arthur. His most significant work was to add to his greatly expanded version of Nennius's sketch of Arthur's victories at home, the narrative of his foreign conquests;[1] to portray both the king and his knights in the colors of contemporary chivalry and courtly romance; and to recount at some length the treason of Modred against Arthur as husband and as king, and Arthur's vengeance, fatal also to himself.

The national epic material of one of the most romantic peoples in the world had thus been put into a definite form supremely appropriate and apparently authoritative. In this form, — the ground having doubtless been already prepared by many less systematic tales on the same subject, — it was made current by popular story-tellers, and swept over mediæval Europe almost in an instant, so that Arthur and his knights were adopted not only as English but as Christian heroes. That the material continued for centuries, partly as a result of Geoffrey's influence, to hold a place of unsurpassed importance in romantic literature, is a fact with which we are not here directly concerned. But whether or not Geoffrey had so intended, his book was taken seriously by the historians. Not only did the French, English, and Latin metrical chroniclers of the two following centuries, — who, whether they wrote for the upper classes or for the populace, were rather poets or rhymers than historians, — continue to paraphrase Geoffrey's story almost entire, but the sober Latinists of the monasteries, with very few exceptions, regarded it with careful attention ; and while there were some among them, even from the first, who discerned its true nature, or viewed it with great distrust, and while most of them, owing largely to the character of their works, did no more than to extract from its pages a few brief notices, there were not wanting others (and that among the most painstaking) to embody it almost verbatim in their compilations, and many more drew upon it very freely. In its almost countless

---

[1] For this he probably took the hint from ancient stories.

repetitions during a very long period, the history, as thus told in chronicles, naturally underwent very great modifications of detail. These were due sometimes to the carelessness or inaccuracy of those who rearranged it, sometimes to their unjudicial and instinctive love of romance and a good story, sometimes to their desire to reconcile it with other historical authorities or with ideas of their own. The narrative necessarily gathered up also some touches from current popular tales about its heroes, and increasingly (especially after the first couple of centuries) from the related very elaborate prose romances, which in their origin had been largely inspired by it. In the long French prose compilations of the fourteenth and fifteenth centuries it was itself treated throughout in a fashion thoroughly romantic. It received occasional notice in Continental chronicles not dealing especially with England, but only in those of England did it hold a place of the largest importance. Naturally the Scottish historians gave it much attention, but often only to travesty it in the interest of national prejudice and animosity. In exceedingly various shapes, then, it reached at last the English prose historians of the sixteenth century. These men were setting out seriously, under the lights and shades of the Renaissance, to compile the authentic history of their country. Credulous as some of these were by nature, and impossible to the time as was a genuinely scientific method, yet they did not fail to question the Arthurian story at every point and to reject, and train the reading public to reject, or distrust its least credible features. Gradually, with the passing of the mediæval spirit, passed away the importance of the story to history, and by the beginning of the seventeenth century, it came to occupy in history only a comparatively insignificant place. For four hundred years and more, this narrative in which there were scarcely a few glimmerings of truth had aided most signally in supporting the usurpation of romance upon the realm of fact, but the age of romance was at last ended, and fact, though not yet swollen with parvenu insolence, could not much longer be largely kept from what was rightfully its own.

ADDITIONAL NOTES

CERTAIN articles which (with one exception) have appeared since the foregoing pages were in the hands of the printer, demand notice here.

PAGE 26

Mr. Anscombe has lately renewed the argument that the scenes of Arthur's battles as named by Nennius are to be identified with places in the region to the south of the Roman walls, that is, in Upper Britain.[1] His reasoning will hardly convince those who have heretofore been skeptical. He prefers the forms of the names in the Vatican MS. (which suit the theory better) and puts more confidence, among other points, both in the historicity of Nennius's list and in the occasional trustworthiness (accidental trustworthiness, perhaps it is only fair to say) of Geoffrey than the majority of students will think justified.

Mr. Anscombe's disagreement[2] with another of my conclusions may be noted. He believes Nennius to be right in saying that Octha and his followers first settled in the North, and suggests that they may have removed to Kent in consequence of Arthur's victories. " The extreme eastern point of Kent was a strange place wherein to station the Saxon auxiliaries who had been hired to defend the Roman province [sic] against the northern peoples of the Picts and Scots."

PAGE 47

Gewissae, the name which Geoffrey gives to Vortigern's tribe, is a Saxon name (Plummer's Bede, II, 89).

PAGES 49 ff.

In some notes on Geoffrey[3] Mr. Ward proposes the following hypothesis about the liber and its connection with the Historia, which seems interesting and possible enough to be here reproduced, though, as he himself says, it is not much more than guesswork.

---

[1] Ztsch. f. Celt. Phil., 1904, V, 103–123 ; cf. pp. 15–16, 26–28, above.
[2] P. 110; cf. p. 25, above.   [3] Anglia, 1901, XXIV, 381–385.

" Archdeacon Walter of Oxford brought home from Brittany an Old Welsh MS., containing many British genealogies and several historical glosses. He had not leisure (perhaps not skill enough) to translate these into Latin, and arrange them. He naturally turned to South Wales, where Robert of Gloucester was Prince of Glamorgan, and Urban was Bishop of Llandaff." Geoffrey was recommended to him, undertook the work, and did it, " from first to last, under the sanction of Archdeacon Walter."

PAGE 90

For another Oriental parallel to Uther's change of form see Oertel, *Jour. Amer. Oriental Soc.*, 1905, XXVI, 186. Professor Oertel also quotes Pausanias, v, 18, 3 : ὡς συγγένοιτο Ἀλκμήνῃ Ζεὺς Ἀμφιτρύωνι εἰκασθείς.

PAGES 96 ff.

In an article on *The Round Table*,[1] Professor L. F. Mott argues plausibly for a connection in folk-lore observances between the Celtic Round Tables on the one hand and, on the other, the druidical circles and the various circular or oval objects in Great Britain which are or have been popularly associated with Arthur. He thinks that they all point back to primitive agricultural festivals, and suggests therefore that Arthur was originally an agricultural god. This last inference is perhaps as likely to be true as any of the theories which have been proposed to explain the mythological elements in the conception of Arthur ; but it does not seem more probable than these other theories, especially in view of the manner in which popular and romantic stories develop. At all events, the character of agricultural divinity does not differ greatly from that of culture hero, which one of these theories assigns to Arthur. Whoever is inclined to accept either hypothesis must readjust for himself the emphasis in part of what has here been said [2] of the growth of the idea of Arthur before Geoffrey. He must picture to himself not an historical (or supposedly historical) figure gradually attracting to itself the débris of various mythological personages, but two distinct figures, one mythological, the other historical, gradually united, with all their attributes.

PAGES 189–191

The arraignment of the existing text of William of Malmesbury's *De Antiquitate Glastoniensis Ecclesiae* has been strongly renewed by Mr. W. W. Newell.[3]

---

[1] *Publ. Mod. Lang. Assoc.*, 1905, XX, 231–264.   [2] Pp. 107–108, above.
[3] *Publ. Mod. Lang. Assoc.*, 1903, XVIII, 459–512.

Mr. Newell makes it appear probable (though there is no absolute proof) that the Arthurian entries in this work (among many other sections) are inter-polations made in the latter part of the twelfth century. It must therefore be doubted whether the idea that Arthur and Guenevere were buried at Glas-tonbury[1] really antedates Geoffrey's *Historia*. The same is true of the story of Arthur and Ider,[2] for the insertion of which, in particular, Mr. Newell has a plausible theory[3]; though it hardly seems to me justifiable (considering the frequent occurrence of such episodes in romantic literature) to assert positively[4] that the ultimate source of this story is Geoffrey's account of the duel between Arthur and the giant of Mont St. Michel.

Mr. Newell's discussion[5] of the discovery of the bodies of Arthur and Guenevere is not altogether in agreement with mine.[6]

I see no reason to alter my statement that the account of this incident given in the *Flores Historiarum* is copied from that in the Coggeshall Chronicle. It is true that the date 1187, which I have given[7] for the latter chronicle, merely marks the year at which Abbot Ralph took up the task of compilation.[8] It seems also to be true that Roger of Wendover more prob-ably began his work on the *Flores* at the year 1188 than at *ca.* 1200, the date which (using round numbers in a case of uncertainty) I have put down.[9] But we must suppose that Ralph wrote before Roger, and Roger's work is still only a compilation up to 1202.

Mr. Newell's conclusion[10] that Giraldus had never heard of a connection between Arthur and Glastonbury before 1191, while it may be true, does not seem to me to be borne out by valid evidence.

Mr. Newell appears definitively to reject Giraldus's assertions about the instrumentality of King Henry II in the discovery of the bodies. But even if Giraldus is wrong, as appears to be the case, in saying, in the *Speculum*, that the king suggested the search to *Abbot Henry*, nevertheless in his ear-lier account (that of the *De Principis Instructione*) Giraldus's statement is[11] that the king had made his communication to *the monks*. It may well be that this is the fact and that in his later version Giraldus may be writing carelessly, or, as Mr. Newell suggests, may have forgotten. Distrust of Giraldus would seem to me better grounded if I could accept the statement[12]

---

[1] See p. 191, above.   [2] Pp. 98–99, above.   [3] Pp. 493–497.

[4] P. 497, note.   [5] Pp. 505–509.   [6] Pp. 189–191, above.   [7] P. 172, above.

[8] It is, therefore, in the absence of definite knowledge about the authorship of the earlier part, the best assignable date for this earlier part, in which occur the bulk of the Arthurian entries.   [9] P. 173, above.   [10] P. 508.

[11] As Mr. Newell's citation (p 507, note 2) shows.   [12] P. 506, note 1.

that the *De Principis Instructione* was not written until 1217. The dates of both the composition and the publication of the treatise as a whole and in its various parts are only inferential and uncertain; but the statement just mentioned seems to be taken inadvertently from Mr. Warner's conclusion [1] that the complete work was *published* about 1217. Mr. Warner's discussion [2] affords good reason (never controverted, so far as I know) to believe that the first *distinctio*, which contains the passage in question, was written (if not published) some time before the year 1200.[3]

However, the statement that the bones were found at a depth of sixteen feet may be false, and if so it is the less unlikely that they may have been found by accident; and the conclusion which Mr. Newell adopts, namely that the discovery was planned, or manipulated, by the Abbot, to enhance the glory of Glastonbury, must always be borne in mind as an alternative to (or possibly as coöperative with) the theory which I have followed, involving machinations of King Henry.

PAGE 213

It has recently been pointed out [4] that the verses said in the *Polistorie del Eglise de Caunterbyre* to have been engraved on Gawain's sword occur also, together with an explicit and extravagant statement in prose of the size of the various parts of the sword, in a manuscript which is said to be of the reign of Edward I, a few years earlier, that is, than the *Polistorie*.[5]

Professor A. C. L. Brown has called attention [6] to the fact that the *Gaban* [7] whom the verses call the maker of the sword is probably the famous smith known in Welsh stories as *Gofan*, or *Govan*, in Irish as *Goibnin*.[8]

---

[1] Giraldus, *Opera*, VIII, xv.   [2] Pp. xiv–xx.

[3] My "about 1194," though it is, I think, not unreasonable, perhaps sounds more definite than our actual knowledge warrants.

[4] *Rom.*, 1905, XXXIV, 279–280.

[5] The verses were printed by Madden in his *Syr Gawayne*. M. Meyer has shown also (*Rom.* XXXIV, 98–100) that the last four verses are a commonplace, known to exist in varying forms in still three other MSS.

[6] *Modern Philology*, 1903, I, 100.

[7] The name has generally been corrupted to *Galan*, etc., in the MSS., unless as Professor Kittredge suggests to me, *Galan* (*Galant*) is here the earlier form and is to be taken as a corruption of *Wayland*.

[8] Professor Rhŷs has brought the same fact to my notice, and adds that the mediæval Irish word for "smith" was *goba*, or *gaba*, genitive *gobann*, etc.

In the article just referred to[1] Brown makes the extremely probable suggestion that the smiths to whose workmanship Layamon ascribes Arthur's burnie and spear[2] were both originally no other than Gofan.   It seems to me that we must accept Professor Kittredge's emendation[3] of Madden's translation, which would make Wygar (i.e. *Wigheard*, battle-hard) the name not of the smith, but of the burnie, and *Wite3e* the name of the smith. *Wite3e* will then apparently be a corrupt form of *Widia*, or *Wudia*, the name given in Anglo-Saxon mythology to the son of Wayland.   But whether this is so, or Madden was right in supposing *Wygar* to be a corruption of *Weland*, or Wygar is an independent person otherwise unknown, Brown certainly seems to be right[4] in saying that Saxon narrators might easily substitute their own legendary smith for the Welsh one whom they found in the story.   It seems altogether probable that the name of the other smith, *Griffin*, whom Layamon calls maker of the spear, is merely a corrupt form of *Gofan*, the more especially, as Brown observes, in view of the verses on Gawain's sword referred to above.   To quote Brown's words : " In Irish and Welsh, wonderful arms are regularly said to be the work of Gobban.[5] He would therefore be the natural artificer of Arthur's magic accoutrements." From all which follows the main conclusion of the article, namely that in these, as in other instances, Layamon is preserving in Saxon disguise original Welsh ideas.

Similarly Brown gives almost certain confirmation to the theory that Layamon's name *Goswhit* for Arthur's helmet is a Saxon translation of a Welsh name.   He points out[6] that most of the names of Arthur's possessions in *Kulhwch and Olwen* contain the idea of "whiteness."   Even *Gwenhwyfar* is "the white enchantress."   " Probably all the belongings of the Celtic Other World had whiteness or luminosity attributed to them."

I am glad to transcribe also from the article just under discussion two minor points.[7]   (1) Layamon's form *Winetlonde*[8] for Wace's *Guenelande* (Greenland) as the country of one of Arthur's subject kings, seems to show that Layamon thought *Gwynedd* (North Wales) to be meant.   (2) *Gille Callæt*[9] means "prudent gillie."

---

[1] Pp. 99–100.   [2] See p. 162, above.

[3] Appended to Brown's article, p. 99, note 4.

[4] And parallel cases bear him out (p. 99, note 5).

[5] Doubtless one should always remember that the name was originally generic, not personal.   [6] Pp. 101–102.   [7] P. 97.

[8] See p. 164, above.   The equation of *Winetlonde* with *Gwynedd* was suggested by Professor Kittredge.   [9] See p. 159, above.

PAGE 218

I have overlooked the fact that the Dorell and Richard whom the French *Brut* names (together with Holdinus) as recipients of fiefs in France from Arthur are evidently identical with Borellus Cenomanensis and Guytardus Pictavensis whom Geoffrey (ix, 12) mentions (with Holdinus) among the Gallic lords present at Arthur's coronation. Why the *Brut* makes them relatives of Arthur does not appear.

PAGE 232

The Guerin de Chartres who appears in Bouchart is evidently the Guerinus Carnotensis whom Geoffrey (x, 4) also represents as a member (though not the chief member) of Arthur's embassy to Lucius. The author of the account in the *Liber de Constructione* [1] applies the appellative Carnotensis, by confusion, to Boso of Oxford.

PAGE 239

The Ricardus cited as authority by Laziardus is probably Richardus Cluniacensis. [2]

PAGE 242

Some further explanation will make clearer the reason for Fordun's objection to Geoffrey's statements about the relationship between Arthur and Anna. Geoffrey (viii, 19 and 20) first represents that Arthur was the eldest child of Uther and Igerna, and that Anna was also their daughter. In the next chapter he says that Uther had given Anna in marriage to Lot. He implies a considerable interval between chapters 20 and 21, but the statement is not altogether plausible in view of his remark (ix, 1) that Arthur was fifteen years old at his accession. It is consistent enough with what Geoffrey says of Lot and Gawain in ix, 11. But in ix, 9 Geoffrey tells us that in the time of Aurelius, Lot had married his (Arthur's) sister. Since Aurelius died, according to the rest of Geoffrey's account, long before Arthur's birth, this statement is in absolute contradiction to both the others. Fordun partly bases his criticism, however, on a misconception of Geoffrey's language in ix, 9, which Fordun, like Boece later, [3] interprets as meaning that Anna was the sister of Aurelius.

Geoffrey's statement (ix, 2) that Hoel of Brittany was the son of a sister of Arthur obviously implies a second sister. The occasional confusion of the two in later chronicles [4] was to be expected.

---

[1] See p. 123, above.   [3] See p. 247, above.
[2] P. 171, above.   [4] See pp. 183, 232, above.

Still later (xi, 2) Geoffrey calls Cador's son Constantine, to whom Arthur leaves the kingdom, Arthur's *cognatus*. (Later versions say, *nephew*.[1]) Geoffrey has represented Cador as Duke of Cornwall, and if we wish to rationalize we may assume that Geoffrey thinks of him as the immediate successor of Gorlois, perhaps, therefore, as son of Gorlois and Igerna and half-brother of Arthur. The *Brut Tysilio* and Hardyng say definitely that Cador was son of Gorlois.[2] That Guenevere is called in later versions a relative of Cador[3] may be partly a careless inference from this statement of Geoffrey, but more probably comes from his earlier one (ix, 9) that Cador brought her up.

PAGE 246

It seems altogether probable that the Vodinus, bishop of London, in Boece,[4] is to be identified with Geoffrey's Archbishop Guethelinus.[5]

[1] See pp. 230, 252, above.
[2] See pp. 117, 251, above.
[3] See pp. 159, 225, 266, above.

[4] See p. 246, above.
[5] See p. 59, above.

INDEX

[The names of some chroniclers and some chronicles are given in the vernacular, of others in the Latin form, in accordance, as nearly as possible, with common usage. In the arrangement of sub-headings Geoffrey's order has been taken as the basis. Names of saints are entered under St., and the order is as if the title were spelled in full. Brackets [] mean that some link of the connection between subject and reference must be supplied by the reader.]

Appendix:

A SUPPLEMENTARY BIBLIOGRAPHY
AND DISCUSSION

by

R. S. LOOMIS

A SUPPLEMENTARY BIBLIOGRAPHY
AND DISCUSSION *

by

ROGER SHERMAN LOOMIS

Fletcher's excellent work on the Arthurian material in the Chronicles, when first published in 1906 as volume 10 of [*Harvard*] *Studies and Notes in Philology and Literature,* established itself at once as a sober and reliable work of reference in a field full of interest but confused by antiquated editions, forged data, and baseless speculation. Long out of print, it was republished in 1958 by Burt Franklin, and is now again published with a supplement bringing the discussion and the bibliography up to date. It goes without saying that, in the sixty years that have passed since this book first appeared, the scholarship on the subject has greatly expanded, and Fletcher, if he were alive, would have taken account of it. For instance, he would doubtless feel obliged to revise drastically his chapter on the life and work of Geoffrey of Monmouth in the light of the researches of H. E. Salter, J. Hammer, J. S. P. Tatlock, and R. A. Caldwell. Would that he might have lived to perform the task of revision himself! But since he died prematurely and the reader should be advised of the additions and changes called for by the advances in scholarship, I have attempted to fill this need.

I do not, however, claim to have produced an exhaustive bibliography on so extensive a field, or to have touched on all the hypotheses proposed. That would call for another book. I have merely attempted a selective listing and a brief review of the conclusions of modern scholarship so far as they affect the materials treated by Fletcher. I follow his order in the treatment of topics, providing a limited bibliography and discussion for each topic. The full bibliography comes at the end. Those who wish to extend their investigations farther will consult J. J. Parry, *Bibliography of Critical Arthurian Literature for the Years 1922-1929* (New York, 1931); J. J. Parry and Margaret Schlauch, *Bibliography of Arthurian Critical Literature for the Years*

---

* Not indexed.

1930-1935 (New York, 1936); annual bibliographies by Parry, succeeded by Paul A. Brown, in *Modern Language Quarterly*, beginning June 1941 and ending June 1962; annual bibliographies in *Bulletin Bibliographique de la Société Internationale Arthurienne*, beginning 1949 and continuing.

GILDAS AND THE SIEGE OF MOUNT BADON (3-8)

Brodeur, 238-48, 255-65, 275-8
Bromwich, 91-4
Bruce, I, 4f; II, 45-8
Chambers, 2-5, 171f, 179-83, 197-201, 234-7
Evans, 89, 93-5
Faral, I, 1-39, 143-6
Hodgkin, I, 118-25 178-82

Jackson (2), 2f, 10
Jackson (3)
Jones, 4-8, 10
Lloyd (1), I, 98, 124-7, 134-43, 160f
Stenton, 2-4, 22f, 30f
Tatlock, 4, 47
Windisch, 38-40, 52-4

* * *

Fletcher's account of Gildas agrees in nearly all respects with later scholarship. Lloyd, however, doubts that the saint was the son of a king, since it was a Welsh convention to provide every saint with a highborn ancestor. The historians Hodgkin and Stenton are less sceptical than Fletcher of Gildas' statement that the first Saxon invasion swept across almost the whole island. Fletcher's reasons for disregarding the failure of Gildas to mention Arthur seem to have been equally cogent for more recent scholars, who without exception regard him as a historical figure. All, except Mrs. Bromwich, would in spite of the silence of Gildas credit Arthur with the victory of Mount Badon. All would date that victory about the year 500, and, except Faral, all would place it in the South of England, though their guesses range from western Kent (Evans) to the border of Wales (Faral). According to Hodgkin, the evidence of burials shows that pagan Saxons had established themselves as far west as Fairford (Glos.) before 500. Then the siege of Mount Badon might plausibly be located about six miles away at Badbury Hill in Great Coxwell (Berks.), which is crowned with earthworks. (See map in Hodgkin, I, p. 124.) Jackson sees no linguistic improbability in the equation of Badon with Badbury, and argues for Badbury Rings in Dorset; nevertheless, the resemblance between the name Badon and one or other of these Badburys may be purely fortuitous. Whatever the site of the victory, the testimony of Gildas that it brought a period of peace, and the witness of Procopius (see Stenton) that Saxons were returning from Britain to the Continent should be accepted as evidence of Arthur's prowess. But the defeat of the Britons by the West Saxons at Old Sarum (Searoburh) in 552 seems to mark the end of the period of peace and the resumption of the drive to the west.

NENNIUS (8-30)

Brodeur, 242-66, 272-8
Bromwich, 92-4
Bruch, I, 6-10
Chadwick, 37-47
Chambers, 1f, 4-13, 197-203, 238-40
Evans, 83-90, 92f
Faral, I, 56-73, 132-54, 168, 234; III, 38f, 61
Hodgkin, I, 122, 125-34

Jackson (1), 44-57
Jackson (2), 4-11
Jones, 7-12, 16
Lloyd (1), 126, 223-6
Lot, 35-7, 68-71, 109-11, 115-9, 129f, 194-6, 216, 224
Stenton, 19-21
Tatlock, 4, 73, 180-2
Windisch, 40f, 69, 142, 145f

*　　*　　*

In general, it may be said that scholars have not discredited Fletcher's account of Nennius and his analysis of the *Historia Britonum*. The state of the manuscripts, however, makes it difficult to arrive at final conclusions. Nennius was apparently the name of a cleric of South Wales, a disciple of Bishop Elbodug of Bangor, who compiled from several sources the medley called the *Historia Britonum*. The latest editor, Lot, ventures 826 as the date of final composition. Mrs. Chadwick suggests ca. 800, perhaps with an appendix of ca. 828-9. The list of Arthur's battles probably goes back to one of Nennius's earlier sources, and Jones, Jackson, and Mrs. Bromwich agree that its ultimate source was a Welsh poem of little historic authority. Jackson (1) has carefully examined the names of the battle sites and has concluded that only two can be identified with certainty, the Silva Celidonis, i.e. the forest region between Glasgow and Carlisle, and Urbs Legionis, i.e. Chester. But there were no Germanic invaders for Arthur to fight about the year 500 in either of these regions. Octha came down from the North, and it was in the South, therefore, according to Nennius himself that Arthur fought, together with the kings of the Britons, against the son (or grandson) of Hengist. Nevertheless, Faral, Jones, and Mrs. Bromwich prefer to see in the victor a hero of the North, like Urien. The bases of this view are the failure of Gildas to connect Arthur with Mount Badon and the reference in the North-British poem, the *God-*

oddin, probably as old as the ninth century, possibly as old as 600, to Arthur as noted for his supremacy in deeds of slaughter. But there is no slightest hint in the poem as to where these deeds were performed. Neither argument is of sufficient weight to counterbalance the absence of any other references to Arthur in the Welsh poetry of the North, the silence of Bede, who was writing in Northumbria in 725, and the combined testimony of Nennius and the *Annales Cambriae,* assigning to Arthur the credit for Mount Badon, which everyone except Faral places in the South. Fletcher's over-cautious statement that Arthur may have been a myth after all is offset by the fact that his name is not that of any Celtic divinity but a normal development from the Roman name Artorius, and by Stenton's conclusion (p. 31) that "four independent authorities [including Gildas and the *Saxon Chronicle*] agree in suggesting a single coherent story" of the period. Another argument for linking Arthur with the South rather than with the North of Britain is supplied by the list of *Mirabilia* included in the *Historia Britonum.* Two of them, linking him with marvels of South Wales and Herefordshire are recorded much earlier than the gloss in 13th-century manuscripts which links him with Wedale in Lothian. Two names in the *Mirabilia* should be replaced by better variant readings, Troynt by Troit, and Anir by Amr. The legendary tomb of Amr, Arthur's son, may therefore be localized, as Jackson (2) pointed out, at the source of the River Gamber in Herefordshire.

THE *ANNALES CAMBRIAE* (31-34)

Brodeur, 251-4, 264, 266, 276
Bromwich, 94
Bruce, 7n, 11f
Chadwick, 47, 57, 66, 74
Chambers, 13-16, 171-4, 199f, 203f, 240f

Faral, I, 221-3, 260; II, 296-9; III. 45
Hodgkin, I, 121
Jackson (1), 56
Jackson (2), 4-8
Jones, 3-9, 11
Tatlock, 60, 183, 319n

*   *   *

Jackson (2) and Jones agree with Fletcher, though with some hesitation, in interpreting "in humeros suos" as a mistranslation of Old Welsh for "on his shield", owing to the similarity of *scuit* (shield) and *scuid* (shoulder). Jackson (2) disputes Fletcher's statement that the entry in the *Annales* regarding Mount Badon was merely an amplification of Nennius' account of the same battle. Chambers computes the dates of

Badon and Camlann as, respectively, 518 and 539 instead of two years earlier, but, however the dates are computed, Jackson (2) and Jones regard them as ten or fifteen years too late. Fletcher's warning that the Camlann entry does not tell us that Medraut was Arthur's nephew, or a traitor, or even that he fought on the opposite side, is echoed by recent scholars. The identification of Camlann with Camboglama, a Roman fort on Hadrian's Wall, is a possibility but no more, according to Jackson (1), and is inconsistent with the view that Arthur was a Southern hero.

WILLIAM OF MALMESBURY (37-40, 104)

Bromwich, 90
Bruce, I, 12, 21n, 38n.
Chambers, 16-9, 249f
Faral, I, 244-52, 260

Jones, 20
Loomis (1), 55f, 64
Loomis (2), 183-5
Tatlock, 206f, 212

*   *   *

Faral and Tatlock question the importance which Fletcher attached to William's famous reference to the "idle tales" (*nugae*) circulating about Arthur in his day, but Bruce, Chambers and Loomis agree with Fletcher. Jones corrects Fletcher's translation of *Britonum* as "Britons" by substituting "Bretons", and Loomis points out that on the testimony of both Geoffrey of Monmouth and Giraldus Cambrensis the Welsh had long ceased to be called *Britones,* and Zimmer and Brugger have proved that the word was habitually applied to the Continental Bretons and the emigrants from Brittany who settled in Britain after the Norman Conquest. All scholars but Tatlock accept Gaston Paris's and Fletcher's equation of Walweitha with Galloway. William's conversion of Walwen (Gawain) into a king of Walweitha, however, though regarded by Mrs. Bromwich as indicative of a genuine historic tradition of Gawain in Scotland, is more probably, as Brugger and Bruce believed, merely an example of the medieval principle of linking place names and personal names on the arbitrary basis of similarity of sound.

GEOFFREY OF MONMOUTH
The Life of Geoffrey (43-6, 82)

Bruce, 17-20
Chambers, 20-4
Faral, II, 1-38
Lloyd (1), II, 523-5

Lloyd (2)
Parry and Caldwell, 72-74
Tatlock, 438-50

* * *

All recent authorities reject the *Gwentian Brut* as a forgery of Iolo Margannwg. Consequently, Fletcher's statement that Geoffrey was an archdeacon of Llandaff and a nephew of Uchtryd, Bishop of that see, has no sound basis. He was probably born at Monmouth of Breton parents, for he referred to himself as *Brito* (not *Wallensis*) and showed in the *Historia,* as Fletcher noted, a contempt for the Welsh in contrast to his admiration for the Bretons. Between 1129 and 1151 he witnessed seven charters concerned with Oxford and the vicinity, and he was probably a canon of St. George's there. The title *magister* and his learning suggest that he taught the Latin classics. Fletcher rightly stressed Geoffrey's relations with Robert, Earl of Gloucester, and rightly doubted whether as Bishop of St. Asaph he ever visited his see. In 1153 he was a personage of such importance as to witness the treaty assuring the succession of Henry of Anjou to the throne. The date of his death was 1155, not 1154.

Editions of the *Historia Regum Britanniae* (43n)

Caldwell	Hammer
Faral, III, 64-303, 364-85	Tatlock, 5f
Griscom	

* * *

Griscom's edition gives a more accurate transcript from the manuscripts than Faral's, but his introduction is quite unsound. Hammer's variant version of the *Historia,* though regarded by him as a late redaction of the Vulgate text, has been shown by Robert Caldwell to be a highly significant early draft, less polished and lacking any dedication.

Dedications and Date of the *Historia* (45)

Bruce, 18	Griscom, 31-98
Chambers, 41-8	Parry and Caldwell, 80f
Faral, II, 10-28	Tatlock, 433-7

* * *

The earliest dedication seems to have been addressed to Robert of Gloucester alone and was probably written shortly after King Henry's death in 1135. The dedication to King Stephen and Robert was written probably in April 1136 when the two met at Oxford, certainly before 1138 when there was a rupture between them. And probably the Robert-Waleran dedication falls between 1135 and 1138 also.

The *Liber Vetustissimus* and Geoffrey's Motives (49-56, 115)

Bruce, 19-23
Chambers, 53-7, 92
Faral, II, 386-96
Griscom, 99-112

Lloyd (1), II, 525-7
Parry and Caldwell, 81f, 86f
Tatlock, 422-32
Windisch, 124-9

*   *   *

With the exception of Griscom and Windisch, scholars agree with Fletcher that Geoffrey's alleged source, the *liber vetustissimus*, brought from *Britannia* (Brittany), either never existed or else contained only some meagre suggestions. Fletcher was too generous in absolving Geoffrey of intentional fraud, but it was an age when charters, saints' lives, and histories were commonly composed or doctored for some practical end. Geoffrey's motives in perpetrating the hoax were in part the desire for fame and consequent advancement in the world, and in part a pride in his Breton stock. There is no reason to suppose that any of his patrons were accomplices in the sham.

Geoffrey's Latin Sources (57-75)

Chambers, 56f
Faral, II, 252-66, 282-7, 296-8
Parry and Caldwell, 61-5

Tatlock, see index under Gildas,
  Nennius, William of Malmesbury and Henry of Huntingdon.

*   *   *

Fletcher's treatment of these sources leaves little room for improvement. Faral exaggerates the influence of classical sources.

Geoffrey's Geltic Sources (75-88)

Bruce, I, 87f
Chambers, 57-80, 85-92
Faral, II, 275f

Loomis (2), 131-44, 161-4
Parry and Caldwell, 83-5
Tatlock, 194-205, 314-6, 381-91

*   *   *

Though Faral and Tatlock tend to minimize Celtic elements, it seems fairly clear that Geoffrey derived some of his material on Arthur indirectly from Welsh or Cornish sources. Personages such as Uther Pendragon, Walvanus, Cajus, and Bedeuerus were surely well-known figures in Welsh tradition, and Eventus (Iwenus) son of Urien was Owain, son of Urien, the historic opponent of Ida in Bernicia.

The emperor Lucius Hiberus was fabricated by Geoffrey out of a hypothetical Welsh Llwch the Irishman (Hibernus), and his wars with Arthur follow somewhat the same pattern as the cognate stories of the wars of Loth and Lancelot with Arthur. Arthur's sword Caliburnus, his lance Ron, and his shield Pridwen unquestionably bear the Welsh names Caledvwch, Rhongymyniad, and Prydwen, though this last name in the *Spoils of Annwn* is that of a ship and not a shield. Fletcher was too charitable to Rhys's theory that Uther was originally a god of death, but Uther's paternal relationship to Arthur may well have had no better basis than the misunderstanding which Fletcher suggests. Their translation of *Annwn* as Hades is completely misleading since it is a term covering the far from gloomy concepts of the dwellings of the pagan gods. The "insula avallonis", where Caliburnus was forged and to which Arthur was borne for the healing of his wounds, was one of these concepts. The story of Arthur's begetting at Tintagel offers in its nomenclature such an authentic Cornish coloring that it is probably based on a local legend.

THE SAINTS' LIVES (77-80, 105-7)

Brooke, 201-33
Bruce, I, 10, 196-203
Chambers, 80-5, 93, 241-8, 263f
Cross and Nitze, 21, 47n, 55
Faral, I, 236-44, 253-6; II, 409-21
Hughes, 183-97

Jones, 21
Lloyd (1), I, 147f,
Loomis (2), 182f, 214-6
Loomis (3), 214-22
Tatlock, 183-94, 243-8

* * *

In the main Fletcher's treatment is sound, but British scholars have added much to our understanding of the backgrounds of the Saints' Lives and of their affiliations with specific ecclesiastical centres. Particularly illuminating are the studies of Brooke and Miss Hughes. Tatlock was mistaken in arguing that Caradoc of Lancarvan was a monk of Glastonbury (*Speculum*, XIII [1938], 141). Caradoc's account of the abduction of Guenevere by Melwas, King of the Summer Country, and her rescue by Arthur, was rightly interpreted as a myth by Fletcher (pp. 94f), but to characterize Melwas as an infernal divinity is to identify him with "gloomy Dis", who abducted Proserpine. As Loomis (3) points out, there was nothing infernal about Melwas, and there was probably a confusion between the Summer Country, an elysian land, and Somersetshire.

MERLIN (91-4)

Bruce, I, 129-43
Chambers, 24-9, 48-50, 95-9
Faral, II, 38-48, 341-77
Jarman, 20-30

Parry and Caldwell, 75-79, 89-92
Tatlock, 171-7
Taylor
Zumthor

* * *

The opinion of Bruce, Faral, and Tatlock that the Welsh poems attributed to Myrddin were composed after Geoffrey had made him famous by the *Historia* and the *Vita Merlini* is rejected by Welsh scholars. Jarman believes that the name Myrddin was not that of a historical person but was simply due to the mistaken analysis of the name Caerfyrddin (Carmarthen) as a compound meaning "Fortress of Myrddin". This accounts for Geoffrey's statement that the boy Merlin was discovered at Kaermerdin. But for some unknown reason this imaginary figure was credited by the Welsh with poetic and pro-phetic powers and eventually the Scottish legend of a prophetic mad-man Lailoken was attached to him. Fletcher was doubtless right in attributing to Geoffrey the arbitrary lifting of the story of Vortigern's tower from Nennius and identifying Ambrosius with Merlin.

GAWAIN (94, 104f, 113)

Bromwich, 89f
Chambers, 17f, 87, 151
Loomis (2), 206-13
Loomis (3), 146-55

Tatlock, 206
Whiting
Windisch, 174

* * *

Though the Celtic scholars, Mrs. Bromwich and Windisch, regard Geoffrey s Walgainus etc. as a substitution for Welsh Gwalchmai, this hypothesis does not account for the consistent termination of the name in *n,* in all non-Welsh texts, nor for Gawain's mythical trait of waxing and waning in strength with the rising and setting of the sun, nor for the names of his brothers. All these data are explained by the deriva-tion of Galvain through Galvagin from the Welsh epithet Gwallt-advwyn, meaning "Bright or Resplendent Hair", which was attached to Gwrvan and also, presumably, to Gwri or Gware.

IDER (98f)

Chambers, 117-21, 267   Robinson, 17-9
Faral, II, 451-7

*   *   *

All three recent authorities agree that the passage in the *De Anti-quitate* concerned with Ider is not to be credited to William of Malmesbury. It is an interpolation concocted by some Glastonbury monk to support the claim of the monastry to certain lands.

ARTHUR'S SURVIVAL AND RETURN (100-2, passim)

Bruce, I, 10, 33-5, 74-82   Loomis (1), 53f, 64-71
Chambers, 17f, 25, 46, 49, 89,   Tatlock, 204f, 212
  105-12, 121-4, 217-32, 249, 265   Windisch, 114f, 259
Jones, 18, 20f

*   *   *

The belief in Arthur's survival was implanted in the Welsh, and more firmly in the Cornish and Bretons. Even in England and in modern times Arthur was believed to be sleeping with his warriors in a cave, and the legend spread as far away as Mount Etna in Sicily. The Alanus cited by Fletcher (p. 101) and Chambers was identified with Alanus de Insulis by mistake.

THE MODENA SCULPTURE (102)

Bruce, 14-7   Loomis (2), 198-208
Chambers, 133f, 151f   Tatlock, 212-4
Cross and Nitze, 22-4

*   *   *

There has been much discussion of the highly significant dating of the Modena sculpture. Foerster's opinion that it goes back to the first decades of the twelfth century, though combated by Tatlock, is supported by nearly all art historians, and is corroborated by the fact that it shows no influence of Geoffrey of Monmouth; that the names of Isdernus and Galvaginus are closer to the Welsh forms than those of Geoffrey; the armor and the sculptural style belong to the early, not the late, twelfth century.

CONTEMPORARY MANNERS IN THE *HISTORIA* (108-14)

Tatlock, 288-304, 308f, 321-80

* * *

Tatlock's treatment of this subject is remarkably detailed and complete.

Alfred of Beverley (116, 171)

Chambers, 46, 260   Tatlock, 210
Loomis (2), 189f

* * *

The testimony of Alfred, writing according to Tatlock about 1143, that stories about the history of Britain were familiar to so many that anyone who was ignorant of them acquired the reputation of a boor, is open to two interpretations. Tatlock believed that these stories were inspired by Geoffrey's *Historia,* and only after they were all the rage did the historian Alfred find and read their source. It seems more likely that these stories were the same as the tales about Arthur which, according to the statement of Ailred of Rievaulx in 1141-2, had caused a novice in his secular life to weep, and the existence of which was attested by William of Malmesbury as early as 1125. Is it conceivable that if every knowledgable person was talking about Geoffrey's book and the stories contained in it, Alfred, the chronicler, should have been the last person to see a copy?

THE WELSH TRANSLATIONS OF GEOFFREY (117-9)

Bruce, I, 22n   Lloyd (1), II, 626
Chambers, 21, 54   Parry and Caldwell, 89
Grișcom, 99-211   Windisch, 124

* * *

Griscom lists in an appendix all the ms. redactions of Geoffrey into Welsh, and provides an English translation of one of them, which had previously been translated most inaccurately. Griscom failed, however, to prove that this text represented the *vetustissimus liber* which Geoffrey claimed as his source. Two of the Welsh texts, *Brut Dingestow* and *Brut y Brenhinedd* have been edited by Henry Lewis and J. J. Parry respectively.

HENRY OF HUNTINGDON (119-21)

Bruce, I, 18n   Parry and Caldwell, 80, 88
Chambers, 19, 41, 44-6, 251f   Tatlock, 431-4
Loomis (1), 56n, 64

*   *   *

Fletcher's translation on p. 120, "his kinsmen the Britons" should be corrected to "your kinsmen, the Bretons", for it renders "Britones, parentes tui". Since Henry addressed Warinus Brito as a compatriot, the latter must have been a Breton established in England.

GEOFFREY GAIMAR (125-7)

Bell, 184-88   Foulon, 94
Bruce, I, 24f   Legge, 27-30, 277
Chambers, 54f, 260f   Tatlock, 452-6, 459

*   *   *

Tatlock gives a full and satisfactory account of Gaimar's reference to his translation of Geoffrey's *Historia*.

WACE'S *BRUT* (127-43)

Arnold, I, lxxiv-lxxxvi   Foulon, 94-103
Bruce, 25-31, 82   Houck
Caldwell   Tatlock, 459-82
Chambers, 101-5

*   *   *

Arnold's edition of Wace supersedes the old one of Le Roux de Lincy, except that it gives no variant readings of proper names. His introduction is sounder in the treatment of the *fables* about Arthur than Tatlock's argument that they were all inspired by Geoffrey of Monmouh. Tatlock is probably right in asserting that Wace, in referring to himself as *clerc lisant,* had no office in mind, and that the title *maistre* meant a teacher. Miss Houck points out that Wace displayed a marked familiarity with the geography of southern England, and she covers fully the matter of his sources. Tatlock's extreme scepticism about Breton tales of the Round Table is properly refuted by Foulon.

DRACO NORMANNICUS (145f)

Chambers, 110-2, 264f   Loomis (2), 61-75

*   *   *

Tatlock in *Modern Philology*, XXXI (1935), 1-18, 113-25, argued, quite rightly, that Etienne de Rouen treated Arthur and his sojourn in the Antipodes in a spirit of mockery, but his further claim that the inhabitants of the Antipodes were conceived as monsters is not supported by the evidence. As king of the Underworld Arthur reappears in later records as dwelling in a hollow mountain or cave.

LAYAMON'S *BRUT* (147-66)

Brook and Leslie, 400-15   Loomis (1), 104-1
Bruce, 28-36   Tatlock, 467, 472-531
Chambers, 105f   Wells, 32-5, 191-5
Gillespy   Wyld

*   *   *

Fletcher's excellent treatment of the poet needs correction in certain details. The modern connotation of the word *elf* as a dwarfish male sprite does not apply to Layamon's *alven*, who correspond to the French *fées*, beautiful females. In fact, there are French parallels to the gifts of the fays to the infant Arthur and to the transportation of the wounded Arthur by fays to the isle of Avalon, as recounted by Layamon. These two additions to Wace's *Brut* and the account of the riot over precedence and the founding of the Round Table are plainly of Breton or Cornish derivation. There is no evidence that Layamon took them from an "expanded Wace", or took anything directly from Welsh traditions, unless it be the name Griffin (a corruption of Gofan) borne by the smith who forged the spear Ron at Carmarthen. Probably the name Wygar (Saxon Wighard) belongs to Arthur's burnie, not to the elvish smith who wrought it; and the name of Arthur's helmet, Goswhit, suggests analogy with Beowulf's *hwita helm*. While Tatlock's adoption of the form Lawman is reasonable enough, it hardly seems necessary to abandon the traditional spelling Layamon, since neither of the two forms exactly reproduces the twelfth-century pronunciation of the name. It was of Danish, not Saxon origin, as Tatlock pointed out, but this derivation and the fact that Layamon reveals some acquaintance with Irish matters hardly justifies Tatlock's hypothesis that the poet was born in Ireland, the son of a Saxon, Leovenath, by a Scandinavian woman. The first volume of a new edition of Layamon by Brook and Leslie has appeared.

GESTA REGUM BRITANNIAE (166f)

Faral, II, 429-32   Paton, 28, 45-7
Loomis (2), 63f

*   *   *

The *Gesta Regum Britanniae* by a Breton author adds to the versified history by Geoffrey of Monmouth a description of the isle of King Avallo which derives partly from Geoffrey's *Vita Merlini* but partly from other sources, classical and Celtic. Interesting features of this Breton elysium are absence of age, disease, and sorrow, and its ruler who is at the same time a *regia virgo* and the mistress of Arthur.

LATIN PROSE CHRONICLES (169-89)

Keeler

*   *   *

Laura Keeler gives a systematic examination of the British chroniclers in Latin, 1300-1500, and devotes considerable attention to the influence of Geoffrey of Monmouth and their attitude toward his credibility. She notes an amusing episode in the Lanercost *Chronicle*, a meeting between Peter des Roches and the living Arthur, and reproduces John of Whethamstede's significant rejection of Geoffrey. She adds an appendix on the Round Tables recorded by the chroniclers.

THE EXHUMATION OF ARTHUR (189-91)

Bruce, I, 77-9   Loomis (1), 66f
Chambers, 112-7, 269-74   Nitze, II, 47-9, 58-72
Faral, II, 437-53   Robinson, 8-14
Keeler, 6, 35f, 91

*   *   *

Bruce is mistaken in asserting that the word *Britones* in the twelfth century was sometimes applied to Welshmen; it referred to Continental Bretons or their descendants who had settled in Britain. Fletcher, Robinson, and Chambers mistranslate Giraldus's words "ab historico cantore Britone"; they mean "from a Breton singer versed in (or dealing with) history". Fletcher is also mistaken in crediting William of Malmesbury with the statement that Arthur and Guenevere were buried at Glastonbury. This statement is one of the many misleading interpolations in the *De Antiquitate Glastoniensis Ecclesiae,* for which William was not responsible. Faral argues that it was not King Henry who hatched the scheme of disinterring the bones of Arthur, but the monks of Glastonbury.

MIDDLE ENGLISH METRICAL CHRONICLES (193-9, 251-3)

Millican, 28-32, 50, 116, 157 Zettl
Wells, 35, 193-202

* * *

Wells gives accounts of the Marquis of Bath's *Arthur,* "Robert of Gloucester", Thomas Castelford, and the Short Metrical Chronicle, newly edited by Zettl. Millican has brief remarks on Kelton and Hardyng.

MIDDLE ENGLISH PROSE CHRONICLES (182, 202f, 220, 250)

Brie   Wells, 204-7

* * *

Brie makes a full study of the *Brut of England* and its Anglo-French source. Wells gives it much briefer treatment, and also discusses Trevisa's translation of Higden's *Polychronicon.*

THE SCOTTISH VERSIONS (241-9)

Kendrick, 65-8, 78f, 84f

* * *

Kendrick treats Boece, Major, and Buchanan.

THE TUDOR CHRONICLES (254-71)

Kendrick, 34-64, 79-111   -   Millican

*   *   *

Both scholars discuss at length the Tudor revival of interest in the early British history according to Geoffrey of Monmouth and the prolonged controversy over its reliability.

A SELECTIVE BIBLIOGRAPHY OF ARTHURIAN MATERIAL
IN THE CHRONICLES, 1905-65

Arnold, I., editor. Wace, *Roman de Brut*, S.A.T.F., 1938-40.

Brie, F., *Geschichte und Quellen der mittelenglischen Prosachronik* The Brute of England *oder* The Chronicles of England (Marburg, 1905)

Bell, A. *Medium Aevum*, VII (1938), 184-98.

Brodeur, A. "Arthur Dux Bellorum", *Univ. of Calif. Pub. in English*, III, no. 7 (1939), 237-84.

Bromwich, R. "Scotland and the Arthurian Legend", *Bulletin Bibliographique de la Société Internationale Arthurienne*, No. 15, pp. 85-95.

Brook, G. L., and R. F. Leslie, editors. Lazamon. E.E.T.S. (1963)

Brooke, C. *Studies in the Early British Church,* ed. N. K. Chadwick (Cambridge, 1958), pp. 201-33.

Bruce, J. D., *Evolution of Arthurian Romance from the Beginnings down to the Year 1300* (Baltimore, Göttingen, 1923; New York, 1927).

Caldwell, R. A. "Wace's *Roman de Brut* and the Variant Version of Geoffrey of Monmouth's *Historia Regum Britanniae.*" *Speculum,* XXXI (1956), 675-82.

Chadwick, N. K., editor. *Studies in the Early British Church* (Cambridge, 1958).

Chambers, E. K. *Arthur of Britain* (London, 1927).

Cross, T. P. and Nitze, W. A. *Lancelot and Guenevere* (Chicago, 1930).

Evans, John. "The Arthurian Campaign", *Archaeologia Cantiana,* LXXXVIII (1963), 83-95.

Faral, E. *La Légende Arthurienne* (Paris, 1929).

Foulon, C. *Arthurian Literature in the Middle Ages,* ed. R. S. Loomis (Oxford, 1959), 94-103.

Gillespy, F. L. "Layamon's *Brut*: a Comparative Study in Narrative Art", *Univ. of Calif. Pub. in Mod. Phil.,* III (1916), 361-510.

Griscom, A., editor. Geoffrey of Monmouth, *Historia Regum Britan-niae* (New York, 1929).

Hammer, J. editor. Geoffrey of Monmouth, *Historia Regum Britan-niae, Variant Version* (Cambridge, Mass. 1951).

Hodgkin, R. H. *History of the Anglo-Saxons* (Oxford, 1935).

Houck, M. "Sources of the Roman de Brut of Wace", *Univ. of Calif. Pub. in English,* V, No. 2 (Berkeley, 1941).

Hughes, K. *Studies in the Early English Church,* ed. N. K. Chadwick (Cambridge, 1958), 183-200.

Jackson, K. H. (1) "Once Again Arthur's Battles," *Mod. Phil.,* XLIII (1945), 44-62.

Jackson, K. H. (2) *Arthurian Literature in the Middle Ages,* ed. R. S. (Oxford, 1959), 1-21.

Jackson, K. H. (3). "The Site of Mount Badon," *Journal of Celtic Studies,* II (1958), 152-5.

Jarman, A. O. H. *Arthurian Literature in the Middle Ages,* ed. R. S. Loomis (Oxford, 1959), 20-30.

Jones, Thomas. "Early Evolution of the Legend of Arthur," *Notting-ham Mediaeval Studies,* VIII (1964), 3-21.

Keeler, L. "Geoffrey of Monmouth and the Late Latin Chroniclers, 1300-1500," *Univ. of Calif. Pub. in English,* XVII, No. 1.

Kendrick, T. D. *British Antiquity* (London, 1950).

Legge, M. D. *Anglo-Norman Literature and Its Background* (Oxford, 1963).

Lloyd, J. E. (1) *History of Wales from the Earliest Times to the Edwardian Conquest,* ed. 3 (London, New York, 1939).

Lloyd, J. E. (2) "Geoffrey of Monmouth," *English Historical Review,* LVII (1942), 460-8.

Loomis, R. S. (1) *Arthurian Literature in the Middle Ages* (Oxford, 1959).

Loomis, R. S. (2) *Wales and the Arthurian Legend* (Cardiff, 1956).

Loomis, R. S. (3) *Arthurian Tradition and Chrétien de Troyes* (New York, 1948).

Lot, F., *Nennius et l' "Historia Britonum".* Paris, 1934.

Millican, *Spenser and the Table Round* (Cambridge, Mass., 1932)

Nitze, W. A., editor, *Le Haut Livre du Graal Perlesvaus* (Chicago, 1932, 1937).

Parry, J. J. and Caldwell, R. A. *Arthurian Literature in the Middle Ages,* ed. R. S. Loomis (Oxford, 1959), 94-103.

Paton, L. A. *Fairy Mythology of Arthurian Romance, Radcliffe College Monograph,* No. 13 (1903); New York, 1960.

Robinson, Joseph Armitage. *Two Glastonbury Legends* (Cambridge, 1926).

Stenton, F. M. *Anglo-Saxon England,* ed. 2 (Oxford, 1947).

Tatlock, J. S. P. *Legendary History of Britain* (Berkeley and Los Angeles, 1950).

Taylor, R. *Political Prophecy in England* (New York, 1911).

Wells, John E. *Manual of the Writings in Middle English, 1050-1400* (New Haven, Conn., 1916).

Whiting, B. J. "Gawain: His Reputation, His Courtesy and His Appearance in Chaucer's *Squire's Tale",* *Medieval Studies,* IX (1947), 189-234.

Windisch, E. *Das keltische Brittannien bis zu Kaiser Arthur. Abhandlungen der phil.-hist. Klasse der königl. sächsischen Gesellschaft der Wissenschaften,* XXIX, No. vi (Leipzig, 1912).

Zettl, E., editor. *The Anonymous Short Metrical Chronicle.* E.E.T.S. (1935).

Zumthor, P. *Merlin le Prophète* (Lausanne, 1943).